Digital Media: The Future

T0191589

Springer

London
Berlin
Heidelberg
New York
Barcelona
Hong Kong
Milan
Paris
Singapore
Tokyo

By the same author

Digital Convergence:
The Information Revolution

ISBN 1-85233-140-2

John Vince and Rae Earnshaw (Eds)

Digital Media: The Future

With 167 figures

 Springer

John A. Vince, MTech, PhD, FBCS, CEng
School of Media, Arts and Communication,
Bournemouth University, Talbot Campus, Fern Barrow,
Poole BH12 5BB, UK

Rae Earnshaw, BSc, MSc, PhD, FBCS, CEng
Department of Electronic Imaging and Media Communications,
University of Bradford, Richmond Road, Bradford BD7 1DP, UK

ISBN 978-1-84996-857-7

British Library Cataloguing in Publication Data
Digital media : the future
    1.Digital communications 2.Multimedia systems
    I.Vince, John, 1941- II.Earnshaw, R. A. (Rae A.)
    384.3

Library of Congress Cataloging-in-Publication Data
Digital media : the future / John Vince and Rae Earnshaw (eds.).
        p. cm.

    1. Multimedia systems. 2. Digital media. I. Vince, John, (John A.) II. Earnshaw, Rae
A., 1944-
QA76.575. D538 2000
006.7--dc21   99-089473

Contents

List of Contributors

Samura Ali
Fakulty of Electrical Engineering
Universiti Teknologi Malaysia
Sekundai Campus
Locked Bag 791
80990 Johor Bahru
Johor Darul Takzim
Malaysia
Email:
smali@suria.fke.utm.my
Home page:
http://www.utm.my/

Jan Allbeck
Center for Human Modeling and
Simulation
Department of Computer and
Information Science
University of Pennsylvania
Philadelphia
PA 19104-6389
USA
Email:
allbeck@gradient.cis.upenn.edu
Home page:
http://www.cis.upenn.edu/

Eric Badiqué
European Commission
ACTS Programme
Email:
Eric.Badique@cec.be
Home page:
http://www.de.infowin.org/
ACTS/

Norman I. Badler
Center for Human Modeling and
Simulation
Department of Computer and
Information Science
University of Pennsylvania
Philadelphia
PA 19104-6389
USA
Email:
badler@central.cis.upenn.edu
Home page:
http://www.cis.upenn.edu/

Roland Mark Banks
BT Laboratories
Martlesham Heath
Ipswich
Suffolk
UK
Email:
roland.banks@bt-sys.bt.co.uk
Home page:
http://www.innovate.bt.com/
showcase/visiondome/

O. Belmonte
Dto. Informática de la
Universitat Jaume I.
Campus del Riu secretary
E-12071
Castellón
Spain
Email:
belfern@inf.uji.es
Home page:
http://www.inf.uji.es/

M. Bermell
Dto. Electrònica i Informàtica
Universitat de València
Campus de Burjassot
Burjassot
Valencia
Spain
Email:
gil@glup.irobot.uv.es
Home page:
http://www.uv.es/

Rama Bindiganavale
Center for Human Modeling and
Simulation
Department of Computer and
Information Science
University of Pennsylvania
Philadelphia, PA 19104-6389
USA
Email:
rama@graphics.cis.upenn.edu
Home page:
http://www.cis.upenn.edu/

Juliet Bourne
Center for Human Modeling and
Simulation
Department of Computer and
Information Science
University of Pennsylvania
Philadelphia
PA 19104-6389
USA
Email:
jcb@gradient.cis.upenn.edu
Home page:
http://www.cis.upenn.edu/

Jerry Bowskill
BT Labs
Martlesham Heath
Suffolk
UK
Email:
jerry.bowskill@bt-sys.bt.co.uk
Home page:
http://www.labs.bt.com/people/

Heather Brown
University of Kent at Canterbury
Canterbury
Kent
CT2 7NZ
UK
Email:
hb@ukc.ac.uk
Home page:
http://www.ukc.ac.uk/

M. Cavazza
Electronic Imaging and Media
Communications Department,
University of Bradford, Bradford,
BD7 1DP, UK
Email:
m.cavazza@bradford.ac.uk
Home page:
http://www.eimc.brad.ac.uk/

Nic Chilton
EIMC
University of Bradford
Bradford
BD7 1DP
UK
Email
n.chilton@bradford.ac.uk
Home page:
http://www.eimc.brad.ac.uk/

Adrian F. Clark
VASE Laboratory
Department of Electronic
Systems Engineering
University of Essex
Colchester
CO4 3SQ
UK
Email:
alien@essex.ac.uk
Home page:
http://esewww.essex.ac.uk/
~alien/

L.K. Comerford
Microcomputer Music Research
Unit
School of Computing and
Mathematics
University of Bradford
Bradford
BD7 1DP
UK
Email:
l.k.comerford@scm.brad.ac.uk
Home page:
http://www.scm.brad.ac.uk/

P.J. Comerford
Microcomputer Music Research
Unit
School of Computing and
Mathematics
University of Bradford
Bradford
BD7 1DP
UK
Email:
p.j.comerford@scm.brad.ac.uk
Home page:
http://www.scm.brad.ac.uk/

Kris Cook
Pacific Northwest National
Laboratory
Richland
WA 99352
Email:
kris.cook@pnl.gov
Home page:
http://www.pnl.gov/infoviz/

Vern Crow
Pacific Northwest National
Laboratory
Richland
WA 99352
Email:
vern.crow@pnl.gov
Home page:
http://www.pnl.gov/infoviz/

D.A. Duce
Rutherford Appleton Laboratory
Department for Computation
and Information
Chilton
Didcot
Oxfordshire
OX11 0QX
UK
Email:
D.A.Duce@rl.ac.uk
Home page:
http://www.itd.clrc.ac.uk/Person/
D.A.Duce/

Nick Dyer
BT Labs
Martlesham Heath
Suffolk
UK
Email:
nick.dyer@bt-sys.bt.co.uk
Home page:
http://www.labs.bt.com/people/

Rae Earnshaw
EIMC
University of Bradford
Bradford
BD7 1DP
UK
Email:
r.a.earnshaw@bradford.ac.uk
Home page:
http://www.eimc.brad.ac.uk/

Chris Flerackers
ANDROME nv
Wetenschapspark 4
B3590 Diepenbeek
Belgium
Email:
cflerack@luc.ac.be
Home page:
http://www.edm.luc.ac.be/

Roger J. Green
Department of Electronic
Imaging and Media
Communications
Bradford University
Richmond Road
Bradford BD7 1DP
UK.
Email:
r.j.green@bradford.ac.uk
Home page:
http://www.eimc.brad.ac.uk/

F.R.A. Hopgood
Rutherford Appleton Laboratory
Department for Computation
and Information
Chilton
Didcot
Oxfordshire
OX11 0QX
UK
Email:
F.R.A.Hopgood@rl.ac.uk
Home page:
http://www.itd.clrc.ac.uk/Person/
F.R.A.Hopgood/

Mikael Jern
Advanced Visual Systems
15 Blokken
DK 3460
Birkeroed
Denmark
Email:
mikael@avs.dk
Home page:
http://www.avs.dk/

David J. Johnston
VASE Laboratory
Department of Electronic
Systems Engineering
University of Essex
Colchester
CO4 3SQ
UK
Email:
djjohn@essex.ac.uk
Home page:
http://www.essex.ac.uk

Beth Hetzler
Pacific Northwest National
Laboratory
Richland
WA 99352
USA
Email:
beth.hetzler@pnl.gov
Home page:
http://www.pnl.gov/infoviz/

Marcelo Kallmann
Computer Graphics Laboratory
Swiss Federal Institute of
Technology
EPFL, DI-LIG
CH 1015 Lausanne
Switzerland
Email:
kallmann@lig.di.epfl.ch
Home page:
http://www.epfl.ch/

Wim Lamotte
ANDROME nv
Wetenschapspark 4
B3590 Diepenbeek
Belgium
and
Limburgs University Centre
Wetenschapspark 2
B3590 Diepenbeek
Belgium
Email:
wlamotte@luc.ac.be
Home page:
http://www.edm.luc.ac.be/

Peter J. Macer
Hewlett-Packard Research
Laboratories
Filton Road
Stoke Gifford
Bristol
BS12 6QZ
Email:
pejm@hplb.hpl.hp.com
Home page:
http://www.hpl.hp.com/

F. Martínez
Institut de Robòtica
Universitat de València
Polígono La Coma
S/N 46980 Paterna
Valencia
Spain
Email:
gil@glup.irobot.uv.es
Home page:
http://www.uv.es/

Richard May
Pacific Northwest National
Laboratory
Richland
WA 99352
USA
Email:
richard.may@pnl.gov
Home page:
http://www.pnl.gov/infoviz/

Dennis McQuerry
Pacific Northwest National
Laboratory
Richland
WA 99352
USA
Email:
dennis.mcquerry@pnl.gov
Home page:
http://www.pnl.gov/infoviz/

Renie McVeety
Pacific Northwest National
Laboratory
Richland
WA 99352
USA
Email:
renie.mcveety@pnl.gov
Home page:
http://www.pnl.gov/infoviz/

Nancy Miller
Pacific Northwest National
Laboratory
Richland
WA 99352
USA
Email:
nancy.miller@pnl.gov
Home page:
http://www.pnl.gov/infoviz/

Grant Nakamura
Pacific Northwest National
Laboratory
Richland
WA 99352
USA
Email:
grant.nakamura@pnl.gov
Home page:
http://www.pnl.gov/infoviz/

Lucy Nowell
Pacific Northwest National
Laboratory
Richland
WA 99352
USA
Email:
lucy.nowell@pnl.gov
Home page:
http://www.pnl.gov/infoviz/

I.J. Palmer
Electronic Imaging and Media
Communications Department
University of Bradford
Bradford
BD7 1DP
UK
Email:
i.j.palmer@bradford.ac.uk
Home page:
http://www.eimc.brad.ac.uk/

Martha Palmer
Center for Human Modeling and
Simulation
Department of Computer and
Information Science
University of Pennsylvania
Philadelphia
PA 19104-6389
USA
Email:
mpalmer@linc.cis.upenn.edu
Home page:
http://www.cis.upenn.edu/

Soraia Raupp Musse
Computer Graphics Laboratory
Swiss Federal Institute of
Technology
EPFL, DI-LIG
CH 1015 Lausanne
Switzerland
Email:
soraia@lig.di.epfl.ch
Home page:
http://www.epfl.ch/

Peter Robinson
University of Cambridge
Computer Laboratory
New Museums Site
Pembroke Street
Cambridge
CB2 3QG
UK
Email:
pr@cl.cam.ac.uk
Home page:
http://www.cl.cam.ac.uk/
Research/Rainbow/

R. Rodríguez
Institut de Robòtica
Universitat de València
Polígono La Coma
S/N 46980 Paterna
Valencia
Spain
Email:
gil@glup.irobot.uv.es
Home page:
http://www.uv.es/

C. Romero
Institut de Robòtica
Universitat de València
Polígono La Coma
S/N 46980 Paterna
Valencia
Spain
Email:
gil@glup.irobot.uv.es
Home page:
http://www.uv.es/

J. Sevilla
Dto. Electrònica i Informàtica
Universitat de València
Campus de Burjassot
Burjassot
Valencia
Spain
Email:
gil@glup.irobot.uv.es
Home page:
http://www.uv.es/

Jianping Shi
Center for Human Modeling and
Simulation
Department of Computer and
Information Science
University of Pennsylvania
Philadelphia
PA 19104-6389
USA
Email:
jshi@graphics.cis.upenn.edu
Home page:
http://www.cis.upenn.edu/

G.K. Stylios
COMIT
University of Bradford
Bradford
BD7 1DP
UK
Email:
g.k.stylios@brad.ac.uk
Home page:
http://www.eimc.brad.ac.uk/

W. Tang
Electronic Imaging and Media
Communications Department
University of Bradford
Bradford
BD7 1DP
UK
Email:
w.tang@bradford.ac.uk
Home page:
http://www.eimc.brad.ac.uk/

Daniel Thalmann
Computer Graphics Laboratory
Swiss Federal Institute of
Technology
EPFL, DI-LIG
CH 1015 Lausanne
Switzerland
Email:
thalmann@lig.di.epfl.ch
Home page:
http://www.epfl.ch/

Nadia Magnenat Thalmann
MIRALab
C.U.I.
University of Geneva
CH-1211
Switzerland
Email:
thalmann@cui.unige.ch
Home page:
http://miralabwww.unige.ch/

Jim Thomas
Pacific Northwest National
Laboratory
Richland
WA 99352
USA
Email:
jim.thomas@pnl.gov
Home page:
http://www.pnl.gov/infoviz/

Peter J. Thomas
Centre for Personal Information
Management
Faculty of Computer Studies and
Mathematics
University of the West of
England
Bristol
Coldharbour Lane
Bristol
BS16 1QY
UK
Email:
Peter.Thomas@uwe.ac.uk
Home page:
http://www.csm.uwe.ac.uk/
faculty/cpim/

Frank Van Reeth
ANDROME nv
Wetenschapspark 4
B3590 Diepenbeek
Belgium
and
Limburgs University Centre
Wetenschapspark 2
B3590 Diepenbeek
Belgium
Email:
frank.vanreeth@luc.ac.be
Home page:
http://www.edm.luc.ac.be/

Pascal Volino
MIRALab
C.U.I.
University of Geneva
CH-1211
Switzerland
Email:
pascal@cui.unige.ch
Home page:
http://miralabwww.unige.ch/

Graham Walker
BT Labs
Martlesham Heath
Suffolk
UK
Email:
graham.walker@bt-sys.bt.co.uk
Home page:
http://www.labs.bt.com/people/
walkergr/

T.R. Wan
COMIT
University of Bradford
Bradford
BD7 1DP
UK
Email:
t.r.wan@brad.ac.uk
Home page:
http://www.eimc.brad.ac.uk/

Janice Webster
Virtual Reality Centre
University of Teesside
Middlesbrough
TS1 3BA
UK
Email:
j.webster@tees.ac.uk
Home page:
http://www.tees.ac.uk/

Paul Whitney
Pacific Northwest National
Laboratory
Richland
WA 99352
USA
Email:
paul.whitney@pnl.gov
Home page:
http://www.pnl.gov/infoviz/

Pak Chung Wong
Pacific Northwest National Laboratory
Richland
WA 99352
USA

Email:
pakchung.wong@pnl.gov

Home page:
http://www.pnl.gov/infoviz/

1
New Media Technologies: The European Perspective

Eric Badiqué

Abstract

A flurry of new, exciting technologies is signalling the birth of a new medium, not yet completely understood, not yet fully imagined. It may exactly fit your own personal needs, or it may simply be good old TV, broadcast to millions; it may be fully immersive, taking you through a bumpy ride on your active chair, or it may simply be a picture on a screen; it may challenge you with high levels of interactivity with audio-visual objects or it may simply give you the best high-definition, multi-channel entertainment you want to have; it may be indexed and easy to navigate or it might just surprise you with things you would have never expected. This new medium will also leverage the same tools to give you telepresence with family, friends and colleagues or allow you to experience places you would never dare or dream of going to. It will redefine group meetings and some levels of social interactions with the help of avatars, virtual humans and intelligent agents. The frontier between "*story-telling*", as in current broadcasting, and "*communication*" will progressively blur, leaving us with a continuum of image-rich and flexible "*infocommunication*" services somewhere between plain old TV and multimodal telepresence. The foundations of these "New Media" technologies have been laid. ACTS and other EU programmes have played their role, helping to develop synergies across the continent. The new IST Programme will take up the "New Media" challenge and aim to catalyse the best of European research in the area. Its success will determine whether some of the most ambitious visions being dreamed up for the 21st century will become reality or not.

1.1 European Collaborative R&D

We are living in exciting times. The construction of Europe is one of the most daring undertakings ever contemplated. Although there are risks and uncertainties, there are also great hopes and promises. Europe is now a reality in many aspects of people's everyday lives, from the freedom of movement across historical borders to new opportunities for trade in one of the world's largest single markets. Along the road to integration, Europe has just passed a major milestone with the launch of the common currency, and negotiations have started to prepare for the addition of five new countries. The European vision is taking shape.

Research and development is one of many aspects in the construction of Europe. Alongside community initiatives dedicated to life sciences, energy, environments and education, the European Union actively supports R&D in Telecommunications and Information Technology through a number of Programmes. They aim at supporting the best research teams to jointly develop, prove and demonstrate the best technology. In supporting excellence, these Programmes help promote enabling technology, contribute to the development of Europe-wide standards and support European industrial, social and cultural policies.

Looking back over 10 years of European R&D in telecommunications, it is important to remember that community R&D is not just a "quick fix". It requires a long-term vision. The RACE (Research in Advanced Communications in Europe) was launched in 1987 and is only now bearing fruit. With important European successes like GSM, MPEG or DVB we are now benefiting from EU cooperation initiated in the 1980s. Community R&D has led to interoperability and affordability through collaboration in RTD, standardization and stimulation by pilots and demonstration. The current Programmes provide a good basis for future developments.

R&D now needs to adapt to a new environment. Commercial and competitive pressure is likely to lead to short-term focus at the expense of long-term vision and corresponding research support. As the complexity of systems increases, so does R&D, demanding multidisciplinary teams and approaches. Technology itself is also blurring the picture. As novel options appear in rapid succession, making the right choice for integration and deployment becomes increasingly difficult.

In this context, a new role for community R&D is taking shape. Continued and reinforced pan-European cooperation will fill some of the void left by former telecom monopolies and ensure coherence in infrastructures and services. It will also ensure the adaptation to multiple players and new technologies. Pan-European programmes will play a role if they place the emphasis on industry-wide consensus rather than technological gadgetry.

1.2 The ACTS[1] Approach: Coherence, Integration and Exploitation of Synergy

The Advanced Communications Technologies and Services Programme (ACTS) was launched in 1994. It will be completed in 2000. ACTS is characterized by five levels of integration within which synergies are being exploited.

1.2.1 Project Level: Collaborative, Pre-Competitive R&D by Multinational Teams

This is where strong European teams are built. They contribute to a European R&D identity across borders and promote exchanges between academic and industrial worlds. The added value is the following:

---

1 http://www.uk.infowin.org/ACTS/

- Working together across cultures and languages
- Investing in a common project with clear and shared responsibilities
- Leveraging complementary expertise
- Bringing the best European researchers and developers together within a common project

Projects can be of various sizes depending on their scope. Some projects count 4 to 6 partners and are particularly focused (AURORA[2] for restoration, MODEST[3] for intelligent surveillance). Others bring together a large number of partners and answer strategic European needs (MOMUSYS[4] for MPEG-4, RACE/dTTb[5] for terrestrial TV).

1.2.2 Project Cluster Level: Complementary, Synergetic Clusters of Projects

Small clusters of projects explore options and contribute to making the right technical choices. They are associated with mechanisms for exchange and comparison of results. They lead to lessons and recommendations of general interest. Examples of ACTS multimedia clusters are:

- 3D acquisition (VANGUARD[6], PANORAMA[7], RESOLV[8])
- Virtual and distributed studio (MIRAGE[9], DVP[10])
- MPEG-4 (MOMUSYS, EMPHASIS[11], VIDAS[12], SCALAR[13], SPEAR[14])
- MPEG-7 (DICEMAN[15], MODEST, HYPERMEDIA[16], STORiT[17])

1.2.3 Domain Level: Multimedia Chain From Production to User Terminal

Bringing together a large number of complementary multimedia projects in content technologies, advanced services, broadcasting and telecom services, the ACTS Multimedia Domain[18] can be considered as a European convergence laboratory. Its

---

2 http://www.ina.fr/Recherche/Aurora/index.en.html
3 http://www.tele.ucl.ac.be/MODEST/
4 http://www.tnt.uni-hannover.de/project/eu/momusys/
   momusys.html
5 http://www.analysys.co.uk/race/pl4/sucstori/sucstori.htm
6 http://www.esat.kuleuven.ac.be/~konijn/vanguard.html
7 http://www.tnt.uni-hannover.de/project/eu/panorama/
8 http://www.scs.leeds.ac.uk/resolv/
9 http://www.itc.co.uk:80/mirage/
10 http://viswiz.gmd.de/DVP/Public/
11 http://www.fzi.de/esm/projects/emphasis/emphasis.html
12 http://www-dsp.com.dist.unige.it/projects/vidas.html
13 http://www.uk.infowin.org/ACTS/RUS/PROJECTS/ac077.htm
14 http://www.uk.infowin.org/ACTS/RUS/PROJECTS/p210.htm
15 http://www.ina.fr/Recherche/diceman.en.html
16 http://www.uk.infowin.org/ACTS/RUS/PROJECTS/ac361.htm
17 http://www-ict.its.tudelft.nl/storit/

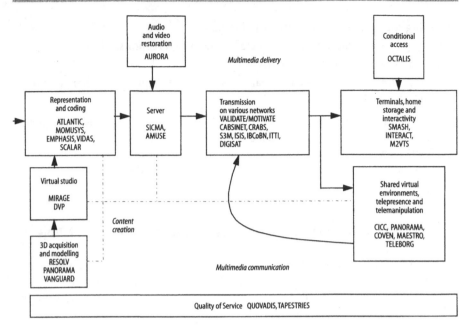

Figure 1.1 The ACTS multimedia creation, delivery and communication chain.

creation, distribution and communication technologies support the new multimedia value chain (Fig. 1.1).

1.2.4 Programme Level: Working in a Wide "Telecom" Environment

As was previously the case for RACE, the ACTS Programme is drawn together as a coherent whole. There are six technical areas in ACTS:

- Interactive digital multimedia services
- Photonic technologies
- High-speed networking
- Mobility and personal communication networks
- Intelligence in networks and services
- Quality, security and safety of communication systems and services

A basic feature of the Programme is the "*concertation mechanism*", which ensures regular exchanges and cross-fertilization between project participants. It also permits ACTS results to be presented coherently and in a form suitable for active dissemination to interest groups outside the Programme. Through various concertation mechanisms, project achievements are collated and presented as Programme level results which take the form of guidelines and recommendations.

---

18 http://www.uk.infowin.org/ACTS/ANALYSYS/CONCERTATION/
MULTIMEDIA/

Operating in a coherent and integrated environment, projects contribute to formulation and implementation of European Telecom policies.

1.2.5 World Level: Contributing to Standardization

Within the ACTS Programme, a major priority has been to ensure that projects
contribute to standardization. In most cases this has been a prerequisite. This
approach has been extremely positive in the large majority of cases and numerous
ACTS projects have significantly contributed and, sometimes profoundly, shaped
emerging standards in groups such as ISO/MPEG[19], DAVIC[20], DVB[21], FIPA[22] or
OPIMA[23]. A genuine contribution to standardization activities ensures relevance
and high-quality work, since projects are literally "constantly audited" by some of
the world's most talented engineers within standardization groups. It also ensures
that the research will have real impact and it supports open standards policies key
to the development of healthy competition. Some examples of highly successful
ACTS multimedia contributions to global standardization are in MOMUSYS,
EMPHASIS, VIDAS, DICEMAN for MPEG-4 and 7, SCALAR and SPEAR for
JPEG2000, and MODEST for FIPA.

1.3 New Media Technologies in ACTS

Within the ACTS Programme, a group of about 30 projects are now delivering
results and contributing to the shaping of new media technologies along three main
axes (see also ACcenTS[24] Newsletter):

• Representation and coding
• New content paradigms
• New communication paradigms

1.3.1 Advanced Representation and Coding of Audio-Visual Material

The work is performed exclusively within the framework of major international
standardization activities (ITU, ISO/IEC...). Significant contributions and, in many
cases, leadership has been provided in areas such as H263+, JPEG2000, MPEG-2/4
and recently also MPEG-7. Collaboration with the COST[25] framework has been
initiated. Emerging tools provide object-based representation, enhanced interaction, 3D sound and graphics, hybrid imaging, indexed content and scalability over
heterogeneous networks.

---

19 http://drogo.cselt.stet.it/mpeg/
20 http://www.davic.org/
21 http://www.dvb.org/
22 http://www.fipa.org/
23 http://drogo.cselt.it/ufv/leonardo/opima/
24 http://www.esat.kuleuven.ac.be/~konijn/accents.html
25 http://www.teltec.dcu.ie/cost211/

1.3.1.1 MPEG 2 Compression Extended to the Entire Content Production Chain

The ATLANTIC[26] project, and its predecessor COUGAR, have helped enable the cost benefits promised by high-efficiency MPEG-2 audio and visual compression to be extended to the entire content production chain. ATLANTIC overturned accepted wisdom by demonstrating that the entire moving image audio-visual programme chain (including concatenated coding, frame-accurate editing, switching, mixer effects and bit-rate changing) can be implemented using low bit-rate, long GOP, MPEG-2 coding. The project demonstrated improvements in technical quality at lower cost and without impairing content creativity. This success opens up the possibility of trading high-quality, full-motion, audio-visual content over practicable networks.

The project has achieved a number of world firsts in applying MPEG-2 coding and bit-stream handling. MPEG-2 compression can now be used for remote signal capture, contribution by satellite or telecoms networks, post-production in a network and server-based environment, content trading, play-out and scheduling, primary distribution to satellite link-ups and regional studio centres, and "drop and insert" for advertisements and regional programmes to secondary distribution by cable and terrestrial networks. At each of these stages the fourfold increase in coding efficiency of MPEG-2 brings savings in network and storage capacity, as well as cost reductions from the economies of scale resulting from using an open international standard.

1.3.1.2 Second Generation Coding: MPEG-4 Standardization

MPEG-4 understands an audiovisual scene as a composition of audiovisual objects with specific characteristics and behaviour, notably in space and time. This conceptual jump makes MPEG-4 the first truly digital audiovisual representation standard. The object composition approach allows support of new functionalities, such as content-based interaction and manipulation, as well as the improvement of already available functionalities, such as coding efficiency, by using only the most adequate representation methodology and coding features for each type of data.

One of the most exciting and powerful consequences of the object-based approach is the integration of natural and synthetic content. While until now the natural and synthetic audio-visual worlds have evolved mostly along parallel roads, the MPEG-4 representation approach allows the composition of natural and synthetic data in the same scene, unifying the two separate worlds. This unification allows us to efficiently code natural as well as synthetic visual data, without undue translations like the conversion to pixel-based representations of synthetic models. MPEG-4 integrates visual objects of various types, e.g. frames, 2D arbitrarily shaped video objects, text, graphics and 3D faces, as well as audio objects of various types, e.g.

---

26 http://www.bbc.co.uk/atlantic/

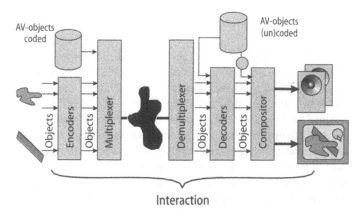

Figure 1.2 Simplified architecture of an MPEG-4 system.

music, speech and structured audio. Therefore, in order to build the final audiovisual scene (Fig. 1.2), not only do the coded representations of the various audiovisual objects have to be considered, but so does the description of their composition.

MOMUSYS has been instrumental in giving European interests a strong influence in MPEG-4 and putting European companies on the leading edge of advanced AV representation technology and new application paradigms. MOMUSYS has become the European platform for ISO/IEC MPEG-4 standardization, validating results in extensive real-user field trials that use MOMUSYS hardware demonstrators as terminals. The main objective of the project has been to develop and validate the technical elements necessary to provide new audio-visual functionalities, like content manipulation, content scalability and content-based access, for mobile multimedia systems.

EMPHASIS has developed a high-performance MPEG-4 video decoder. A generically optimized version (i.e. platform independent) has been presented with success at several MPEG meetings. This decoder is now being further developed by Philips Digital Video Systems for audio and video streaming within three types of network: satellite link, Internet and LAN. One major achievement of EMPHASIS is a fully functional and completely synthesized VHDL description of an MPEG-4 rendering coprocessor, also supporting perspective transformation. The individual modules of the coprocessor can be reused for other applications and will therefore become the basis for building future MPEG video decoding systems.

One partner of EMPHASIS has developed an MPEG-4 player capable of displaying MPEG-4 bit streams containing natural audio, natural video and synthetic 3D objects. The player has been integrated with a portable 3D transformation engine specifically developed for cost-sensitive applications such as digital TV. Basic research has also been carried out in EMPHASIS on the 3D rendering of audio objects in simulated acoustic environments. This led to the development of new efficient schemes for the reproduction of acoustic scenes by stereo headphones and multi-channel loudspeaker systems.

1.3.1.3 MPEG4 on the Internet

COMIQS's[27] objective is the technical and service validation of a set of new paradigms introduced by recent and ongoing innovations in ISO/MPEG-4/VRML and the Internet IETF. Within the convergence process of interactive multimedia applications – ranging from entertainment to engineering, the COMIQS achievements will be validated in the field of Electronic Commerce. COMIQS's added value and differentiation reside in all-media integration (3D virtual catalogue integrating digital high-quality multimedia with video, photo-realistic images and high-quality sound), increased interactivity (objects contained in motion pictures, audio tracks, 3D objects), real-time streaming, placement of MPEG-4 into the Internet context, and Quality of Service management. The project partners are already contributing to the IETF/MPEG-4 liaison.

1.3.1.4 MPEG-4 Intellectual Property Rights

MIRADOR[28] defines, develops and promotes an extensive framework for copyright protection, compliant with the MPEG-4 Intellectual Property Rights group specifications, including still pictures, video and audio protection. The objectives of the project are to deliver an MPEG-4 watermarking suitable for audio, pictures and video objects to be used in MPEG-4 productions, to integrate these technologies with MPEG-4 codecs, to promote the technology so that a better understanding of watermarking technology is reached by rights holders, and to introduce the first watermarked MPEG-4 production acting as a shop window for the project.

1.3.1.5 TV Screen Customization

The CUSTOM-TV[29] project develops, demonstrates and validates the technology for user-friendly screen customization and interactive programme selection in a multimedia broadcast environment by introducing the multimedia elements of the MPEG-4 standard and the object description of the MPEG-7 standard into existing Digital Visual Broadcasting (DVB) services. This system will demonstrate the compatible coexistence of MPEG-2 with MPEG-4 and MPEG-7, contributing to faster acceptance of these new standards.

1.3.1.6 Distributed Internet Content Exchange with MPEG-7 and Agent Negotiations

MPEG-7 is a nascent standardization effort within ISO/IEC. Its aim is to specify standard description technology to facilitate identification, retrieval and filtering

---

27 http://www.ccett.fr/comiqs/welcome.htm
28 http://www.tele.ucl.ac.be./MIRADOR/
29 http://www.irt.de/customtv/

of content. In the context of content production, it is significant because it will create the possibility to search all media archives simultaneously, over computer networks for instance, in the way that we search the WWW today for text documents. This has the potential to drastically reduce pre-sales expense. Importantly, MPEG-7 does not specify how content is made available; an MPEG-7 description may be associated with an analogue tape, for instance. DICEMAN will open up valuable databases of multimedia content by making them easier to search, using advanced forms of descriptions and indexing and advanced forms of user interfaces. It will enable the location of the best content for a given purpose, both locally and globally, over electronic networks, using agent-based assistants to users and provider. The project will enable the exchange and trading of multimedia content over electronic networks using standardized interfaces to electronic databases. At the time of writing DICEMAN had already taken a major leading role in the MPEG-7 standardization group.

1.3.1.7 Multimedia Object Descriptors Extraction

MODEST is defining and developing a framework for the analysis of video sequences in order to extract high-level semantic scene interpretation. It is based on the segmentation, tracking and indexing of moving objects in video scenes and the index interpretation by the use of Intelligent Physical Agents (IPA). The work is performed in the scope of the MPEG-4, MPEG-7 and FIPA standards. The project will be demonstrated in a video surveillance application. At the time of writing, the project was actively contributing to MPEG-7 specifications and was in charge of the "real-time systems" group within the FIPA (Foundation for Physical Intelligent Agents) international specification group.

1.3.1.8 Hypermedia Service Environment

HYPERMEDIA investigates the handling and delivery of continuous multimedia (audio-visual) material in a hypermedia service environment. This sort of environment allows users to navigate in hyper-space and explore databases owned by the various players in the service chain (content providers, network providers, service providers etc). HYPERMEDIA's users will be professionals – the communications and media organizations which are the service providers for the general public. User requirements are evolving, and the most significant development is demand for improved navigation techniques. This implies that multimedia services will have to evolve into hypermedia services. HYPERMEDIA develops video indexing tools that increase the possibilities for interactivity. Service providers and other professional users will be able to use these tools on their audio-visual materials to offer improved navigation and search facilities. There is a clear market opportunity for services that handle and deliver continuous audio-visual materials. This "continuous audio-visual market" will have a value chain of services. HYPERMEDIA will demonstrate a solution addressing all aspects of this market (metadata, video indexing tools, databases architecture, network architecture, intellectual property rights services) and develop an exploitation plan based on the results of its trial.

1.3.1.9 Standardization of Second-Generation Still Image Representation and Coding

The SPEAR project aims at giving the JPEG group work better visibility by having at least six of the most active experts work together and disseminate the results of their work in their respective countries. Meetings between experts will help them converge their national interests to a European common position. At the time of writing, the SPEAR team was actively involved in the JPEG group, representing European companies' interests in a coherent manner.

MPEG-related activities within ACTS have been coordinated by the ACTS MPEG Forum[30].

1.3.2 Use of Innovative Tools to Develop New Content Paradigms

Within a group centred on "Technology for Content Creation", ACTS projects have developed and shared new approaches to 3D acquisition and modelling, distributed and low-cost virtual studio, capture and animation, and restoration of audiovisual heritage. This group has carried out an analysis of likely future trends in content creation within a digital environment and has produced recommendations within a compendium document[31] which is publicly available (see also the "The MEDICI Framework, New Technologies for Cultural Heritage"[32]).

1.3.2.1 3D Acquisition Technology for Consumers

The RESOLV system uses a laser range finder and video camera to produce cost-effective copies of real environments rapidly. An interior is scanned from many positions to provide a complete model that is realistic enough to create the sense of "being there" for telepresence and navigation applications. The absolute accuracy of the laser range finder is sufficient for use in surveying. The AEST (Autonomous Environmental Sensor for Telepresence) plans and navigates to appropriate capture positions after overall guidance from the operator. The tripod or trolley-based EST is a lightweight alternative that can be used in a wider variety of locations.

VANGUARD has developed novel techniques for 3D image acquisition. These avoid the need for expensive hardware by using readily available consumer electronics and software for the creation of 3D models from uncalibrated video

---

30 http://www.ccir.ed.ac.uk/mpeg/
31 http://www.ina.fr/Ext/SIC/
32 http://www.medicif.org/

sequences. All this serves to make 3D acquisition technology much more accessible to the average amateur enthusiast. VANGUARD's goal was ambitious – at the outset even the theoretical feasibility still had to be proven. Today, the project has succeeded and the consortium's theoretical work has, to a large extent, defined the state of the art in this area. Practical results from the project have been demonstrated at several fairs (ACF, EITC, CGIX, IBC etc.). At ACF a VANGUARD demo received a Golden Eye Award for its three-dimensional reconstruction of the archaeological site at Sagalassos (Turkey). Two of VANGUARD's academic partners have now founded spin-off companies having the commercial exploitation of 3D acquisition technology as their core business. At the time of writing, one of these spin-offs (Eyetronics) was already working with a special effects company in Hollywood.

1.3.2.2 The Coming of Age of Virtual Reality Television

Reducing the cost of virtual studios...

Three-dimensional (3D) virtual reality opens the way to realistic "walk-throughs" and theme park experiences in the home as well as exciting broadcast services. Most virtual environments start off as 3D models made by computer, but some are also being obtained from live video. All 3D images need to be viewed in a form that retains the important depth information, so they are not reduced to a single plane on the screen. MIRAGE has successfully developed a lightweight telepresence camera and integrated this with a number of important elements of programme production and subsequent display.

MIRAGE has developed affordable and practical virtual production systems and techniques, and has successfully demonstrated 3D programme production and display. At the heart of the virtual studio is a fully robotic production system, controlled by a single operator, to select shots with computer graphic or pre-shot video backgrounds. The system is PC-based and obtains the highest broadcast quality with photo-realistic, pre-(field)-rendered backgrounds. Full camera motion control, also including roll, is provided by the MIRAGE developed Powerpod head. The MIRAGE Virtual Edit Suite (VES) will be used for real-time virtual production in 3D using the lightweight camera developed within MIRAGE. The VES is a high-end system delivering high-quality graphics without the need for frame-by-frame rendering and giving perfectly anti-aliased high-definition textures. Its user interface follows traditional edit suite practice.

...and producing content in a distributed environment

Distributed video production (DVP) refers to situations in the broadcasting industry where the cameras, recorders, switchers, mixers and other equipment used in professional video production (or post-production) are located at several sites linked by high bandwidth networks. At the consumer fair in Berlin and at the International Broadcasting Convention IBC '97 in Amsterdam, the ACTS project DVP presented a weather forecast TV show assembled from distributed virtual studios. For the first time in a complex setup, different techniques such as distributed virtual studio, animated virtual characters and a 3D flight over Germany (with animated weather effects) were seamlessly integrated into a single TV weather forecast production environment. For the IFA fair, a virtual studio was connected to an SGI Onyx rendering machine at the German national research centre for information technology (GMD) at Birlinghoven via high-bandwidth ATM. Control data generated by the camera and the virtual character animators at Berlin were submitted to GMD via 2 Mbps ATM circuits. At GMD the virtual set, background as well as foreground, and the virtual character were rendered at high quality in real-time. From Bonn to Berlin the generated video in professional contribution quality was sent via 92 Mbps ATM circuits.

One particular advantage of the DVP distributed Virtual Studio system over local installations revealed itself at the IFA: Compared to Virtual Studio productions on site, the time to set up the complete system to be ready for production was very short due to the distributed configuration. Hardware was already pre-configured at the different sites and only remote control had to be established. DVP results are strongly influencing worldwide drives initiated within EBU and SMPTE[33]. Joint task forces on compression algorithms, file formats, transfer protocols, system management, metadata and interfaces have also been launched successfully. A number of manufacturers are now showing early ATM adapter products designed to support this DVP technology.

1.3.2.3 Digital Archive Restoration

Since the advent of film and video recording, a unique record of this century's cultural and historical events has been compiled by broadcasters, producers and archivists. A huge wealth of this archive material is held and it has particular problems in the form of video noise, film grain, dirt and other defects. Television channels, archivists and film producers all hold numerous archive programmes which, taken as a whole, make up a unique record of history, artistic and cultural development and of all aspects of life in this century. Each type of video and film format has its own share of particular degradation, with problems increasing with each replay.

Restoration solutions at an acceptable cost are therefore indispensable for the large-scale utilization of television archives, thus contributing, through revenue generated, to the preservation of our audio-visual heritage. The AURORA project aims to create tools to restore television archives efficiently. Present methods are highly labour-intensive. The AURORA project has produced hardware allowing a large proportion of defects to be removed automatically so that manual operation is only required for a small proportion of the processed programme, and has assisted with advanced user interfaces, hence reducing costs and raising quality. A prototype of the AURORA real-time restoration system was demonstrated successfully at the IBC'98 exhibition in Amsterdam. The prototype is a forerunner of the next generation of cost-effective restoration equipment aimed at opening up archives for documentary, educational and entertainment purposes.

---

33 http://www.smpte.org/engr/ebumeet1.html or http://www.ebu.ch/pmc_home.html

1.3.2.4 Quality Evaluation

The quality of new digital services will depend on program content, the choice of coding scheme and the allocated service bit rate. It will be important for content providers to be able to ensure that their programs are adapted to the chosen coding scheme and delivery medium. An automated quality assessment tool capable of calculating the expected quality of the delivered services will be well suited for this task. Future stereoscopic television services will require the control of filming parameters to enhance stereoscopic presentation and minimize viewer eyestrain. New subjective assessment methods are required to determine optimum filming parameters. TAPESTRIES[34] is developing an automatic quality assessment tool for MPEG-2 encoded services. Subjective quality assessment methodologies adapted to the evaluation of MPEG-4 encoded services are also under investigation. In TAPESTRIES new subjective quality assessment criteria based on viewer "presence" are being investigated for the quality evaluation of stereoscopic services.

1.3.3 Use of Multi-Modal Interfaces, Advanced Delivery Mechanisms and Innovative Content Tools to Develop New Communication Paradigms

The "Telepresence and Shared Virtual Environments" group[35] has functioned as a think-tank to produce recommendations and guidelines regarding networking requirements, usability and safety of new telepresence services. It has also been analysing the potential of tele-operation, telepresence, VEs and virtual humans in terms of their impact on society, for example through the development of telework.

1.3.3.1 Telepresence: It's as Real as it Gets Without Physically Being There

Telepresence extends the video conferencing concept so that participants can use non-verbal aspects of communication (eye contact, spatial perception, body movement, gestures, facial expressions) in the same way as they would in a face-to-face meeting.

Telepresence in the medical field...

Two complete imaging systems for video communication with multi-viewpoint capability have been developed within PANORAMA. The first system is a real-time 3D videoconferencing system with viewpoint adaptation which uses a stereoscopic image sequence as input. The second system is based on a true 3D reconstruction of the scene using a trinocular camera setup. The Surgical Research Unit OP 2000 (Germany) implemented computer, video, communication and laser technology in the clinical routine. OP 2000 built up interfaces for ACTS PANORAMA and tested these developments in the medical environment.

---

34 http://www.itc.co.uk/s-and-t/ACTS/tapestries/
35 http://www.uk.infowin.org/ACTS/ANALYSYS/CONCERTATION/
   CHAINS/SI/HOME/CH_SID/

A network for the first field trials was implemented using experimental 20–30 GHz transponders of the national satellite "DFS Kopernikus". This method of linking the codecs was chosen for its easy availability, great flexibility and the possibility of making point-to-multipoint connections. Today, use is made of the more commonly available 12–14 GHz band, where the necessary earth stations can be both smaller and cheaper.

...telepresence brings music to their ears...

A multi-site musical rehearsal is one of the most demanding telepresence/teleconference applications in terms of synchronization and audio/video quality. The advantages of such an environment can be numerous, both in gaining time and money and in bringing together artists and ideas from around the world. However, the musicians and conductor require not only high-quality audio and video, but also three-dimensional sound space rendering and very low transmission delays. Within the ACTS-DVP project a two-site environment for conducting distributed musical rehearsals was developed. Trials have been performed and the qualitative and quantitative performance of the system measured based on a methodology developed within the project.

Two major distributed musical rehearsal trials took place between GMD (Sankt Augustin, Bonn) and the University of Geneva on November 1996 and May 1997 with the GRAME EOC orchestra. The modern music pieces retained for the rehearsal were P. Boulez's "Dérives" for six instruments and H.P. Platz's "Piece Noire", for 12 instruments. The musicians were located in Geneva while the conductor was in St Augustin. The total duration of each rehearsal was 6 hours. Objective evaluation results indicate that the overall quality of the DR system is initially about 40% of a normal localized rehearsal. The results also indicate clearly that the performance of the orchestra improves dramatically with two or three 10 minute training sessions. After these short training sessions performance reached the 100% level.

...telepresence through your personal avatar...

The project VIDAS has developed an MPEG-4 compliant coder/decoder capable of analysing a videophone sequence, segmenting the speaker's region, extracting face calibration and animation parameters (according to MPEG-4 specifications) and applying them to a suitable 3D head model which is capable of synthetically reproducing the sequence.

Any human face can be represented faithfully through synthetic 3D models, which are calibrated and animated by means of a very compact stream of parameters according to the syntax defined for Face and Body Animation (FBA) in MPEG-4. The ACTS VIDAS project has played a very central role in the FBA group, by contributing sequences to the Test Data Set and by providing source code for a 3D head model. Known applications of this technology range from video games to multi-modal interactive interfaces or movie production.

...telepresence within shared virtual environments...

Collaborative Virtual Environments (CVEs) actively support human–human and human–machine communication through shared 3D spaces. CVEs find uses in such diverse applications as virtual meeting rooms (e.g. business conferencing), shared visualizations (e.g. architectural walk-throughs), cooperative working (e.g. car design) and a variety of cultural experiences (e.g. virtual museums). COVEN (COllaborative Virtual ENvironments) was launched in October 1995. Its aim is to comprehensively explore the issues in the design, implementation and use of CVEs at scientific, methodological and technological levels.

COVEN has recently developed and held trials of a new technique that represents a breakthrough in the use of CVEs – a technique which will make working with CVEs easier, more efficient and highly flexible, hence giving users more control over their environment. One essential ingredient to the success of CVEs is their ability to make efficient use of group communication, as collaborative applications require high interaction and low latency.

The project has successfully tested a complement to the MBone – called the DIVEBONE[36] (from the Swedish Institute of Computer Science) – which runs on top of the COVEN prototype platform DIVE (Distributed Interactive Virtual Environment). DIVEBONE builds an application-level multicast backbone. It uses algorithms and principles that are similar to the MBone, while restricting network traffic to DIVE-specific packets. Within this scheme, each member site operates an application that connects to its nearest DIVEBONE neighbours. The COVEN DIVEBONE trials, a "world first" for CVE applications, have already demonstrated beyond doubt the advantages and efficacy of the concepts over existing techniques.

...telepresence for virtual tennis...

A real-time, virtual and networked interactive tennis game simulation was presented at the opening and closing session of Telecom Interactive '97 in Geneva, Switzerland. It was further demonstrated at the opening ceremony of Virtual Humans '97 Conference in Los Angeles, at the Virtual Technologies booth of the SIGGRAPH '97 exhibition, and at various other conferences. In this demonstration the interactive players immersed themselves in the virtual tennis court environment using head-mounted displays, magnetic sensors and data gloves. Several underlying technologies supporting this simulation were developed within the framework of the ACTS COVEN project.

...and telepresence for entertainment

Building on COVEN, VPARK is extending an existing Shared Virtual Environment system and creates a Virtual Amusement Park by integrating several applications on the platform. The Virtual Amusement Park is developed as a major infrastructure to be used at a Pan-European level, offering users the possibility of incorporating their own applications in the future. The Core System Architecture is modular, flexible and open. The internal modules, forming the core of the system, provide basic functionality at a relatively low level: visual database management, animation of virtual humans, rendering and networking. The current system supports a networked virtual environment that allows multiple users to interact with each other and their surroundings in real time. The users are represented by

---

36 http://www.sics.se/dive/dive.html

3D virtual human actors with realistic appearances and articulations. In addition to user-guided agents, the environment can also include fully autonomous human agents. The current system incorporates different media: sound, 3D models, facial interaction, textures mapped on 3D objects and real-time movies. It is being extended in several ways. A more advanced network structure is being implemented, allowing better scalability in terms of the number of users supported. New basic functions are being integrated. The system's core and interfaces are being extended to support more multimedia objects: generalized images, speech sequences, video, text. User interfaces are developed for defining face and body behaviours.

1.3.3.2 The Next Telepresence Frontier: Tele-Manipulation

Systems for real-time, physical telepresence in real remote environments...

The TELEBORG[37] project aims to develop the required hardware and software infrastructure for real-time physical telepresence in real remote environments. This requires data input and output devices representing a great number of physical parameters further than image and audio. Such devices monitor kinaesthetic and haptic data such as motion and force. The project initially deals with the development of low-cost bandwidth-optimized data input devices which will include kinaesthetic and force-reflecting functions. These are "data gloves", "data arms" with force-feedback sense, and helmet-type screens with head orientation sensors as well as active seats for overall body dynamics monitoring. In parallel, adequate data output devices will be developed to serve as "physical supports" for the remote user. They will include dual camera mountings and manipulators, performing head–eye coordination, hand–eye coordination etc. The number of degrees of freedom and force-exerting capacities will depend on the particular application.

High-performance telepresence may open the possibility of teleworking in industrial sectors ("blue collar teleworking"), requiring equipment driving or guidance (such as material handling or part assembly), or in sectors involving unpleasant working conditions (heat, dust, chemical pollution etc.). The possibility of machine guidance through tele-manipulation of machine driving panels opens an extremely wide range of applications from chemical industry to civil works. The impact on working conditions for the users may be enormous. Telepresence peripherals (helmet screens, force-reflecting gloves etc.) may become standard educational tools in the near future. Using such devices, students may be able to perform "hands-on" experiences in virtual "didactic" environments from mechanics, atomic scale chemistry, etc.

...tele-manipulation for remote surgery...

MIDSTEP[38] has developed two demonstrators for telesurgery, one for an interventional ultrasound demonstrator (telescanning) and one for minimal

---

37 http://www.de.infowin.org/ACTS/RUS/PROJECTS/ac216.htm
38 http://www.uk.infowin.org/ACTS/RUS/PROJECTS/ac214.htm

invasive surgery (laparoscopy). With the telescanning demonstrator, the remote clinician is able to serve a number of facilities to take a biopsy with the help of an ultrasound system. The laparoscopic demonstrator allows the performance of ultrasound scanning with surgeons in the operation room and a remote ultrasound radiologist. The project contributes to the progress of R&D in telepresence, focusing on the following areas:

• audio and video image acquisition and processing
• augmented reality and perception by the human in a remote environment
• robotics
• ergonomics and human–computer interface
• standardization trials and participation in new standards definition
• bandwidth requirements for networking and audio–video compression in networking
• security and safety for processing and communication quality in telemedicine

...and tele-manipulation for maintenance

The MAESTRO[39] project has demonstrated the use of telepresence for the maintenance, installation and repair of mechanical (or electromechanical) equipment. It is particularly dedicated to the training of complex maintenance/installation scenarios for remote users, such as SMEs which cannot afford complex on-site training equipment. The resulting technology should enable users to train themselves to deal with maintenance tasks by connecting to a "Virtual Showroom" where they can learn maintenance procedures through computer-augmented video-based telepresence.

The following technologies have been either investigated, developed or integrated within the MAESTRO platform:

• broadband networking including monitoring and adaptation of the quality of service
• video-based telepresence
• teleoperation techniques (e.g. simple robotic arms, joystick-based and/or dataglove-based teleoperation)
• augmented reality and real-time registration of CAD models of equipment on its video image
• hypermedia data management for technical documentation
• human–computer interaction, based on speech interfaces

1.3.3.3 Fitness for Purpose of Video Telephony and Telepresence

The primary aim of VIS-à-VIS[40] is to examine the configuration requirements for consistent and accurate communication through video telephony in comparison

---

39 http://www.uk.infowin.org/ACTS/RUS/PROJECTS/ac233.htm

with standards of real-world face-to-face communication; i.e. identifying the veracity of video telephony and its "fitness for purpose". The key objectives are to define objective face-to-face video telephony criteria and measurement tools for advanced communication service tasks, to conduct experiments to determine the veracity of different configurations on the basis of face-to-face psychological criteria and to create recommendations and benchmark tests for determining "fitness for purpose" to enable reliable procedures for a rapid and flexible video telephony service introduction. The results of the experiments shall be formulated as fitness-for-purpose guidelines. The guidelines shall be appropriate for manufacturers, suppliers and user groups and shall include specific recommendations for current and future technology standards and service implementation requirements.

1.4 Future Perspectives: The IST[41] Programme

The information society builds on the convergence of information, communication and networking technologies. The Information Society Technologies (IST) Programme was launched on 15 March 1999 and will last for four years. It is designed to help create a user-friendly information society by building a global knowledge, media and computing space which is universally and seamlessly accessible to *all* through interoperable, dependable and affordable products and services. The structure and scope of the new IST Programme were inspired by the following:

- The need for universal access to *general-interest services* by citizens using highly capable digital devices.
- The requirement for organizations to constantly shift the boundaries of their operations and collaborations, reinvent existing activities, and competitively exploit *new business models and markets.*
- The importance of *exploiting Europe's creative and technological assets*, its rich heritage and diversity and its highly educated human capital to produce, organize, package and deliver new digital interactive information products and services.
- The strategic necessity to ensure that Europe develops a *proper and competitive technological basis* to achieve these goals.

1.4.1 Structure of the IST Programme

As a result, the IST Programme is structured as four interrelated Key Actions, each with specific objectives (Fig. 1.3). It consists of a set of complementary activities that are derived by grouping together the technologies, systems, applications and services and the research and development and take-up actions with the greatest affinity or interdependence. The Programme also caters for long-term research

---

40 http://www.uk.infowin.org/ACTS/RUS/PROJECTS/ac314.htm
41 http://www.cordis.lu/ist/

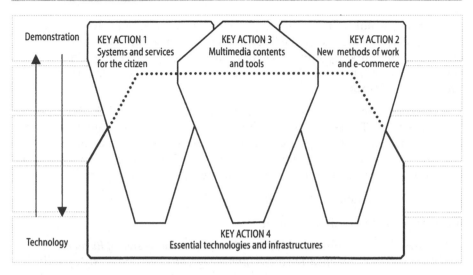

Figure 1.3 Integrated Key Actions.

within the "Future and Emerging Technologies" domain of activity. The objectives of the proposed Key Actions are as follows:

- *Key Action I – Systems and services for the citizen*
  Foster the creation of the next generation of user-friendly, dependable, cost-effective and interoperable general-interest services in the area of education and training, health, special needs, administrations, environment and transport.
- *Key Action II – New methods of work and electronic commerce*
  Develop technologies to enable European workers and enterprises, in particular SMEs, to increase their competitiveness in the global market-place.
- *Key Action III – Multimedia content and tools*
  Improve the functionality, usability and acceptability of future information products and services to enable linguistic and cultural diversity and contribute to the valorization and exploitation of Europe's cultural patrimony.
- *Key Action IV – Essential technologies and infrastructures*
  Promote excellence in the technologies which are crucial to the information society, to accelerate their take-up and broaden their field of application. The work will address in particular the convergence of information processing, communications and networking technologies and infrastructures.
- *Future and emerging technologies*
  Support research which is of a longer-term nature or involves particularly high risks.

1.5 Digital Media Futures in IST

The development of digital media technologies will naturally be widely supported by the IST Programme. This will be the case for essential technologies as well as applications, demonstrations and trials. An important aspect is likely to be effective combination of pluri-disciplinary technologies such as interfaces, coding and processing, networking, human factors and service engineering. This will be encouraged through the setting up of dedicated cross-programme projects and supporting activities.

The following is an attempt to provide some guidance on support of "Digital Media Futures" within IST. The text consists of direct quotes from the IST Work Programme. It is not exhaustive and is based on a largely personal interpretation of the IST Action Lines projected onto this conference's main themes. The corresponding IST Action Lines as specified in the workplan are given at the end of each paragraph.

1. Digital Information and Creativity

Authoring and new forms of content

"The Programme will promote more creativity and better design of European multimedia content in key application areas (knowledge, business and lifestyle publishing and geographic information) through the development of advanced content technologies. The objective will be to improve multimedia authoring, design and production systems for handling radically new combinations of highly visual and interactive media forms, including 3D and virtual reality. The aim will also be to explore new forms of multi-sensory contents enabling enhanced user perception and interaction, and to develop and evaluate the needed architectures, models and tools. The work is expected to capitalise on European strengths in design, cultural diversity and audiovisual production creativity by involving directly creators and designers. It should include the integration of new forms of content with novel delivery mechanisms in new media" (Action Line [AL] III.2.1 and III.5.1).

2. Interfaces for New Media

Adaptable multi-sensory interfaces

"The objective is the development and demonstration of integrated multi-sensor subsystems using advanced sensor, actuator and display technologies including image and auditory scene processing. The scope includes the development of new interaction paradigms and inter-mediation technologies supporting intelligent multi-modal, multi-sensorial user interfaces for portable and/or wearable information appliances and systems. The approach should aim at affordability, ease of use and accessibility and be targeted to both consumer and professional individual and group users. The scope also includes the development and demonstration of technologies for advanced displays, including, as appropriate, integrated driver, image processing, touch-sensing and control electronics, aiming at low-cost, mass-market applications. The work is to be complemented by take-up actions" (AL IV.6.1).

3. Art, Design, and Virtual Communities

Digital preservation and access to scientific and cultural heritage

"The work will address new ways of representing, analysing, manipulating and managing different kinds of digital cultural objects from different media sources, with special attention given to surrogates of fragile physical objects. The work should focus on the sustainable development of valuable digital repositories in Europe's

libraries, museums and archives. The aim will also be to improve access by citizens and by professionals to Europe's fast-growing science and culture knowledge base, through developing advanced systems and services supporting large-scale distributed, multi-disciplinary collections of cultural and scientific multi-media resources. The technological focus is on rich representations, powerful immersive features such as 3D visualization, real-time virtual object manipulation and group interactivity, whether for multimedia retrieval, virtual galleries, mass media events or audio-visual distribution. Work is expected to develop new mixed-economy models for exploitation, repackaging and re-use. Work should also address interoperable access to distributed resources, whether through cross-domain resource discovery, interfaces or new architectures and standards, or whether through digital archives integrating library and museum objects"(AL III.2.3 and III.2.4)

Large-scale shared virtual and augmented environments

"The objective will be to develop and demonstrate models, languages and technologies for shared virtual and augmented environments and to explore human interaction in them, for both professional and consumer uses. The scope includes multi-sensory interaction within both reality-based and non-real virtual and augmented environments and their seamless integration with audio-visual representation and coding techniques. The technological work should be complemented by large-scale demonstrators of new applications and by social and psychological research addressing both novice and experienced users" (AL III.4.2).

4. Animation and Virtual Humans

Real-time simulation and visualization technologies

"The intent will be to develop and demonstrate large-scale and/or real-time distributed simulation and visualization systems for design, to support control and business processes, for training and general-interest applications. Support to multi-scale multi-physics simulations, interoperability and re-usability of software components on heterogeneous distributed systems, and support for collaborative work, are particular priorities. In addition to demonstrations and assessments, complementary work is expected to include both first-user and best-practice actions. The R&D will also cover new and improved virtual-reality modelling languages, virtual-presence concepts such as telepresence, avatars and autonomous agents, scalability and interoperability over distributed heterogeneous platforms and networks" (AL IV.4.1 and IV.4.2).

5. Digital Media

A new "Digital Medium" is emerging from the confluence of new forms of content and digital art, novel interfaces, virtual communities and intelligent avatars. In addition to the opportunities mentioned above, advanced information management will be a priority of IST. As part of more forward-looking activities, research into a universal information ecosystem will also be supported.

Information management methods

"The objective will be to develop and validate advanced information management methods and tools for very large-scale, co-operative, information repositories. The work is intended to form a bridge between multimedia content applications,

personal information systems and the enabling technologies, generic systems and open architectures. It should specifically cover techniques for the storage and management of information in higher orders of magnitude than presently widely available and advanced search and retrieval based on novel processing techniques, taking into account the likely distributed and heterogeneous nature of such repositories. The work is to be complemented by take-up actions" (AL IV.3.4).

Universal information ecosystems

"The work will aim at the creation of an "universal information ecosystem" in which every single "knowledge entity" (whether a person, organization or entity acting on their behalf) can be globally, yet selectively, aware of the opportunities afforded by all others at any point in time. "Knowledge entities" will seek to achieve their objectives by identifying those most appropriate to collaborate with and the most effective ways in which to do so, dynamically self-organizing and establishing new organizational structures as needed. This initiative will explore novel scenarios, techniques and environments in a context where more and more people and organizations need to communicate, co-operate, and trade with each other in a truly open and global environment. It will combine experimental and theoretical research, bringing together interdisciplinary expertise in networking technologies, distributed systems, software engineering, computational logic, artificial intelligence, human computer interaction, as well as economics, organizational theory and social sciences in general" (Forward and Emerging Technologies P2).

1.6 The Way Forward

The following recalls some important general recommendations for future collaborative projects.

Focus and European Added Value

When planning a collaborative project, it is essential to ensure that objectives are clear and sufficiently focused and that the added value of performing the work in a European environment is proven. The objective should be to develop enabling technology which will benefit the widest part of society as opposed to technological gadgetry. It should concentrate on generic aspects such as cost reduction, ease of use or technology transfer. It should also focus on areas that have an important development potential and encourage the development of completely new markets. Finally, it should contribute to European policies and help address fundamental issues such as access to cultural heritage, privacy, IPR protection and security.

Standards and Interoperability

Ensuring interoperability across Europe and beyond, through standardization, is an essential role of European collaborative R&D projects. Digital media research should aim at encouraging the ubiquitous deployment of reliable 3D and mixed content over the Internet and broadcasting networks. It should directly contribute to worldwide specification and standardization groups such as MPEG, VRML/Web3D[42] and AICI[43]. Requirements from content representation and coding research and application development should influence the design of future networks.

Multidisciplinarity

The confluence of several technological domains is the essence of digital media. Future research in this area will need integration and further development of the best available tools in mathematics, computer vision, computer graphics, interfacing, networking, artificial intelligence and agents technology. It will also need a constant and effective exchange with creators and content owners. Research fields such as shared virtual environments, telepresence, tele-operation and augmented reality are cases in point.

Vision

Above all, vision, radical innovation and the search for new frontiers are essential prerequisites. This area offers us some of the most exciting prospects in the form of a digital medium which promise to be highly visual, interactive, distributed, lifelike, three-dimensional, high-fidelity, intuitive and intelligent.

The foundations of "New Media" technologies have been laid. ACTS and other EU programmes have played their role, helping to develop synergies across the continent. The new IST Programme is taking up the challenge and aims to catalyse the best of European research in the area. At the moment the new IST Programme is only an empty box, waiting to be filled with attractive and promising projects. It is Europe's Programme and it is a unique opportunity for its research community, its industry and its citizens.

Acknowledgements

Sincere thanks are due to the following individuals who, through their work and commitment, have contributed to this overview: F. Allan, J. Barda, C. Bertin, P. Bisson, P. Brooks, R. Buschman, J.H. Chenot, A. D'amico, C. Dosch, R. Earnshaw, H. Fuchs, P. Gardiner, N. Gilchrist, C. Girdwood, L.van Gool, S. Gourrier, E. Ideler, M. Kaul, N. Kladias, R. Koenen, D. Konstantas, F. Lavagetto, D. Leevers, B. Macq, V. Normand, V. Papantoniou, P.F. Penas, F. Pereira, C. Simon, R. Storey, L. Ward.

---

42 http://www.web3d.org/
43 http://toocan.philabs.research.philips.com/misc/aici/

Disclaimer

The opinions expressed in this article are those of the author and do not necessarily reflect the views of the European Commission.

2

From "Web Site" to "Online Presence"; From "Internet" to "Information Society"

Peter Thomas

Abstract

Anyone who has read a newspaper in the last two years knows that the Internet is growing at a phenomenal rate.

Most businesses have Internet connections, there are a growing number of home users of the Internet, and governments around the globe are getting online – and developing information economy strategies to harness the emerging global information infrastructure.

The consensus is that the Internet will have a tremendous impact on how business will be done in the future. Analyses of the Internet legislative, policy, standards, commerce and security contexts suggest that most business sectors will be radically affected. Currently, publishing, finance, entertainment, information and education are changing rapidly because of the Internet, and some predictions suggest that by the end of 2000 billions of dollars of financial assets will be managed via the Internet.

2.1 Online Business

Currently the Internet is demographically and economically skewed. For example, there are more men than women Internet users; most users live in the USA, Asia and Europe; the most often used access mechanism for Internet access is via a commercial ISP.

This means that the level of economic activity on the Internet is limited. The real applications that will drive the development of online commerce are still overwhelmed by entertainment content, and are hindered by a lack of consensus on secure transaction mechanisms.

In addition, the Internet authorities are finding it difficult to regulate the Internet, and the lack of high-speed infrastructure means that many users have to contend with slow and unreliable Internet connections.

However, this picture is changing:

- There are more and more PCs in homes and users are anxious to use them to communicate.
- Many businesses are developing secure transaction mechanisms and there is a strong desire to conduct business – both government and commercial – online.
- The Internet population will also continue to increase – some predictions suggest as much as fivefold increases – and that increase will change the demographics towards women, children and an older population of users.
- The Internet will also be increasingly global, with more users outside major population centres.
- More of the working population will conduct their everyday business online.
- The Internet's infrastructure will become more stable as telecommunications providers increasingly compete for a share of online business.
- Government action – through national "information economy" agencies – will create new legislative and policy frameworks and new alliances between companies who provide the backbone services and applications for the Internet.

All of this means that business online will flourish as new Internet consumer markets grow and a core of business is conducted online. There will also be a growth in "net-enabled" activities such as customer support, information, communications and marketing.

The "digital businesses" at the forefront of these developments are likely to be in financial services, banking, information and entertainment. These businesses will perform transactions online, may deliver their products in physical or digital form, and will create new online products and services which use the Internet as a value-added component.

Among these businesses, new forms of competition will emerge as companies jostle for a position in the value chain, looking for the most effective ways to add value online. The customers of these businesses will of course be harder to satisfy, since they will be conditioned to expect online services. It will be difficult for businesses to enter a market and maintain a position unless online services are constantly improved and updated.

For most businesses in the future, technology infrastructure and know-how will be a key competitive differentiator.

2.2 From "Web Site" to "Online Presence"

As more activities such as customer support and feedback are handled via the Internet, businesses can learn more about their customers via sophisticated Web sites that allow the gathering of customer preference information.

The provision of interactive and information-rich channels to make customers aware of products and services will allow better communications with customers, from whose transactions the most commercially valuable information can be extracted. In this way, online services will be directly linked to corporate strategy, market positioning and product development.

This means that businesses should consider the Internet not as an add-on but as a core part of business strategy. And this suggests not just a Web site but an "online presence"; a view of the Internet as a resource which can be harnessed – and changed – to create new opportunities.

The most obvious focus is the corporate Web site. Most corporate Web sites are "brochureware" – the electronic equivalent of glossy promotional material. They are non-interactive, usually designed to be congruent with corporate identity, and technologically limited.

To provide real added value to customers, Web sites must become "online presences" designed to exploit the unique features of the digital medium. Intelligent context-sensitive interactions, coupled with changing and rich multimedia-based content, are essential to do this.

Of course, many companies are finding this difficult to do, and simply recut existing marketing materials into digital form. Unfortunately, these materials, designed as visual communication, do not create unique and engaging experiences for online consumers.

The availability of new generations of Internet tools, platforms and environments for developers and users means that this situation is changing: Java and Internet desktops, accompanied by sophisticated push technology tools and Internet middleware, are becoming widely available.

One of the key requirements for the creation of an effective online presence is *rich content* – timely, accurate, well-designed, customized and multimedia-based information which mixes both active and passive content. This rich content is Internet-specific – it is newly created content, either designed for the Web or created from the interaction of an individual consumer with an online presence at the point of contact.

Rich content is, however, not enough, and needs to be supported by an *active, intelligent information infrastructure* online. The aim is create for the consumer a uniquely tailored interaction – anything from a personalized quotation based on age, gender and income information to interactive two-way communications with a company. Supported by "smart tools" – applets and Wizards – users can quickly retrieve the information they need and make decisions quickly – an example might be an interactive loan repayment calculator embedded in property details which would allow potential buyers to calculate their monthly repayments.

An active, intelligent information infrastructure also allows consumers to take action – to buy or sell or to make contact with a business – and to make decisions as to how they interact with a business in the future: whether they wish to be notified automatically of relevant information, whether they want to be the recipients of pushed information or whether they participate in online events.

2.3 From Internet to Information Society

The step from Web site to online presence is part of a larger movement in reshaping the Internet and other information and communications technologies to change the way we work and live – affecting communications, relationships and the structure of communities.

What is coming to be known as the *information society* will allow individuals – as consumers or employees – quick, inexpensive and on-demand access to vast quantities of entertainment, services and information. It will provide the ability to interact at a distance with many commercial and government services, and to do so from any location.

The potential benefits to members of the information society are considerable: new products and services; access to, and control of, large volumes of information; and greater convenience, choice and quality of information-based services. The convergence of the IT, communications and information industries that we have seen in this decade will become seamless in the future information society.

However, the information society is not yet here, and some of the underlying infrastructure – technical, social, regulatory and financial – does not yet exist, although the uptake of information society applications (such as EDI, video-conferencing, online information services, teleworking and intranets) is growing.

Predictions about the future shape and course of the information society are hard to make. For example, the Internet is currently seen as the main delivery channel for digital content to desktop multimedia PCs – but this may not be true in 10 or 20 years, when advanced mobile digital services may carry digital content to handheld portable terminals.

Also, qualitative information about the uptake of new products and services is hard to assess, since the information society will be driven by technologies and applications which have significant impacts daily it is this information which is most useful.

And of course, the interplay between demographics and purchasing power on the demand side, and the accessibility of high-quality content on the supply side, will have a significant and unpredictable impact on the developing information society.

2.4 Key Enablers

It is now agreed that there are several key enablers of the information society:

- *Access to infrastructure*: the information society requires fast access to the advanced (currently Internet) infrastructure.
- *Appropriate pricing of information services*: pricing has significant impacts on the speed of uptake of products and the usage of services.
- *High-quality content*: in the consumer market, products and services are dependent on high-quality content.

- *A supportive culture:* studies around the globe suggest that those countries which have a supportive culture will make the transition to an information society smoothly. This includes a commitment to innovate, a competitive market-place (particularly in telecommunications), strong investment in information and communications technologies, and the development of centres of excellence which promote the information society.

2.5 Moving Into the Information Society

For most nations, moving into the information society will not be a simple task. As a recent UK Department of Trade and Industry (DTI) report [1] suggests, countries face significant competitive threats if they do not take immediate advantage of information and communication technologies.

At the heart of the information society are businesses and their competitiveness. Improvements in business processes, increased efficiency and new business opportunities are all available to those businesses that quickly take up information society technologies. Timeliness, control and increased choice and quality are all possible benefits of increased use of information and communication technologies.

But barriers, such as the high costs of networking, hardware and software components, the lack of an appropriate skills profile among the workforce, a lack of "digital literacy" and understanding of information society benefits, and access to advanced communications infrastructure are all significant.

As is also recognized, to encourage businesses to fully integrate these technologies into their corporate strategies requires strong support from government.

While working to providing a secure regulatory environment – and increasing consumer confidence in the information society by action on issues such as authentication, privacy, access to unsuitable content and consumer protection – governments around the globe are realizing that the development of the information society needs to be market-driven.

This is especially true in the area of electronic commerce [2], where the majority of digital transactions will occur in an open, global, electronic market-place.

2.6 The Australian Context

One of the nations which is enthusiastically pursuing the opportunities of the information society is Australia, and particularly the state of Victoria in southern Australia. Victoria's *Victoria 21 Strategy* [3] aims to build a strong global communications and multimedia industry and to establish Victoria as a major creative centre for development export of multimedia content, set in the context of a developing technical and multimedia literacy and usage in a highly advanced multimedia and communications infrastructure.

Victoria has recognized that the IT&C (including electronics) sector will be one of the largest industries by the end of the century, representing unparalleled convergence in communications, computing and context provision, all based on previous developments in underlying microelectronics and photonics industries. The computing, communications and media industries are rapidly converging to create a period of immense growth, all centred around the explosion of digital media content, a move toward mass consumer markets and global digital trading of knowledge-based products and services. The sector, overwhelmingly influenced by large global multinationals, will be one of the driving forces for sustained wealth creation and enhancement of the quality of life, and provides the enabling context for growth and development of existing and new businesses which can exploit the development of IT&C technologies – including the new multimedia content and information industries. In comparison with the shift from vertical integration of the mainframe era to the commoditization of the PC era, the convergence of computing, communications and media/content industries will bring about a dramatic reorganization in the value networks for these industries, particularly as communications and computing products start to be selected for their ability to deal with the latest content.

The challenge has been taken up enthusiastically by Australian State and Federal agencies, in particular the Victorian State Government's *Multimedia Victoria* agency, and the recently established Federal *National Office for the Information Economy* (NOIE) [4].

Multimedia Victoria has been active in supporting industry development and economic adjustment by providing strategic leadership for rapid change, participating in partnership projects with the private sector to build Victoria's capacity, and ensuring an appropriate business environment of regulation, skills development and infrastructure provision.

Multimedia Victoria is seeding the development of the information society in areas such as

- *Education and the Internet:* ensuring that every citizen is capable of using multimedia communication tools and that every child has access to email and networked resources via VICNET, which provides public electronic access to information services and the Internet from public library terminals across the state and stimulates community use networked technologies.

- *Multimedia enterprise:* the inner-city suburb of South Melbourne has become a content development precinct and is a hive of creativity, film production and software – a government-owned building, the Tea House, has become the hub of this precinct.

- *Multimedia investment:* the Multimedia 21 Fund is a A$21 million resource to stimulate local content development.

- *Investment recruitment:* IT and communications investment in Victoria, facilitated by the Victoria 21 program, has generated over A$813 million in new projects and created 4600 jobs.

- *Electronic commerce:* the International Electronic Commerce Business Centre in Melbourne is a centre of excellence where research, information and demonstration projects are made available to businesses in all sectors of the economy.

- *Access to infrastructure:* the establishment of a single, broadband wide area network across all government sectors in Victoria will link together every government site in the State, including every school, hospital, and police station.
- *Integrated Electronic Service Delivery:* the ESD infrastructure, implemented by government in partnership with the private sector, will allow Victorian citizens and business access to government services 24 hours a day, seven days a week through multimedia kiosks at popular locations such as shopping malls, through the Internet via computers at home or work, or through telephone via Interactive Voice Response.

At Federal level, NOIE is tasked to develop, coordinate and overview national policy relating to the regulatory, legal and physical infrastructure environment for the information economy, including facilitating electronic commerce, ensuring consistency of Australia's positions in international fora, and overseeing policies for applying new technologies to government administration, and information and service provision. *The National Information and Online Services Strategy* which NOIE will develop will set out national goals, roles and priorities for action in the context of a regulatory and legal framework for information and online services.

References

[1] http://www.dti.gov.uk/converg/index.htm
[2] See http://www.ecommerce.gov/
[3] http://www.mmv.vic.gov.au/
[4] http://www.noie.gov.au/

3

Human–Computer Interaction with Global Information Spaces – Beyond Data Mining[1]

Jim Thomas, Kris Cook, Vern Crow, Beth Hetzler, Richard May, Dennis McQuerry, Renie McVeety, Nancy Miller, Grant Nakamura, Lucy Nowell, Paul Whitney and Pak Chung Wong

Abstract

This chapter describes a vision and progress towards a fundamentally new approach for dealing with the massive information overload situation of the emerging global information age. Today we use techniques such as data mining, through a WIMP interface, for searching or for analysis. Yet the human mind can deal and interact simultaneously with millions of information items, e.g. documents. The challenge is to find visual paradigms, interaction techniques and physical devices that encourage a *new human information discourse between* humans and their massive global and corporate information resources. After the vision and the current progress towards some core technology development, we present the grand challenges to bring this vision to reality.

3.1 Introduction

Today's world is rapidly changing to become an information-rich and analysis-poor suite of societies. The rapid growth of the Internet, wireless communication, multimedia home and office servers, and the data interoperability among massive digital libraries will enable virtually everyone to have access to huge amounts of information on almost any topic. We also observe the business world rapidly changing from many smaller corporations focused on single or few products towards today's large international corporations providing a wide range of complementary services and products. These corporations and close partnerships are

---

1 Pacific Northwest National Laboratory is managed for the US Department of Energy by Battelle Memorial Institute under Contract DE-AC06-76Rl0-1830.

aimed at providing focused-market socially acceptable solutions to customers while reducing the support structures and single product competition.

Our technology suite for information analysis must advance to support these changes in the world around us. The vast majority of the technology mindshare has been directed toward providing collection of and access to this information. Now we must redirect at least a portion of our mindshares to providing technology for effective

1. searching that brings back relevant and to the extent possible complete informa-tion spaces
2. visual paradigms that enable the human mind to process in parallel vast quanti-ties of information
3. interaction paradigms that allow a higher order interaction closer to the cogni-tive processes
4. physical devices which allow humans to take advantage of their many senses

These emerging technologies will lead to a new human information communica-tion – a discourse – that enables discovery, understanding and presentation/reuse of information. We no longer want to interact with the computer. We want to interact directly with the information resources.

As a technical community, we are not starting from scratch [1–11]. Great progress is being made in academia, government, and industrial laboratories. Several disci-plines are offering parts of solutions, including information visualization, knowl-edge engineering and management, intelligent agents, human–computer interaction, information appliances, collaboration science, cognitive science, perceptional engineering, and statistics, to name a few. Yet we see mostly good but incremental technological inventions. What we need is a fundamentally new approach and suite of technologies that will enable humans to interact with millions, if not billions, of information units in real time. We propose such a vision and some technology steps towards the goal of developing a New Human Informa-tion Discourse.

3.2 The Vision

Here are some thoughts on how such a discourse might proceed. As an individual, I can describe my situation, my knowledge and my need for information. The avail-able information resources relevant to my situation and time are then brought to me with supporting logic and help enable me to (1) discover enough information to seek further information, (2) understand and translate information into knowl-edge, insight, and actions, and (3) reuse and present this knowledge within my context and situation.

I must be able to ask questions and get knowledgeable information from experts. Human experts are yet another form of information resource that must be included in the solution space, through intelligent agents, avatars, or direct communication. I must be able to determine the quality of what is there and most importantly what is not there within the information resources. I must be able to find and interact with fine-grained detailed information objects within a known context. This could also be stated as working on the parts of an information space while understanding the whole of the space. I must be able to understand and translate between the contexts of the information resources and the contexts of my knowledge and situation spaces. And I must feel comfortable with my display and interaction devices, which allow the presentation and real-time interaction with these massive information resources.

This seems like a major leap in capability. Yet if we look at the defining characteristics of this vision and some emerging technology examples, we can see that this new human information discourse is almost within reach. That is the outline for the remainder of the paper. We will first look at visual paradigms and what we have learned to date. Then we will present several examples of higher order interaction techniques. We proceed to a discussion of some interesting physical interaction tools. Then we conclude with some of the grand challenges we face in moving toward the new human information discourse.

3.3 Visual Paradigms

There is an increasing body of literature in the area of visual paradigms [12–38], with a dedicated workshop and even metrics proposed for evaluating visual paradigms [31]. Most focus on specific analysis and implementation of a single paradigm. When faced with a complex analysis problem in large information spaces, analysts will likely combine a number of information exploration methods and paradigms [33]. For example, getting an overview of the information can mean many things, including

- getting a sense of the major themes in the information and how strongly they are present
- understanding how the themes relate to one another
- seeing how the information relates to another information collection or to a standard ontology
- getting a summary of the attributes of the information, such as source, date, and type of document

In this section, we briefly describe two tools based on visual paradigms: SPIRE (Spatial Paradigm for Information Retrieval and Exploration) and WebTheme [10,17]. We present fundamental lessons learned from inventing, developing, delivering, and refining the technology in these tools.

The SPIRE system was explicitly designed to help information analysts to deal with masses of text documents. SPIRE automatically produces a suitable knowledge base of themes (key words) that can be used to distinguish groups within the document collection under analysis. The system then creates n-dimensional vectors characterizing each document with respect to those topics. The document vectors are clustered and projected from n-space into 2-space; the lower order projection is used to create the visual representations. In the ThemeView™ visualization, themes

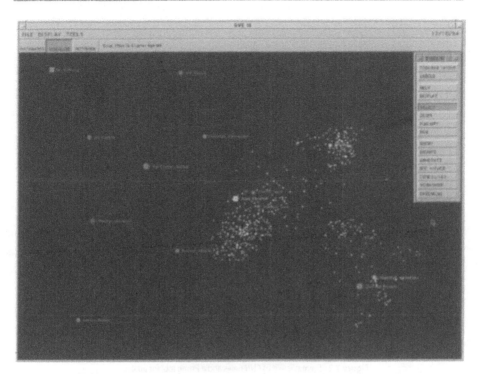

Figure 3.1 Galaxies visualization of documents and document clusters within a textual database.

within the document spaces appear as a relief map of natural terrain, where taller peaks show dominant themes. It is particularly good for helping an analyst to jump-start his or her understanding of the collection – it conveys the main themes in a collection and an overall sense of how they are related. Figure 3.1 illustrates a sample initial Galaxies display for a document space. Figure 3.2 illustrates a ThemeView™ for the thematic space.

Within global information spaces we also must address digital libraries [39–41] and Web information spaces [42–45]. WebTheme™ consists of a WWW harvesting and visualization server, which produces visual representations of the contents of WWW pages.

WebTheme (Fig. 3.3) is designed to operate in conjunction with the SPIRE text engine and a Netscape WWW server. Although SPIRE and the WebTheme server run on a Unix computer, WebTheme can be accessed by Netscape or Internet Explorer on a variety of computers.

This suite of technologies has been used for competitive analysis with patents, combined science articles, masses of strategic organizational planning documents, resumes, science and medical research, national security applications, metadata management, and many others. Actual use has greatly exceeded our initial expectations and the technology continues to expand based on feedback from the users.

Some of the fundamental lessons learned are:

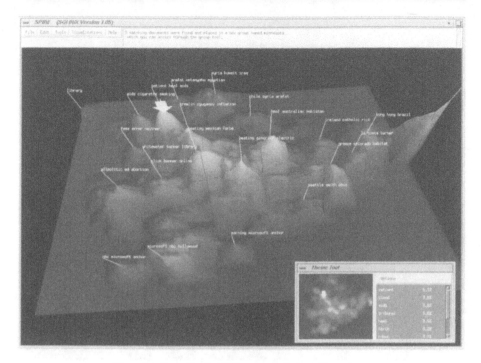

Figure 3.2 ThemeView™ of CNN news and a Probe tool for analysis.

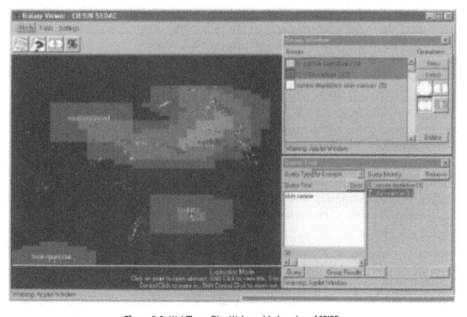

Figure 3.3 WebTheme™: a Web-enabled version of SPIRE.

- People can deal with large amounts of visual information given a good logical and physical paradigm. Within the Galaxies visualization space 20 000–100 000 document analyses are workable. Within the Themeview™ much larger information spaces can be understood.
- People think and interact beyond WIMP interface technologies. More often than not people must decompose their thinking processes to map into one-word or one-click interfaces now available within WIMP.
- Scaling to analyze large information spaces changes everything, from the visual paradigms to the underlying mathematics and the ways in which people keep track of their analysis and interactions. The influence of scale for the analysis of global information spaces should not be underestimated.
- In large information spaces, finding what is missing is as important as finding what is there.
- People bring a lot of knowledge and situation-dependent information to most analysis tasks. This information must be considered as an integral part of the analysis processes and the information space.
- Insight and decision making from these large information spaces are not usually dependent on a single unit of information, but on the interrelationships of multiple information objects.
- A fundamental issue within large information spaces is the quality and integrity of the information. The human mind can usually make some initial judgements with visual paradigms that allow analysis of the entire information space.
- The underlying mathematical signatures and associated metadata signatures within these information spaces are fundamental and must be developed in concert with the visual and interaction paradigms.
- The n-space internal information representations are a good foundation for information exploration and analysis.
- Time and space are universal dimensions that must be exploited with most large information spaces.

Visual paradigms are one of the key components to the new human information discourse. Tightly coupled to visual paradigms are interaction techniques [46–65] that bring life to the analysis process for global information spaces. In many cases and references included it is impossible to separate the two.

3.4 Higher Order Interaction Techniques

For many years we have been using and developing effective interfaces using today's WIMP interfaces [3]. These have worked very well up to the point where both the largeness and complexity of our information spaces and tools to analyze them become limiting factors. Today, on all our desktops, it is often very difficult to even find the files and information of importance for any current situation analysis. Experience shows that we each have 2000–4000 files on each desktop, all nested in a complex hierarchy of windows and folders within folders, down to long lists of files.

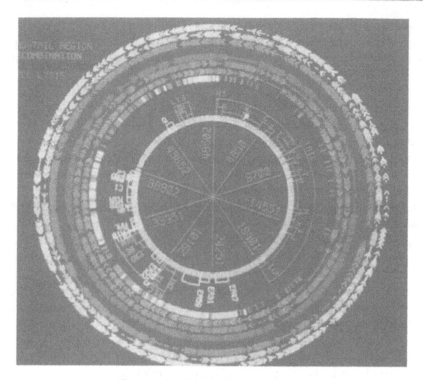

Figure 3.4 Cage/Gem genetic engineering system.

Several of the application domains – specifically chemistry and genetic engineering – have had to develop visual approaches that allow humans to interact with millions of information units. Doing so has required a different suite of interaction techniques, which we call Higher Order Interaction Techniques (HOIT). One such discipline example is genetic engineering [51]. Figure 3.4 displays over one million information items in an interactive environment allowing dynamic engineering for new biological forms [52]. Techniques such as "whole–part relationship", "Progressive disclosure", and "relative positioning" were all absolutely required for large space analysis.

The whole–part relationship allows users to see the whole (context) while working on the parts. Progressive disclosure allows users to see the maximum complexity possible for a specific view and have the system dynamically change visual paradigms to ensure visual completeness. Relative positioning enables users to rely on visual information proximity as a key within their information spaces.

Another example of a higher order interaction technique comes from a private energy use situation analysis [58], where the goal was to illustrate the theory versus actual experiment results. In Fig. 3.5 we see a transparent surface that illustrates the theory, while the solid surface illustrates actual energy use over a three-week period. The combination of both the theory and the experimental values provided the required insight for decision making.

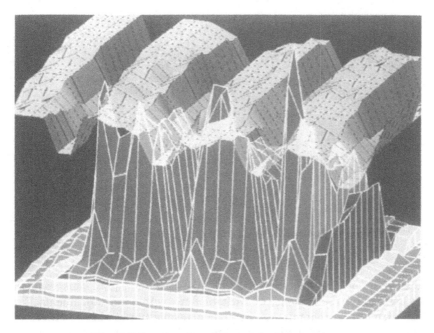

Figure 3.5 Theory/experiment higher order interaction technique.

Another such higher order interaction technique is relationship discovery. As shown in Fig. 3.6, one can see potential relationships based on "rainbows" that connect information units. Initial white arcs are expanded into colored segments based on the types of possible relationships. Evidence may also show the likelihood of strong dis-associations depicted as arcs below the information plane.

Figure 3.6 Relationship discovery rainbows visualization.

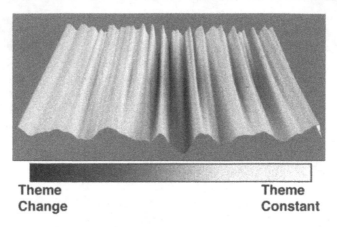

Theme   Theme
Change   Constant

Figure 3.7 TOPIC-O-GRAPHY™ of a long text document.

Another HOIT is that enabled by TOPIC-O-GRAPHY™ [32]. This technology allows users to tell the sequence of thematic flows within long documents. This is critical when one is attempting to illustrate plausible stories in and between large information spaces. Correlating information units that are part of other information units into stories will become a critical capability within large and complex information spaces.

In the example in Fig. 3.7, the beginning of the document is illustrated by the start of the signals and curves. Thematic changes are automatically recognized and depicted as changes within the curves, with the end being on the far right. Now that this technology can identify the location of specific themes, one can do automatic table of contents generation, automatic theme recognition, and automatic chunking for cluster analysis, enabling the user to see the thematically relevant structures.

One of the fundamental interaction capabilities required is the ability to represent and interact with information flows (another HOIT) across multimedia information spaces independent of the media, and number of information units. A good example can be found in Tufte's book on *Visual Explanations* [8], illustrating the thematic flows of music and artists over time (pages 90–91).

Another example is ThemeRiver™ (Fig. 3.8), which illustrates the thematic flows of Castro's speeches over time as topics inside a river. Then potentially related external events are illustrated across the top by the dated events that may or may not have had an influence on the thematic changes.

Another issue is the identification of the black holes in information spaces. This can be illustrated by looking at a Galaxies visualization within Fig. 3.1. Why are there no information units in some regions within this space? What would be the pertinent topics and themes if there were information units there? In large information spaces this is critical to establish confidence in understanding the interrelationships and to facilitate the discovery processes.

A final example of another HOIT is the information hypercube [31]. Within this example a fixed information topic space is defined and the information units are

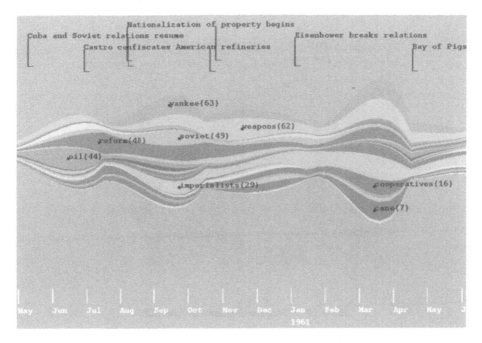

Nationalization of property begins

Cuba and Soviet relations resume

Castro confiscates American refineries

Eisenhower breaks relations

Bay of Pigs

yankee(63)

weapons(62)

reform(48)   soviet(49)

oil(44)

imperialists(29)

cooperatives(16)

cane(7)

May   Jun   Jul   Aug   Sep   Oct   Nov   Dec   Jan   Feb   Mar   Apr   May   J

1961

Figure 3.8 Information flows – ThemeRiver™ visualization.

then mapped into space ordered by the most important to least important topics. This can be visualized as a large 3D cube, with the information units partially populating the cube. Here the empty or sparse regions have explicit meanings.

In summary, these higher order interaction techniques allow the user to address large information spaces through information flows, information relationships, fixed information spaces, comparing the theory and experimental evidence, relative proximity positioning, and progressive disclosure. These are only a start toward a sufficient suite of powerful interaction techniques.

3.5 Physical Devices

Within most of our offices today we have an implicit information organization. This often has the computer at the center of the workspace. In most cases the actual workspace is much larger and encompasses a large desk space. This information workspace can be organized in several manners. A common organization scheme is based on time. To the left of our workspace is the historical filing and stacks of reference materials. Then to the right is the phone, the schedules, and the near-term action items. This workspace will include very different displays and interaction devices [66–76].

One design for a new workspace that attempts to achieve many of the goals as stated above is the HI-SPACE [68]. This is illustrated in Fig. 3.9.

Figure 3.9 HI-SPACE (Human Information workSPACE).

Within this prototype implementation there are no devices that tether the users to their workspace. The users' hands or any handheld object serve as pointing devices. There is a blending of physical objects (PHIcons) and logical objects (information units) through tangible interface constructs. By using gesture, tangible interfaces, and voice recognition a more robust interaction system can potentially be created. When combined with portable information appliances, this type of physical information workspace would allow interaction among people and large information spaces, in a mode that supports discovery, understanding, and information reuse.

3.6 Grand Challenges

While there has indeed been much progress towards the described vision, there are still many grand challenges, illustrated below.

1. New visual and interaction paradigms with appropriate combinations that enable billions of information objects to be analyzed.
2. New visual and higher order interaction paradigms must become intelligent, such that the system can be adaptive and suggestive to help user selection of these techniques; a guided human information discourse is required.
3. Fundamentally new underlying mathematical and statistical approaches for multimedia information signature generation, information summarizing, and information context understanding.
4. New physical interaction devices that require no special tethering, allow for large visual spaces, and easily blend with our logical massive information spaces.

5. New metrics that allow the developers to compare and measure the improvement of new visual, interaction, and physical techniques.

In summary, we have described a vision of some defining characteristics for management and analysis of large information spaces. Some emerging technologies for visual paradigms and examples of higher order interaction techniques give hope that there are effective visual and interaction paradigms for massive information spaces. Combined with a sample physical/logical human information workspace, this leads us to believe that it is within our future to go beyond current data mining into a fundamentally new human information discourse.

Acknowledgements

There are many staff within the suite of information synthesis and visualization programs who have made significant technical contributions towards the development of the illustrated tools. The list of more than thirty people is referenced through http://www.pnl.gov/infoviz/. In addition, we wish to thank the many sponsors of supporting work, including DOE, DARPA, CIA, NASA, NAIC, Navy, ARMY, FBI, and several commercial companies.

References

General

[1] Card, S.K., Mackinlay, J.D., and Shneiderman, B. (eds.) *Readings in Information Visualization: Using Vision to Think*, Morgan Kaufmann Series in Interactive Technologies, San Francisco, 1999.
[2] Cleveland, W. *Visualizing Data*, Hobart Press, Summit, NJ, 1993.
[3] Foley, J.D., van Dam, A., Feiner, S.K., and Hughes, J.F. *Computer Graphics Principles and Practice*, 2nd edn. Addison-Wesley, Reading MA, 1990.
[4] Heath, L.S., Hix, D., Nowell, L.T., Wake, W.C., Averboch, G.A., Labow, E., Guyer, S.A., Brueni, D.J., France, R.K., Dalal, K., and Fox, E.A. Envision: A User-Centered Database of Computer Science Literature. *Communications of the ACM*, 38, 4 (April 1995) 52–53.
[5] Schneiderman, B. *Designing the User Interface*, 3rd edn. Addison-Wesley, Reading, MA, 1998.
[6] Tufte, E. *The Visual Display of Quantitative Information*, Graphics Press, Cheshire, CT, 1983.
[7] Tufte, E. *Envisioning Information*, Graphics Press, Cheshire, CT, 1990.
[8] Tufte, E. *Visual Explanations*, Graphics Press, Cheshire, CT, 1997.
[9] Tukey, J.W. *Exploratory Data Analysis*, Addison-Wesley, Reading MA, 1977.
[10] Wise, J.A., Thomas, J.J., Pennock, K., Lantrip, D., Pottier, M., Schur, A., and Crow, V. Visualizing the non-visual: Spatial analysis and interaction with information from textdocuments, *Proc. IEEE Information Visualization '95* (1995), 51–58.
[11] Wong, P.C. and Bergeron, R.D. 30 years of multidimensional multivariate visualization. In Gregory M. Nielson, Heinrich Mueller, and Hans Hagen (eds.) *Scientific Visualization: Overviews, Methodologies & Techniques*, IEEE Computer Society Press, Los Alamitos, California, 1997.

Paradigms and Metrics

[12] Ahlberg, C. and Shneiderman, B. Visual information seeking: Tight coupling of dynamic query filters with starfield displays, *Proc. ACM CHI94 Conference: Human Factors in Computing Systems* (1994), 313–321 and color plates.
[13] Ahlberg, C. and Wistrand, E. IVEE: An information visualization & exploration environment, *Proc. IEEE Information Visualization '95* (1995), 66–73.

[14] Asahi, T., Turo, D., and Shneiderman, B. Using treemaps to visualize the analytic hierarchy process, *Information Systems Research* 6, 4 (December 1995), 357-375.

[15] Becker, R.A., Eick, S.G., and Wilks, A.R. Visualizing Network Data, *IEEE Transactions on Visualization and Computer Graphics* 1, 1 (March 1995), 16-28.

[16] Chalmers, M. and Chitson, P. Bead: Explorations in Information Visualization, in *Proceedings of SIGIR '92* (Copenhagen, Denmark, 21-24 June 1992), 330-337.

[17] Crow, V., Pennock, K., Pottier, M., Schur, A., Thomas, J.J., Wise, J., Lantrip, D., Fiegel, T., Struble, C., and York, J. Multidimensional Visualization and Browsing for Intelligence Analysis, in *GVIZ '94 Proceedings of Graphics and Visualization Conference*, Richland, WA, 1994.

[18] Egenhofer, M. and Richards, J. Exploratory access to geographic data based on the map-overlay metaphor, *Journal of Visual Languages and Computing* 4, 2 (1993), 105-125.

[19] Eick, S.G., Steffen, J.L., and Sumner, E.E. Jr. SeeSoft - a tool for visualizing line-oriented software statistics, *IEEE Transactions on Software Engineering* 18, 11 (1992) 957-968.

[20] Fairchild, K.M., Poltrock, S.E., and Furnas, G.W. SemNet: three-dimensional representations of large knowledge bases, in Guindon, R. (ed.), *Cognitive Science and its Applications for Human-Computer Interaction*, Lawrence Erlbaum, Hillsdale, NJ (1988), 201-233.

[21] Hearst, M.A. and Karadi, C. Cat-a-cone: an interactive interface for specifying searches and viewing retrieval results using a large category hierarchy. In *Proceedings of ACM SIGIR '97*, Philadelphia, PA, 27-31 July 1997, ACM Press.

[22] Hemmje, M., Kunkel, C., and Willett, A. LyberWorld - A Visualization User Interface Supporting Full Text Retrieval, in *Proceedings of SIGIR '94*, Dublin, Ireland, 3-6 July 1994, pp. 249-259.

[23] Hetzler, B., Whitney, P., Martucci, L., and Thomas, J. Multifaceted insight through interoperable visual information analysis paradigms, *IEEE Information Visualization*, 1998.

[24] Chi, E. Huai-hsin, E., Barry, P., Riedl, J., and Konstan, J. A spreadsheet approach to information visualization. In *Proceedings of IEEE Symposium on Information Visualization, InfoVis '97*. IEEE.

[25] Huang C., McDonald, J.A., and Stuetzle, W. Variable resolution bivariate plots. *Journal of Computational and Graphical Statistics*. 6(4), 383-396, 1997.

[26] Inselberg, A. Multidimensional detective. In *Proceedings of IEEE Symposium on Information Visualization, InfoVis '97*. IEEE.

[27] Jerding, D.F. and Stasko, J.T. The information mural: A technique for displaying and navigating large information spaces, *Proc. IEEE Information Visualization '95*, 43-50.

[28] Keim, D.A. and Kriegal, H. VisDB:Database exploration using multidimensional visualization, *IEEE Computer Graphics and Applications* (September 1994), 40-49.

[29] Korfhage, R. To see or not to see - is that the query?, *Communications of the ACM* 34 (1991), 134-141.

[30] Krohn, U. Visualization of navigational retrieval in virtual information spaces. In *Proceedings of the Workshop on New Paradigms in Information Visualization and Manipulation*, Baltimore, MD, 2 December 1995, pp. 26-32.

[31] Miller, N.E., Hetzler, B., Nakamura, G., and Whitney, P. The need for metrics in visual information analysis, in *Workshop on New Paradigms in Information Visualization and Manipulation*, November 1997, Las Vegas, NV.

[32] Miller, N.E., Wong, P.C., Brewster, M., and Foote, H. TOPIC ISLANDS™ - a wavelet-based text visualization system, *IEEE Visualization*, 1998.

[33] Mukherjea, S., Foley, J.D., and Hudson, S. Visualizing complex hypermedia networks through multiple hierarchical views, *Proc. ACM CHI95 Conference: Human Factors in Computing Systems* (1995), 331-337 and color plate.

[34] Nowell, L.T., France, R.K., Hix, D., Heath, L.S., and Fox E.A. Visualizing search results: some alternatives to query-document similarity. *Proceedings of the 19th Annual International ACM SIGIR Conference on Research and Development in Information Retrieval*, Zurich, Switzerland, August 1996, pp. 67-75.

[35] Olsen, K.A., Korfhage, R.R., Sochats, K.M., Spring, M.B., and Williams, J.G. Visualization of a document collection: the VIBE system. *Information Processing and Management* 29, 1 (1993) 69-81.

[36] Rushall, D. and Ilgen, M. DEPICT: documents evaluated as pictures, visualizing information using context vectors and self-organizing maps. In *Proceedings of IEEE Symposium on Information Visualization, InfoVis '96*. IEEE, 1996.

[37] Spoerri, A. InfoCrystal: a visual tool for information retrieval. *Proceedings of Visualization '93*, San Jose, California, 25-29 October 1993, pp. 150-157.

[38] Thomas, J.J., Shawn, B., Brown, J.C., Pennock, K., Schur, A., and Wise, J. Information visualization: data infrastructure architectures, *Scientific and Statistical Database Management Conference*, 28–30 September 1994.

Digital Libraries Paradigms

[39] Rao, R., Pederson, J. O., Hearst, M. A., Mackinlay, J. D., Card, S. K., Masinter, L., Halvorsen, P. K., and Robertson, G. G. Rich interaction in the digital library. Communications of the ACM, 38, 4 (1995) pp. 29-39.
[40] Roussinov, Dmitri and Ramsey, Marshall. Information Forage through Adaptive Visualization, in Proceedings of Digital Libraries 98, The Third ACM Conference on Digital Libraries (Pittsburgh, PA, June 23-26, 1998) pp. 303-304.
[41] Sahami, Mehran; Yusufali, Salim; and Baldonado, Michelle Q.W. SONIA: A Service for Organizing Networked Information Autonomously, in Proceedings of Digital Libraries 98, The Third ACM Conference on Digital Libraries (Pittsburgh, PA, June 23-26, 1998) pp. 200-209.

Web Visualization

[42] Andrews, K. Visualizing cyberspace: information visualization in the Harmony Internet browser, in *Proceedings of Information Visualization '95*.
[43] Card, S.K., Robertson, G.G., and York, W. The WebBook and the WebForager: An information workspace for the World-Wide Web, *Proc. ACM CHI96 Conference: Human Factors in Computing Systems* (1996), 111-117.
[44] Chi, E.H., Pitkow, J., Mackinlay, J., Pirolli, P., Gossweiler, R., and Card, S.K. Visualizing the evolution of Web ecologies, in *Proceedings of CHI '98*, Los Angeles, 18-23 April 1998, pp. 400-407.
[45] Zamir, O. and Etzioni, O. Web document clustering: a feasibility demonstration, *Proceedings of SIGIR '98*, Melbourne, Australia, 24-28 August 1998, pp. 46-54.

Interactions

[46] Bartram, L., Ho, A., Dill, J., and Henigman, F. The continuous zoom: a constrained fisheye technique for viewing and navigating large information spaces, *Proc. ACM User Interface Software and Technology '95* (1995), 207-215.
[47] Bederson, B.B. and Hollan, J.D. PAD++: A zooming graphical user interface for exploring alternate interface physics, *Proc. ACM User Interfaces Software and Technology '94* (1994), 17-27.
[48] Chimera, R. Value bars: an information visualization and navigation tool for multiattribute listings, *Proc. ACM CHI92 Conference: Human Factors in Computing Systems* (1992), 293-294.
[49] Cutting, D.R., Karger, D.R., and Pederson, J.O. Constant Interaction-time scatter/gather browsing of very large document collections, in *Proceedings of SIGIR '93*, Pittsburgh, PA, 27 June-1 July 1993, pp. 126-134.
[50] Ebert, D., Shaw, C., Zwa, A., Miller, E., and Roberts, D.A. Minimally-immersive interactive volumetric information visualization. In *Proceedings of IEEE Symposium on Information Visualization, InfoVis'96*. IEEE.
[51] Douthart R.J., Thomas, J.J., and Schmaltz, J.E. Simulated cloning in the CAGE environment, *Nucleic Acids Research*. IRL Press, Oxford, 1986, pp. 285-297.
[52] Douthart, R.J., Thomas, J.J., and Schmaltz, J.E. Color Graphics Representations of large sequences in the GEM environment, *Nucleic Acids Research*. IRL Press, Oxford, 1988, pp. 1657-1666.
[53] Fishkin, K. and Stone, M.C. Enhanced dynamic queries via movable filters, *Proc. ACM CHI95 Conference: Human Factors in Computing Systems* (1995), 415-420.
[54] Furnas, G.W. Generalized fisheye views, *Proc. ACM CHI86 Conference: Human Factors in Computing Systems* (1986), 16-23.

[55] Goldstein, J. and Roth, S.F. Using aggregation and dynamic queries for exploring large data sets, *Proc. ACM CHI95 Conference: Human Factors in Computing Systems* (1995), 23–29.

[56] Hearst, M.A. TileBars: visualization of term distribution information in full text information access, in *Proceedings of CHI '95*, Denver, CO, 7–11 May 1995, pp. 59–66.

[57] Inselberg, A. The plane with parallel coordinates, *The Visual Computer* 1 (1985), 69–91.

[58] Lucas, R.G., Taylor, Z.T., Miller, N.E., and Platt, R.G. *Characterization of Changes in Commercial Building Structure Equipment and Occupants*, PNL-7361, 1990, Pacific Northwest Laboratory, Richland, WA.

[59] Mackinlay, J.D., Rao, R., and Card, S.K. An organic user interface for searching citation links, *Proceedings of CHI '95*, Denver, CO, 7–11 May 1995, pp. 67–73.

[60] Pederson, J.O., Cutting, D.R., and Tukey, J.W. Snippet search: a single phrase approach to text access, in *Proceedings of the 1991 Joint Statistical Meetings*, American Statistical Association, 1991.

[61] Pickett, R.M. and Grinstein, G.G. Iconographs displays for visualizing multidimensional data, in *Proceedings IEEE Conference on Systems, Man, and Cybernetics*, Beijing and Shenyang, PRC, May 1988, pp. 514–519.

[62] Robertson, G.G., Card, S.K., and Mackinlay, J.D. Information visualization using 3D interactive animation, *Communications of the ACM* 36, 4 (April 1993), 56–71.

[63] Robertson, G.G. and Mackinlay, J.D. The document lens, Proc. *1993 ACM User Interface Software and Technology* (1993), 101–108.

[64] Sarkar, M. and Brown, M.H. Graphical fisheye views, *Communications of the ACM* 37, 12 (July 1994), 73–84.

[65] Shneiderman, B. The eyes have it: a task by data type taxonomy for information visualizations, in *Proceedings for IEEE Symposium on Visual Languages*, 3–6 September 1996, pp. 336–343. IEEE Service Center.

Physical Devices

[66] Krueger, M. *Artificial Reality II*. Addison-Wesley, Reading, MA, 1990.

[67] Matsushita, N. and Rekimoto, J. HoloWall: designing a finger, hand, body, and object sensitive wall, *UIST '97 Proceedings*, pp. 209–210.

[68] May, R.A., Thomas, J.J., Lewis, R.R., and Decker, S.D. Physical human information workspace, *Proc. Western Computer Graphics Symposium '98*, 23–26 April 1998, pp. 25–31.

[69] McNeill, D. *Hand and Mind: What Gestures Reveal About Thought.* University of Chicago Press, Chicago, IL, 1992.

[70] Norman, D. *The Psychology of Everyday Things.* New York: Basic Books, 1988.

[71] Omologo, M., Matassoni, M., Savaizer, P., and Giuliani, ?. Hands-free speech recognition in a noisy and reverberant environment. *ESCA-NATO Workshop on Robust Speech Recognition for Unknown Communication Channels*, Pont-a-Mousson, France, 17-18 April 1997.

[72] Svaizer, P., Matassoni, M., and Omologo, M. Acoustic source location in a three-dimensional space using cross-power spectrum phase, *Proc. ICASSP*, Munich, Germany, April 1997.

[73] Thomas, J.J. A New human information discourse, Fraunhofer Institute for Computer Graphics opening invited address at IGD Ceremonial Event, 28–30 October 1997.

[74] Ullmer, B. and Ishii, H. The metaDESK: models and prototypes for tangible user interfaces, *UIST '97 Proceedings*, pp. 209–210, 1997.

[75] *Virtual Reality: Scientific and Technological Challenges*, National Research Council, National Academy of Sciences, Committee on Virtual Reality Research and Development, National Academy Press, December 1994.

[76] Wellner, P. Interactions with paper on the digital desk. *Comm. ACM*, 36(7) (July 1993), 87–96.

4

Transparent Access to Video Over the Web: A Review of Current Approaches

Peter J. Macer and Peter J. Thomas

Abstract

This chapter is a technical review of computer tools which aim to provide manageable computer-based representations of video sequences. The paper is part of a series of publications (see Macer and Thomas 1996a,b; Macer et al. 1996; Macer and Thomas 1999a–e) which describe work in the development of solutions to the problems of accessing video sequences on computer, particularly over the Web. Several approaches are reviewed here, which range in approach from those which use a highly abstract representation, dissimilar in nature from the medium of video and which rely on conventional, rigid information retrieval techniques such as database querying, to those in which the representation is similar in nature to the video which it represents – for example images taken from the video sequence itself and which use less traditional, more *ad hoc* retrieval techniques. The chapter is intended to provide a comprehensive, coherent, critical review of those approaches which are based on abstract representations using conventional retrieval techniques, and those which employ more literal representations using newer retrieval techniques. The systems discussed are introduced in an approximate order of decreasing abstraction and increasingly *ad hoc* retrieval techniques.

4.1 Introduction

The startlingly rapid growth of computer and communications technologies in the latter half of the twentieth century, and the associated increase in both the quantity and quality of information generated, stored, and made accessible through these means has caused the twentieth century to be dubbed "the information age". Indeed, it is said that the *New York Times* contains as much information every day as the average 17th century person encountered in a lifetime. But increasingly, it is not only the traditional *textual* information found in newspapers that is being produced, distributed, archived, and accessed. Relatively new media types – such as video – are also becoming increasingly important. In the UK, 86% of homes now have videocassette recorders, and in 1989, for the first time, the number of video-tapes rented exceeded the number of books borrowed from public libraries.

As well as changes in the types of media in which information appears, the methods used for its dissemination and access are also changing rapidly. There are now more than 45 million people in over 200 countries who have full or partial access to the Internet – the global network of information serving computers, which grew from 0.4 million hosts in 1993 to some 1.7 million in 1996, while one particular subsection of the Internet – the World Wide Web – has grown at an even more extraordinary rate: an estimated 650 000 Web site servers were in existence world-wide in January 1997, compared with 230 000 six months earlier, 100 000 a year earlier, and a mere 10 022 two years earlier.

These changes, both in the nature of information itself and its quantity and avail-ability, impact every aspect of modern society to an extent that been likened to the industrial revolution of the eighteenth century. But this new revolution – the Infor-mation Revolution – is, like its predecessor, not without cost. Even as long ago as 1945, it was recognized that the ever-increasing quantities of knowledge and infor-mation available were useless unless efficient ways of "selecting" the required information could be found. This phenomenon – that of being overwhelmed with information and unable to manage it efficiently – has become known as *informa-tion overload*.

We are not, however, powerless against this tide of information, and ironically it is the computer – one of the very tools that has brought about the phenomenon of information overload – that enables the potentially overwhelming quantities of information presented to us to be managed. The potential "magic lens" for finding, sorting, filtering, and presenting relevant items of information has been realized by the various computer-based tools that have been developed to allow the storage, indexing, and retrieval of information.

4.2 Information as Video

One particular type of data – video – poses particular problems. Video may be stored on computers in exactly the same manner as other forms of information, such as text, images, and audio, and when considered at the lowest level is no different from these media: the information is simply binary data residing in memory or stored on CD-ROM, hard disk, tape or some other storage device. On a higher level, however, video has a number of properties that set it apart from these media, and presents a particular challenge to its efficient storage and retrieval. These properties are:

• *The high volume of data needed to encode even short sequences of video*: because any communications channel will have a finite bandwidth, the large volume of raw data required for digital video sequences makes accessing video sequences from remote servers a relatively time-consuming and potentially expensive task, with even small sequences taking many minutes or even hours to download, particularly if the server and client are geographically distant. It is therefore important to ensure that the video data being retrieved by the user is exactly that which meets their requirements. Downloading more – or different – data than that which is actually required is more expensive in the case of video than with virtually any other medium.

- *The temporal component of video*: video, like images and rendered text, is displayed over a spatial area – typically a television screen. It clearly has a spatial component. But, like audio, video information changes over time: it also has a temporal component. Video may therefore be classified as a *spatio-temporal medium*. Unfortunately, this means that, to a large extent, it has all the restrictions of temporal media, rather than the advantages of spatial media. Although an individual frame of a video sequence may be treated as a still image and understood at a glance, much of the important information in a video sequence is contained within its temporal component, and is not shown by a single still image. Like audio, if users wish to understand a ten-minute sequence of video they must take ten minutes to watch the whole sequence.

- *The opacity of images (and hence video) to computers*: Textual information stored on computers is relatively easy to catalogue, search, and access because it is symbolic. Images, on the other hand, are not generally constructed from an easily identified and finite set of primitives, and because of this their content and structure cannot easily be analyzed and matched by computers in the same way as with text. They are therefore said to be "opaque".

Although video is conceptually a continuous medium, in which the image is smoothly and continuously changing, in practice, video is stored and displayed as a series of discrete still images shown in rapid succession. This would seem to suggest that visual content querying techniques (i.e. Flickner *et al.*, 1995; Fountain *et al.*, 1996; Mokhtarian *et al.*, 1996; Picard, 1995) could be directly applied to each individual frame in order to provide visual content querying and indexing of the video sequence as a whole. While this is indeed the approach taken by some systems, the procedure is hampered by the large number of still-image frames contained in even short video sequences (up to 25–30 frames per second). Because of this large number of images and hence the large amount of data that must be processed, searches even within a single video sequence can require a significant amount of time, let alone those involving a library of video sequences. Visual content querying techniques may not therefore necessarily lend themselves to the problem of querying moving image (video) databases, despite the apparent similarity of the video and still images. Because of these difficulties in applying what intelligent image database techniques there are to video sequences, they can be said to be opaque to computers to an even greater extent than still images. All of the problems associated with the retrieval of image data are therefore repeated and heightened with video data.

The concept of using computer tools to provide a more manageable representation of video sequences is not novel, and there are a variety of computer-generated representations available. These range from those which use a highly abstract representation dissimilar in nature from the medium of video and which rely on conventional information retrieval techniques such as database querying, to those in which the representation is similar in nature to the video which it represents – for example, images taken from the video sequence itself and which use less traditional, more *ad hoc* retrieval techniques.

4.3 Approaches to Handling Video

This scale – from abstract representations using conventional retrieval techniques to more literal representations using newer retrieval techniques – is a convenient way of classifying the various approaches, and in the following sections each of the relevant systems are introduced in an approximate order of decreasing abstraction and increasingly *ad hoc* retrieval techniques.

4.3.1 Traditional Database Methods: ViMod

ViMod is just such a data model using a basic representational unit of video called a *temporal interval*. This is defined as "a finite closed interval in the physical time required to present a video". It is unclear how temporal intervals within a video sequence are identified, but the loose definition would suggest that it is simply a matter of human judgment as to what constitutes an appropriate partitioning. Each temporal interval is described by a set of features that fall into five different categories:

- *Video Q (Qualitative) features* are dependent on the content of the video itself, are described over a temporal sequence, and require qualitative descriptions.
- *Video R (Raw) features* are similarly those that are dependent on the content of the video itself, and are described over a temporal sequence, but can be measured as raw data.
- *Image Q-features* are again dependent on the content of the video, but may be specified with reference to a single frame, rather than requiring that a number of frames are considered. Like *Video Q-features* they cannot be described in terms of raw data, but require qualitative descriptions.
- *Image R-features* are dependent on the content of the video and pertain only to single frames, but can be measured as raw data.
- Finally, *Meta-Features* are those features that are not directly dependent on the content of the video sequence itself. They generally apply to the complete video and rarely to smaller time intervals

For each temporal interval identified in the video sequence, attribute values in each feature category are determined and stored in an appropriate computer file structure, with a reference to the corresponding section of the video sequence. This provides a data model of each temporal interval, which may be indexed and queried by a suitable database management system.

It is certainly the case that the data model used by ViMod is appropriate for querying by conventional database methods. However, it is less clear that the limited and inextensible set of features described are sufficient to model video sequences in enough detail to provide a useful and flexible classification. Indeed, because of the "richness" of the medium of video, and the diversity of genres and subject matters, it is doubtful that *any* finite, pre-defined data model could capture all of the information required for any and all applications. In addition, although the *Video* and *Image R-features* described in the data model, such as the *Audio Levels* and *Colour Histograms*, may be extracted by automatic processes, the other three feature classes – and indeed the partitioning of a video sequence into "temporal intervals" itself – will certainly require manual classification. Jain and Hamapur indicate that they have developed software tools to aid this process, but it will remain a long way from being the wholly automated task. The inflexibility of pre-defined data models and the need for laborious manual classification are both limitations inherent in this type of system identified by Oomoto and Tanaka (1993). In order to address these problems, while still exploiting the advantages of a textual database approach, they have developed *OVID* (Object-oriented Video Information Database).

4.3.2 Object-Oriented Databases: OVID

Like ViMod, OVID provides a framework for the user to enter textual information about each segment of a video sequence and some database management tools to allow the resulting data structures to be indexed and queried. However, in contrast to ViMod, OVID does not use a rigid and pre-defined data model for all video clips, but allows arbitrary attributes and their associated values to be defined and added incrementally as the classification process takes place. In addition, the system seeks to reduce the amount of manual classification required by using object-oriented techniques to allow some attribute/value pairs to be automatically *inherited* from one data model to another, and from one video segment to another.

Oomoto and Tanaka assert that scenes in a video are often overlapped by – or entirely included within – other meaningful scenes, so a number of video-objects (the data structure used by the system to represent a single scene) may describe the same section of video. When this occurs, OVID provides a mechanism to allow some of the data describing the sequence to be shared between the video-objects. When new attribute/value pairs are defined by the user to describe a certain feature of the sequence which the video-object models, they are classified by the user as being either *inheritable* or *non-inheritable* attributes. Inheritable attributes belonging to a video-object are automatically assigned to any other video-object whose temporal interval is contained within the temporal interval of the former video-object. Non-inheritable attributes do not have this property.

By defining as inheritable those attributes and values that must logically be the same for a given scene as they are for its subsuming scene, there is no need to manually enter identical information for different but similar video objects. For example, if a scene taking place at night-time is defined as a video-object A, and another object B is defined over some portion of object A, then the object B must also be a night-time scene. Therefore A can be given an inheritable attribute "situation" with a value "night", so that B automatically inherits the same attribute and value. This behavior is called *inheritance-based on interval inclusion relationship*. Similarly, if the intervals of two video-objects overlap, a new video-object is automatically generated for the overlapping time period, inheriting those attributes and values common to both.

Once an OVID database of video-objects has been generated, two methods are available for retrieving information. The first is by use of *VideoSQL*, a query language specifically designed as part of OVID. Users can formulate VideoSQL queries such that the system will return video-objects in which a given attribute has a certain value, or which are defined over a certain frame or sequence of the raw video. The system has a hierarchy of attribute values defined, specific to each database, such that a particular value (e.g. "car" or "boat") can be defined as a more specific example of a different value (e.g. "vehicle"). The system can use this information to return video objects where attribute value is a more specific example of the VideoSQL query.

The second method for retrieving specific video-objects from the database is by using the *VideoChart*, which represents video-objects in a graphical form. A scale along the top of the screen shows the frame number of the raw video increasing from left to right, below which each video-object is represented by a horizontal bar showing the extent and location of the time interval that the video-object covers, and labeled by its unique object identifier (oid). Each video-object is represented by a bar on a different horizontal line, while video-objects consisting of more than one interval are drawn on the same line.

VideoChart therefore allows users to visualize the temporal relationships between video-objects and determine which parts of the raw video have been classified as having a rich structure of overlapping scenes and sub-scenes, and which are more simply structured. The user may interact with the representation by selecting any bar from the chart to play the video clip that it represents, examine the attributes and values defined for it (including any it inherits from interval inclusion relationships), or save the object to a buffer so that VideoSQL queries can later be applied to it.

4.3.3 A Mathematical Approach: Video Algebra

The idea of the inheritance of attributes and attribute values between scenes is also used by Weiss *et al.* (1995) in *Video Algebra*, which – as the name suggests – is an algebraic method of describing the structure of video sequences. The fundamental entity dealt with in video algebra is a *presentation*, defined as a "multi-window spatial, temporal, and content combination of video segments". Presentations are described by video expressions. The most primitive video expression creates a single window presentation from a raw video segment, while more complex compound video expressions are constructed by combining simpler ones using video algebra operations such as concatenation ($P_1 \oplus P_2$), union ($P_1 \cup P_2$), and difference ($P_1 - P_2$).

The model also permits the association of arbitrary content descriptions to each video presentation. Although the model does not define the form of this description, the prototype system developed by Weiss *et al.* uses a Boolean combination of attribute/value pairs in a similar fashion to that used in OVID. When a new video expression is defined, an attribute called "text" is automatically generated, and a text string value corresponding to the closed caption text (subtitles) is assigned to it (the idea of storing the closed caption text associated with video sequences and using it as an index to the content is also used by Brown *et al.* (1995) to retrieve video clips from an online archive of news broadcasts). Video algebra also allows other attribute/value pairs, such as the names of the actors featured or a title for the sequence, to be manually defined. The components that make up each video expression inherit all of the descriptive attribute/value pairs that are defined for the expression itself. Thus all of the content attributes associated with a parent video node are also associated with all of its descendant nodes.

This inheritance model, used in both video algebra and OVID is, of course, the standard model for inheritance in object-oriented systems, with properties of the more general parent objects being inherited by the more specific child object. However, it is not at all clear that it is an applicable model in this circumstance. The object-oriented approach assumes a class hierarchy with "type of" associations, i.e. a child class is a more specific *type of* the more general parent class (e.g. "cars" are a more specific type of "vehicle"). It cannot be said, however, that a short video sequence is a more specific type of the longer sequence from which it was taken. The model used in video algebra is actually nearer to being a "part of" or *aggregation* hierarchy, where each simple object is *part of* the more complex object (i.e. each presentation is an *aggregation* of simpler presentations). It can be argued therefore, that in video it make little sense for properties of complex expressions to be inherited by simpler components. Rather, the features of each component part should be combined to produce a description of the expression as a whole, in the same way as occurs with the video sequences themselves when individual shots are edited together to form a longer sequence.

The video algebra system supports content-based access by enabling the user to query the attribute/value content descriptions associated with each video expression using a simple predicate query language. Weiss *et al.* also describe one of the features of the system as being the support for "browsing and navigation": "Browsing operations enable the user to inspect the video expression and to view the presentation defined by the expression. The user can play back any expression or browse and traverse the organizational hierarchy with "Get-Parents" and "Get-Children" operations".

Although this system may be appropriate for the authoring of multimedia materials (complex algebraic operations such as conditions, loops and transitions make it a potentially powerful tool for this purpose), it is difficult to see how the extreme abstraction of video sequences into algebraic expressions makes its content more accessible, as is claimed. The automatic parsing of closed caption text into a form in which it can then be used as an index to the sequences is a clever innovation, and goes some way to addressing the problem that textual classification is generally an entirely manual process, but the usefulness of this technique would seem to be somewhat negated by the inheritance scheme apparently operating in the "wrong" direction, i.e. with shorter video sequences inheriting the entire text from the much longer sequences of which they are part, rather than short sequences having a short textual caption, each of which combine to produce a longer caption associated with the longer "parent" expression.

4.4 Using Images

While text is an ideal classification and indexing medium in terms of the ease with which it may be queried and manipulated by computer, it is not without certain disadvantages. The trend towards the use of graphical user interfaces (GUIs) rather than textual command line interfaces attests to the general acceptance that, in many cases, people find it easier to work with pictures (icons, in the case of GUIs) than with text.

4.4.1 Iconic Representations: MediaStreams

MediaStreams (Davis, 1993) follows the trend towards iconic representations by defining an iconic visual language for video annotation. This system avoids breaking the raw video into smaller units – as is the case in the previously described approaches – by simply annotating the intact sequence with icons that denote objects and actions at the points at which the objects and actions occur. Davis points out that systems which split sequences into smaller units impose a single fixed segmentation, and claims that because MediaStreams imposes no fixed "chunking", it provides more flexible access to the video sequence. Before annotating a video sequence with iconic representations of its content, a "palette" of icons which are to be used must be built up. This is achieved using the "Director's Workshop" tool, which has over 2200 iconic primitives, arranged in a logical hierarchy of increasing specificity of meaning. The user navigates through the hierarchy and selects the required icons to move to the palette, from where they may later be used to annotate the video. If no icon primitives exist for a required object, action, or concept, a compound icon may be constructed by selecting multiple primitives. For example, a compound icon indicating that "the scene is located on top of a street in Texas" may be constructed by locating and selecting the icons for "Texas", "Street", and "on top of". The new compound icon appears as a horizontal row of its primitives, and is added to the icon palette.

Once an initial palette of icons has been built up, the annotation process may begin. The user drags relevant icons from the palette and drops them on the "Time Line" – an abstraction of the video sequence in which the passage of time is represented spatially, progressing from left to right across the screen, similar to the *VideoChart* view used in the OVID system. Once dropped onto a time line an iconic description extends from its insertion point in the video stream to the next scene break. The user may create new compound icon sentences while the annotation process is taking place, and compound icons created in this way are added to the icon palette and may themselves be used as icon primitives.

Davis claims that iconic annotation enables "quick recognition and browsing" and "visualization of the... temporal structure of video content", and that "global, international use of annotations" makes clear "visual similarities between instances or subclasses of a class (visual resonances in the iconic language)". Davis's thesis is that the use of iconic rather than textual annotation and classification enables more efficient visualization and browsing, and because icons – unlike textual languages –

are internationally recognizable, they have the added advantage of being accessible to a wider range of people.

Certainly, the argument that pictures – or icons – can in some circumstances convey information more efficiently than text is compelling: the adage 'a picture is worth a thousand words' does seem to apply. It is also true that pictures can be used to convey the same message across cultures, and many stylized pictures in the form of icons, signs and symbols are recognized internationally. However, even given the ability to produce compound icons from those primitives provided, it seems perhaps unlikely that the diversity of objects, actions, and abstract concepts present in video could be unambiguously represented by a relatively small set of icons. For instance, it is unclear how any set of general-purpose icon primitives could adequately and uniquely identify a specific actor in a video sequence.

The problem is that while a finite set of icons is eminently suitable for denoting a finite set of actions, as is demonstrated by the use of button bars and the like in GUIs, they are less suitable for representing the limitless possibilities that occur in video.

4.4.2 Using Images from the Video: Salient Stills

If a pictorial rather than textual representation of the video stream is to be used, it may be more appropriate to make use of the large number of high-resolution pictures that are contained within the video sequence itself, rather than a finite set of limited resolution icons that are pre-defined without reference to the video. This is indeed the approach used by many video representations.

"Salient Stills" (Teodosio and Bender, 1993) is just such a system, and produces a single still image from the temporal sequence of frames present in a given video sequence. The system analyses the camera motion occurring between frames and applies the appropriate translation and/or scaling factor to each image such that objects and features in each frame align accurately with the same objects and features in the next.

All of the frames thus processed are then combined into a single image, discarding duplicated parts of each frame. Thus, if the original video sequence was a panning shot, the resulting salient still would be a wide "panoramic" image, encompassing the entire range of the camera's pan. Alternatively, if the camera had zoomed in on a particular object during the shot, the resulting salient still would be a variable resolution image showing the whole of the wide angle view in relatively low resolution, but displaying progressively higher resolution nearer to the part of the image that was the centre of the zoom.

It is claimed that the variation in resolution caused by zoom shots "draws the attention to the salient parts of the scene that commanded the attention of the camera operator". This may indeed be the case, although professionally produced video tends to contain relatively few zoom shots, so in order to fully exploit this characteristic of salient stills the video would have to be shot with the resulting salient still in mind, rather than the video sequence itself. A further problem with this technique is that it can only represent continuous sequences of frames, i.e. single shots. Video in which transitions like cuts and dissolves occur will have to be split into individual shots before the salient stills process is applied. This is not in itself an insurmountable problem, but it is worth noting that the salient stills technique does not carry out this procedure itself.

The major problem with this system, however, is that while it is clearly a powerful method of representing shots in which a moving or stationary camera films a relatively static scene, problems may arise if the objects in the video sequence are themselves moving. It is unclear how the system behaves in this circumstance, or how much user intervention is required to produce a different, perhaps more optimal, result than this default behavior.

The literature indicates that features from the original video sequence are included in the salient still if they are present in at least 50% of the frames showing the same area. Thus transitory objects are entirely removed from the salient still. This may be appropriate in some applications but a different strategy will certainly be required in other examples. The salient stills system does allow transitory objects to 'composited back' into the still – in the cellist example, an additional salient still is shown in which the music assistant appears a number of times, giving a 'stroboscopic' effect, and showing his path across the stage. A human operator, however, must instigate this process, and it is unclear as to how much additional human intervention is required to give a satisfactory result.

4.4.3 Using Three Dimensions: VideoSpaceIcons and Micons

The VideoSpaceIcon system (Tonomura *et al.*, 1993) uses a very similar concept to that used in Salient Stills, i.e. that of scaling and translating each frame from the original video sequence to match the camera motion, and combining the resulting images to produce a single picture showing the entire scope of the original shot. This system, however, uses a different algorithm to combine the images into a single picture, and provides additional information about the temporal sequence.

Rather than including in the finished still image those details that appear in over 50% of frames, VideoSpaceIcon simply uses the most recent version of duplicated parts of the scene. Hence the last frame from the video sequence is shown in its entirety, while only those parts of the penultimate frame showing a different spatial area from the last frame are visible, and so on. While this is still not without problems (e.g. a moving object occurring close to the trailing edge of a pan shot will leave a trail of multiple copies of itself across the image) it does have the advantage that the operation of the algorithm is easier for the user to understand (thinking of the image as a stack of photographs is an adequate mental model), so it is easier to predict the outcome of applying the system to a given piece of video footage. It is possible that the reverse is also true: i.e. it is easier to accurately envisage the original video sequence from the finished still.

In addition to the "Salient Stills style" of representation, VideoSpaceIcon gives additional visual information about the video sequence: above and to the left of the still representation are "X-ray views" of the original video sequence. These are generated by performing an edge detection operation on each frame of the video and then summing the results of this process vertically up each column of pixels (in the top-view X-ray), or horizontally along each row (in the side-view X-ray), resulting in two separate one-dimensional arrays of pixels. When each of the frames has been processed in this way, the one-dimensional arrays are displaced by an amount corresponding to the horizontal or vertical camera motion and then combined to form two-dimensional images. These images, resembling radiological X-ray photographs, are designed to show the movements of the objects in the original video sequence over time, although – like a radiological photograph – it is rather hard for an untrained observer to interpret the image in any great detail.

These three elements – the combined frame video still and the top- and side-view X-rays – combine to make up a VideoSpaceIcon, which is conceptually a three-dimensional block with the combined still on the front face, the top-view X-ray on the top surface, and the side-view X-ray along the side face.

A similar three-dimensional solid representation is used by Smoliar and Zhang (1994) in their "micons" (movie icons). In this representation, the front of the block simply shows the first frame of the video sequence, (i.e. no compositing of multiple frames is used) while the top and side show only the pixels on the top and side edges of each consecutive frame following on from the first frame (i.e. no "X-ray" effect is used). The browsing tool developed by Smoliar and Zhang allows the user to examine "slices" through the micon taken either vertically – thus revealing a single frame from the selected point in the video sequence; or horizontally – revealing a single row of pixels from all of the frames in the sequence. The latter operation allows the user to gain an impression of the motion of the objects present in the sequence over time.

This system has the advantage that it is easier to understand slices through the micon than to interpret the X-ray views used in VideoSpaceIcon, but suffers the drawback that the user needs to specify where the micon is to be sliced in order see the motion; with the X-ray views all of the available information is available to the user *a priori*. Additionally, because the computer must be able to generate cross-sectional views at any point in the micon, all of the data from all of the frames must be available, so there is no saving in data size due to temporal redundancy. A micon of a video sequence could therefore actually have a larger data structure than a MPEG compressed version of the same sequence (assuming similar frame sizes were used for each).

4.4.4 Using Time Lines: VideoMap

Tonomura *et al.* (who proposed VideoSpaceIcon) also describe a representation of video sequences called VideoMap (Tonomura *et al.*, 1993). This consists of a number of horizontal time-lines (i.e. representations in which time progresses from left to right across the screen), each showing a different time-varying data set extracted from the original video sequence. The data sets shown are as follows:

- An intensity histogram showing the intensity values of all pixels in each frame, quantized into 16 levels. Each quantized frequency value is represented by a gray scale in which white represents a high frequency and black a low frequency of occurrence.

- The average intensity, drawn as a line graph, and showing how the average pixel intensity varies over time.
- The intensity histogram difference, again drawn as a line graph, showing a measure of the difference between the intensity histograms of successive frames. A peak in the graph indicates the likely presence of an editing point in the video sequence.
- The top and side X-ray views, as described for VideoSpaceIcon. In this mode, however, the X-ray views are not displaced to account for camera motion, so the camera motion itself may be interpreted by examination of these two time lines. If both the top and side X-ray views consist primarily of parallel horizontal lines, the camera was motionless throughout the shot; if the lines present on the top-view X-ray are sloping, the camera panned left or right during the shot; if the lines present on the side-view X-ray are sloping, the camera tilted up or down during the shot; if the lines on both views diverge or converge, the camera zoomed in or out during the shot.
- The hue histogram, which is similar to the intensity histogram except that it shows the hue value of the pixels in each frame (rather than the intensity) quantized into 256 levels.

While the information that these various time-lines provide is interesting and perhaps potentially useful, it would seem that there may be better ways of conveying the same information. The X-ray views, for example, take up a large amount of the available screen space and require some knowledge or experience to interpret their meaning, yet only provide little if any more information than whether a particular shot is a pan, a tilt, or a zoom shot. This information could be represented with a much more economical use of screen space, and be more easily understood, by the use of three small icons, or even the words "pan left", etc. Similarly, the intensity and hue histograms and the average intensity graph seem to convey very little information other than indications of when editing points occur (a user could not, for instance, recognize a particular shot or sequence from these three representations alone), and as this information is already presented quite effectively in the inter-frame intensity difference plot they would seem to be rather redundant.

The topmost time-line on the VideoMap, however, is perhaps a more useful representation of the original video. By automatically detecting the peaks in the inter-frame intensity difference, the computer is able to identify the editing points (cuts) in the video sequence and so extract the first frame from each shot. These are shown at the appropriate places along the top of the screen to coincide with the start of each shot on the various time-lines below.

4.5 Summary

There have been a number of attempts to produce computer-based alternative representation of video sequences. They range from those based on very formal and rigid methods, like traditional databases and algebra, in which the representation is typically highly dissimilar to the medium of video itself, to those which use much looser and unstructured browsing techniques and are generally much closer in nature to the video sequence that they represent.

Table 4.1 Summary of approaches for transparent access to video.

Textual representations	ViMod (Jain and Hampapur, 1994)	Strong reliance on traditional database methods. Video represented by pre-defined attribute/value pairs.
	OVID (Oomoto and Tanaka, 1993)	Similar to ViMod, but uses Object-oriented techniques to reduce classification task. Arbitrary attributes can be added at any stage.
	Video Algebra (Weiss *et al.*, 1995)	Represents video as algebraic constructs. Allows database search techniques to be applied to associated attribute/ value pairs
Representations using images	MediaStreams (Davis, 1993)	Uses an extensible set of combinations of icons to annotate the video sequence.
	Salient Stills (Teodosio *et al.*, 1993)	Combines each frame of a video shot to produce a single "panoramic" image.
	VideoSpaceIcon (Tonomura *et al.*, 1993)	Similar to "Salient Stills", but uses more intuitive algorithm to produce panoramic image. Also provides "X-ray" views to indicate motion
	Micons (Smoliar and Zhang, 1994)	Stacks each frame of video sequence one behind the other to from a 3D solid. Micon may be "sliced" vertically to show any individual frame, or horizontally to show motion.
Representations using sequences of stills	VideoMap (Tonomura *et al.*, 1993)	A number of time-lines showing image properties such as colour histograms, average intensity, X-ray views, etc. Also shows "shot reference" sequence of frames taken from the video itself.
	PaperVideo (Tonomura *et al.*, 1994)	The first frame of each shot of a video sequence printed onto paper.
	(Taniguchi *et al.*, 1995)	Summarizes 24 hours of a TV channel's output by displaying frames sampled at regular intervals. Uses two-level hierarchy to provide more detailed view of each single hour's broadcasts.
	VideoTiles (Falchuk and Karmouch, 1995)	Another "sequences of stills" representation. Provides multi-level hierarchy to allow users to "zoom-in" on areas of interest .
	(Smoliar and Zhang, 1994; Zhang *et al.* 1995)	Similar to VideoTiles but with more intuitive representation of hierarchy and temporal flow.
	(Chen and Wu, 1995)	Another "Sequence of stills" representation, but with an alternative approach to "chunking" time.

Table 4.1 shows this range of previously suggested representations and summarizes some of their features. It also shows the general trend from the formal information retrieval methods to more unstructured techniques, and from highly abstract representations to those more similar to the medium of video.

References

Brown, M.G., Foote, J.T., Jones, G.J.F., Sparck Jones, K., Young, and S.J. (1995) Automatic content-based retrieval of broadcast news, *ACM Multimedia '95*, 5–9 November 1995, San Francisco, CA.

Davis, M. (1993) Media streams: an iconic visual language for video annotation, *Proceedings of the IEEE Symposium on Visual Languages*, August 1993.

Flickner, M., Sawhney, H., Niblack, W., Ashley, J., Huang, Q., Dom, B., Gorkani, M., Hafner, J., Lee, D., Petkovic, D., Steele, D., and Yanker, P. (1995) Query by image and video content: the QBIC system, *IEEE Computer*, September, pp. 23–32.

Fountain, S.R., Tan, T.N., and Sullivan, G.D. (1996) Content-based rotation-invariant image annotation, *Colloquium on Intelligent Image Databases*, IEE, 22 May 1996, pp. 6/1–6/6.

Jain, R., and Hampapur, A. (1994) Metadata in video databases, *SIGMOD Record*, 23(4), December, 27–33.

Macer, P. and Thomas, P. (1996a) From video sequence to comic strip: summarizing video for faster WWW access. *Proceedings of 3D Graphics and Multimedia on the Internet, WWW and Networks*, British Computer Society Computer Graphics & Displays Group, 16–18 April 1996.

Macer, P. and Thomas, P. (1996b) Video storyboards: summarizing video sequences for indexing and searching of video databases. *IEE E4 Colloquium Digest on Intelligent Image Databases*, Savoy Place, 22 May 1996.

Macer, P. and Thomas, P. (1999a) browsing video content. *Proceedings of BCS HCI Group Conference, The Active Web*, January, Staffordshire University, UK.

Macer, P.J. and Thomas, P.J. (1999b) Evaluation of the Rosetta video summarizing system (in preparation).

Macer, P.J. and Thomas, P.J. (1999c) Video browsing using storyboards (in preparation).

Macer, P.J. and Thomas, P.J. (1999d) An empirical comparison of algorithms for representative frame selection in video summarizing (in preparation).

Macer, P.J. and Thomas, P.J. (1999e) Accessing video over the Web (in preparation).

Macer, P., Thomas, P. Chalabi, N., and Meech, J. (1996) Finding the cut of the wrong trousers: fast video search using automatic storyboard generation. *Proceedings of CHI'96 Human Factors in Computing Conference*, Vancouver, April 1996.

Mokhtarian, F., Abbasi, S, and Kittler, J. (1996) Indexing an image database by shape content using curvature scale space, *Colloquium on Intelligent Image Databases*, IEE, 22 May 1996, pp. 4/1–4/6.

Oomoto, E. and Tanaka, K. (1993) OVID: design and implementation of a video-object database system, *IEEE Transactions on Knowledge and Data Engineering*, 5(4), 629–643.

Picard, R.W. (1995) Light-years from Lena: video and image libraries of the future, *International Conference on Image Processing*, Washington DC, October, pp. 310–313.

Smoliar, S.W. and Zhang, H.J. (1994) Content-based video indexing and retrieval, *IEEE Multimedia*, Summer, 62–72.

Teodosio, L. and Bender, W. (1993) Salient video stills: content and context preserved, *ACM Multimedia '93*, June, pp. 39–46.

Tonomura, Y., Akutsu, A., Otsuji, K., and Sadakata, T. (1993) VideoMAP and VideoSpaceIcon: tools for anatomizing video content, *INTERCHI'93*, April 1993, pp. 131–136.

Tonomura, Y., Akutsu, A., Taniguchi, Y., and Suzuki, G. (1994) Structured video computing, *IEEE Multimedia*, Fall, 34–43.

Weiss, R., Duda, A., and Gifford, D.K. (1995) Composition and search with a video algebra, *IEEE Multimedia*, Spring, 12–25.

5

Ubiquitous Communications and Media: Steps Toward a Wearable Learning Tool

Nick Dyer and Jerry Bowskill

Abstract

Advances in miniaturization have led to a growing field of research in "wearable" computing. This paper looks at how such technologies can enhance computer-mediated communications, with a focus upon collaborative working.

An educational experiment (MetaPark) is discussed which explores communications, data retrieval and recording, and navigation techniques within and across real and virtual environments.

In order to realize the "MetaPark" experiment, an underlying network architecture is discussed that supports the required communication model between static and mobile users. This infrastructure (the MUON framework), is offered as a solution to provide a seamless service that tracks user location, interfaces to contextual awareness agents, and provides transparent network service switching.

5.1 Introduction

Since the birth of computers, it has been a design goal of hardware manufacturers to make systems as small and compact as possible. This led on to the migration from monolithic mainframe computers to desktop workstations, and then to portable computers. In more recent years a trend has emerged for full-function "palmtop" computers, such as the Toshiba Libretto, and even "wearable" computers [1]. The authors use the term *wearable* to refer to all computing devices that are designed to be mobile. While portable computers are carried to a location and used when the user is stationary, mobile computers are designed to be used while the user is moving around and active in other tasks.

The authors are researching new forms of "telepresence" based on networked wearable computers. Figure 5.1 illustrates two forms of wearable: a commercial belt

The Hip PC -
The Xybernaut MA IV

✕ 233MHz Pentium MMX
✕ Head Mounted Display
✕ 64MB of RAM
✕ Win®95
✕ 2.1GB hard drive
✕ Speech recognition

a   b

Figure 5.1 a Xybernaut wearable computer. **b** A modified palmtop computer.

mounted computer from Xybernaut (http://www.xybernaut.com/) (Fig. 5.1(a)) and a palmtop modified by the authors to include a head-mounted display, an external battery pack and a "chorded" keyboard (Fig. 5.1(b)).

The authors believe that such devices, in combination with location and other forms of "context" awareness, enable "ubiquitous communications" in which users are given appropriate communications channels and multimedia information based on their location and task within a real world environment. A specific research focus is on using wearables to allow people in a real-world environment to access remote people and multimedia information held within an online collaborative virtual environment. This is detailed further in Section 5.2.

The concept of fusing real and virtual space, a form of collaborative mixed reality, is being explored through the development of an educational environment called "MetaPark". MetaPark is currently under construction and consists of a collaborative virtual environment modelled on a real park which is used by schools in central Ipswich as a learning resource. Section 5.3 of this document explores the proposed MetaPark experiment.

MetaPark is being built using an experimental MUON framework for mobile multimedia applications. Section 5.4 describes the authors' experience of using palmtop and wearable devices as novel interfaces onto virtual environments and describes work in progress on using the same devices as "portals" to virtual world content and inhabitants within the real-world park. The underlying network framework is described, which supports wearable applications.

Finally, a discussion in Section 5.5 summarizes the chapter.

5.2 Ubiquitous Communications

Most applications for commercial wearable computers, typically belt-mounted PCs running the Windows operating system, have been restricted to tasks involving mobile data input or retrieval. However, body-worn networked computing devices are suited to many applications, and the impact on personal communications will be significant. For example, a networked wearable computer can behave as a mobile phone, an audio-graphic conferencing terminal, a video conference terminal or a virtual conferencing terminal (Walker *et al.* [2] present an overview of telepresence technologies.) Let us not forget the mobile phone itself, the most widely used networked wearable on the planet. Although the physical devices have a limited multi-modal interface they typically contain a 250 MIP processor and can act as a "thin client" to network embedded services, for example allowing users to send and receive email, fax and video.

5.2.1 Context

Much of the near-term research activity around wearables is addressing "contextual information services", primarily "mobile location services". These aim to deliver timely and location-specific media such as traffic reports or tourist information to either mobile phones or palmtop PC terminals [3]. Our research focus is the application of wearables within computer-supported collaborative working, achieving "ubiquitous telepresence" by combining more traditional audio-visual conferencing with collaborative virtual environments. MetaPark is a practical embodiment of these ideas, a persistent online space that provides contextually appropriate access to colleagues, services and information. In concept this is similar to the idea of "co-habited mixed realities" [4]; as "wearers" move through the real world they also move through either literal or abstract virtual environments. For example, when entering our research laboratory the wearer is connected to an augmented reality conferencing session with other team members who are working remotely.

Thus we are moving toward a "ubiquitous telepresence" in which telecommunication is being dynamically mediated based on a "contextual awareness" of the wearer's current location, task, availability, skills and social profiles (Fig. 5.2). Even in a desktop service, context plays a significant role. For example, an incoming communications request could be handled differently, depending on factors such as my availability, my relationship with the caller, terminal characteristics (including any specialized hardware in my computer), and other ongoing and scheduled activities. The same initial contact might result in a video conference, audio connection or voicemail.

Context is that much more important in a wearable setting, with many more permutations of terminal type, network connectivity, user activity and perceptual loading. In handling all the service options, there will be an important role for personal agents and profiles to manage the mushrooming complexity. Our initial application development, as described later in this chapter, is agent- and profile-based, which provides unified access to a range of contextual data and additional intelligence, intended to reduce the demands on the user. Faced with a proliferation of services in an era of wearable computing, we would suggest that there is an important role for a "context provider" to present the user with at least a degree of consistency and integration. The role of context provider would include consistency in areas such as billing and authentication, but could also avoid duplication of profiles and real-time contextual data such as location and availability.

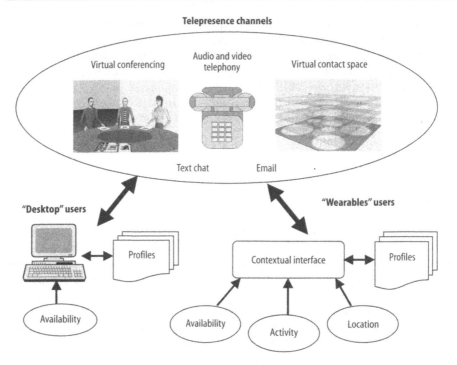

Figure 5.2 Ubiquitous telepresence.

The goal is to deliver "seamless service": a re-purposing of interface and content which delivers appropriate functionality to the user across a range of devices and in a variety of settings. Seamless service would include transitions between different bandwidths and terminals, in an extension of the handover between base stations in existing mobile services. An early and simple example of a contextually sensitive interface is a mobile phone with different alert and messaging settings for use when driving or in a meeting. At present, much of the context must be entered manually, although the phone can respond unprompted to the in-car adapter. In the future there will be much more direct input from sensors and other networked devices.

The vision is of "ubiquitous telepresence", sharing many features with Mark Weiser's [5] earlier work on "ubiquitous computing", and "ubiquitous media" by Buxton *et al.* [6]. It is motivated by technology trends in miniaturization and performance, which will enable an unparalleled range of hardware and services – an explosion in the technical possibilities which serves to emphasize the importance of user studies in informing future developments.

Our vision of wearables as contextual communications devices is being explored based on our previous research and subjective evaluations of wearable communications. A Wearable Communication Space (WearCom) [7], for example, allows a wearable computer user to communicate with multiple remote people in a virtual environment that supports high-quality audio communication, visual representations of the collaborators and an underlying spatial metaphor. Using a body-worn networked computer with a monocular head-mounted display, we are able to place

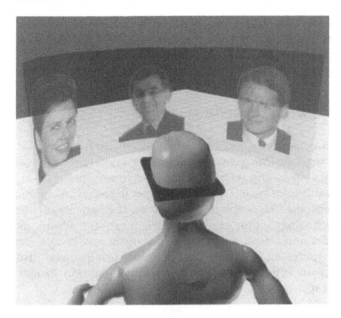

Figure 5.3 A spatial conferencing system.

the wearer within a virtual display space in which conventional screen information can be spatialized relative to the user's head orientation. With this display configuration the WearCom conferencing space allows remote collaborators to appear as virtual avatars (representations of people) distributed about the user (Fig. 5.3). Each avatar is a still image of the respective participant; however, future avatars could be more complex virtual representations or live video streams, depending upon the acceptable visual perceptual loading of the remote user. All audio streams are spatialized in real time so that they appear to radiate from the corresponding avatar.

Just as in face-to-face collaboration, users can turn to face the collaborators with whom they wish to talk, while still being aware of the other conversations taking place. Users could also move about the space, enabling them to choose their own viewpoint and the spatial relationships between the collaborators. In this way the space could support dozens of simultaneous users, similar to current collaborative virtual environments. Since the displays are see-through and see-around, the user could also see the real world at the same time, enabling the remote collaborators to help them with real-world tasks. These remote users may also be using wearable computers and head-mounted displays, or could be interacting through a desktop workstation. Preliminary indications suggest that spatial cues significantly improve the effectiveness of multiparty conferencing, which is particularly significant for mobile communications as the user has typically more distractions than a deskbound user. In previous research we similarly found that users can locate information more rapidly with this type of spatial information display than with the more traditional desktop metaphor information displays [8]. Spatial displays also scored more highly during subjective evaluations.

Taking an educational field-trip scenario, we then looked at how real and virtual environments could be connected together with wearable devices acting as the technological bridge, and this is illustrated in the next section.

5.3 MetaPark – An Overview

MetaPark has evolved as a goal after a number of years' research into the use of collaborative virtual learning environments using a variety of interface and interaction modalities, including interactive video environments (IVE) and wearable augmented reality information spaces. This paper describes an experiment that has a manifold purpose. We want to demonstrate the benefits of using wearable computing technology within an educational context, with a focus upon the effectiveness of communication, data retrieval, navigation, and data recording. The central idea is to create a "co-habited mixed reality" using a literal virtual representation of a real-world park which is accessible either online or via moving through the real world space itself.

5.3.1 Background Research

Figure 5.4 illustrates a collaborative virtual environment: a multi-user 3D world implemented by the authors using the Microsoft DirectX API libraries. This abstract world includes an amphitheatre in which inhabitants can gather to view a broadcast TV or video stream and a "virtual fish tank", populated with autonomous fish. Our concept was to prototype a space in which children would visit to learn about ecology.

While the interface to the virtual environment illustrated above was imagined as classroom-based, not mobile, a novel mechanism was developed to make interaction between users and virtual artefacts more convivial and compelling. Artificial creatures in the virtual environment respond to the presence of specific users in a physical environment.

User identity and location information are gathered via "smart badge" devices; thus individuals become part of the user interface.

The aim of our application was to demonstrate the concept of graphics responsive to user identity in the context of our educational ecology research. The tank contains fish models, each of which is associated with a particular badge. The identity badge (Fig. 5.5(a)) is based on the "iRX 2.0" design available from the Personal Information Architecture group at MIT [9]. When the fish are loaded into the "environment" a polling mechanism performs the following actions:

• Check for iRX communications on the serial port
• Update the position for the fish
• Render the 3D scene on the screen

The iRX devices (nicknamed "crickets") transmit a continuous stream of codes that have to be converted into a stream of ASCII characters. Each device sends a unique two-byte sequence that repeats at regular intervals. To check for the presence of an

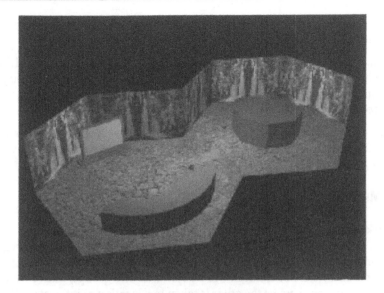

Figure 5.4 An educational shared space.

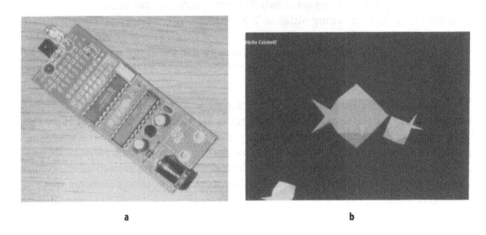

a   b

Figure 5.5 a Infrared iRX badge. **b** A virtual fish attracted to the user.

iRX badge, and thus the user, the serial port is continually read and a buffer of 100 bytes is filled. When this happens, a procedure is called to count the number of "hits" (bytes that match a particular cricket signature). If a specified threshold is reached, the relevant fish is marked as active.

Updating the fish positions was divided into two categories – active and inactive fish. For inactive fish (those that have not been selected to meet a user), a random direction is calculated and the fish moves along the vector until a boundary limit is reached, when a new direction is then calculated. The active fish (selected in response to a user identity) is sent to the front of the screen, as shown in Fig. 5.5(b), where it rotates until the iRX device is removed from detection range. The fish then swims back and becomes inactive again.

The authors acknowledge the rationale of "tangible" user interfaces as advocated by Hiroshi Ishii *et al.* [10], where a central theme is the combination of "graspable" foreground media and ambient background media that provide subtle cues to unseen form or function.

The rendering section uses DirectX Retained-Mode to create and render the 3D scene and a 2D-overlay plane is added to display the transparent text layer used for displaying messages for the user.

5.3.2 MetaPark Design

MetaPark will build on the previous collaborative virtual world architecture, but with an emphasis on mobile terminals and interaction with the virtual world via corresponding interactions with a matching real-world environment. For the MetaPark study a class of children will be split into two groups, one of which will remain in a classroom, while the other is taken to a location of interest (in this case Christchurch Park, Ipswich). The field workers at the park will be given wearable computers that will contain park-related information, communications software, a GPS unit and data recording utilities. The group in the classroom will work on a computer that has a 3D representation of the park as a real-time simulation. Our intention is for the children at both locations to use the same wearable interface devices, although the classroom devices will be used to navigate a virtual world displayed on a large room-based display.

The positional data from the remote GPS system will be used to place a virtual representation of the remote group within the 3D park model. This will allow the class group to follow the path of the remote group as they explore the environment, as well as allowing the path data to be saved. The communications software will allow the remote and classroom children to text chat and talk to each other so that each group can exchange information and ideas as well as taking location-specific notes (Fig. 5.6).

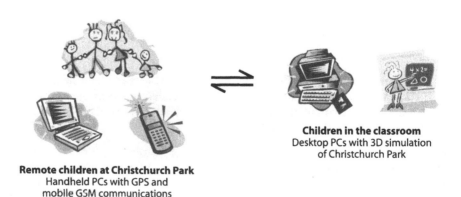

Children in the classroom
Desktop PCs with 3D simulation
of Christchurch Park

Remote children at Christchurch Park
Handheld PCs with GPS and
mobile GSM communications

Figure 5.6 A MetaPark overview.

In order to promote information exchange and communications between the children, the content would have to be contrived such that the remote and classroom groups receive different types of information, and each group would be given different objectives which rely upon help from the opposite group.

To facilitate the technical communications between each computer unit, we are designing a network infrastructure that supports text chat and binary file transfer, and additionally allows transparent transitions between different service providers (wireless LAN, modem, infrared). Known as the MUON Framework (see below), this network architecture also tracks the user's location, based upon a predefined beacon list, and will also provide rudimentary information about the user's current level of activity. Using these cues, the classroom group should be able to alter their communications strategy as the remote group undergoes different state and location changes.

The virtual environment running within the classroom is not limited to a single connection. It will also support remote collaborative access, so that other groups can join the MetaPark experiment, providing further input to the children's activities by communicating with the remote group as well as other virtual groups.

The next section explains our approach to the underlying communications network architecture.

5.4 MUON Framework

In order to support the communications model for the MetaPark project, it was necessary to design a network architecture that allows mobile users to communicate without the need to concern themselves with the underlying technical issues which this implies. The solution to this was a client–server network support system called the MUON (Mobile User Object Notification) Framework.

5.4.1 Defining the Problem

The provision of communications channels for wearable computing addresses the following issues:

- Maintaining connectivity for mobile users wherever they may be
- Offering the best bandwidth based on the user's location and resource availability
- Supporting multiple service providers (wireless radio LAN, infrared connection, GSM modem)
- Ability to switch automatically between service providers without user intervention
- Supporting user-to-user asynchronous and synchronous communications
- Supporting location awareness and spatial placement of information
- Supporting user availability awareness and contextual communications based on this information
- Provide a gateway between the network and external software agent systems

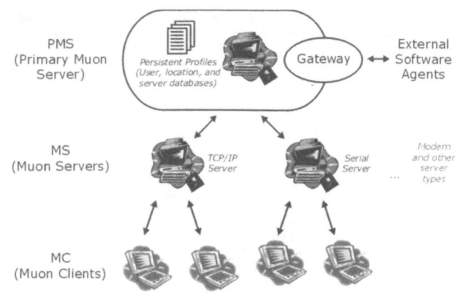

Figure 5.7 MUON framework components.

5.4.2 System Components

The basic components of the network are described below and illustrated in Fig. 5.7.

- *MUON*: fundamental to the network solution is the concept of a MUON object. This structure defines the data packets sent as traffic over the network. The idea was that client-destined data on the network would be saved in a server-based persistent database. A notification message would be generated and sent to the client, containing information about the type of data and allowing the user to choose to retrieve the data in accordance with their current situation.
  For the client–server architecture, a three-layer approach was adopted where the lower layer consists of the clients which participate on the network. The middle layer server acts as a direct host to the clients, and the topmost layer consists of a Primary Muon Server (PMS), which is responsible for managing the network and maintaining persistent databases. These are described in more detail below.
- *Muon Client (MC)*: this component provides the connectivity between the user and the rest of the network, allowing messaging to occur between other users, servers, and external software agents. It also integrates the user location and activity awareness module and sends this data up the hierarchy to the PMS.
- *Muon Server (MS)*: a server is established for each type of service provider (initially LAN, modem, and serial) to provide clients with an initial connection point and to provide the network infrastructure to pass data between clients and the system. A prioritized list of service providers is set for each client, to automatically detect connectivity with higher bandwidth servers and allow the client to automatically move to the optimal server (e.g. moving seamlessly from GSM

modem to radio LAN when entering a building). Conversely, if a connection is dropped, the system will move a client onto a different server to maintain network connectivity via a different service provider (e.g. moving from radio LAN to GSM modem on exiting a building).

- *Primary Muon Server (PMS)*: the function of the PMS is to manage the entire network, keep the client profile and location databases up to date, provide logon security using client authentication, and manage a list of current servers. When messages are sent to an inactive client, the PMS records these in the recipient's profile, which is retrieved by the client when they next log on. Also, the PMS manages the location messages (e.g. if a message is posted in the photocopier room to notify people of a fault, the PMS will store this information and send it to any clients that subsequently visit that location).

5.4.3 Synchronous and Asynchronous Communications

The most common form of asynchronous communication is email. The MUON Framework supports a similar asynchronous messaging system that allows users to send text and binary (pictures, files, etc.) data to offline recipients. This data is then stored on the PMS in the recipients' persistent databases, ready for when they next log on.

When two (or more) users are online simultaneously, a dialogue can be arranged between each client. This semi-synchronous communications medium is more commonly known as text-chat.

For synchronous communications, both users must be online and have enough available bandwidth to cope with the continuous stream of data between each other. Audio and video communications channels are then possible. The MUON Framework will not provide synchronous communications services directly, but will support external IP-based services by negotiating the connection and disconnection processes between the users.

5.4.4 Location Awareness

To facilitate location awareness, the client requires a mechanism that determines its current position within a pre-defined mapping of physical space. This was tackled by the use of radio location beacons and client receiver modules. The beacons are autonomous units that transmit a specific code that is used to denote location. As a transmission medium, infrared offers an inexpensive discreet solution (as shown by the IR beacon in Fig. 5.5(a)). However, its dependency on a line of sight makes it awkward for wearable computers, where the user must direct the receiver towards the beacon to allow transmission to occur. A more suitable alternative for wearable users is short-range radio, and the authors have modified the iRX design to include a low-power AM transmitter and receiver. These devices are inexpensive and can transmit a signal that can be received with sufficient accuracy even where physical obstructions cause radio attenuation. The major disadvantage is that these devices all transmit at the same frequency and can therefore cause interference when used in close proximity with each other. To alleviate the problem, the strength of the beacon must be balanced between providing adequate coverage for each specific location and enough attenuation to prevent interference with neighbouring beacons.

From a software viewpoint, the PMS maintains a master database of each named location matched with its respective beacon code. When a client receives a beacon message (by passing close enough to a beacon for the receiving device to interpret a location code), it passes this up to the PMS, which replies with the matching location name. In this manner, the PMS can track each client as it moves around its environment, and a user can interrogate the system to find the location of another client.

The issue of privacy can be managed by allowing each user to switch dynamically between broadcasting or hiding their location as they see fit.

5.4.5 Location-Based Messaging

With the ability to determine location, the network can also provide another service: location-based messaging. This is where a message can be directed to a location instead of an individual user. As users with location tracking devices move around their environment, they receive messages that have been "posted" to their current location. Conversely, they may post messages at specific locations. To illustrate, a location message could be posted to someone's desk to inform passers by (or those specifically looking for them) that the person is on leave for the next two weeks, and should be contacted via email only for important messages. The location messages are sent to the PMS and stored in the beacon database. When messages have expired, the PMS deletes them accordingly. Each message is assigned a unique ID that is used to amend a user's database each time a location message is read, to prevent continuous notifications being sent for messages they have previously received.

5.4.6 Transparent Network Switching

One of the key functions provided by the MUON framework is network switching. This is the ability to switch automatically between different service providers when either the connection drops or a better bandwidth is available under a different service provider. The supported service providers are wired LAN, wireless radio LAN, infrared via serial, direct serial connection, and modem (including GSM mobile modem). The PMS and Muon Servers are connected only via wired LAN. Clients can select the best service providers available at log-on time, and monitor the availability of other services based on a pre-defined prioritized list.

5.4.7 Availability and Contextual Awareness

The nature of wearable computers dictates that users can be in many states of availability, according to their current situation. It is also the job of the wearable computer to determine which is the most appropriate form of feedback for notifying the user of system events, such as new messages. It is inappropriate for users to be issued a visual notification if they are running down a street; an audio notification would be safer! Also, if the user were engaged in a meeting, it would be appropriate for the wearable computer to limit the availability of the user to receiving urgent messages only. Although these issues are not addressed directly by the MUON framework, it has been a design goal from the outset to allow MUON clients to employ the features of agent technologies that provide user availability information and allow the system to respond to this information accordingly. Also, switching the context of messages could be controlled by an external agent that would feed information into the MUON client, allowing visual and audio notifications to be triggered appropriately. The provision for this type of service is accounted for by the use of "gateways", which connect the PMS to agent servers allowing information to be exchanged between various applications. This allows clients to utilize these services without the need to have a pre-defined IP address (as some of the agent servers require this) or be continuously connected to the network, as the PMS (which does have a unique IP address) acts as the go-between.

5.5 Discussion

This experiment provides avenues for a number of research threads. While the MetaPark environment is still being developed, the authors have been able to demonstrate elements of the system. For example the underlying network framework has been implemented, sample collaborative virtual environments have been constructed, and an intuitive mechanism for interfacing between personal devices and large displays or real world objects has been demonstrated. The authors are currently waiting for an accurate 3D terrain model of the target site to be created.

From a technical viewpoint, the network architecture that supports remote communication between the real and virtual MetaPark visitors provides a technical challenge of significant complexity. When the system is functionally complete a more intensive period of evaluation will commence. In particular, the authors hope to understand the relationships between the virtual and real space communities, the types of learning that occur, and the communications mechanisms used.

In terms of evaluation, longitudinal studies will be important in assessing the benefits of applications that sound intriguing on paper and make compelling demonstrations. Such work will provide qualitative understanding of the practical appeal of ubiquitous telepresence, but with radically new hardware there is also scope for a more constrained, quantitative assessment of the options in presenting and interacting with wearable interfaces.

References

[1] T. Starner, S. Mann, B. Rhodes, J. Levine, J. Healey, D. Kirsch, R. Picard, and A. Pentland, Augmented reality through wearable computing, *Presence* 6(4), 1997.
[2] G. Walker and P. Sheppard, Telepresence – the future of telephony, *BT Technology Journal* 15(4), October 1997.
[3] Pascoe, J. Adding generic contextual capabilities to wearable computers, *Proc. 2nd international symposium on wearable computers*, 19–20 October 1998, pp. 92–99.
[4] Van de Velde W. Co-habited mixed realities, *Proc. international workshop on "community ware"*, *IJCOAI*, Tokyo, Japan 1997.
[5] Weisner, M. The computer for the 21st century, *Scientific American*, 265(3), 94–104, 1991.

[6]   Buxton, W. Living in augmented reality: ubiquitous media and reactive environments. In
      K. Finn, A. Sellen, and S. Wilber (eds.) *Video Mediated Communication.* Erlbaum, Hillsdale,
      NJ, pp. 363–384, 1997. http://www.dgp.utoronto.ca/OTP/papers/bill.buxton/
      augmentedReality.html.

[7]   Billinghurst, M., Bowskill, J., Jessop, M., and Morphett, J. A wearable spatial conferencing space,
      Proc. 2nd International Symposium on Wearable Computers, 19–20 October 1998, pp. 76–83.

[8]   Billinghurst, M., Bowskill, J., Dyer, N., and Morphett J. An evaluation of spatial information
      displays on a wearable computer, *IEEE Computer Graphics and Applications*, November/December
      1998, pp. 24–31.

[9]   MIT iRX2 Infra Red Transceiver. http://ttt.www.media.mit.edu/pia/Research/
      iRX2/.

[10] Ishii, H. and Ullmer, B. Tangible bits: towards seamless interfaces between people, bits and atoms,
      in *Proceedings of Conference on Human Factors in Computing Systems (CHI '97)*, Atlanta, March
      1997, ACM Press, pp. 234–241.

6

Grafting the User Interface onto Reality

David J. Johnston and Adrian F. Clark

Abstract

One of the most obvious but neglected ways of increasing the intuitive nature of human–computer interfaces is to integrate computer-mediated interaction with real-world activities. The interface no longer exists within a vacuum, and the real world itself provides valuable cues to both the user and computer system.

A combination of virtual objects and the real world within an interactive system (known as Augmented Reality or AR) provides an ideal technological opportunity to exploit such naturalistic mechanisms in novel applications.

At Essex University we have constructed a mobile wearable computer, which, through the use of a semi-immersive VR headset and Global Positioning System (GPS) technology, supports an archaeological reconstruction application.

In conjunction with the Colchester Archaeological Trust, we have developed a VRML model of the Roman buildings which once stood in a site to the south of Colchester that is now known as the Gosbecks Archaeological Park. As the user walks around the park, consistent moving stereoscopic views of virtual ancient buildings are presented in the headset. The experience is one of being present in a past age populated by "in-period" avatars or virtual humans.

A virtual guide leads each user round the site; the tour may be individually customized to the visitor's capabilities and interests, and supported by other multimedia such as video and spatialized audio.

The technical work is currently in progress. The goal is to build such a system using inexpensive "off-the-shelf" components in order to demonstrate the viability of ubiquitous computing and the synergy between wearable computers and augmented reality.

6.1 Introduction

Archaeological sites hold a wealth of information about the past, yet to the uninformed eye a visit is often a disappointment. Unfortunately, most of us have neither access to an enthusiastic archaeologist to decipher the available evidence nor the appropriate academic expertise to imagine how the site might have once appeared. *In situ* physical reconstruction is in current disfavour, and organizations such as English Heritage have strict prohibitions regulating construction upon sites of historic importance.

One solution to this conundrum is to develop multimedia computer systems to guide visitors around. Such systems must clearly be wearable and interactive, to allow users to explore freely at their own pace. A tour can also be personally customized to reflect the capabilities and interests of the individual. It is imperative that the system provides a basic navigation facility to ensure that what is physically present in front of the user tallies with the content of the computerized tour.

There are two navigational choices. The first approach is to provide the user with navigational instructions. In this instance the user must inform the system that instructions have been completed, and the system breaks down if a mistake has been made. The second approach is to measure the location of the user automatically. The positional information is then used to control the tour itself.

Additionally, with the user's coordinates at the disposal of the computer system and by using a virtual reality headset, it is possible to provide an immersive experience of the site as it might once have looked. This combination of virtual objects with reality in an interactive system has become known as Augmented Reality (AR). Though augmented reality was initially developed as a visualization technique, it has subsequently developed into a research topic in its own right. Azuma's survey [1] is definitive, and [2] presents a good summary of the distinctions between AR and the more familiar VR.

An avatar (or virtual being) may serve as a tour guide. As well as providing an audio commentary, the avatar can be physically followed around the site. Progress through the tour is mediated through interaction with the avatar, who will present choices at various places *en route*. It will also be possible to populate the site with other avatars in period costume in order to represent the site as a once-living community. Other multimedia types, such as video and music, may also be incorporated to enrich the presentation.

6.2 The Gosbecks Archaeological Park

To the south of Colchester in Essex lies the Gosbecks Archaeological Park [3], which contains both Roman and Celtic remains. Little evidence is visible above ground, though aerial photography and excavation clearly reveal the ground plans of a number of buildings.

The largest Roman theatre in Britain was at Gosbecks. Nearby was a Romano-Celtic temple surrounded first by a ditch and then by a vast colonnaded covered corridor (or portico) which could accommodate the whole audience of the theatre. The portico forms a square of approximately 100 m × 100 m. A VRML model of this construction is shown in Fig. 6.1.

Much is known about Roman architecture from surviving buildings. Roman buildings, certainly those that fulfilled civic function, are generally formulaic; that is,

Figure 6.1

much of the structure can be inferred from a small amount of information – say, the ground plan and a column width. The rules that underpin Roman architecture were detailed by Vitruvius, a Roman architect and engineer of the first century BC, in his ten-volume work *De Architectura*, [4] which is the only complete architectural work to survive from antiquity. These rules have informed the construction of our VRML models. From the existing ground plan, archaeologists can reconstruct the Roman theatre, but only to one of two possible principal forms. Augmented reality has many advantages as a reconstruction technology, in that both possibilities can be represented.

6.3 Wearable Computers

Recent years have seen major improvements in hardware technologies – processor speeds and power consumption, disk capacity and robustness, etc. This has inspired the emergence of viable "wearable computers", small computers that may be carried upon the person while in use. The current generation of wearables is typically based around PC/104 cards, actually designed for the construction of embedded systems. These cards are roughly 100 mm square and are able to plug together vertically. A complete system, comprising processor, display adaptor, disk controllers, disk drive, etc. is able to fit into a package of about 150 × 120 × 120 mm, which can be attached to a (strong!) belt. Power is supplied from rechargeable camcorder batteries. Output is usually achieved by some kind of head-mounted display (HMD) and input by a chord keyboard/mouse or by voice.

The system constructed at the University of Essex and used for this work follows this design and employs a 586 (Pentium) class processor, a 1 Gbyte disk drive, Virtual i-O's "I-glasses" for output and HandyKey's "Twiddler" for input. It is

Figure 6.2

capable of running Linux or Windows 95; the former was used for the work described here. It is illustrated in Fig. 6.2.

The full specifications is as follows:

- Main system
  - PC/104 card comprising Cyrix 133 MHz 586 microprocessor with IDE, floppy, keyboard, serial ports, 20 Mbyte RAM
  - PC/104 VGA card (Trident chipset, 0.5 Mbyte)
  - PC/104 Single PCMCIA type II controller + slot (expandable for two cards)
  - 1.0 Gbyte 2.5-inch IDE hard disk
  - 3–4 hour battery life (running Linux; half that running Windows 95)
- Input–output
  - Twiddler keyboard
  - Virtual i-O "I-glasses" (NTSC version)
  - Palm Pilot Professional
  - PCMCIA AV conference card (audio I/O, video input only)
  - PCMCIA D-LINK DE650 Ethernet card (10Base2/T)
- Power supply
  - 12 V DC input, basic PSU, +5 V, +9 V output
  - Batteries: 2 × Duracell DR11 (6 V @ 3.6 Ah) NiMH
- Software
  - Windows 95
  - Linux (RedHat 5.2)

The wearable used for this work, being based on a 586 and hence having performance roughly equivalent to that of a 75 MHz Pentium, is really somewhat underpowered. However, faster processors currently available in the PC/104 form factor are not low-powered, so there is little option.

A second wearable is in the process of being constructed around a Toshiba Libretto 100 "mini-notebook", which features a P166 MMX processor; the performance of this system will be more satisfactory.

Wearable computer technology heralds an age of novel mobile computing applications such as the immersive archaeological tour described above. Conventional peripherals such as keyboard and monitor are clearly impractical, and miniaturization allows radical form changes. Though there is consensus that a wearable will not be just a "PC in a rucksack", there is much debate over the architectural and physical form that a wearable will eventually take. Through miniaturization, the wearable may take the physical form of a pen or a mobile phone, though this will be largely determined by the nature of the interaction with the device itself. The architecture, for example, instead of a conventional centralized CPU, may be a number of compute nodes distributed about the body that can intercommunicate as well as connect to services and peripherals in the outside world via short-range radio. However, our research is largely independent of the eventual form of a wearable and is concerned primarily with issues of function and usability.

The omnipresence of wearables heralds a new form of communications network where the nodes are people. This is known as a "piconet" [5], and it would allow, for instance, the interaction of many visitors to the same archaeological site. Within a piconet, communication sub-networks are continually being dynamically created and destroyed as individuals move in and out of radio-communication range of each other. Bluetooth [6] is an emerging relevant standard for short-range, high-bandwidth, radio-frequency digital communication.

6.4 Achieving Immersion

We achieve user immersion in the historic scene through the use of a head-mounted display (HMD). In fact, we use our HMD in a semi-immersive mode by removing an opaque strip of black plastic from the front of the headset. In this manner, a semi-transparent view of the computer graphics is optically combined with the real-world scene. The technologies peculiar to AR are less familiar than those of virtual reality, which may be adapted for AR use, so it is worthwhile categorizing the range of approaches available.

- *Optical See-through Head Mounted Display (HMD)*: a head-mounted display which merges virtual and real worlds optically by using a half-silvered mirror. This is the approach we have taken for our initial prototype.
- *Video See-through HMD*: virtual images are overlaid on video images of the real scene. There are some advantages to this approach, as correct registration of the two images has already been achieved. It is easy to handle occlusion between real

and virtual objects, and computer vision techniques are more easily accessible, as the source data already exist. The latency in both real and virtual paths can be more easily controlled to be in synchrony, but a reduced-resolution "reality" has many obvious disadvantages for the wearer.

- *Video See-through Head-Up Display (HUD)*: this partially covers the dominant eye of the viewer so that a virtual floating window is presented in front of the viewer's face. It has been found that an image presented to a single eye is minimally intrusive, although depth information through stereoscopy in the virtual scene is lost.

- *Video See-through Palmtop*: this is a less common type of system described in [7] which uses a magnifying glass metaphor and a palmtop computer to merge virtual images with real ones within the window of the palmtop's display. This is less invasive than a head-mounted display and is claimed to have performance benefits and a more favourable user reaction. The palmtop contains a miniature gyro sensor to determine the orientation of the device and a vision-based recognition system to detect the rough position of the device in the real world and of objects placed in front of it.

Our HMD, the "I-glasses" from Virtual i-O, has built-in tilt sensors that measure the view orientation of the user's head. This is presented in terms of yaw, pitch and roll viewing angles. However, the I-glasses provide no information on the position in space of the wearer's head, and it is necessary to obtain this information from some other source in order to generate an immersive view.

Indeed, to form a correct stereoscopic view of a virtual object requires many other parameters [8]: the field of view; the inter-pupillary distance; the accommodation (focus and depth of field of the eyes); and the vergence (or angular disparity) of the eyes. The technology to measure the latter two quantities does exist but is esoteric and expensive. In short, it is currently impractical to mimic fully all the possible depth cues of reality, but any software architecture developed should be capable of carrying this information for future compatibility. Note that it is difficult to isolate view determination entirely from technology. For example, with a holographic display system many of the parameters described above would not be necessary.

We decided to use the Global Positioning System (GPS) [9] for position determination with our prototype. This represents the current state of the art in navigation. Using a constellation of American Department of Defense satellites, a position fix can be obtained anywhere on the Earth's surface to an unprecedented accuracy. The nominal accuracy of 100 m (using $100 equipment) may be enhanced using a variety of techniques to around 5 mm at an update rate of 10 Hz (using $50 000 equipment).

The high-performance systems are generally supplied as expensive integrated solutions to the surveying industry or high-end navigation market in bulky boxes or as large rucksacks. So, although these are suitable in terms of performance, bulk and cost mitigate against personal use. We therefore investigated how the maximum accuracy could be obtained from GPS technology while still maintaining viability as an affordable and wearable technology.

6.5 Required Accuracy

Critical factors in the usability of position determination technology are the issues of range and accuracy. For example, GPS technology only works outdoors or within a short distance of a window, whereas more accurate magnetic positioning systems work indoors but have ranges of only a few metres. The limited range of most positioning technologies is at odds with the complete freedom of movement demanded by a wearable user. The availability of GPS, and its untapped potential in the augmented reality domain, have guided us initially towards an outdoors application.

Quantitative positioning specifications qualitatively affect application usability. For example, to overlay a virtual object in the field of view of a user one metre out of position may be acceptable if that object is a virtual building in the distance, but this would not be acceptable if the object were supposed to be a virtual human at a typical distance for social interaction.

We have a rule-of-thumb benchmark for human interaction with virtual architecture which is the basic ability to walk through a door. A typical door width of around one metre implies that a sub-metre accuracy of 10 cm is around the maximum acceptable.

The problematically demanding tracking requirements for augmented reality are presented in succinct form by Azuma in [10]. It is suggested that, to maintain a reasonable degree of registration between the virtual and the real, an angular accuracy of 0.5° and a total system latency of under 2 ms are required. These are exceedingly difficult figures to achieve in practice, but nonetheless represent a usefully documented baseline. It is no accident that the state-of-the-art HiBall Tracker system from UNC [11], with which Azuma has been involved, has achieved these figures. This indoor system uses special ceiling panels housing LEDs, and a miniature head-mounted camera cluster called the HiBall. This specification is:

update rate:	> 1500 Hz
latency:	< 1 ms
position noise:	< 0.2 mm
orientation noise:	< 0.03°

The wearable urban navigation system described in [12], which labels real-world objects via an optical see-through display, claims to be usable despite using a GPS positioning system which gives an accuracy of "only" 1 m.

Our system's performance falls between these two extremes, and we suggest that high levels of interactivity for an application like archaeological reconstruction can be achieved at more modest levels of accuracy than those cited by Azuma. It is important to note that at Gosbecks there are no visible remains on the ground, so less than accurate registration with the ground plan of the Roman buildings will not be noticed. The buildings must, however, retain that characteristic of buildings of remaining roughly in the same location!

6.6 A GPS Solution

Much conflicting information exists regarding the positional accuracy of GPS technology. Confusion arises from the fact that the accuracy depends on many factors, and a short explanation of the calculations will reveal why.

A basic GPS calculation measures the time of flight of a radio signal from a number of satellites to a single receiver. The time is measured by looking at the data content of the radio message, which follows a known repeating pseudo-random pattern. A position which is most consistent with these measured ranges is calculated by a least-squares technique. This is nothing more than a basic triangulation problem. Accuracy will obviously depend on the number and configuration of the available satellites. For example, if all the satellites are near the horizon, then the measured altitude will be more prone to error than otherwise.

The satellites broadcast on two frequencies called L1 (1575.42 MHz – largely for civilian use) and L2 (1227.60 MHz – largely for military use, as the signals are encrypted). The timing information for the civilian signal is deliberately degraded in accuracy, resulting in a slowly varying random error in positional fix. When this happens (which is most of the time), Selective Availability (or SA) is described as being on. The nominal accuracy of GPS with SA on is 100 m. It is 15 m with SA off.

The radio waves are delayed by their propagation though the atmosphere, and this introduces range errors, but the satellites also broadcast parameters for a (time-varying) atmospheric model that allows some corrections to be made. However, if both L1 and L2 signals are received, the effects of atmospheric delay can be almost totally compensated for because a law of physics states that the relative delay is described by a factor gamma which is equal to the square of the ratio of the two frequencies.

By using a second receiver at a known location, a technique known as differential GPS (DGPS) can be employed. Provided the base station and the mobile station are sufficiently close together, it can be assumed that the signal delays at both locations from the same satellite are identical. As the location of the base station is known, this delay can be calculated and used to correct the pseudorange of the mobile station. The error for differential GPS is generally quoted as being some proportion of the baseline distance between the fixed and mobile stations. Differential GPS calculations are much simpler than for a single receiver, because many errors are exactly cancelled out. For example, it is neither necessary to apply atmospheric model corrections nor to use the different propagation properties of the L1 and L2 frequencies.

Basic differential GPS is called differential code GPS because the message content is used to measure journey time. An enhancement is called differential phase GPS, where the phase of the signal is also used to obtain a more accurate pseudorange measurement. Of course, a phase measurement in itself, even if continuously monitored, can only provide a relative distance measurement; hence intelligent filtering techniques are used to combine both code and phase measurements to obtain the best aspects of either, yielding a more accurate yet absolute measure. The error for differential phase GPS is generally quoted as being 1 part per million of the baseline distance between the fixed and mobile stations.

The downsides to differential GPS are threefold: a second GPS receiver is required; the location of this receiver must be known very accurately; and the information from this receiver must be propagated to the mobile station in real time. Due to these common requirements and the high setup overhead involved, there are a number of differential GPS correction service providers who broadcast such signals by satellite, FM radio and maritime beacon in a format that adheres to the RTCM 104 standard [13].

There is a consequent choice between service subscription and setting up one's own base station with some form of (radio) link. Subscription costs are high, and even the cheapest differential receiver (for the free maritime beacon service) is of the order of $400. Yet, criticisms are levelled against do-it-yourself DGPS because, unless a large enough common subset of satellites are within range at both locations and sufficiently high-quality information can be obtained, results have been reported as worse than with a single receiver. On the other hand, the error of differential GPS, up to separations of around 30 km, bears a linear relationship to the length of the baseline. Do-it-yourself DGPS allows the length of the baseline to be accurately controlled; subscription users are at the mercy of their service provider's nearest base station.

We have decided to go for a do-it-yourself differential GPS system operating at the L1 frequency, based upon two AllStar [14] boards (made by CMC in Canada) which are typical of the latest OEM products that provide phase information but cost only a few hundred dollars. The model option we chose supplies raw data at 10 Hz, which enables our system to achieve near real-time responsiveness. Most GPS units provide a position fix at most once a second. We were guided in our choice by the nature of the Gosbecks site itself. The horizons are wide and open, and there are no buildings in the vicinity that could introduce multi-path errors or impede line of sight to the satellites. The augmented reality GPS-based urban navigation system described in [12] noted that, due to occlusion by buildings and trees, the necessary line-of-sight access to a sufficient number of satellites for position determination was often not available. The irony is that virtual reconstruction of the Roman buildings is aided by their ruinous nature.

Note that, to save considerable expense, we are performing the final position calculation ourselves using homebrewed GPS code. It is expensive to buy compute power in a GPS product, but cheap to buy compute power in a PC. The computational core of our code is based upon the freely available Pascal batch-processing source [15] that has been written and mounted on the Web by Sam Storm van Leeuwen. We have translated this code into C and have similarly mounted it on the Web [16]. However, the subsidiary benefit of using homebrewed code is that we have complete control over the architecture of our system and can tune the code to our particular application for greater accuracy.

6.7 The Output Stage

The VRML models were developed in collaboration with the Colchester Archaeological Trust. Tcl scripts, informed by the rules of Vitruvius [4], were used to generate the VRML models [17].

We have designed a software interface specification called the Virtual Position Device Interface (VPDI), which abstracts the notion of a position- and view-determining device from any particular hardware. Writing to this interface simplifies the task of integrating positional technologies.

We considered various ways of integrating the output of our DGPS system, through the VPDI interface, to VRML browsers to control the viewpoint. Our software has been developed on top of Linux, so we were looking for a public domain Linux VRML browser with source that would allow us to make our own customizations.

We regard Linux as an easy-to-use development platform – and the public domain software modules from which we have built our system may readily change throughout its evolution. We would like the production system to be portable at the level of source, if not of object, code and are trying to avoid dependence on any proprietary methodology.

We have altered the freely-available FreeWRL browser [18], which has been produced at Harvard, so that the viewpoint is controlled through the VPDI interface. FreeWRL is written in Perl and C, and we have added our own Perl and C code extensions. We wrote a positional device emulator for a joystick that enabled us to test out this software initially. This openness of the FreeWRL source make the whole operation much simpler than interfacing to a proprietary browser such as CosmoPlayer. Our ultimate goal is to move our VPDI code within a Java node of VRML, so that any VRML browser can be driven by positional mediation.

The I-glasses use a yaw, pitch and roll representation of orientation, whereas FreeWRL uses a quaternion representation. Code within the VDPI interface interconverts between matrix; raw, pitch and roll; and quaternion forms. Limitations were discovered in FreeWRL, such as the lack of support for concave polygons. The deficiencies were reported to the author, in the hope that over time these bugs would be fixed.

We have also evaluated VRwave [19], another public domain VRML browser available under Linux, this time written in Java. We found little difference between these packages – though the rendering and interface of VRwave was richer, FreeWRL had a slight edge on performance. We decided to continue our development with FreeWRL for the meanwhile.

Due to the complexity of our archaeological model, with the replication of many basic architectural units such as the columns in Figs. 6.3 and 6.4, we have had difficulty in obtaining real-time visualization of the full model. However, for the initial prototype we have reduced the complexity of the model to prove the principle of real-time performance for the system as a whole. It is less important for us at present to make the right choice of software module, and more important for us to make any choice by which we can obtain a working system within which we can testbed.

We are currently working on modifying FreeWRL to produce stereo output for the I-glasses.

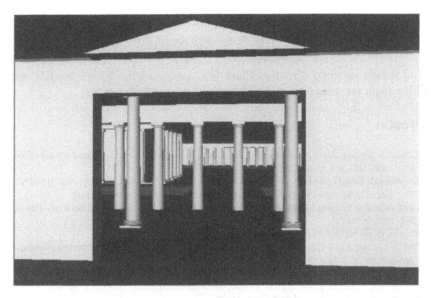

Figure 6.3

Figure 6.4

6.8 Conclusions

Our system demonstrates the viability of more natural interfaces in practical applications, and that the underlying archaeological reconstruction is feasible using augmented reality techniques.

Further work is required to improve the performance and accuracy of the system and to take the demonstration system that proves the principle further in the direction of a production system of direct benefit to the visitor to Gosbecks.

Special thanks go to Dr Christine Clark for developing the VRML models and to Neill Newman for designing and building our wearable computer.

References

[1] Ronald T. Azuma, A survey of augmented reality, *Presence: Teleoperators and Virtual Environments*, 6(4), 355–385, August 1997.

[2] Augmented Reality Review vs. Virtual Reality. http://www.uk.infowin.org/ACTS/ANALYSYS/CONCERTATION/CHAINS/ si/home/ch-sid/arvvr.html.

[3] The Colchester Archaeological Trust, Gosbecks Archaeological Park, *The Colchester Archaeologist*, 1994–1995, Issue 8.

[4] Marcus Vitruvius Pollio, *De Architectura*, first edition, Como, 1521.

[5] Roy Want and Andy Hopper, Active badges and personal interactive computing objects, *IEEE Transactions of Consumer Electronics*, February, 1992.

[6] Bluetooth: A Global Specification for Wireless Connectivity. http://www.bluetooth.com/.

[7] Jun Rekimoto, The magnifying glass approach to augmented reality systems, *International Conference on Artificial Reality and Tele-Existence '95*.

[8] David Drascic and Paul Milgram, Perceptual issues in augmented reality, *Proc. SPIE, Stereoscopic Displays and Virtual Reality Systems III* (eds. Mark T. Bolas, Scott S. Fisher and John O. Merritt), Vol. 2653, pp. 123–134, January–February 1996

[9] Navstar GPS Space Segment/Navigation User Interfaces, 2250 E. Imperial Highway, Suite 450, El Segundo, CA 90245-3509. ICD-GPS-200, Revision C, Initial Release, October 1993.

[10] Ronald Tadao Azuma, Tracking Requirements for Augmented Reality, *Communications of the ACM*, 36(7), 50–51, July 1993.

[11] University of North Carolina, *Wide-Area Tracking: Navigation Technology for Head-Mounted Displays*, April, 1998. http://www.cs.unc.edu/~tracker/.

[12] Steven Feiner, Blair MacIntyre, Tobias Hollerer and Anthony Webster, A touring machine: prototyping 3d mobile augmented reality systems for exploring the urban environment, *The First International Symposium on Wearable Computers*, October 1997, pages 74–81.

[13] RTCM Recommended Standards for Differential Navstar GPS Service, 655 Fifteenth Street, NW, Suite 300, Washington, D.C. 20005 USA. Version 2.1, January 1994.

[14] *User's Manual*, Allstar P/N 220-600944-00X, 500 Dr Frederik Philips Boulevard, Saint-Laurent, Quebec, Canada HAM 2S9, June 1998, Publication No. 1200-GEN-0101.

[15] Sam's GPS Software Pages. http://callisto.worldonline.nl/~samsvl/software.htm.

[16] David Johnston: Personal page. http://vase.essex.ac.uk/projects/gps/djjweb/.

[17] C. Clark and A. F. Clark, VRML interfaces to information systems, *Proceedings of the International Conference on Virtual Environments on the Internet, WWW and Networks*, April 1997.

[18] FreeWRL Home Page. http://www.fas.harvard.edu/~lukka/freewrl/.

[19] The VRwave Home Page. http://www.iicm.edu/VRwave/.

7

Challenges for the World-Wide Graphics Web

F.R.A. Hopgood and D.A. Duce

Abstract

The use of computer graphics on the World Wide Web is growing. For many years the only graphics that appeared on the Web were low-resolution gif images and plug-ins such as VRML. However, in 1999 there have been a number of developments that suggest that the presence of genuine computer graphics at the heart of the Web will grow during the year. The World Wide Web Consortium (W3C) has released a Web Profile for CGM that has commitments from a number of major players that they will implement and use. W3C has had four submissions from members for Scalable Vector Graphics (SVG) on the Web.

Independent of the SVG activity is the work on producing a standard API to Web-based information via the Document Object Model (DOM). This requires the definition of base functionality for interaction on the Web including interaction with computer graphics such as SVG. The question is: does the Web present new challenges or opportunities for computer graphics? That is the topic addressed in this chapter. The first section gives some indication of the changes taking place on the Web, while the second indicates the areas of interest to computer graphics.

7.1 The Web in 2000

7.1.1 Introduction

The move from HTML to XML and the separation of style from content means that the view of the Web by 2000 will be as shown in Fig. 7.1.

Web content should by then be defined in XML rather than HTML and specialist Document Type Definitions (DTDs) will have appeared to deal with multimedia and computer graphics. SMIL and SVG are used as illustrations. For improved searching, there will be a need to improve the quality of metadata associated both with Web pages and graphics within Web pages. The Resource Description Framework (RDF) will be the notation for defining such metadata.

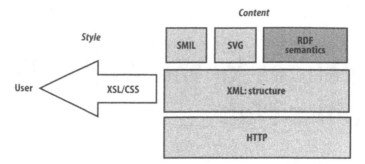

Figure 7.1 The Web in 2000.

It is unlikely that plug-ins will survive very much longer. There is little incentive for browser suppliers to implement such features internally unless there is significant demand and the plug-in suppliers then face a never-ending load in maintaining the plug-in's availability across a range of browsers. In consequence, CGM and VRML on the Web are likely to die and be replaced by XML DTDs.

While not needing a full understanding of the components above, an introduction is needed to give a flavour of how the Web will look in 2000.

7.1.2 XML

XML is a subset of SGML (Standard Generalized Markup Language, ISO 8879) for use on the Web. It retains SGML's basic features but in a form that is much easier to implement and understand. XML can be processed by existing commercial SGML tools and a rapidly growing number of free ones of its own.

The main characteristic of XML is user-defined tags. A simple example is:

```
<?XML version="1.0"?>
<exam>
<question>Who was the last King of England</question>
<answer>George VI</answer>
<question>How many queens were named
  Elizabeth</question>
<answer>Two</answer>
</exam>
```

Elements are the most common form of markup. They are delimited by angle brackets and define the content they enclose. Three elements (question, answer and exam) are used in the above example.

This could be used for transmitting the answers to an exam paper from one site to another. If the two parties involved had agreed the format, there is no reason why a formal Document Type Definition (DTD) needs to be specified.

However, to formalize the format of the exchange, the DTD for the above would be something like:

```
<!ELEMENT exam (question, answer)+ >
<!ELEMENT question #PCDATA>
<!ELEMENT answer #PCDATA>
```

This states that the syntax of an exam paper consists of a set of questions each followed by answers, each of which is of type PCDATA (Parseable Character Data).

One of the attractions of XML is that there is a rigid adherence to the syntax, which means that the parsers are much smaller and more efficient than the equivalent HTML parser, which has to handle a more forgiving syntax such as the ability to omit end tags.

7.1.3 CSS

Two aspects of any document are content and style. The content gives the information to be presented and the style defines how the information is presented. Most publishers have a House Style that is a consistent way of presenting information. The same information printed by two publishers may look quite different.

XML defines content. What is needed is the ability for publishers to have control of style.

The aim of Cascading Style Sheets (CSS) is to give the page developer much more control on how a page should be displayed by *all* browsers.

A *style sheet* is a set of *rules* that controls the formatting of XML elements on one or more Web pages. Thus, the appearance of a Web page can be changed by changing the style sheet associated with it.

A style sheet rule consists of two parts: a *selector* that defines what XML elements are controlled by the rule and a *declaration* that says what the required effect is. Thus a simple rule is:

```
question { color: blue }
answer { color: red }
```

This says that all the questions in a page should be displayed in blue and the answers in red. Here, question is the *selector*, color is the *property* that is to be changed, blue is the *value* that the property is changed to, and color: blue is the declaration.

CSS is concerned with how the text looks on the paper, but also has some graphical support in terms of the elements. Thus, question is a *block-level* element. Block-level elements have an area that contains the content of the text in the element. CSS provides control of how that content is placed on the page.

The core content area can be surrounded by padding, a border and a margin. The padding has the same background as the element, the border can be set to have a different background while the margin is always transparent, so that the background of the parent element shows through. So a simple graphic consisting of blocks of text with borders around can be displayed using XML and CSS.

7.1.4 XSL

The Extensible Style Language (XSL) is not designed to replace CSS; XSL is aimed at activities such as rearranging the document that are not supported by CSS. XSL and CSS share the same underlying concepts and use the same terminology where possible.

With XSL, you can specify the print styling of Web documents at least as well as in a typical word processor. XSL comes in basically two parts:

• a language for transforming XML documents
• a vocabulary for specifying formatting semantics

We will just give a flavour of the first. The XML source document is considered as a tree. So, for example, a fragment of XML might be:

```
<today>
<garden>
<item>Find mower</item>
<item>Cut grass</item>
</garden>
<leisure>
<item>Read book</item>
<item>Watch TV</item>
<item>Have dinner</item>
</leisure>
<work>
<item>Drive to work</item>
<item>Learn XML</item>
<item>Drive home</item>
</work>
</today>
```

which would have a tree as shown in Fig. 7.2.

The associated text strings would hang off the item nodes.

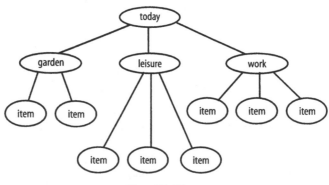

Figure 7.2 XSL tree.

In XSL, you can then define a set of rules (written in XML) that transform this *source tree* into a *result tree*. You do this by defining *patterns* that identify nodes in this tree and associating a *template* that defines an action to be applied. The two parts define a *template rule*.

The simplest style sheet is:

```
<xsl>
</xsl>
```

which does not look too exciting. However, there is a built-in template rule which says if no template rule exists for a node, just process the children nodes of that node in order. So the XSL style sheet above would start at the top and do a tree walk where the default process for the leaves is to output the content of the node, thus transforming the tree into:

```
Find mower
Cut grass
...
```

Now suppose we would like to generate a Web page (we could have said XML, RTF or troff as well). The simplest thing to do would be something like:

```
<xsl>
<template match="item">
<P>
<process-children/>
</P>
</template>
</xsl>
```

We have omitted some detail, but the example gives a flavour of what the style sheet would be like. The tree walk would eventually get to an item node, and this time there would be a pattern rule to apply. The action is to output an HTML paragraph. The process-children command causes all the children nodes of the node in question to be processed in order. In our case, this would just cause the text to be output, so we would have:

```
<P>Find mower</P>
<P>Cut grass</P>
<P>Read book</P>
...
```

Clearly, some differentiation has to be made between what are XSL rules and what is output, which gets us into how you differentiate XML namespaces – but we will not go into that here! It gets more interesting when you start using the full complexity of the pattern matching you can do. We can give specific actions for nodes dependent on position. So we could have:

```
<template match="garden">
<P>
<process-children/>
</P>
</template>
<template match="garden/item[first-of-type]">
<process-children/>
</template>
<template match="garden/item[last-of-type]">
<text>THEN</text>
<process-children/>
</template>
```

producing:

```
<P>Find mower THEN Cut grass</P>
```

The major difference between CSS and XSL is the ability to define a different order for the output in XSL, so we could have:

```
<template match="today">
<process select="leisure/item[first-of-type]">
<process select="work">
<process select="leisure/item[last-of-type]">
<process select="garden">
<process select="leisure/item[first-of-type]">
</template>
```

The item node selector has a qualifier added which indicates which child node is being processed. In this example, we read a book, learn XML at work, have dinner, do the garden and read a book again before going to bed, and we don't watch TV at all! This illustrates that you can process information twice (useful for Contents pages, for example) and can ignore parts of the tree.

7.1.5 SMIL

The Synchronized Multimedia Integration Language (SMIL, pronounced "smile") allows the integration of a set of independent multimedia objects into a synchronized multimedia presentation. Using SMIL, presentations such as a slide show synchronized with audio comments or a video synchronized with a text stream can be described.

A typical SMIL presentation has the following characteristics:

• The presentation is composed of several components that are accessible via a URL, e.g. files stored on a Web server.
• The components have different media types, such as audio, video, image or text.

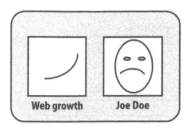
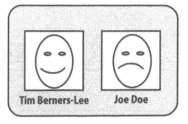

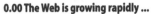

0.00 The Web is growing rapidly ...   1.00 "Tim, what do you think?"

1.05 "This is very exciting"

Figure 7.3 Interactive newscast screenshots.

- The start and end times of different components have to be synchronized with events in other components. For example, in a slide show, a particular slide is displayed when the narrator in the audio starts talking about it.
- The user can control the presentation by using control buttons known from video recorders, such as stop, fast-forward and rewind. Additional functions are "random access", i.e. the presentation can be started anywhere, and "slow motion", i.e. the presentation is played slower than at its original speed.
- The user can follow hyperlinks embedded in the presentation.

SMIL has been designed so that it is easy to author simple presentations with a text editor. The key to success for HTML was that attractive hypertext content could be created without requiring a sophisticated authoring tool. SMIL achieves the same for synchronized hypermedia.

Imagine a news broadcast on the growth of the Web. In the first scene (see left-hand side of Fig. 7.3), a graph on the left-hand side of the screen displays the growth of the Web. The right-hand side of the screen is taken up by a video of an anchor person commenting on the graph. The graph and the commentator's video are set up on a background.

In the second scene (right-hand side of Fig. 7.3), the graph is replaced by a video showing Tim Berners-Lee, and the anchor person starts to interview him. During the interview, the user can click on Tim's video, and Tim's homepage will be brought up (via a hyperlink). Figure 7.4 gives the timeline for these events. Some components do not appear in the figure:

- The image "Web Growth" is shown from time 0:00 to time 1:00.
- The text "Web Growth" is shown once the image has been displayed; the text "Joe Doe" is shown from time 0:00 until the end of the Joe Doe video.
- The text "Tim Berners-Lee" is shown while the video of Tim is being displayed.
- The user can follow a hyperlink connected to Tim's video and text while they are shown.

This scenario can be implemented using the following SMIL document:

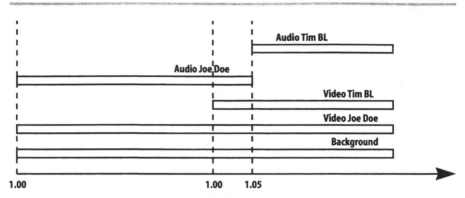

Figure 7.4 Schedule for interactive newscast scenario.

```
<smil>
 <head>
  <layout type="text/smil-basic">
   <tuner id="left-video" left="20" top="50" z="2"/>
   <tuner id="left-text" left="20" top="120" z="2"/>
   <tuner id="right-video" left="150" top="50" z="2"/>
   <tuner id="right-text" left="150" top="120" z="2"/>
  </layout>
 </head>
 <body>
  <par>
   <img href="bg"/>
   <seq>
    <par>
     <img href="graph" loc="left-video" dur="45s"/>
     <text href="graph-text" loc="left-text"/>
    </par>
    <par>
     <a href="http://www.w3.org/People/Berners-Lee">
      <video href="tim-video" loc="left-video"/>
     </a>
     <text href="tim-text" loc="left-text"/>
    </par>
   </seq>
   <seq>
    <audio href="joe-audio"/>
    <audio href="tim-audio"/>
   </seq>
   <video id="jv" href="joe-video" loc="right-video"/>
   <text href="joe-text" loc="right-text"/>
  </par>
 </body>
</smil>
```

7.1.6 SVG

The Scalable Vector Graphics specification should be well established by 2000. Like SMIL it is an XML DTD and is aiming at presenting simple vector graphics on the Web. SVG supports two intended uses:

• Standalone SVG files which represent complete drawings. These standalone SVG files might have been created by a graphics authoring program. If destined to be part of a Web page, these files might be included/referenced using XPointer by a parent document such as an XML Web page.

• SVG "fragments" which represent snippets of graphics which are interspersed (often inline) among the content of a parent document such as an XML Web page.

The following shows a trivial standalone SVG file with no content:

```
<?xml version="1.0"?>
<g xmlns="http://www.w3.org/...">
  <!- Insert drawing elements here ->
</g>
```

The simplest drawings can be described by a sequence of drawing elements. The following example draws a rectangle:

```
...
<g>
  <rectangle x="100" y="100" width="100" height="100" />
</g>
```

An SVG "document" can range from a single SVG graphics element such as a rectangle to a complex, deeply nested collection of grouping and graphics elements.

This example shows a slightly more complex (i.e. it contains multiple rectangles) standalone, self-contained SVG document:

```
<?xml version="1.0"?>
<g xmlns="http://www.w3.org/...SVG_1.0...">
    <rect ... />
    <rect ... />
    <rect ... />
    <rect ... />
</g>
```

The <g> element is the general-purpose element for grouping and naming collections of drawing elements. A complete, standalone SVG drawing typically is bracketed between a <g> and a </g>. If several drawing elements share similar attributes, they can be collected together using a <g> element. For example:

```
...
<g>
```

```
<g fillcolor="red">
  <rect x="100" y="100" width="100" height="100" />
  <rect x="300" y="100" width="100" height="100" />
</g>
<g fillcolor="blue">
  <rect x="100" y="300" width="100" height="100" />
  <rect x="300" y="300" width="100" height="100" />
</g>
</g>
```

A group of drawing elements, as well as individual objects, can be given a name. Named groups are needed for several purposes, such as animation and reusable objects. The following example organizes the drawing elements into two groups and assigns a name to each group:

```
...
<g>
  <g id="OBJECT1">
    <rect x="100" y="100" width="100" height="100" />
  </g>
  <g id="OBJECT2">
    <circle cx="150" cy="300" r="25" />
  </g>
</g>
...
```

The general rendering model is PostScript-like. So a rectangle is a special case of the general path primitive which is filled or stroked. Groupings can be used to specify new coordinate systems.

7.1.7 DOM

On 1 October 1998, Level 1 of the Document Object Model became a W3C Recommendation. A basic HTML document has a static data format which the browser renders. If the user wants to vary the presentation by using, for example, scripts, there is a need to access the content and structure (information) that defines the document. The DOM object model provides a common framework for how scripts reference the elements of a document; how styles are applied to elements; and how scripts can change styles. Suppose we have this simple HTML page:

```
<HTML>
<HEAD>
<TITLE>My Document</TITLE>
<STYLE type="text/css">
H1 {color: black}
</STYLE>
</HEAD>
<BODY>
<H1>The DOM</H1>
<P ALIGN="Left">For <B>all</B> you need to know</P>
```

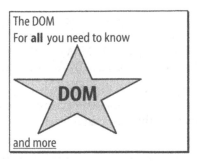

Figure 7.5 Typical Web page.

```
<A HREF="dominfo.html">
<IMG SRC="dom.gif">
and more!</A>
</BODY>
</HTML>
```

This would appear something like Fig. 7.5, and would probably have been transformed to an internal form resembling the structure in Fig. 7.6.

What DOM is trying to achieve is to provide a standard Applications Programming Interface (API) for manipulating this internal form using a programming language such as ECMAScript. To do that you need to have a model of all the bits that make up the document. Even a simple document, such as the one above, has quite a bit of detail and structure once you start examining it (as we can see from the diagram).

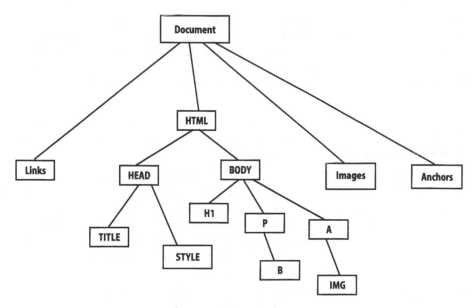

Figure 7.6 Structure of a Web page.

The emphasis in DOM Level 1 is on how you access things, not how you represent them. It is envisaged that the internal structure may vary significantly depending on the type of product that is using the DOM. A browser and editor might have the document information stored quite differently for performance reasons.

If this had been an XML document, the structure and content would be quite similar except that the node labels would vary according to the defined markup. In consequence, DOM has been defined so that it works equally well with both HTML and XML.

Using DOM Level 1, you can access and make changes to the document, the images associated with it, how it is styled etc. A script can refer to an element by giving an absolute reference or by giving its position relative to another entity. The script can add, shuffle and delete elements in the document.

Given an object, you can find out where in the document tree it is located. You can refer to the parent or the child of an object as well as its siblings. You can use these references to walk up or down the document tree.

DOM Level 1 is basically a framework. It defines what an element object and an attribute is and how you can access them. It does not have much navigational functionality to let you search through collections of entities.

The next stage, past Level 1, will be to define reactions that a document can make itself to events that apply to it. DOM will ensure that the functionality introduced by Netscape and Microsoft with their Dynamic HTML offerings can be implemented in a standard way. For example, it would allow the document to change the style of the H1 title, say, when the mouse passes over it.

7.1.8 Resource Description Framework (RDF)

To add value to the data available on the Web, we need to find ways to represent information about that data; that is *metadata*. Metadata is data about data and can be used for many applications, such as searching and cataloguing. An example of metadata is a Platform for Internet Content Selection (PICS) label that is added to a Web page to allow filtering of the Web content arriving at a browser.

W3C's main thrust in this area is the Resource Description Framework (RDF), which is the language being developed to represent metadata. RDF has a key aim that it should be machine readable. It should allow an agent to make intelligent decisions based on the metadata it encounters.

Given an application domain, such as library cataloguing, there will be a need to define the domain vocabulary to be used (author, title etc.). RDF does not itself define the vocabulary but provides a language to define vocabularies. Frequently, you may need to assemble metadata from more than one vocabulary (for example, a library catalogue and commercial data such as price). In consequence, RDF must be able to differentiate between metadata coming from different vocabularies. The work in W3C has been split into two main parts:

• *RDF Syntax Working Group*: to define the RDF data model and RDF syntax.
• *RDF Schema Working Group*: to define a language to define vocabularies.

The first W3C Recommendation is *RDF Model and Syntax Specification*, which was released on 22 February 1999.

RDF is a way of defining the value of a property associated with a resource. So RDF can express statements like:

```
The value 3 is the violence rating of
http://www.mad.com/
```

The property name is `violence`, the property value is 3 and the resource of the property is the Web page in question. Resources do not have to be Web pages; a resource could be a whole Web site defined by a specific URL. You can even make statements about statements.

```
John Smith asserts that "The value 3 is the violence
rating of the following Web page".
```

Here `asserts` is the property, `John Smith` is the value and the previous statement is the resource. And we don't have to stop there. You can have `"I believe that John Smith asserts that..."` and so on. To write an RDF statement of this type, we need a syntax and, of course, XML is the syntax we use:

```
<RDF:Description
about= "http://www.mad.com" >
<PYC:violence> 3 </PYC:violence>
</RDF:Description>
```

Because we have properties that are part of RDF and properties defined for our example PYC rating, we need to differentiate between them, which is why the prefixes `RDF:` and `PYC:` appear. These naming conventions will be defined as part of the XML Namespace specification. Before the RDF statements above, we would need to specify where the `RDF` and `PYC` namespaces are defined. We still have not given the meaning of the property `violence` and any constraints that there may be on the property value (whether 3 is a number in the range 0 to 5 or in the range 1 to 10, say).

The aim of the *RDF Schema Specification* is to define the properties of a resource. It does not specify the vocabulary to be used. What it allows you to define is the vocabulary and the constraints to be put on the property values. To help in this it provides some basic datatypes and some resources and their properties (specified in the standard RDF Data Model).

```
<rdf:Description ID="violence" >
<rdfs:subClassOf resource="#PYCLabel" >
</rdfs:subClassOf>
<rdfs:range href="#Integer"></rdfs:range>
</rdf:Description>
```

The assumption here is that the core vocabulary for RDF schemas is defined in the `rdfs` namespace. This fragment specifies a property with name `violence` that is a subclass of the class PYCLabel defined elsewhere. The value of the property has to be an integer and we have not put any restrictions on its range of values. That would take quite a bit more RDF to achieve!

It is feasible that there will be several rating systems around for Web pages and we may have another rating system which has aggression as a label in its label list. By having some idea of the meaning of violence and aggression in the two label lists, the possibility of translating between the two rating systems is enhanced.

7.2 Challenges for Computer Graphics

The constraints and opportunities placed on computer graphics by the Web are many. Some of these could be usefully discussed here.

7.2.1 Specification in XML

Assuming that any new graphics system will be defined as an XML DTD, this has a number of implications:

1. The rather long-winded tags mean that getting files that will transmit efficiently may be a problem.
2. Working within an environment that includes other XML DTDs means that there may be vocabulary problems. Almost certainly primitives such as text will exist in other DTDs.
3. How do we embed graphics in a Web page? How do we embed Web content in the computer graphics? Figure 7.7 illustrates the problem. The mathematics is a separate DTD. The user may be specifying the styling to apply to the list in another box and so on.

7.2.2 CSS

CSS has been specified as the Recommendation that defines style within the Web. If future graphics systems are to work within a Web environment, more attention has to be taken to the separation between style and content.

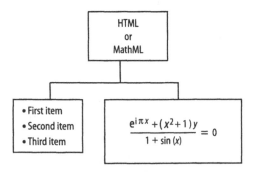

Figure 7.7 An example of HTML and MathML embedded in Web graphics.

Apart from the use of bundled primitives in GKS and PHIGS, little attention has been put into deciding which attributes or parameters represent style or content. For example, many graphics systems decided on whether a value associated with a primitive is an attribute or a parameter purely on the likelihood of the value being the same for a set of primitives or different. Those that tend to be the same for a set of primitives become attributes, the others become parameters.

Another question is whether the styling available in CSS is up to the job. Colour control is almost certainly not sufficient. The box model of CSS may not be sufficient for the juxtaposition of graphics. If viewing a 3D scene is seen as a styling, CSS provides no support. Consequently, any future graphics system may well cause the current reference model adopted for CSS to be changed.

7.2.3 XSL

XSL gives some considerable scope for more fundamental style changes than those in CSS. It should be possible to rearrange the content significantly. How could that effect future graphics? In Fig. 7.7, it would be possible to do an XSL transformation that had the boxes going from left to right rather than top to bottom. Semantically they are probably the same, so it is a style issue. Presenting only a subset of the graphics is currently handled by filters in GKS and PHIGS. How would such a presentation be controlled in a Web-based system. The GKS and PHIGS namesets would need to become attributes associated with XML elements. Does XSL have the power to do the current and future transformations needed in computer graphics?

7.2.4 DOM

How interaction is specified in the future will be controlled by the Document Object Model. That means that objects to be interacted with need to be clearly visible in the DOM and events arising from interactions with the DOM must have the appropriate level of control. As the DOM interaction model is still under development, it is unclear whether the facilities provided will be adequate for computer graphics or not. We suspect that they will be no better than the facilities provided by something like the X Window System and will not have the rich interaction models currently available in graphics systems.

7.2.5 Metadata

Apart from some simple attempts to provide hooks between graphics and the associated databases, not a great deal has been done in terms of metadata in computer graphics systems. With the need to use graphics in areas where trust is important, there will be a rise in the metadata attached to graphics.

A related issue is the need to search for textual information on the Web. So there is a need to be able to define complete text paragraphs in one go rather than splitting them into individual lines, as frequently happens in current computer graphics systems (or even words or characters in the case of PostScript!).

7.2.6 Constraint-Based Graphics

Due to the wide range of devices and browsers around, it is difficult to be precise about the layout of Web-based material. In consequence, a style where the constraints on the graphics are defined and the final layout is defined by the browser is appropriate. However, only a few systems have been developed that handle this in an expert way.

7.3 Summary

Starting off with a belief that the Web presents few challenges to computer graphics, you are moved to a position where the challenges are significant. The Web does cause the graphics programmer to look at things differently. The need to interwork and to recognize that the graphics are not the only part of the complete display will cause many established modes of working to be revised. We do not offer solutions; just present problems!

References

The various W3C Recommendations mentioned in the text can be found at the W3C site:
    http://www.w3.org/.

XML
    http://www.w3.org/TR/REC-xml/
    http://www.w3.org/TR/REC-xml-names/

CSS
    http://www.w3.org/TR/REC-CSS2/

XSL
    http://www.w3.org/TR/WD-xsl/

SMIL
    http://www.w3.org/TR/REC-smil/

DOM
    http://www.w3.org/TR/REC-DOM-Level-1/
    http://www.w3.org/TR/WD-DOM-Level-2/

RDF
    http://www.w3.org/TR/REC-rdf-syntax/

MathML
    http://www.w3.org/TR/REC-MathML/

SVG
    http://www.w3.org/TR/WD-SVG/

PICS
    http://www.w3.org/TR/REC-PICS-services/
    http://www.w3.org/TR/REC-PICS-labels/

8

Watermarking of Digital Images – Current Techniques and Future Prospects

Roger J. Green and Samura Ali

Abstract

Worldwide computer break-ins and unauthorized access to computer data are increasing. Securing the information stored in or communicated between personal computers has become an essential business practice as the number and applications of these machines increase. Conventionally, for example, the Data Encryption Standard (DES), although established some time ago, may be used to encrypt complete image data, but this can be quite time-consuming for, say, 640×480 pixel image files [1, 2].

This chapter reviews watermarking and encryption of images, and then describes ImgCrypt [3]. This provides secure image encryption and "wipe options" to prevent unauthorized access to one's personal image collection. The ImgCrypt package uses the DES algorithm, together with pixel position transformation and neighbourhood encryption, to perform encryption and decryption functions.

Comparison may be made between this method and the conventional text-type method using DES. ImgCrypt encrypts the image data approximately 50 times faster than text-type methods. It is also a very secure encryption, and would not normally allow an intruder to get anywhere near to the image key. Message authentication is also applied here to verify that the contents of the image have not been altered and that the source is authentic.

8.1 Introduction

The rapid growth of the Internet has been accompanied by an increased ease with which the artistic or intellectual property of originators can be gathered and disseminated by others. In addition, this information can be modified and re-represented, often as original work but effectively plagiarized from one or more sources. The difficulty comes in establishing uniquely the author, or authors, of created works in the many forms. Of particular interest is the image, and many techniques exist whereby such data can be gathered, especially as digital cameras and high-resolution scanners are now readily available. Currently, the highest proportion of images is available as hard copy, in the form of books, magazines, or some other such publication. A growing number of images, and maybe ultimately all of them, are to be found as digital representations, and therefore able to be copied via simple techniques. Interestingly, such copying techniques are not well covered by mechanical copyright legislation, because the process is predominantly electronic.

Consequently, it is becoming of particular interest to protect images and also to make images less usable by others. These requirements define watermarking and image encryption, and it is the purpose of this paper to review some techniques, and to introduce a simple, user-friendly example of how these can be achieved for a standard BMP image file.

8.2 Elementary Watermarking and Identification Measures

Although now computer-based, the concept of watermarking is very old, and the earliest documents incorporated quite visual images or patterns to define author-ship, ownership and authenticity. An example image is shown in Fig. 8.1, in which an imprint is added to an original image in an indelible manner.

Clearly, this technique has its drawbacks. An image may be manipulated using one of the commercial packages, such as Photoshop™ by Adobe, so that apparent authenticity is "restored". Also, the watermarking degrades the original image content. A less visible way to watermark an image is to modify the data representing it in a strategic way, such that the casual observer cannot see any differences in it compared with the original. In this case, how can data be modified? A simple way is to examine the content of the image data file and to modify some of the data words in a prescribed format, and to include checking so that, at the receiving end, parity

Figure 8.1 Example image with visible watermark.

a   b

Figure 8.2

and codewords can be examined. If an image has been copied and manipulated, then the checks can reveal where the changes have occurred and to what extent. One of the problems with this approach is the sensitivity of the inclusions/modifications to standard manipulation processes, e.g. format changing, aspect ratio changes, and colour and brightness modifications. In some circumstances, simple greyscale changes can completely remove watermarking.

An example of a digital image, both before and after concealed watermarking, is shown in Fig. 8.2. Figure 8.2(a) is the original image and Fig. 8.2(b) is the coded and watermarked image. In addition, the first image was saved as a BMP file, and the second as a PNG format file, so that the watermark was carried through the format change process. In some circumstances, a certain fragility of the watermark is desirable to show tampering. In others it is not, so that identification under adverse circumstances of manipulation can still be demonstrated. The embedded watermark image is shown in Fig. 8.3.

. No part of the watermark image may be seen by eye within the image. A clue as to how this is done may be seen by examination of the classic image Lena (Fig. 8.4).

Figure 8.3 Watermark included in Fig. 8.2(b).

Figure 8.4 Original Lena image (256 × 256).

Suppose a greyscale version of this image is split into its image planes (Figs. 8.5, 8.6 and 8.7). Then it is possible to see that certain parts of the information representing the image, although contributing to it, are not visibly important.

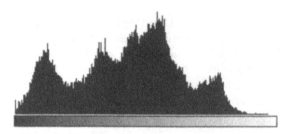

Figure 8.5 Grey level histogram.

Figure 8.6 The four least significant bit planes of the Lena image of Fig. 8.4.

Figure 8.7 The four most significant bit planes of the Lena image of Fig. 8.4.

Two noisy toddlers

Bang ! Bang ! on the drums !

a   b

Figure 8.8 **a** Watermarked image. **b** Embedded watermark image.

It is tempting to suggest that the lowest four bit planes are unnecessary in this particular image. In fact, if they are tampered with, under certain circumstances of inserted texture, such modification can lead to visible artefacts. However, it may be seen that many images are, in fact, insensitive to the exact structure of information inserted into the lower order bit planes. The problem with this, and other spatial-domain approaches, is that transformation between image formats, particularly those involving frequency domain processing, leads to reduction or even elimination of such watermarks. Nevertheless, such watermarks can be easily incorporated as a first line of defence, and take the form of images, text, or other kinds of data file in files which replace the bit planes. For the most part, the eye is not particularly sensitive to the lower order bits, which have less visual significance. This technique can also be extended to colour images, with the added advantage that different watermarks can be added to the primary colour planes, or a given watermark can be distributed between the colour bit planes. Such an image, and the embedded watermark, are shown in Fig. 8.8.

The embedded watermark is not readily discernible, but is easily extracted by simple software. In particular, because of low hue discrimination, a relatively heavy degree of watermarking may be placed in the blue and red channels respectively. Nevertheless, the spatial structure of the watermark can lead to a greater or lesser degree of ruggedness in a noisy, corrupting process, such as compression and format changing. The watermark is not, however, able to protect viewing of an image by unauthorized eyes, and that is where encryption becomes necessary, as well as methods for authentication of images for copyright validation, for example.

In comparison, frequency domain approaches can lead to a secure and rugged protection or identification watermark, especially if they are optimized to maintain spectrum throughout varied compression methodologies. An excellent survey of contemporary work in this field is given in [4], and an interesting approach is given in a paper by Smith and Comiskey at MIT Media Labs [5]. In their paper, it was stated that an image might be considered as noise, and a watermark as a signal

a   b

Figure 8.9 a Raw image file. **b** JPG file with high compression.

embedded within it, which is quite justifiable when one considers the Lena image shown in Fig. 8.4.

The majority of frequency domain approaches, in essence, borrow from the signal processing and communications domain, in respect of signal-in-noise extraction, using matched filtering and spread spectrum techniques. Therefore the techniques are applicable to a wide variety of digital media, including sound and music files also. The essence of frequency domain methods lies in their ability to exploit the compression technique while still being detectable and verifiable. For example, one which was optimized for DCT-compressed images would involve spatial frequencies which were low compared with the basic image coding block of 8 × 8 pixels. If such a watermark were to involve high spatial frequencies, these could easily be filtered out in the compression process. Consider again the Lena image. When it has been subjected to a high degree of DCT processing and coding, the resulting image may be compared with the original, as shown in Fig. 8.9.

The main visible differences are in the clarity of the images and in the greyscale rendition. In terms of watermarking, the grey level image data may then be compared, and this shows that the DCT process adds high-frequency noise to the different planes, thus potentially upsetting any deliberately added data. In effect, the random noise of the original image planes becomes structured, which leads to the possibility of greater visibility of that noise. Even the least significant bit planes show the differences (Fig. 8.10).

A similar comparison may be made with D4, the fourth least significant bit plane (Fig. 8.11).

The artefacts of greatest visibility in the least significant bit planes tend to be high spatial frequencies, while in the more significant bit planes they are the lower spatial frequencies. This can give clues concerning the spectra required to exist in a

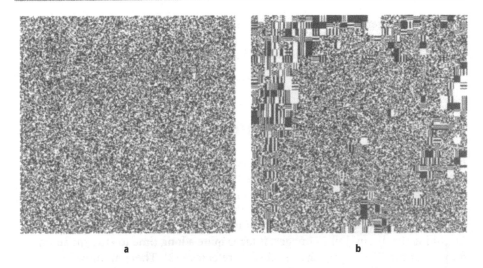

a   b

Figure 8.10 **a** D0 of original image. **b** D0 of DCT processed image.

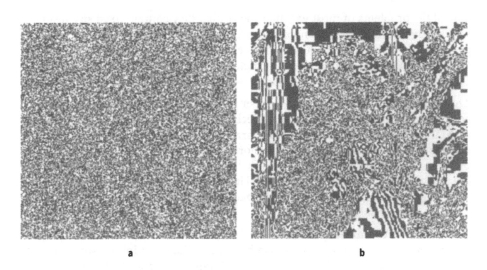

a   b

Figure 8.11 **a** D3 of original image. **b** D3 of DCT processed image.

robust, frequency-domain watermark. Generally speaking, digital watermarks with lower spatial frequencies of high amplitude survive frequency domain coding and manipulation of images, which makes sense because lower spatial frequencies generally contribute to the average grey levels in images, whereas the higher frequencies relate to the sharpness.

There is an increasing number of companies developing proprietary software for image watermarking [6, 7, 8 for example], and there is also significant work in academia around the world, such as at EPFL, Switzerland, associated with the ACTS "TALISMAN" project [9], and at Cambridge University, UK [10]. Details of exact methodologies tend, for obvious reasons, not to be revealed fully in published works. In addition, image format issues are of as much importance as techniques because of the differing compression effects on data, whether image material or watermarks.

8.3 Encryption and Authentication

In this area, the objectives can, and do, overlap with the concepts of watermarking, except there is the additional advantage that an image (or, for that matter, other digital media) becomes unusable to an unauthorized person or institution. Most encryption algorithms do not care about the intellectual or artistic content of a file, which is considered merely as data bytes upon which some mathematics operates. Confining the discussion to images, it takes quite a long time to encrypt an image fully using the DES approach, decribed in reference [2]. There are now improved methods which do not necessarily process each pixel, but instead use a well-representative sample [10].

One of the problems of most graphics files is that they contain fixed size headers, which vary only slightly in content from file to file. An "intruder" who knows the approximate contents of the header of an encrypted file could possibly decrypt the header and subsequently use this information to decrypt the whole file. A short key might easily be discovered in this way.

The objectives of the subject of this paper were to develop a fast, secure, and low-cost encryption package using the DES technique, suitably modified, together with an XOR cipher and pixel position transformation. The procedure for encryption is as follows: firstly, pixel position transformation is undertaken to scramble the picture, and the DES algorithm is used to develop a group of pixel keys. These keys are used repeatedly to encrypt every pixel in an example 640 x 480 resolution image file, using a modified XOR cipher. The package bypasses the header file and only encrypts the raw data.

The procedure begins by segmenting the image data stream into blocks of 64 bits, scrambling the data in an 8 by 8 data block, and then continuing with the DES process (detailed in references 1 and 2). Pixel transformation is fairly straightforward. A matrix of the following kind is used to rearrange the pixel data:

```
29 25 42 44 14 34 06 46
19 48 07 52 16 50 59 08
20 21 02 58 49 36 30 22
57 01 40 56 12 55 35 13
60 18 61 05 33 09 38 62
26 04 37 51 15 24 47 63
27 32 43 64 27 45 31 23
17 10 03 41 53 39 54 11
```

Each number represents the pixel data which finally remains at a given pixel position. For example, the top left entry, 29, is the data which was previously at position

29 (where now 12 resides). Five other rearrangement matrices exist for the whole encryption/decryption process. As a starting point, for a 640 × 480 image the first 640 pixels are divided into 10 blocks of 64 pixels (8 × 8 as above), and each rearrangement matrix is moved according to another set of criteria defined by the encryption key. Exactly the converse process occurs when decryption takes place.

In addition to implementing the main encryption/decryption algorithm, it is necessary to process the encryption key, in order to generate subkeys, which are necessary in the DES process. The key consists of 64 bits, of which only 56 are active. In every byte of the key, the eighth bit is an odd parity bit. This gives some internal validation of the key itself.

In order to run the main algorithm, 16 subkeys are generated, 48 bits in length, to be used at the 16 stages of the DES algorithm. The software to generate an encrypted file is bidirectional, with a flag used to determine whether encryption or decryption is required. The flag is incorporated within the encryption key at the outset.

The XOR cipher technique applied in this work consists of firstly encrypting the first row of pixels in the image using the pixel key. The first pixel in each row except the first row is not encrypted, because this pixel acts as a key also and should remain unchanged. The XOR cipher technique starts with the second pixel in the second row and finishes with the last pixel in the last row. During encryption or decryption, each pixel is XORed by the pixel key and its four nearest neighbours, as shown in Fig. 8.12.

The unencrypted values of the first row are used during encryption. For decryption, the first row data is decrypted first before being XORed with the next row's data.

Encryption protects against passive attack (eavesdropping), but protection against active attack (falsification of data and transaction) is also desirable. This latter implies message authentication [11]. The two most important aspects of this are to verify that the contents of the message have not been altered and that the source is authentic. One authentication technique is to use a secret key to generate a small block of data, known as a message authentication code (MAC). A variation in the MAC that has received much attention is the one-way hash function. Figure 8.13 illustrates one way in which a message can be so authenticated.

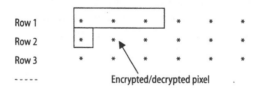

Figure 8.12 Selected neighbours for XOR ciphering.

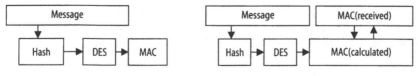

Figure 8.13 Message Authentication code using DES.

One of the simplest hash functions is to take the bit-by-bit exclusive-or (XOR) of every block. This can be expressed as follows:

$$C_i = b_{i1} \oplus b_{i2} \oplus \ldots \oplus b_{im}$$

where:

C_i = ith bit of the hash code, $1 \le i \le n$

m = number of n bit blocks in the input

b_{ij} = ith bit in the jth block

$\oplus$ = XOR operation

The result is an m-bit hash code, for which, in this case, m is set to 128 bits. The hash code is then encrypted using the secret key encryption (DES). The sender then sends the message and the MAC to the receiver. The recipient performs the same calculation on the received message, using the same secret key, to generate a new MAC. The received code is compared to the calculated code. If they are the same, the program will tell the recipient that the contents of the message have not been altered and that the source is authentic. If not, a warning message will appear on the screen.

8.4 Security Considerations

The security of a system employing the DES depends only upon the key, and not the availability of the algorithm or equipment used to implement the algorithm. Therefore the key is very important in determining the overall system security. Guidelines to be used in selecting a key are:

1. Consider the key to be a single, 56 bit number.
2. Avoid bias in selecting a key.
3. Change the key as frequently as practical.

Assuming that the key is kept secure, with the technique described it is extremely difficult for an unauthorized person to decode an intercepted message into its original form. This is because there are 2^{56} different images that can possibly be decoded from the encoded image data.

8.5 Demonstrations of ImgCrypt

The ImgCrypt program to implement all the above functions can deal with 256 grey level or colour image files, 640×480 pixels in size, and in BMP format. Consider the monochrome image shown in Fig. 8.14. When decrypted, the original image is seen, as shown in Fig. 8.15.

The technique is similarly effective on 256-colour images.

Figure 8.14 **a** Monochrome source image. **b** Encrypted file using ImgCrypt.

Figure 8.15 **a** Output using correct key. **b** Output using incorrect key.

In benchmark tests, it was found that ImgCrypt was around 50 times faster than the basic DES algorithm. The authentication part of the package was found to be sensitive to an error in a single pixel.

8.6 Future Avenues

In the future, images are going to carry with them all kinds of information, other than watermarks and authentication data. Digimarc [6] have developed the means to include Web page links, financial information, news events, and so on, in their processed images, making the way easier by bundling software with image manipulation packages such as Photoshop™. Other data forms can be included. To make an image a multimedia event, sound or Midi files may be added. If they are incorporated within the spatial domain, access may be public. If the frequency domain is used, then intervention and unlawful modification is more difficult, except if one has the correct spectral key.

In addition, images may be compounded with one another, in bit planes or mixed between them, depending on the objectives and the acceptable colour palettes and grey scales. In the future, different aspect ratio interpretation data may be embedded, to allow for the multiplicity of image display formats already available and the display hardware technical capabilities. In future, an image may not only be equal to a thousand words, but may even contain them.

8.7 Conclusions

ImgCrypt is based on the DES algorithm, and also employs pixel position transformation, but is faster. The package has been developed to include the DES algorithm, if the user wishes to make comparisons. Message authentication has been added, to increase the capabilities. The length of the key code means that it is quite difficult to break into an image file, once encrypted. The data in the image file is encrypted at around 300 kbps, fast enough for many purposes. The package has been specifically designed to protect personal image files of aspect ratio 640 × 480, although it can readily be adapted for other sizes. The software runs very effectively on even modest PCs.

References

[1] *Data Encryption Standard*, FIPS Publication 46, National Bureau of Standards, US Department of Commerce, Washington DC, January 1977.
[2] *DES Modes of Operation*, FIPS Publication 81, National Bureau of Standards, US Department of Commerce, Washington DC, November 1981.
[3] http://cosimo.die.unifi.it/~piva/Watermarking/watermark.html.
[4] http://www.media.mit.edu/pixeltag/.
[5] http://www.signumtech.com/.
[6] http://www.digimarc.com/.
[7] http://www.generation.net/~pitas/sign.html.
[8] http://ltswww.epfl.ch/~kutter/watermarking/JK_PGS.html.
[9] http://www.cl.cam.ac.uk/~fapp2/steganography/index.html.
[10] S.M. Ali, Secure encoding of digital images, *M.Sc. dissertation*, Bradford University, UK, September 1998.
[11] W. Stallings, *Data and Computer Communications*, 5th edn. Prentice Hall, Englewood Cliffs NJ, 1996.

9

An Evolving Vision of Sound: An Intuitive User Interface for Creative Control of Complex Musical Objects

P.J. Comerford and L.K. Comerford

Abstract

This chapter describes the evolution of a user interface for sound control of a complex synthesis system such as Bradford Enhanced Synthesis Technology (BEST). It examines the issues involved in providing sound control tools which allow for creativity while managing a massive body of data. The differences between the technical possibilities and the real needs of the user are highlighted, and practical solutions arrived at are detailed.

9.1 Bradford Sound Synthesis Technology

The Bradford Musical Instrument Simulator (BMIS) and its successor, Bradford Enhanced Synthesis Technology (BEST), were designed and developed in the Microcomputer Music Research Unit (MMRU) of the School of Computing and Mathematics at the University of Bradford. It is a modular microprocessor-controlled system, using the additive synthesis algorithm for the production of complex musical sound [1]. It is implemented using Field Programmable Gate Arrays (FPGAs), so that design flexibility can be maintained relatively easily. BEST is used as a research tool in the exploration of musical sound, and has been exploited commercially, principally at the high end of the pipeless classical organ market in the UK and abroad. About 2500 instruments based on the Bradford system have been sold worldwide, including installations at cathedrals and abbeys.

In additive synthesis, sound is built up from the basic "building blocks" of sine waves, combined at different amplitudes and frequencies to produce different sounds. This means that the system has tremendous flexibility, since the behaviour of each component of the sound is under the control of the user to define and alter. (This is why synthesis organs are different in concept from organs based on sampling technology, which use recordings of sound; it is not possible to change samples in the sort of detail available in a synthesis system.) The detail with which the complex sounds can be defined in additive synthesis systems such as BEST has implications for the user interface – it is no use having the potential to create sounds of great accuracy and complexity if there is no mechanism by which the user can control and alter these sounds simply and with precision.

BEST has a modular structure; up to eight sound generation modules can be linked together. Each of these modules has a waveform memory capacity of four million 16-bit words, and has eight independent output channels (64 in all), each with a sample output rate of 42.7 Ksamples. 16-bit waveform storage resolution and 24-bit amplitude resolution are preserved over a range of 48 dB. The modular structure permits the use of a large number of independent sound sources, which makes the system capable of producing a high level of ensemble in organ simulation. It also influences what is required of the user interface, as it is essential to be able to have quick access into the required part of what is necessarily a massive body of sound-defining data.

9.2 Why Does On-Site Voicing Matter?

The capability to alter sound in detail on-site, a process known as "voicing", is important because, in relation to the auditioning of musical effects, the influence of acoustic is profound – so much so that Pierce [2] can comment

> When does music sound good? In a good hall.

Conversely, a poor acoustic can give rise to unfavourable judgements upon sound heard within it.

The effect which a building will have upon sound perception is, broadly, determined by the balance between sound which reaches the listener directly from the sound source and that which arrives indirectly having reflected off one or more surfaces.

Direct sound influences the perception of sound location, as sound generally appears to emanate from the direction in which it was first heard, and by definition direct sound arrives at the listener before indirect sound. Direct sound has the effect of enhancing subjective "clarity" (clarity of sound is a subjective perceptual judgement, but a physical "clarity measure" is defined as the ratio of early arriving sound (direct sound and early reflections within 35 ms) to late arriving sound).

When indirect sounds are reflected off surfaces in the physical environment in which the sound event occurs, the reflections [3]

> create a multitude of representations of the same auditory event, although each representation will differ to some degree.

These multiple reflections add sound energy to direct sound, and therefore make the instrument appear louder than if the listener heard direct sound only [4].

When indirect sound arrives at the listener perceptibly later than direct sound (e.g. 80 ms behind direct sound), each note seems to last longer and the gaps between notes seem shorter. In such a case, notes tend to blur into one another. The action of late reflected indirect sound which causes this effect is known as reverberation.

Given that the acoustic environment can have such a significant effect on the perception of sound, the importance of being able to voice on site becomes apparent, particularly when dealing with a large and therefore immobile instrument such as an organ, which, because of its size, is likely only ever to be heard in one acoustic. This is the case with pipe organs as well as with synthesized sound, as evidenced by the comment of Sumner on the importance of changing the sound of an instrument to suit, or to compensate for, its acoustic, that [5]

> many [pipe organs] are spoilt because they are not well conceived in terms of their environment.

An interesting example of the influence of buildings on sound is the perceived effect of acoustic upon organ attack transients, that is, upon the portion of sound which occurs before the sustained tone of each note is reached. This is often a period of great disorder, with partials growing in very individualistic patterns of both amplitude and frequency. Transients play a similar role in musical sound to that of consonants in speech – they aid articulation. Transients break up sustained sound; by their disordered nature they emphasize note initiations (even when many sound sources are active concurrently), because [6]

> the auditory system will treat a sudden change of properties as the onset of a new event

and they establish note identity, thus aiding sound recognition.

A reverberant acoustic will prolong the perceived length of a transient. On one hand, this can have a useful effect by accentuating note beginnings within the blend of sound created by the multiple resonances, but on the other it may produce unacceptable effects as the very unstable frequencies of the transient period are extended and clash audibly with the succeeding more orderly pitches of the sustained tone. The transient characteristics suited to achieving ideal articulation will thus vary from acoustic to acoustic. Pollard [7] has noted that, because the time delay effect occurring between striking an organ key and hearing the post-transient note is altered by the acoustic, the notes of the organ must be voiced so that the overall "rise-time" (i.e. perceived total attack period) is short enough to be able to play fast music in the stated acoustic. This is analogous to the modification of playing styles which takes place between repeated performances in different acoustics; in a very reverberant environment, individual notes must be more detached and staccato to distinguish the notes, whereas in a dry acoustic playing must be more legato to cover the gaps between notes. The need for such variations is known to professional orchestral musicians, who can be required to play the same repertoire on successive nights in venues with contrasting acoustics. It is also illustrated by the "detached" note style with which organists often play initial hymn lines in reverberant cathedrals or churches.

The characteristics of the building acoustic may also impose a general colouration on the perception of sound heard within it, attenuating some frequencies while accentuating others. To a greater or lesser extent, all aspects of the sound will be affected by the acoustic of their environment, and in such circumstances the ability to have detailed control of the partials' content, profiles, stability, tuning and so on, of each component of the sound is indispensable if satisfactory results are to be achieved.

9.3 Specialist Requirements for Sound Control in Pipeless Organ Applications

As well as its use in the context of research into the nature and perception of musical sound, BEST is also used in the pipeless organ industry. The overall requirements in practice of the sound control interface for the data management and voicing of a synthesis organ may be summarized under three interlinked headings: creative accessibility, intuitive manageability and speed.

- *Creative accessibility*
  As noted above, an advantage of the synthesis approach to sound production is that, unlike a sampling system, the behaviour of each building block of the sound can be precisely defined by the voicer. Accessibility means providing the tools to give the voicer access to this data interactively, so that online and immediate changes can be made to all features which control the sound being created.

- *Intuitive manageability*
  The many parameters used to define each sound in a synthesis system mean that the interface must provide helpful and intuitive ways to manage the data proliferation. The complexity of the sound objects being controlled needs to be hidden as far as possible from the voicer during the voicing process. Provision for natural navigation through the sound data is very important, especially for new users, if the creativity necessary for voicing is not to be stifled.

- *Speed*
  It is essential that changes to sound can be auditioned within a very short time, because of the shortness of memory in listening to such subtle changes as are often involved in organ voicing. This means that all features which affect sound, as opposed to the hardware-related aspects of the synthesis data such as switch definitions, must be included in the online controls, and also that online changes should be processed extremely fast.

A fourth consideration arises in relation to the pipeless organ industry. It is a field peopled for the most part by small companies. This means that there is little industrially based funding available for interface development, which in turn serves to concentrate the mind of the interface developer upon what is absolutely essential in the way of interface tools to enable creativity, to aid the process of turning sound concepts into sounds, rather than upon whether the interface is "wizzy". This factor is considered further below (see Section 9.5).

9.4 Interface Evolution

From the start, what set the Bradford system apart and contributed to its reputation for excellence was the quality and complexity of the sounds it was capable of producing, and the recognition that the sound should be alterable in detail on-site to suit the acoustics of the building, i.e. the need for voicing capability. The alterations would be made by a "voicer" with specialist knowledge of instrument sound, who would create and refine the sound of the instrument.

9.4.1 Version 1

The first sound control interface was an alphanumeric package called "Interactive Voicing", developed at the University of Bradford, which gave immediate online access to the characteristics which determined how notes should sound. This data included not only waveform content but such parameters as the stability of different notes of each stop, note-by-note tuning, decay envelopes, pitch changes triggered by increased note use in a department, and so on.

The IV package reflected the sound definition structures used in the data: access to features was hierarchical, accessing the data controlling each particular characteristic by moving down through the levels of the data structure using unique alphanumeric six-character names to identify each level and feature (Fig. 9.1).

Some changes were implemented as they were typed in, while others required the stop-switch controlling the changed sound to be reselected. This second type had the advantage of allowing the all-important instantaneous "before and after" comparison to be made, which is so helpful when assessing very subtle changes in voicing.

Figure 9.1 In this example of an Interactive Voicing screen, the "stop" control gives access to sound defining data identified by a particular name "sflaut"; the "c[hange]" control allows alterations to be made to the data defining one of the waveforms, "4", associated with this stop name. The numerical values shown are the relative amplitudes of each partial, and these are changed by typing in new values.

The basic structure of the specification – not the sound characteristics described above, but such features as the number and position of switches on the console, keyboard ordering, allocation of output channels, and so on, was also defined in data and therefore easily alterable, but was not accessible online via IV.

9.4.2 Version 2

Many additional features and new approaches have been added during subsequent interface evolution, and the speed of processing has greatly increased since the original interface was implemented. Throughout, the premise that sound characteristics should be alterable on-site has been retained.

Sound parameters which were previously altered alphanumerically are now accessible graphically, using a Visual Basic package called "Digital Enhanced Voicing" (DEV), developed by an industrial partner of the University of Bradford, Wyvern Classical Organs. DEV works under Windows and overlays a structure similar to that of the original Interactive Voicing. It also gives access to various data-related organizational functions.

The effect of making the sound-control data available in graphical format brought a new dimension to the sound creation process. It made the voicing mechanisms more accessible to new users, which has been important as the use of the technology has spread more widely in the pipeless organ industry. For example, it is easier to identify a prominent partial when it is displayed as a high bar on a histogram than as a high number in a list of numbers. Ease of use increases speed of achieving results, which in turn helps the creative process, since it reduces the length of the intense concentration needed to implement and assess an idea in sound.

It is worth noting that not all sound characteristic controls lend themselves equally well to graphical control as opposed to numerical definition. This is partly a function of the sound features themselves. For example, to tune individually each note of a particular stop it is useful to have a separate slider or histogram bar control which can be adjusted for each note until the required frequency is set up (see Fig. 9.2), but to apply a new temperament it is easiest to type in or select a code name for that temperament.

By the same token, to apply an overall deviation of frequency to each note of a stop, selected at random from within a defined maximum range, it is easier to type or select the percentage defining the range of deviation than to make the adjustment note by note. In practice, a combination of graphical and numerical controls allowing both gross and fine adjustments is the ideal.

In some cases the data structures by which sound features are represented in the synthesizer impose limitations on the design of data control tools. For example, in BEST there can be multiple tremulants, each with varying degrees of amplitude and frequency deviation across the spectrum, but for each tremulant definition there is only one rate of deviation. Thus a *numerical* rate control per tremulant is as effective to use as a slider to control this variable – indeed, more effective, as it allows the varied rates of different tremulants to be more easily compared.

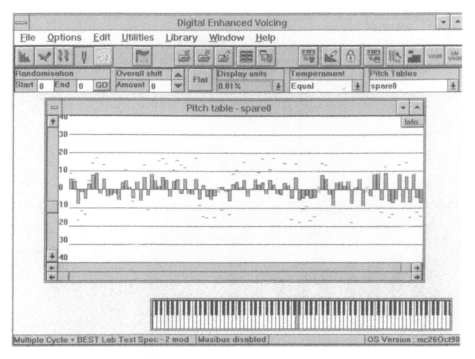

Figure 9.2 A Digital Enhanced Voicing screen, showing the interface for changing note frequencies for a designated stop; the histogram-like display shows the note-by-note deviation from the strict frequencies of the current temperament; altering the bar height causes an immediate change to the audible note frequency.

9.4.3 Version 3

A recent major advance in the technology has been the development by the MMRU of Bradford Enhanced Synthesis Technology (BEST). This system has many new features; from the standpoint of the user interface, the most significant is that it includes a facility for specifying and playing complex multiple cycle waveforms. The waveforms are, as before, synthesized from sine waves, but each partial now has its own independent separately controllable amplitude and frequency profiles for the all-important attack transient period. This development has required the creation of a new comprehensive graphical interface for specifying, controlling and generating the complex multiple cycle waveforms.

The interface package, called "Envelope Studio" (ES), is written in Visual C++ and was developed at the University of Bradford. It is designed to run concurrently with DEV so that those parts of the sound not specified in the waveform content by ES can nevertheless be simultaneously accessible for change.

ES has two main functions: automation of the organization of data relating to multiple cycle waveforms, and provision of tools to the user for creation and alteration of those waveforms. It has familiar Windows-type buttons, drop-down menus and dialogue boxes. For all the most frequently used functions menu items are duplicated by toolbar buttons.

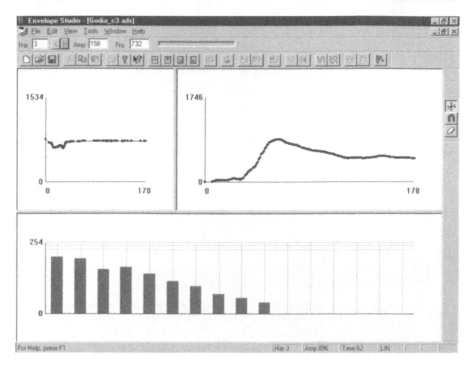

Figure 9.3 An example of an Envelope Studio screen showing the partials' content of an organ waveform in the lower pane, and the frequency and amplitude attack profiles of its third harmonic partial in the upper panes. All partials are alterable with the tools shown on the right toolbar.

When used for voicing, a particular waveform is selected by clicking on the required note on an on-screen keyboard. This opens a three-pane window for the relevant note of the designated stop (see Fig. 9.3). The lower pane contains a histogram-type display of the relative amplitudes of each of the partials of the sound in the sustain state of the note (excluding random amplitude and frequency movements) – that is, the partials' content of the note. The upper two panes change with each partial of the waveform; they are the frequency profile (in the left pane) and the amplitude profile (in the right pane) for the selected partial during the attack transient. Partial profile selection is via forward/back buttons on the action bar, or by right mouse click on the relevant partial in the lower pane. The three panes can each be resized to and from full screen by a single click of a toolbar button, to facilitate detailed changes.

There are three specialist freehand waveform control tools for use in waveform voicing:

• *pointer tool*
  This allows detailed changes to amplitude and frequency profiles for each partial by moving individual waveform points, or by the addition of extra points. The same tool also allows changes to be made in the lower pane to the level of individual partials of the spectrum.

- *drag tool*

  This allows quick reshaping of the amplitude and frequency profiles for each partial by dragging any portion of the existing profile into a new shape. The same tool can also be used in the lower pane to change the levels of partials by dragging to give the waveform a new spectrum.

- *erase tool*

  This allows point-by-point removal of unwanted details in the amplitude and frequency profiles for each partial.

Data relevant to the current position of these freehand tools in the active pane is shown in the status bar; this information will also vary, depending upon the pane in which the tool is positioned.

In addition to the freehand controls which allow the detailed redrawing of amplitude and frequency profiles for each partial and the partial spectrum of each defined note, ES provides a range of macro-like controls to aid the implementation of more automated operations. For example, temporal shifts can be made to profile waveforms without the need for redrawing (see Fig. 9.4).

Similar macro-type commands in dialogue boxes are also available for making amplitude changes to the waveforms; instead of repeatedly specifying the same

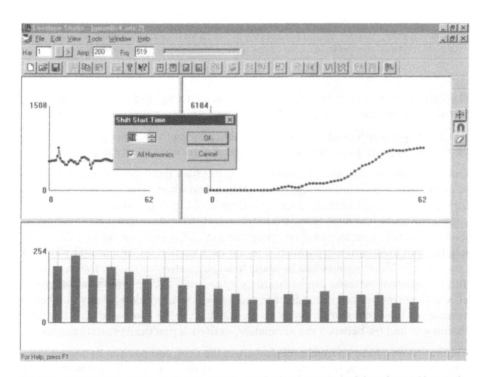

Figure 9.4 In this example, shifting the start time by 18 ms as defined by the user in the dialogue box would cut out the "dead time" at the beginning of the amplitude profile (upper right pane) for this partial, and would remove some of the larger frequency "blips" shown (upper left pane). The control can be used to apply such time shifts to individual partials or to every partial in the active waveform.

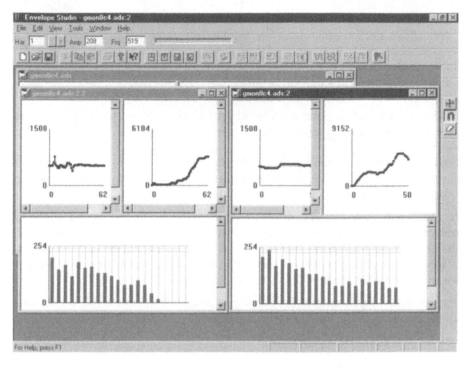

Figure 9.5 The screen shows three different versions/subversions of a waveform used for a particular note. The different versions can be instantly auditioned for comparison, and accepted, rejected, or stored for later consideration.

change to individual partials, the user can define an amplitude change to be made to groups of selected partials, to individual notes, or to complete stops, as required.

A copy and paste facility allows for the automated copying of partials' profiles between partials of the same waveform, between different notes or from one stop to another.

One important requirement identified during interface development was the ability to make "before and after" comparisons of the sound which is being changed. Therefore, unlike normal Windows packages where the "duplicate" function produces a copy of the active file which is updated concurrently with the original, ES has a special item on the Window menu called "New Version". This makes a copy of the active window, but maintains a separate history for each version under a unique filename (see Fig. 9.5). Thus changes can be made to an alternative version of the waveform, and the different versions can be heard independently to compare their perceptual effects. New versions can be made of any active waveform window, so any number of versions of the same sound, or of its derivatives, can be compared. Loading and listening to and fro between the alternative versions is practically instantaneous.

This has proved to be an invaluable feature in the field; comparison between subtly altered sound is immediate and repeatable, so problems of audio memory which often dog audio comparisons of slight changes are avoided. In addition the knowledge that there is an instantly accessible "backup" available in case of disaster encourages the boldness of creativity necessary to voicing.

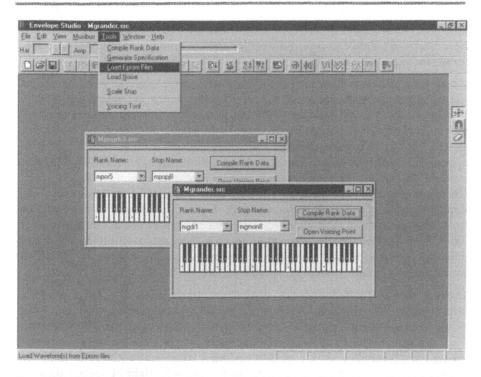

Figure 9.6 In addition to providing tools for waveform modification, Envelope Studio is used for organization of all the data relating to multiple cycles and for waveform generation and loading.

As well as giving control of the amplitude and frequency profile waveforms and of the harmonic content of the note, ES has an organizational role in waveform control data compilation, automated waveform memory allocation, waveform generation, and waveform and data loading (see Fig. 9.6). The tools available to the user at any time depend upon the mode in which ES is being used. ES also gives access to text-editing tool.

9.5 Current Sound Control Interface Development

The MMRU is fortunate to have had practical experience in using the BEST interface for sound research and in the voicing of synthesis instruments on-site in diverse acoustics (including five cathedrals). This, in addition to feedback from users of the interface in the pipeless organ industry, has provided unique and invaluable experience to inform the realistic development of effective interface tools which perform their function adequately and very fast.

Interface development is an ongoing part of the Bradford project, particularly as the new technology throws up new areas of sound for control. In this connection, one part of a European Commission-funded research project, coordinated by the

University of Bradford and involving one other university and six industrial partners, has been planned to concentrate upon the examination of interface enhancements for synthesis systems.

A number of different directions would be possible for interface developments. For example, a multidimensional soundscape through which the voicer could move seeking an ideal sound seems superficially appealing. However, in practice in a voicing context the adjustments to be made to the sound produced by a system such as BEST are at a far more detailed level than lends itself to such a broad-brush approach. Another approach would be the development of an automated "expert system" for voicing. But, unless such a system were exceptionally sophisticated (incorporating acoustic feedback among other features), any removal of the detailed control of sound alterations from the hands of the human voicer would be unacceptable to those with experience of what is actually needed in this kind of work. Such an advanced system would be difficult to attain within the budgetary constraints of the industry; a simplified automated system, working as a glorified tone-control, would not be an acceptable substitute.

Instead, the EC-funded research is to concentrate upon the more practical approach of evaluating improvements by advancing the interface through evolutionary enhancements from present systems, rather than by starting from scratch. This also suits the ethos of the specialist pipeless organ industry; such companies create a small number of high-quality custom instruments, without having large research resources to devote to enhancements and with tight budgetary imperatives, so they prefer and need to have small incremental advances in succession as quickly as possible, rather than wait for a much more ambitious and less certain result (the "bird in hand" principle).

In summary, interface speed is the requirement of critical importance, with ease of use a close second. Users judge the elegance of the interface by these factors rather than, for instance, its incorporation of multimedia features.

Areas which have been identified as most likely to bring benefit to speed and ease of interface use are currently under examination, and include:

- *Improved navigation tools* to access the very complex sound data more naturally and intuitively in terms of its relation to sound structures, not data structures. Specifically, this means consideration of two alternative approaches:
  - *Accessing all the data associated with a particular stop*
    Where the interface is used to control organ sound, this has the advantage of tying in with the way most organ voicing in the field is approached. The user specifies the required stop, and is presented with sound features relating to the stop, from which an area for change is selected. The development of DEV has moved in this direction.
  - *Accessing data through the concept of "phases of note life"*
    In this approach, the user specifies the portion of a note in which changes are to be made (e.g. attack, sustain), and moves through the sound features related to that phase before selecting a sound to be altered. This would have the advantage of being more accessible to the general music user less familiar with the concept of organ stops.

- *Easier to use help* mechanisms to link data structures to sound structures. Context-sensitive help mechanisms to provide assistance with using voicing tools and also give online information about the effects of changing the sound defining data, are a fruitful area for development.

Acknowledgements

The authors gratefully acknowledge the work of their colleagues over a number of years in the development of voicing interfaces: Mr John McFerran, Dr Miles Marks, Dr Nick Briggs, and Mr Leslie Newell. Furthermore, many of the opportunities for the authors to experiment with the use of the interface in fieldwork have been provided by Mr Richard Wood, MA.

References

[1] Comerford, P.J. Simulating an organ with additive synthesis. *Computer Music Journal*, 17(2), Summer 1993.

[2] Pierce, J.R. *The Science of Musical Sound*. Scientific American Books. revised 1992.

[3] Handel, S. *Listening: an Introduction to the Perception of Auditory Events*. 1989

[4] Rasch, R.A. and Plomp, R. The listener and the acoustic environment, in Deutsch, D. (ed.) *The Psychology of Music*. Academic Press, 1982.

[5] Sumner, W.L. *The organ*, 4th edn. McDonald and Jane's, London, 1973.

[6] Bregman, A.S. Auditory scene analysis: hearing in complex environments, in McAdams, S. and Bigand, E. (eds.) *Thinking in Sound: the Cognitive Psychology of Human Audition*. Clarendon Press, Oxford, 1993.

[7] Pollard, H.F. Time delay effects in the operation of a pipe organ. *Acustica*, 20(4), 1968.

10

Integrating Paper and Digital Documents

Heather Brown and Peter Robinson

Abstract

This chapter outlines two very different approaches to using physical paper documents as natural input devices to computers. The DigitalDesk is a computer-enhanced desk that uses a video camera to detect and recognize paper documents, while Xerox's "Intelligent Paper" is specially produced paper containing invisible marks that uniquely identify each sheet. Both allow the visible contents of the paper to be matched to a corresponding digital document. This, in turn, allows natural actions, such as pointing to an item on a page, to be used to initiate computer actions. The overall effect is to blur the conventional distinction between paper and digital documents.

The chapter describes the basic mechanisms used in the two approaches and looks briefly at some existing and potential applications. It then looks in more detail at a specific application area: allowing printed documents to act as natural interfaces to the additional information found in digital versions encoded according to the Text Encoding Initiative (TEI) guidelines.

10.1 Introduction

Many papers have been published about the relative merits of paper and digital documents, and many hypertext designers have attempted to make their systems easier to use and understand by incorporating familiar paper-like features into the interface [1, 2]. Hypermedia is widely recognized as a marvellous way of finding information and the usability and appearance of digital documents is continually improving [3], but users still prefer to print out documents of more than a few pages because they find reading from paper more convenient and pleasant than reading from a screen.

Several recent projects have attempted to incorporate the advantages and convenience of paper into portable computer systems. A report on one of these, the *The Virtual Book* project [4], gave the following succinct summary of the strengths of paper and digital documents when describing their goals for the design of a portable digital book to compete with paper:

> The task, then, was two-fold: come as close to paper as possible in the dimensions of legibility, ergonomics, robustness, and similar attributes; then, surpass it in other attributes such as searchability, flexibility, and interactivity.

The resulting prototype, *Lectrice*, has a high-quality 10.4 inch diagonal display surrounded by a frame containing several physical buttons. These buttons and a pen are used to manipulate the documents displayed. The device can be attached to a computer network via a physical "tether" or radio link, or it can be used as a standalone device. Users found it comfortable to read from a Lectrice when sitting back on a couch and it was described as "an agreeable bed companion: it provides its own light and turns pages almost silently".

A rather different approach to mimicking the advantages of paper in a portable computer system is shown by the *XLibris Active Reading Machine* [5] and the *Dynomite* portable electronic notebook [6]. These concentrate more on merging "the benefits of paper note-taking with the organizational capabilities of computers" and use "digital ink" to mimic standard paper note-taking mechanisms instead of making users change their way of working to suit the computer.

In spite of this awareness of the relative merits of paper and digital documents, and the increasing recognition of the need to bring the advantages of paper into the digital world, little has been done to incorporate actual physical paper into computer systems. For most users, computer-based documents are almost invariably manipulated via a screen and mouse or keyboard and remain essentially separate from paper documents.

This chapter reports on two novel ways in which physical paper can become an integral part of an interactive computer system, allowing familiar and convenient printed paper documents to provide access to the powerful facilities associated with digital documents. Section 10.2 outlines the basic mechanisms used by the DigitalDesk [7] and Xerox's "Intelligent Paper" [8], explains how they allow paper to become an active part of a computer system, and describes some existing and potential applications.

Section 10.3 then looks in more detail at a potential application designed to exploit the detailed scholarly information that may be recorded in digital documents coded according to the Text Encoding Initiative (TEI) guidelines [9]. A TEI text may provide information about the state of old manuscripts, include details about the different versions of a work, and give linguistic information or notes about the work provided by scholars. Section 10.3 shows how a modern printed transcription of a work could act as the starting point for exploring the additional information in a TEI text.

10.2 New Technology for Integrating Paper Into the Computer Interface

10.2.1 The DigitalDesk

The Cambridge University Computer Laboratory and the Xerox Research Centre in Cambridge (formerly Xerox EuroPARC) have collaborated for several years on research into the use of video in user interfaces. The approach has been to add computational properties to the conventional office environment rather than replicating the office on a computer screen [10, 11]. The original DigitalDesk was developed by Pierre Wellner, a student at Cambridge University sponsored by Xerox [12]. In addition, the collaboration has produced *BrightBoard* [13], a computer-enhanced whiteboard, and a *Digital Drawing Board* [14], a version of the DigitalDesk for use in computer-aided design.

The DigitalDesk itself consists of an ordinary desk enhanced by

- a conventional computer system linked to a central document registry
- a video camera and projector mounted above the desk pointing down at the desktop
- an LED-tipped pointing device

Figure 10.1 shows how the parts of the overall DigitalDesk system are related.

Images from the video camera are processed to recognize documents (sheets of paper or the pages of open books) on the desktop and to match them up with corresponding digital documents stored in the central registry. Once this has been done, the computer system can associate positions on the paper pages with the appropriate digital information. User actions can then be initiated *from the page* using the pointing device, and the system can respond via the conventional computer screen or by projecting information down onto the desktop. In particular, it can project information directly onto the page – to highlight certain parts of the text, for example, or to superimpose additional information onto diagrams or graphs. Projecting coloured rectangles onto the page to highlight words or sections of text is an effective way of making the text "live". It is similar in many respects to the

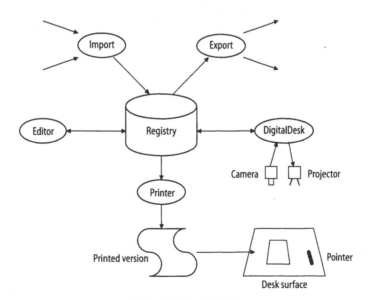

Figure 10.1 The DigitalDesk.

dynamic use of colour to highlight text on a screen. The overall effect is to involve the paper in the system in a completely new way.

The recognition of pages from the video images is crucial to the operation of the DigitalDesk. In some early applications an easily detected identifier was printed on each page to aid recognition. This worked well, but limited the use of the desk to specially printed documents. The recognition system was later improved so that normal printed documents could be used. The updated system works in four stages.

1. The video images are processed to find the areas representing pages on the desktop.
2. These areas are then examined to find the positions of all lines of text.
3. Details of word spaces and ascenders/descenders are extracted for each line.
4. The pattern of lines on a page and the patterns of spaces, ascenders, and descenders for each line are then used to find the best match with a page in the central registry.

The current DigitalDesk technology is not capable of performing accurate optical character recognition. Figure 10.2 shows the resolution achieved for text after initial thresholding of the video image. It demonstrates that characters are unclear, that almost nothing in the way of font information is available to help with the recognition, and that the lines of text may not be horizontal in the image. For a book that does not lie completely flat on the desk, there is the added problem that the lines may be slightly curved. Figure 10.3 shows part of a page image after the base and x-height have been found for each line and further processing has been undertaken to identify the spaces between words and the ascenders and descenders within each word. The pattern of spaces/ascenders/descenders is then assembled into a "line barcode" and the line barcodes for the page are checked against similar barcodes derived from the electronic text. For a relatively small document registry, this method gave an accurate page match in a reasonable time (a few seconds). Once the corresponding digital page has been found in the registry, the position of each word in the electronic text can be mapped to a known position on the page.

Figure 10.2 Text in a thresholded image.

Figure 10.3 Line image showing extracted features.

The LED-tipped pen is easily recognized in the video image, so pointing to a position on the page with the pen can be interpreted in much the same way as moving a cursor to a position in a window on a computer screen. Similarly, clicking with the pen can be interpreted in much the same way as a mouse click and can therefore initiate an action associated with the visible text at that position.

The DigitalDesk thus involves physical paper in two novel ways. It allows the paper to act as an input device – each page acting rather like a fixed screen image. Its ability to project information onto the page also allows the paper to act in a limited but interesting way as an output device. (A further form of input, of course, is to draw on a piece of paper using a real pen or pencil and then capture the image.)

10.2.2 DigitalDesk Applications – Interactive Mathematical Notebook

An interactive mathematical notebook [15] was developed to demonstrate the potential of the DigitalDesk in teaching. This was a paper notebook that could be carried round and used in the normal way, but it took on additional features when placed on the DigitalDesk. Figure 10.4 shows a page from the notebook and (inset) a section of the video image showing it in use on the DigitalDesk. The page is part of a tutorial on the graphs of quadratic equations. The student can experiment with quadratics by writing coefficients into a general equation on the page and seeing the resulting graph projected onto a space on the page.

As this application used the earlier page recognition system, each page in the notebook contained a clear page identifier in an OCR font. This can be seen at the top right in Figure 10.4, together with a thick horizontal line that made it easier to recognize pages (and their orientation) in the video image.

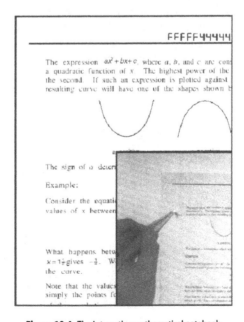

Figure 10.4 The interactive mathematical notebook.

10.2.3 DigitalDesk Applications — the "Active Alice" Grammar Lesson

The first major application using the new page recognition system to provide grammar lessons for children based on normal printed books with electronic versions available as part of the British National Corpus [16, 17]. The application was called "Active Alice" [18] because the book chosen as the first example was a simplified version of *Alice's Adventures in Wonderland* [19].

The Alice text, in common with all texts in the BNC, is an SGML [20] text containing markup giving the part of speech of every word in the text. The BNC classifies words according to 57 different *word class codes*. Some of the commonly used word classes are:

AJ0	adjective (e.g. hot, strange)
AJC	comparative adjective (e.g. taller, worse)
AV0	adverb (e.g. suddenly, immediately)
CJC	coordinating conjunction (e.g. and, or)
DPS	possessive determiner (e.g. their, her)
NN1	singular common noun (e.g. book, sister)
NP0	proper noun (e.g. France, Alice)
PNP	personal pronoun (e.g. you, she)
VBD	past tense of verb to be (e.g. was, were)
VVG	-ing form of lexical verbs (e.g. living, thinking)
VVB	base form of lexical verbs (e.g. live, think)

The following (slightly simplified) version of the first two sentences of the electronic text shows that the word class codes are easy to extract from the text for use in the application.

```
<w NP0>Alice <w VBD>was <w VVG>beginning <w TO0>to
<w VVI>get <w AV0>very <w AJ0>bored.
<w PNP>She <w CJC>and <w DPS>her <w NN1>sister <w VBD>were
<w VVG>sitting <w PRP>under <w AT0>the <w NN2>trees.
```

When the book is placed on the DigitalDesk and identified, two windows of information are projected down onto the desk, one either side of the book. The area to the right is used for lesson information about word types, while the area to the left is used mainly for a quiz. These are both designed to involve the printed text where possible. Figure 10.5 shows the initial window that appears to the right of the book and the additional information that would appear below it if the user clicked the pen on the **Verbs** menu item.

If the user subsequently chooses **More about tenses** in the "Verbs" window, a third small window appears beneath the others giving information about different tenses and how certain forms of verbs may be derived by adding "ed" or "ing". There is always a **Show me...** item in the second level window. Selecting this involves the book in the lesson by highlighting all the words of the relevant type on the open pages (by projecting coloured rectangles down onto the book). About 30 different

Active Grammar System	Verbs
To find out about words on the page, simply point to them with the pen. To find out about different types of words, point to the word type in the list below.	Verbs are words about doing (*singing*, *walk*, *played*), but they may also be about thinking, feeling or possessing. Verbs have different tenses to express actions in the past, present, or future. To *be*, to *have*, and to *do* are special verbs used in many different ways
Adjectives (describing words) **Adverbs** (how/where/when/...) **Determiners** (a/the/my/some/that/...) **Nouns** (words for things) **Pronouns** (I/you/we/they/mine/...) **Verbs** (doing words)	**More about verbs** **More about tenses** **More about be/have/do**
Others	**Show me the verbs in the book**

Figure 10.5 Initial information (left) and information about verbs.

windows of information are directly available on the right of the book. The **Others** menu item in the initial window provides access to information on prepositions, conjunctions and some less common word types.

If the user clicks the pen on a word in the book, the word is highlighted by a coloured rectangle and information about the word is projected onto the area to the left of the book. Figure 10.6 shows the information that would be projected if the user clicked on the word "her".

A permanent quiz window invites the user to answer questions or find certain types of words. The problems always involve the currently open pages of the book. Some typical problems are

• Find 2 nouns
• Find a comparative adjective
• Find 3 different pronouns
• Find 2 words from the verb "to have"
• Are the highlighted words adjectives or adverbs?

The interface is designed to involve the book as far as possible and to use consistent colour coding for words of a given type – blue for adjectives and green for verbs, for example. Thus the words shown in italics in Figs. 10.5 and 10.6 appear in colour in

Determiner – possessive
A determiner explains which noun we mean (*a* bull, *your* house, *many* books, *that* field). "*her*" is a possessive determiner – one that explains who owns the noun or nouns (*my* gloves, *his* pen, *their* books).

Figure 10.6 Feedback on "her".

the projected information, and the same colour coding is used when highlighting words in the book.

10.2.4 Intelligent Paper

In 1998, Xerox announced a new technology known as Intelligent Paper. This was described in a paper in the *Proceedings of Electronic Publishing 98* [8], and the information in this section is taken mainly from that paper.

The basic idea is that every sheet of Intelligent Paper should be uniquely identifiable to any computer attached to the World Wide Web. The only special equipment needed for this, apart from the paper itself, is a pen-like pointing device connected to the Web via a conventional or radio link. The pen can detect which sheet of Intelligent Paper it is pointing at and transmit this information to a Web-based computer.

Each sheet of Intelligent Paper is covered with special markings, invisible to the human eye, that uniquely identify both the sheet of paper and the position within the sheet. The pointer device can read these marks and, when the pen is clicked on the page, transmit the *page-id* and *position-within-page* over the Web to a network address derived from the *page-id*. A program at this address interprets the page/position information and takes action. Typically this results in information being sent back over the Web to a screen or printer close to the user. Figure 10.7 illustrates a possible use. The user has an Intelligent Paper tourist map of Paris giving places of

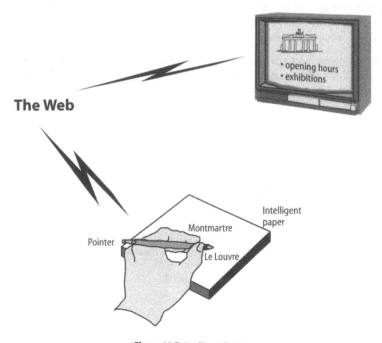

Figure 10.7 Intelligent Paper

interest, such as the Eiffel Tower and the Louvre. To see information about the Louvre displayed on a screen, the user simply points to the Louvre on the map.

The overall system is intended to work in the following way. Publishers buy supplies of Intelligent Paper from authorized producers. They print and distribute the paper in the normal way. They also develop Web-accessible software that associates specific actions with given positions on given sheets of paper. Intelligent Paper looks and feels just like any other paper, so users retain all the normal advantages of portability, feel, and flexibility. Thus maps, books, and catalogues can still be used in all the normal ways. As explained in [8], however, "if the user owns a pointer and is near a peripheral device connected to the Web, the paper document assumes the behaviour of a touch-sensitive screen. It becomes enriched with arbitrarily complex information, provided by the document's publisher at its Web site".

The underlying technology of Intelligent Paper uses two layers of ink. Figure 10.8 shows a map of Europe printed on Intelligent Paper. The top layer is normal visible ink. The lower layer provides the identification information and is known as the code layer. This is printed in invisible ink and uses a special technology known as Xerox DataGlyphs™. DataGlyphs may be used in a variety of ways, but in one of the simplest variants they allow cells approximately a quarter of an inch square to be laid out in a grid pattern. Each cell is printed so that it contains approximately 150 bits of data. Pages up to 5 feet square only need 16 bits of data to represent the *position-within-page*, so this allows 64 bits to represent a unique *page-id* and still leaves plenty of spare bits for security purposes, error correction, and future special applications.

The pen can be thought of as a camera that can view a complete cell. In practice it can see just enough of the DataGlyphs to determine not only the contents of a cell but also the position of the cell relative to its field of view. This allows it to determine its *position-within-page* to a high degree of accuracy.

A pen click causes the *page-id* and *position-within-page* to be routed over the Web to the publisher's Web site as a request for an action. Several routing mechanisms can be used for determining the Web address from the page identification. To keep

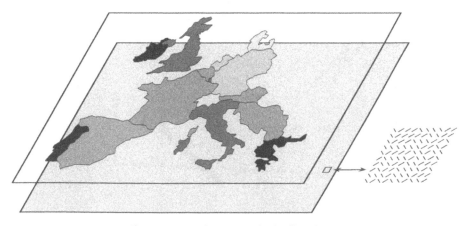

Figure 10.8 Map of Europe printed on Intelligent Paper.

the routing tables needed to associate *page-ids* with URLs down to a reasonable size, these may work in several stages. Once the request reaches the publisher's Web site, the responsibility for matching it up with the correct digital page and interpreting and acting on the request is entirely up to the publisher. Routing the resulting information back to a Web-addressable computer near the user is a problem that could be addressed in a number of ways. One solution could be the use of "Intelligent Confetti", as described in the next section.

Intelligent Paper provides a new and very different way of using paper as an input device to a computer system. The "hardware" needed (Intelligent Paper and a specialized pointer) is much less cumbersome than the DigitalDesk, but a large Web-based software and routing infrastructure is needed to realize the full potential of Intelligent Paper as an input medium for any Web-based computer. Once this infrastructure exists, however, the possibilities are enormous.

10.2.5 Intelligent Paper Applications

The Xerox paper describes two applications in some detail and suggests some future possibilities. This section focuses on one application called *Reading Othello* and outlines a few of the future possibilities mentioned.

The *Othello* example is based on the actions a student might take when reading her Intelligent Paper version of Shakespeare's *Othello*. Ariane is a French student of English Literature. She is lying in bed, in front of her Web-addressable TV, reading her version of *Othello*. This looks like any other *Othello* except that some pages have boxes printed across the top looking like menu items on a screen. Some actions that Ariane might take are described below.

1. She comes across a word she does not understand, so she clicks on the word and sees an explanatory note about the word displayed on the TV screen.
2. She wishes to hear the scene, so she clicks on the PLAY SCENE box at the top of the first page of the scene and hears the scene recited.
3. She wants to browse the Web site for the book, so she clicks on the MAIN WEB PAGE box and sees the initial Web page for that version of *Othello* displayed. The pen now starts to act like a mouse for the TV screen. Moving the pen on the page moves a cursor on the screen and clicking the pen acts like a mouse click. This allows her to browse the Web site.
4. Browsing the site leads her to a particularly relevant page. She wants to make a note of it for future use, so she pencils a note in the margin of the book, and clicks the pen on the LINK box at the top of the page and then on the pencilled note. This sets up a new action associated with the position of the pencilled note on that page. Later on, if she clicks the pen on her pencilled note, the relevant Web page will be displayed.

The LINK facility outlined in action 4 provides an interesting way of adding individually tailored information to pre-printed Intelligent Paper documents.

Other potential Intelligent Paper publications might be

- **maps:** providing access to tourist information and timetables for public transport
- **pocket encyclopedias:** providing access to complete multimedia versions
- **product catalogues:** providing access to order forms and multimedia information on products

A final variation is the possible use of Intelligent Confetti – small round stickers carrying a *page-id* only. These could be used to make additional facilities available when stuck on sheets of Intelligent Paper or, more importantly, used to identify Web devices to be used for output. This would allow a user to set up the return address for actions by clicking first on their Intelligent Paper and then on the Intelligent Confetti on the required output device.

10.3 Using the Text Encoding Initiative

10.3.1 Introduction to the TEI

The TEI is an application of SGML designed specifically for capturing a wide variety of information about literary texts. It covers complex literary and linguistic structures, different versions of texts, the state of old manuscripts, scholarly commentaries about texts and much more. The TEI guidelines are comprehensive; they occupy 1300 pages and cover the use of more than 400 different elements.

The British National Corpus (BNC) uses the TEI guidelines, so the "Active Alice" project described in Section 2.3 was an example of accessing a TEI text from paper. Like all BNC texts, the Alice text used only a small subset of TEI facilities to record simple information about parts of speech. Several major TEI projects, however, have captured detailed scholarly information about old works (see [21] for a list of TEI projects). The Canterbury Tales Project [22], for example, created TEI versions of the 54 manuscripts of Chaucer's Wife of Bath's Prologue. A CD-ROM version of these [23] provides detailed comparisons of different versions and full collations of all the witnesses to the Prologue.

An interesting way to exploit the effort put into creating these rich TEI versions is to use a modern paper version of an old work to access the additional scholarly information in the TEI version. The rest of this section introduces a small selection of TEI facilities relevant to this application and Section 3.2 looks in more detail at a specific example.

Old manuscripts contain many deletions and insertions. Deletions may be made by crossing out or erasing. Insertions are typically written above the original line or in a margin. The two are frequently combined when text is replaced. Such a replacement might be indicated in the TEI text as follows:

```
Descending by <del type=overstrike>the easy slope</del>
<add place=supralinear hand=DW>the beaten road</add>
that led
```

The del element indicates that the original text "the easy slope" was deleted by drawing a line through the text (type=overstrike) and the add element indicates that "the beaten road" was then added above the original line (place=supralinear). hand=DW specifies that the new text was written in a different handwriting identified by the name "DW". Different types of deletion (e.g. erasure) and addition (e.g. leftmargin, overleaf) could have been specified and several other attributes are available to provide further details.

Elements such as gap, damage and unclear can be used to indicate that the original text was illegible or not clear enough to be transcribed with confidence. Where the text for a damaged section has been guessed or suggested by a scribe or scholar, it can be indicated by a supplied element. For example

```
<damage cause="rubbing">
<supplied reason="illegible" resp="PR3">
at this season </supplied> </damage>
```

might be used to specify that a scholar identified by the name "PR3" was responsible (resp="PR3") for supplying the text "at this season" as a likely interpretation of text that was illegible due to rubbing of the manuscript.

Variations on these elements, including nested additions and deletions, may be sufficient to cover changes and problems within a single manuscript, but further elements – including app, lem, and rdg – are needed to encode information about different versions and copies of the same work. app is used to indicate the presence of some "critical apparatus". lem and rdg distinguish base or "lemma" versions of a text from different "readings" given by other scribes or in other versions. The following simple example (taken from the TEI Guidelines) shows how variations of a single word from four different versions might be coded.

```
<app>
<lem wit="El Hg">Experience</>
<rdg wit="La" type="substantive">Experiment</>
<rdg wit="Ra2" type="substantive">Eryment</>
</app>
```

The wit attribute identifies the different "witnesses" or sources. At the start of the manuscript there will be a witlist element containing information which relates the names used to identify the witnesses (El, Hg, La, and Ra2 in the example) to a description of the relevant people or manuscripts. Where many variations exist, rdgGrp elements could be used to subdivide the appropriate lem and rdg elements into several different families or "reading groups".

Two further examples should be sufficient to give an idea of the range of TEI information that might be available in a manuscript. The first of these is related to verse. TEI elements used for verse include lg for line groups, l for lines, and seg for segments within lines. Attributes for these elements can be used to give details of metrical analysis, rhyme patterns, and the type of verse. Thus

```
<lg type=stanza met="-+-+-+-+/-+-+-+"
rhyme="ababcdcd">
```

might be used to introduce a stanza and specify its metrical pattern and rhyme. If a line within the stanza did not conform to the overall metrical pattern, a met attribute could be used as shown below to override the pattern given by the line group element.

```
<l n=2 met="--+-+">
```

The final, rather different, example concerns information about names and places. The TEI provides name and rs (referring string) elements for names and places. name is used for proper nouns and rs for general-purpose names. For example

```
In June <name type=person key=SM3 reg="Smith, Dr John">
Smith</name>moved to <name type=county>Kent</name>.
Later
in the year <rs type=person key=SM3>the Doctor</rs>
```

Here the key attribute provides a unique identifier for the person or place concerned, and reg gives a regularized or standardized version of the name. More detail may be encoded than shown above. For names, this could include forenames, surname, titles referring to rank or role (e.g. Lord, Colonel), nicknames, and embellishments like "Junior", "de la", or "IV". For places, information can be given about the country, region, settlement (town), and relative position or distance from another place. If used consistently, these elements make it easy to find every reference to particular people and places in a work.

10.3.2 The Wordsworth Project

The Wordsworth Trust [24] and staff at the Universities of Newcastle and Kent have held discussions about a project to create TEI versions of a selection of Wordsworth's manuscripts. The motivation for this is to allow scholars to access information over the Web instead of having to travel to Dove Cottage to inspect the manuscripts. If the project goes ahead, the resulting TEI texts could also be accessed via the DigitalDesk or Intelligent Paper. This section outlines some of the possibilities assuming the TEI versions contain the type of information outlined in Section 10.3.1.

Traditionally, humanities scholars have published weighty books containing transcriptions of manuscripts and comparisons of different versions, together with numerous footnotes describing the state of the manuscripts and giving information about the history or interpretation of the text. *The Thirteen-Book Prelude by William Wordsworth*, edited by Reed [25] is a good example. Wordsworth's *Prelude* is a poem of approximately 8000 lines, but the Reed version consists of two substantial volumes containing total of 2300 pages. They form part of a series known as *The Cornell Wordsworth*, which aims to present "clean, continuous 'reading texts' from which all layers of later revision have been stripped away" and also to provide "a complete and accurate record of variant readings, from Wordsworth's earliest drafts down to the final lifetime (or first posthumous) publication". They do this by providing three main versions

- the clean reading text
- transcriptions giving a printed approximation of all the insertions and deletions in the originals
- photographs of the manuscript pages

Extensive notes are provided explaining the history and state of the various versions and giving additional information about the meaning of the text. The following is a typical example taken from the transcriptions.

$$[9^r]$$

While yet
[? Then never]
~~Ere I~~ [? had] travell'd from my native hills
And afterwards when thought the
 gorgeous
 Alp
I roamd $\left\{\begin{array}{l} my \\ [?] \end{array}\right.$ pleasures were entirely

The positioning and spacing of the text is a close representation of that used in the original manuscript. The items in square brackets within the text represent doubtful or illegible words which would be encoded using gap and unclear elements in a TEI version. The "[9^r]" at the start identifies the sheet of the original manuscript. The numbers in brackets to the right of the text refer to the book and lines in the manuscript and, where appropriate, give the corresponding line numbers in the clean reading version. These numbers are used to link footnotes to the appropriate text.

Similar information concerning the manuscripts could be encoded using the TEI guidelines, although it would require the use of advanced versions of the features described in the previous section. For Web access or CD-ROM versions, this information could be made available via a standard hypertext interface. For the DigitalDesk or Intelligent Paper, a printed version containing the clean reading text could be used as the starting point.

On the DigitalDesk this would work as follows. Once a page of the work has been recognized, the user is presented with a menu of the various types of information available for the work. The user selects one or more of these. Areas of the open pages are then highlighted (using a colour code linked to the menu) to show where this type of information is relevant. To access the details, the user then points to a specific highlighted area. Further feedback may be given via information projected onto the paper/desk or via the computer screen. As a specific example, the user could ask to see all the places where a particular manuscript differs from the reading text. Highlighting all such areas on the page would provide a vivid illustration of the pattern and level of the differences. Full details of the other version would be projected onto a separate area of the desk or presented via a screen.

Should the reader wish to check up on references to particular names, the system might give information at two or three different levels. Initially, all names on the open pages could be highlighted. The user could then point to a particular highlighted name to ask to see the additional information. At this point the user could also have the option of asking for a list of all references to the same person or place (this could be given by displaying appropriate text extracts on the screen or by giving page references for the paper version).

The system would work in a rather similar way with Intelligent Paper, but the initial selection of the type of information required would probably be made by pointing to menu boxes printed on the page. Instead of highlighting areas on the page to show where additional information is available, the system would display an appropriately highlighted version on a Web-connected computer screen. Further levels of information would then be requested by pointing to the appropriate text on the page or by using the pen as if it were a mouse for the screen.

10.4 Summary

Much effort has been expended in replicating the qualities of paper on a computing device. Although great progress has been made, there is as yet no real alternative to the paper document that can be folded up and stuffed in a pocket. This paper has described two experimental systems for bridging the gap between the paper and digital worlds. Both approaches allow physical paper to act as a starting point for accessing and exploring the dynamic world of digital information.

Although the current DigitalDesk prototype has significant limitations in its recognition system, it has already shown that many applications are feasible. Its ability to project information onto the paper provides an eye-catching and attractive way of involving the paper at all stages, not just as a starting point for accessing the digital information.

Intelligent paper opens up a whole new world of Web-based applications and has potentially far-reaching implications for publishers. Although it does not provide an immediate equivalent of the DigitalDesk's ability to highlight information on the paper, it is an extremely flexible technology that fits well with the ubiquitous nature of the Web and advances in mobile computing. The LINK facility, referred to in Section 10.2.5, brings a whole new meaning to annotations on paper.

Acknowledgements

The authors would like to thank Robert Harding, Steven Lay, Dan Sheppard, and Richard Watts for their contributions to the DigitalDesk and the Active Alice project; Marc Dymetman and Max Copperman for the inspiration provided by their paper on Intelligent Paper and for their willingness to allow us to quote from it and use their figures to illustrate the explanations given in Sections 10.2.4 and 10.2.5; and members of the Wordsworth Trust and staff at the Universities of Newcastle and Kent for ideas about the Wordsworth project.

References

[1]   Victoria A. Burrill, VORTEXT: VictORias TEXT reading and authoring system, in *Text processing and Document Manipulation* (ed. J.C. van Vliet), pp. 43–57, Cambridge University Press, 1986.

[2] Abigail Sellen and Richard Harper, Paper as an analytic resource for the design of new technologies, in *Proceedings of the ACM SigChi Conference on Human Factors in Computing Systems, CHI'97* (ed. Steven Pemberton), pp. 319–326, ACM/Addison-Wesley, 1997.

[3] Andrew Birrell and Paul McJones, Virtual Paper, *Project Web Page*, Digital Equipment Corporation Systems Research Center. http://www.research.digital.com/SRC/virtualpaper/home.html.

[4] David Chaiken, Mark Hayter, Jay Kistler, and Dave Redell, *The Virtual Book*, SRC Research Report 157, Digital Equipment Corporation Systems Research Center, November 1998.

[5] Morgan Price, Bill Schilit, and Gene Golovchinsky, XLibris: the active reading machine, in *CHI 98 Summary*, pp. 22–23, ACM Press, 1998. http://www.fxpal.xerox.com/papers/pri98.pdf.

[6] Bill Schilit, Lynn Wilcox, and Nitin "Nick" Sawhney, Merging the benefits of paper notebooks with the power of computers in Dynomite, in *CHI 97 Extended Abstracts*, pp. 22–23, ACM Press, 1997. http://www.fxpal.xerox.com/papers/sch97.pdf.

[7] William Newman and Pierre Wellner, A desk that supports computer-based interaction with paper documents, *Proceedings of the ACM Conference on Human Factors in Computing*, Monterey, 1992.

[8] Marc Dymetman and Max Copperman, Intelligent Paper, in *Electronic Documents, Artistic Imaging, and Digital Typography* (eds. Roger D. Hersch, Jacques Andre and Heather Brown), pp. 392–406, Springer-Verlag, LNCS, 1998.

[9] C.M. Sperberg-McQueen and Lou Burnard (eds.), *Guidelines for Electronic Text Encoding and Interchange (TEI P3)*, ACH/ACL/ALLC (Association for Computers and the Humanities, Association for Computational Linguistics, Association for Literary and Linguistic Computing), Chicago/Oxford, 1994.

[10] Peter Robinson, Virtual offices, *Proceedings of Royal Society Discussion Meeting on Virtual Reality in Society, Science and Engineering*, BT Publication SRD/R5/1, 1995.

[11] Pierre Wellner, Interacting with paper on the DigitalDesk, *Communications of the ACM*, 36(7), 87–96, July 1993.

[12] Peter Robinson, Dan Sheppard, Richard Watts, Robert Harding and Steve Lay, A framework for interacting with paper, *Proceedings of Eurographics '97*, (eds. D. Fellner and L. Szirmay-Kalos), Vol. 16, No. 3, 1997.

[13] Quentin Stafford-Fraser and Peter Robinson, BrightBoard – a video augmented environment, *Proceedings of the ACM Conference on Human Factors in Computer Systems*, Vancouver, 1996.

[14] Kathy Carter, Computer aided design – back to the drawing board, *Proceedings of the International Symposium on Creativity and Cognition*, Loughborough, 1993.

[15] Peter Robinson, Dan Sheppard, Richard Watts, Robert Harding and Steve Lay, Animated paper documents, *Proceedings 7th International Conference on Human-Computer Interaction*, HCI'97, San Francisco, August 1997.

[16] Gavin Burnage and Dominic Dunlop, Encoding the British National Corpus, in *English Language Corpora: Design, Analysis and Exploitation* (eds. Jan Aarts, Pieter de Haan and Nelleke Oostdijk), pp. 79–95, Amsterdam and Atlanta: Editions Rodopi, 1993.

[17] G. Leech, 100 million words of English, *English Today*, 9(1), 1993.

[18] Heather Brown, Robert Harding, Steve Lay, Peter Robinson, Dan Sheppard and Richard Watts, Active Alice: using real paper to interact with electronic text, in *Electronic Documents, Artistic Imaging, and Digital Typography* (eds. Roger D. Hersch, Jacques Andre and Heather Brown), pp. 407–419, Springer-Verlag, LNCS, 1998.

[19] Lewis Carroll (retold by Jennifer Bassett), *Alice's Adventures in Wonderland*, Oxford Bookworms, Oxford University Press, 1994.

[20] Charles F. Goldfarb, *The SGML Handbook*, Oxford University Press, 1990.

[21] TEI home page, http://www-tei.uic.edu/orgs/tei/index.html, and list of applications, http://www-tei.uic.edu/orgs/tei/app/index.html.

[22] The Canterbury tales project, http://www.shef.ac.uk/uni/projects/ctp/index.html.

[23] Peter Robinson, *The Wife of Bath's Prologue on CD-ROM*, Cambridge University Press, 1996.

[24] Wordsworth Trust Home Page, http://www.wordsworth.org.uk/.

[25] Mark L. Reed (ed.), *The Thirteen-Book Prelude by William Wordsworth*, Volumes I and II, Cornell University Press, 1991.

11

"Smart" Documents with ActiveX 3D Data Visualization Components

Mikael Jern

Abstract

The scientist and engineer can now exercise sophisticated visualization techniques to help understand the information that has come from experiments and, increasingly, from simulations run on high-performance computers. But the techniques available to present this information to other engineers and decision-makers within reports are much more basic: just 2D and pseudo-3D graphs and diagrams, as used for many years. With the increasing use of electronic documents, distributed by intranet and Internet, the opportunity to provide interactive visualization techniques within scientific and engineering reports has become practicable. This new technology of components allows the author of a report to distribute a Microsoft Word document with an embedded 3D data visualization viewer. Additionally, although the benefits of visualization are recognized, the take-up of very flexible, general-purpose applications have been limited due to their cost and the steep learning curve associated with their use.

This chapter explains the advantage of using low-cost, configurable, advanced 3D data visualization components based on Microsoft's ActiveX components, which can be embedded and distributed in documents and reports. With the increasing use of electronic documents, distributed by Internet and corporate intranets, the opportunity to provide interactive visualization techniques within scientific and engineering reports has become practicable.

Customizable components allow the author of a report to distribute the relevant electronic information coupled with an embedded data analysis viewer "smartdoc", which allows the recipients to interactively examine the data in the same way as the original analyst. Instead of being a dumb document, the "smartdoc" would be a complete data exploration application through which a reader could, via embedded ActiveX visualization/analysis components, explore the data underlying the report. Instead of being a static summary document the report becomes much more like a very natural interface or portal onto the data. Additionally, although the benefits of visualization are recognized, the take-up of very flexible, general-purpose applications to build specific, relevant, tools that can be distributed and shared within the company.

This chapter demonstrates with several examples how to develop visualization components based on Microsoft's ActiveX/COM architecture. These customizable components can be used by sophisticated programmers in their own applications as well by users who simply wish to visualize multivariate data viewing in an Excel spreadsheet.

11.1 Introduction

The widespread popularity of Web technology has created several new interactive visualization models, such as HTTP/CGI, VRML, Java applets, ActiveX and Beans. The Web first started out as a giant URL-based file server for publishing electronic documents. The explosive growth of the Web has dramatically changed user expectations concerning the delivery of information to a client and led to the acceptance of the three-tier client–server: the database and/or simulation, the Web server and visualization, and the Web client.

The Web is a client–server system. In other words, browsers (the clients) get information from other computers (the servers). The Common Gateway Interface (CGI) technique is today used to access most server environments. The universal Web browser, easy distribution of the application and centrally administrated code, solve many of the largest problems facing client–server computing and we can find amazing Web-based visualization applications. The Web introduced a new user interaction model, in which the client GUI, based on HTML, is less functional and relies upon the data or application servers for visualization traditionally executed on the client. The HTML user interface form submitted from the client is today the basic unit of any client–server interaction, but this technique is not suitable for highly interactive visualization with data stored in a data warehouse on the server-side.

CGI is not perfect. HTTP with CGI is very slow and cumbersome, and represents a stateless protocol, which is not suitable for developing modern Web-based interactive visualization applications. The main problem is that CGI-based Web applications require HTTP and the Web server to mediate between the applications running on the clients and the server.

Just as HTML, GIF and PNG allow text and 2D images to be browsed on the Web, Virtual Reality Modeling Language (VRML) provides the same function for 3D graphics. VRML is seen as an abstract functional specification of virtual worlds providing a universal file format and Internet standard for 3D, going for a solution that can be scaled up or down to fit different implementation capabilities. VRML allows users to view and navigate though 3D virtual worlds and hyperlink to new worlds. VRML 97, based on the VRML2 specification, has now become a formal ISO standard. There are several VRML plug-ins available, such as Platinum's CosmoPlayer (previous controlled by SGI) and Microsoft's Internet Explorer.

Java applets have been used to overcome some of the limitations with HTTP/CGI. Java, a platform-independent language, allows the creation of client-side applets, which are automatically downloaded from the server and executed on the client. Java applets can significantly increase the visual data interaction between the client application and user, and allow tasks to be executed on the client. Java applets are interpreted on the client by the Java Virtual Machine, which is usually embedded in the Java-enabled browser such as Netscape's Navigator or Microsoft's Internet

Explorer. Java applets, however, are downloaded every time they are used and performance therefore depends on the available bandwidth. Java applets will therefore not always provide the performance required for interactive data visualization.

11.2 "Thin" vs. "Fat" Clients

11.2.1 "Thin" Client

A "thin" client, by definition, has minimal software requirements necessary to function as a user interface front-end for a Web enabled application. In a "thin" client model (Fig. 11.1), nearly all functionality is delivered from the server side by a "visualization engine" while the client perform more simple display and query functions based on HTML forms, GIF or PNG images and 3D VRML worlds.

The most appealing aspect of the "thin" client to visualization users is that the overall cost of software and maintenance can be dramatically reduced. The "thin" client allows the application developers to eliminate the notion of software distribution at the client level (no license issue!), and eliminate the notion of maintaining local software and supporting multiple operating systems on remote clients.

The interaction between the visualization engine and the client "Web browser" with a VRML viewer plug-in is described in the "visualization on demand" application (Figure 11.1). The user interface is created with a standard HTML form. This form contains a number of fields to be set by the user, which controls not only the data to be visualized, but also the visualization attributes, such as isosurface level, color mapping and legend. The user accesses the visualization engine through this HTML page in a Web browser.

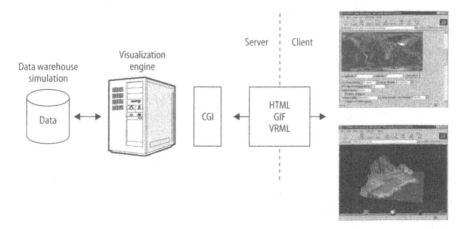

Figure 11.1 "Visualization on demand" – a schematic view of the Web client–server architecture showing a "thin" visualization scenario based on a "visualization engine". A virtual VRML scenario is defined on the basis of a simulation or other analytical expressions are generated interactively with CGI scripts. The HTML user interface form (upper picture on the client-side) permits the user to control the visualization method and its attributes dynamically. A VRML scene (lower picture) is produced by the visualization engine based on the parameters specified in the HTML form.

On submission of the form a CGI script is executed on the server. The script contains the sophistication necessary to guide the visualization software in producing appropriately laid-out graphics and the attribute information and data request specified in the form. This is then passed to the visualization engine, where it is used to set parameters. The requested data is accessed from a data warehouse or simulation, the mapping instructions are executed and the geometry is created, which is finally converted into the standard VRML 97 file format. The VRML is transferred to the client and viewed by the favored VRML browser. No special licensed visualization software is needed at the client-side.

The effectiveness of VRML viewers for communicating information about 3D environments can be dramatically enhanced by attaching annotations and hyperlinks to the 3D scenes. Links in VRML work in precisely the same way that they do within HTML; thus, pointing to an object with a link will first highlight the object's "visual cue" and "descriptive text". By clicking on the selected object, more data attributes can be made visible, another VRML created or a new application is invoked. These hyperlinks can be used to develop "information drilldown" in a 3D space. The WWW Anchor node in VRML provides the framework to have links (interaction) to other worlds, animations, sound and documents.

11.2.2 "Fat" Client

In the data visualization analysis context, it is clear that visualization tools need to be more than simply presentation vehicles. They need to be tightly integrated into the "*data navigation paradigm*". The notions of slice and drilldown through a data space need to be mapped into the data visualization navigation concept. Therefore, the concept of a "thin" client raises the issue, "Where should the data visualization take place to provide maximum data exploitation?"

Real-time visual data manipulation does not translate well into a "thin" client. While the VRML file format allows distribution of 3D visualization scenes to the Web, the user has no direct access to the underlying data sources. The "mapping" of numerical data into geometry format (VRML) takes place on the server-side. The user interaction is here dependent upon the network bandwidth. The VRML browsers can be considered to be more efficient as "presentation" tools.

Web-based component technology can be used to overcome the limitations of the "thin" client approach. Java allows the creation of "applets" and "beans", and we have Windows/COM components. These "fat" clients (Fig. 11.2) can significantly increase the data interaction between the client application and the end user, allowing tasks to be executed on the client.

Highly interactive user interface tasks are delivered that provide point-and-click navigation through multidimensional data structures. Visual User Interfaces (VUI) such as information drilling and moving a cutting plane through a volume data set are supported.

Web component technology based on Microsoft's ActiveX architecture can be used as a framework for a component-based visualization system. Visual data manipulation is provided at the client side through industry-standard components. Highly

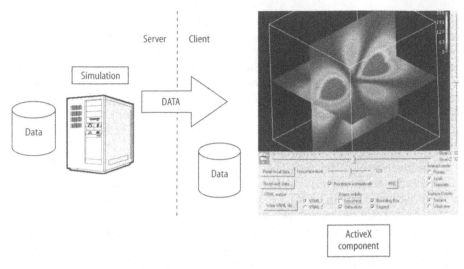

Figure 11.2 The application "fat client" component scenario. The simulation runs on the server-side, producing large amounts of volume data. The mapping of numerical data into geometry and rendering is performed at the client side. The user can interactively manipulate the data. The visualization process is fully controlled by the end user. This special visualization ActiveX component was developed with the commercial visualization software AVS/Express and performs "data slicing" and isosurface generation through a volume data set.

interactive user interface tasks are delivered that provide point-and-click navigation and information drill-down through multidimensional data structures. Visual data interfaces such as information drilling and moving a cutting plane through a volume data set etc. can be supported.

Unlike Java applets, which remain on a system only while they are used, ActiveX components stay on the system. Therefore they do not need to be downloaded each time they are going to be used. In this way they are similar to browser plug-ins. Clearly, full-featured visual data analysis tools based on the ActiveX component technology has many advantages over the rudimentary offerings of Java applets and HTML query forms.

11.3 What's so Special About Components?

A component is a task-specific piece of software that has well-defined interfaces and can be used multiple times in different applications. The published interfaces of a component guarantee that it will behave as specified and can communicate with other components.

What makes a component unique is that it can expose its properties, events and methods to any standard Independent Development Environment (IDE), such as Visual Basic, Delphi, Visual Café etc. A component can also provide customization features that allow for the modification of its appearance and functionally.

11.3.1 Why Component-Based Development?

- Avoids *ad hoc* reuse, enforces coherent interface
- Reliable – immutable interfaces
- New services can be added to a component (just add new interfaces)
- Strong infrastructure exists today (DCOM, ActiveX, CORBA, JavaBeans)
- Standard Independent Development Environments glue components together

Creating software components for specified functions encourages reuse of these parts in multiple applications, thus reducing overall application development time. By assembling applications from components (Figs. 11.3 and 11.4), programmers have the option of creating a "part" from scratch or reusing a part from a library of existing components.

The general concepts of object-oriented design and programming are starting to be well understood by a new generation of programmers. The necessary infrastructure to assemble applications from components is now becoming available. The underlying technology, however, is perhaps not yet ready for any large-scale production

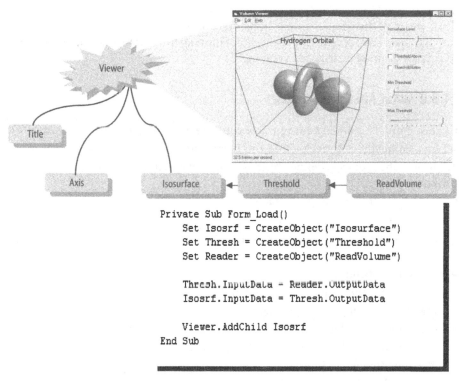

```
Private Sub Form_Load()
    Set Isosrf = CreateObject("Isosurface")
    Set Thresh = CreateObject("Threshold")
    Set Reader = CreateObject("ReadVolume")

    Thresh.InputData = Reader.OutputData
    Isosrf.InputData = Thresh.OutputData

    Viewer.AddChild Isosrf
End Sub
```

Figure 11.3 An application ActiveX/COM component "Volume Viewer" constructed from low-level "atomic" components and an infrastructure "Visualization Engine" consisting of a viewer, data model and event mechanism. A developer can assemble a new ActiveX control with a customized set of interfaces by combining Visual Basic's built-in controls (which are, in fact, also ActiveX controls) with other existing ActiveX controls (in our case, the "atomic" visualization components) and tying them together with a few lines of Visual Basic code.

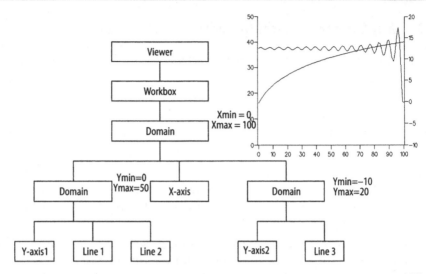

Figure 11.4 The scene tree and layout management of a line graph application components with two *y*-axes using different scaling. The application component is constructed from a library of atomic visualization components (viewer, axis, line, text, domain, ...).

deployment of distributed applications. Networks such as the Internet and corporate intranets have accelerated the trend of moving from large, standalone systems to smaller-grained distributed systems.

11.3.2 What Are Components?

- Latest industry-standard for reusable software development
- Two architectures: ActiveX/COM and JavaBeans
- Self-describing objects defined by interfaces that specify properties, methods, and events
- Interface separated from implementation

11.3.3 What Are Components Good For?

- Inherently distributable
  - Internet/intranet deployable (COM and JavaBeans)
  - Standards for object management
- Easier application deployment
  - Dynamically loaded
  - Versioned/constant interfaces
  - Increased quality and reliability
  - More easily reusable than class libraries

As a consequence, the notion of component-based programs has come to represent the next step in developing new applications that easily plug in to the existing infrastructure through well-defined interfaces. Assembling applications or high-level application components from modular components increases the overall reliability and maintainability of an application, because individual components are usually tested, well specified, and designed to have agreed-upon functionality. In addition, component-based development offers increased flexibility for developing applications more quickly. Application components need to be developed to meet the specifications of at least one of the major "request broker architectures". These include CORBA, Microsoft's DCOM and Sun's JavaBeans.

11.4 ActiveX Visualization Components

The Component Object Model (COM) and its successor DCOM (Distributed COM), developed by Microsoft, are methodologies for the creation of binary software components. Thus COM allows developers to create software building blocks which can be used by their clients without intimate knowledge of the component, but still lets them leverage the expertise of the developer.

DCOM also allows for network-enabled interprocess communications and so makes it feasible to let software entities running on different machines work together as if the components were located on the same machine. In fact, from the programmer's point of view it does not make a difference if the components are located on the same or on different machines. Thus DCOM can, for example, be used to let several machines connected via a network work in parallel on the same problem.

ActiveX (or OCX in older terminology) controls are components which can be inserted into a Web page or any application capable of hosting ActiveX controls in order to reuse packaged functionality that someone else has programmed. For example, the ActiveX controls introduced in this paper allow you to enhance your Web pages and Office 97 applications with advanced 3D visualization.

ActiveX controls can be embedded within Web browsers such as Internet Explorer, applications such as Office 97, or programming environments like Visual Basic, Visual C++, Visual J++, Power Builder, and Borland's Delphi. Since ActiveX controls can be written in any language, they let application developers use the performance offered by languages such as C and C++ to solve a specific time-critical problem, but still allow them to use tools like Visual Basic or Delphi (or even Java using the Java–ActiveX bridges) for the overall design of their applications.

11.4.1 Creating ActiveX Visualization Components

The commercial visualization software AVS/Express was used to prototype, design and construct a customized ActiveX component which supports advanced visualization techniques such as isosurfaces, cutting planes, glyphs, volume rendering, and interactive features such as drilldown, picking, rotating, zooming and scaling.

AVS/Express uses a visual programming paradigm which is noticeably different from what the average programmer is used to. You create a visualization application by connecting the input and output ports of different objects with each other, thus

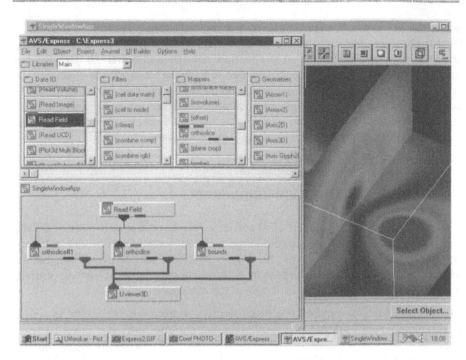

Figure 11.5 The Network Editor in the commercial visualization software AVS/Express. This OOP environment is used to design, customize and create an ActiveX visualization component. The component is exported through C++ wrapper classes embedded in an application template (ActiveX control). The network for building a volume data viewer component is described here.

subsequently applying the visualization techniques conveyed by the individual objects to the data which gets passed from one object to the next in the queue (Fig. 11.5).

For ActiveX controls maximum performance is imperative, and the user interface contained in a standard high-level module is not suitable. Therefore the visualization network for an ActiveX control usually consists of pure low-level visualization modules. The parameters for these low-level modules (e.g. an isosurface level) will be controllable by a user interface designed and developed with standard Visual Basic tools. The visualization components developed in AVS/Express can be embedded into any Windows-based application capable of hosting ActiveX controls and were designed for use with any ActiveX hosting development tool, including Visual Basic, Delphi and Visual C++.

The first step in the process of creating an ActiveX control is the design of the actual visualization control (data viewer). Using the Network Editor and the usual visual programming techniques, you assemble the objects ("read data", "slice", "isosurface", "3D Viewer" etc.) that you need for your visualization component and draw connection lines between the selected objects to indicate data references. The Network Editor shown in Fig. 11.5 demonstrates the defined network for a component, which can perform both vertical and horizontal slices through a volume data set. When the component is designed and tested, you can then "save and export" the result through C++ wrapper classes, which can then be embedded into a generic code template for ActiveX controls.

An important design decision is to define a stable and well-defined interface for the visualization component consisting of so-called properties of the ActiveX control. These properties can be anything from an "isolevel number" or "cutting plane section" to a "viewing attribute (rotate, scale, translate)".

11.4.2 Using Visual Basic to Add the User Interface

The visualization component developed in our example has many properties (Table 11.1) but no user interface that controls them. In order to facilitate using the controls in a Windows environment and to spare the user the effort of implementing a user interface, we have created the user interface control in Fig. 11.6 with Visual Basic (VB).

Table 11.1 A list of all the properties and methods of a sample ActiveX visualization control for viewing Volume Data as described in this chapter.

Structured data control		
Property Name	Data Type	Description
AutoUpdate	BOOL	While AutoUpdate is FALSE, Express will not update the screen. Use this if you have a lot of property changes which would normally trigger screen updates. This can save a lot of screen redraws.
Dims	Long array	Read-only. Returns the data set's extents. Example Express.Dims[0] returns the dataset's extents in the x-direction
DoRNC	Method	Performs a reset/normalize/center operation on all visible objects.
FileName	String	Sets the name of the data file to read. This can be a local file or a URL
InteractMode	Long	Changes the control's behaviour on mouse operations. 0 = rotate, 1=scale, 2=translate
IsoValue	Float	Sets the data value used to generate the isosurface
MinMax	Float array	Read-only. Returns the minimim/maximum data value. 0 = minimum, 1=maximum Example: Express.MinMax[0] returns the minimum data value.
ReInit	Bool	If TRUE, ReInit calculates the slices in the center of the dataset and sets SliceXY and SliceXZ accordingly. Additionally, the isosurface value is set to the center of the data range.
ShowBounds	Bool	Toggles the bounding box
ShowIsosurface	Bool	Toggles the display of the isosurface
ShowLegend	Bool	Toggles the display of the legend
ShowSlices	Bool	Toggles the display of the orthoslices
ShowWireframe	Bool	Toggles between display of surfaces and wireframe mode
SliceXY	Long	slice index in XY direction
SliceXZ	Long	slice index in XZ direction
VRMLFileName	String	Set this to a valid filename to generate a VRML file. This file will use the format given by the VRMLFormat property
VRMLFormat	Long	Type of VRML file to output 0 = VRML1, 1 = VRML 2

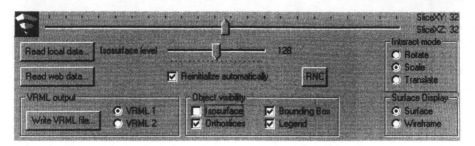

Figure 11.6 The user interface controlling the visualization component is designed and constructed with Visual Basic. Sliders control cutting plane and isosurface levels. The user can also specify VRML level, object visibility, data reader etc.

An important aspect of component creation is the ability to combine components into new components via a mechanism called COM aggregation. A developer can assemble an entirely new ActiveX control with a customized set of interfaces by combining VB's built-in controls (which are, in fact, also ActiveX controls) with other existing ActiveX controls (in our case, the visualization component) and tying them together with a few lines of Visual Basic code. This task is comparatively simple and can be performed even by non-expert programmers after a few hours. The new ActiveX component, which contains both the user interface as well as the visualization control, is assembled in VB.

In VB the forms and dialog boxes are created that will be the basis for the application's user interface. VB enables you to interactively assemble and test your user interface including forms, dialogs, menu bars, labels, file selection and persistently set the properties for the objects you have created. In VB, you will also write the code necessary to integrate the visualization control with the user interface. These event procedures contain the reference to the visualization code to be executed when the event occurs. For example, moving the "slider control" will trigger an event to redraw the cutting plane.

In the final step, we have created a new control with VB, which contains the user interface as well as the "visualization viewer" control via COM aggregation (see Figure 11.2).

11.4.3 "Smart" Documents

With the increasing use of Microsoft's electronic documents (Office 97), distributed by Intranet and Internet, the opportunity to provide easy-to-use, advanced interactive data visualization techniques within electronic documents on the powerful PC desktop has become possible. Customizable components allow the author of a report to distribute the relevant electronic information coupled with an embedded data analysis-viewer "smartdoc", which allows the recipients to interactively examine the data in the same way as the original analyst. Instead of being a dumb document, the "smartdoc" would be a complete data exploration application through which a reader could, via embedded ActiveX visualization/analysis components, explore the data underlying the report. Instead of being a static summary document the report becomes much more like a very natural interface or portal onto the data. Additionally, although the benefits of visualization are

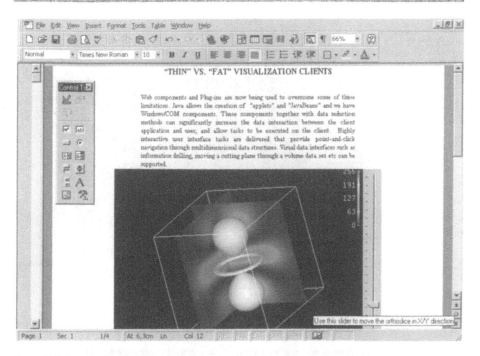

Figure 11.7 Example of a visualization ActiveX control embedded in a Word 97 document to perform data slicing and isosurface generation of large volume data on the PC desktop. This new technology of components allows the authors of a report to distribute it with a specific "data viewer", for example, allowing the recipients to interactively examine the data in the same way as the original analyst.

recognized, the take-up of very flexible, general-purpose applications to build specific, relevant, tools that can be distributed and shared within the company.

To embed the newly assembled visualization ActiveX control, described above, into an application that can act as a container, simply register the ActiveX control. You can then import the ActiveX control into any desired container and immediately start using it. For instance, in Internet Explorer you bring the control into the ActiveX Control Pad. You don't have to write any more code.

To instantiate such a control in an Office application (such as Word97 in Fig. 11.7 and Excel in Fig. 11.8), move your mouse pointer over the toolbar area and press the right mouse button. A popup menu with a choice of additional toolbars will appear. Select "Control Toolbox" and move the mouse pointer to the new toolbar. Click on the "Additional controls" button and select the visualization control from the list of available registered components.

The customized ActiveX visualization control contains only those graphics objects used by the application, which makes the application small and more efficient compared with using a standalone visualization application on the PC desktop.

The size of the ActiveX visualization component in this paper is about 3 Mbyte, but it needs to be installed only once on each client's system. Once the ActiveX control resides on your computer it will not need to be downloaded again. For example, the

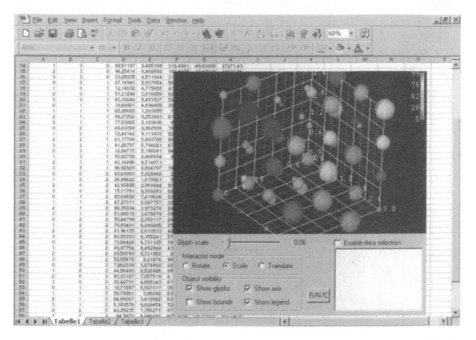

Figure 11.8 A 3D Glyph ActiveX component interfaced with Excel. The user selects multivariate data to be viewed from the rows and columns in a spreadsheet.

Word 97 document shown in Fig. 11.7 contains the embedded ActiveX component. When the document is transferred over the Internet, it will only refer to the component, and thus the total size of the document will remain small (30 kbyte). Any project can therefore exchange Word97 documents with embedded advanced 3D visualization over the Internet using pre-installed ActiveX components at the client side. Local stored data is accessed by a "data reader" in the component or transferred over the Internet using the "URL reader".

11.5 Excel Glyph Component

The next ActiveX visualization component provides a higher level view of multivariate data through a 3D Glyph Component interfaced with Excel. In this scenario, the user can view multivariate data in an Excel spreadsheet. The user explores various aspects of a multidimensional dataset using a 3D glyph visualization paradigm with value-based filtering and data "drilldown".

Click on the "Additional Controls" button in Excel and select the Glyph ActiveX control from the list of available registered components. After instantiating the control, the user then selects the data in Excel to be viewed with a simple mouse drag operation. Select the data from the rows and columns and be rewarded with a 3D mesh bearing the glyphs on each node. Obviously, the size of this mesh depends on the number of selected data values.

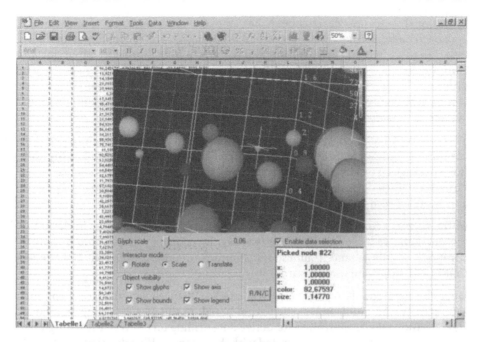

Figure 11.9 In the 3D Glyph ActiveX component, the user identifies the points of interest by clicking on the visualization object (sphere) and obtaining the object identification (node #22 in this figure). See the text for more details.

The component is fully integrated with Excel. The selected data to be viewed is automatically transferred from Excel to the component. The glyph is represented by its location in 3D space (x, y, z) described by the first three column values. The fourth column value is size, the fifth is color, and the remaining columns can be viewed after picking the glyph and performing a "drilldown" (Fig. 11.9). The "Column Assignment" interface controls which column of data is interpreted for which visualization variable.

In the 3D Glyph display, the user identifies points of interest by clicking on the visualization objects and obtaining the sequenceID. This ID is then used to explore additional information about the multivariate data represented by that point. Pulling additional annotation information from the Excel data or triggering other references results in searches through the intranet or Internet. This visual user interface (VUI) technique is an example of "data drilldown", in which interaction with the graphical objects is used to extract more detailed information in order to effect additional investigations.

11.6 Conclusion and Future Trends

In this exploding world of abstract data, there is great potential for information visualization to increase the bandwidth between us and an ever-growing and ever-changing world of data. The result will be greatly improved *time-to-insight*.

Traditional software development has moved to a Web component-based approach building smaller, single-purpose building blocks. Technologies like Sun's Java language with JavaBeans and Microsoft's ActiveX provide an important component of cyberspace – the ability to create an object that behaves similarly in different applications and on different computers. I can create an interactive component on my computer and distribute it to you in cyberspace, and it will still behave in the same way when you use it.

With ActiveX technology, Windows programmers will have a much easier time combining traditional Internet connectivity programs with powerful desktop software packages. For example, with the ActiveX components, projects can exchange "smaller" Office documents over the Internet that refer to these already available and installed components at the client-side.

In the future, a component's location on the network will become as irrelevant to the developer as its source language is today. Developers will expect to be able to compose, distribute, and troubleshoot solutions wherever, whenever. Distributed COM (DCOM) is one way forward.

Over the next couple of years, we will see the Web evolve in giant steps into interactivity and multi-user participation based on the new emerging standards. Visualization will develop into interactive data drilling on the Web providing visualization technology closely integrated with the database. Visualization on the Web will become even more active and dynamic, with JavaBeans and ActiveX components streaming down the Internet to the Web client.

The future trends and improvements in Visualization for the Web can be summarized:

- 3D visualization on affordable and powerful PC desktops
- Customizable components based on the ActiveX framework
- Multivariate visualization techniques – glyph "iconic" representation
- Descriptive visualization – presentation quality, perception and clarity
- Visual User Interface (VUI) – "information drilldown" on the Web
- "Smart" documents – 3D visualization embedded in Office documents

Acknowledgements

This work was partly supported by the European Community in the ESPRIT Project CONTENTS (EP 29732).

About the European Project CONTENTS

The objective of the CONTENTS Project is to develop customizable application components for the interactive visual analysis of data on powerful PC platforms. The data of interest are large multivariate data sets (engineering, medical and commercial) generated by simulation/modeling/measurement running on HPC platforms in a distributed and heterogeneous environment (including NT-based Intel parallel processor and suitable UNIX platforms).

The components will be based on the emerging industry-standard ActiveX/DCOM architecture, and will be properly "bridged" towards CORBA-based architectures for multi-platform portability and compatibility. CONTENTS will help to improve European awareness of object-oriented component technology in a distributed environment based on the industry standard DCOM.

These interactive visualization components will be embedded within electronic documents, allowing the author of a report to distribute the relevant electronic information coupled with an embedded high-performance data analysis-viewer "smartdoc", which allows the recipients to interactively examine the data in the same way as the original analyst. Instead of being a dumb document, the "smartdoc" will be a complete data exploration application through which a reader can, via embedded high-performance visualization/analysis components explore the data underlying the report.

Industrial partners British Aerospace and Unilever, and the medical research hospital DFC of the University of Florence, will drive the project with their pragmatic practical user needs.

Leading edge industrial partners AVS, AET and Intecs will provide their high-tech competence and experience in data reduction and visualization, image processing and management, multi-platform component design and re-engineering.

The project will enable SME technology providers to investigate the potential of providing their tools as distributed components to supply baskets of techniques for particular applications.

Organization	Country	Role
Advanced Visual Systems	DenmarkK	Lead Partner
Advanced Engineering Technology	Italy	Technology Partner
Intecs Sistemi	Italy	Technology Partner
British Aerospace	UK	End User
Unilever	UK	End User
Dipartimento di Fisiopatologia Clinica	Italy	End User

12

3D Fashion Design and the Virtual Catwalk

Pascal Volino and Nadia Magnenat Thalmann

Abstract

More than the development of a simple technique or algorithm solving a precise problem, cloth simulation and garment animation require a collection of new advances in many different areas, such as mechanical simulation, collision detection, geometric modeling, and user interfaces. This chapter summarizes the state-of-art technologies available, and which are all needed for developing the realistic and efficient simulation of complex garments. Final design and catwalk examples are provided to illustrate the new advances.

12.1 Introduction

Anyone dreaming about a particular garment model should be able to materialize it on a computer screen. Virtual simulation and animation of complex garments, however, require a very complex assembly of techniques, which are not only related to mechanical modeling and numerical simulation, but also to new interactive design to enable any user to reproduce efficiently and accurately his or her design ideas. While virtual fashion design is an important outcome of these developments, they will also benefit a wide range of application, from computer graphics to industrial CAD and prototyping applications, all with their specific needs.

Garment simulation is still a very dynamic research topic, and the techniques are still in constant evolution, as they start being efficient enough to foresee real applications in the domain of virtual fashion and garment prototyping. MIRALab has been actively involved in these developments, and since 1990 several garment simulation models have been developed in regard to this evolution (Fig. 12.1). Using the appropriate technologies, it is now possible to duplicate precisely actual fashion show garment models in virtual catwalk shows, widening the perspectives brought to virtual creation.

Figure 12.1 Evolution of garment simulation in MIRALab.

The purpose of this chapter is to present an overview of the various techniques that are available for garment animation, and to discuss their relevance and difficulties for creating efficient models for fashion design. The evolution of these techniques used in MIRALab is discussed as an example leading to the models and catwalk simulations described at the end of this presentation.

12.2 Designing Garments

The traditional garment industry builds garments by defining "patterns", or fabric shapes, which are cut into the material and seamed together around a mannequin. Existing CAD systems help the fashion designer in the design process by providing tools for drawing the 2D patterns with a gradation process for defining several garment sizes, and with specifications on how the patterns should be seamed together. The subsequent assemblies around a mannequin and redesign are, however, purely manual tasks, whereas the designer works on real paper or fabric models.

The easiest way to design accurate virtual garment models is to reproduce this intuitive methodology for creating the shape of the cloth surface. The garment patterns should then be assembled around a virtual body using a simplified form of mechanical simulation. Modeling garments from seamed patterns was first presented in [1]. A collection of patterns representing the cloth are seamed together to build the complete garment. While the early development did not include any dedicated design software, a specific pattern editor was first presented in [2]. The current garment design software described [3] takes advantage of this scheme for designing precise and complex models (Fig. 12.2), and furthermore provides tools for performing cutting and seaming directly on the 3D simulation, using interactive mechanical simulation.

Among the various other techniques to be considered is the creation of garments directly from the expected 3D shape. In this way, tight dresses or underwear can be created directly to fit the underlying body. However, development algorithms, such as presented in [4], are required to turn these surfaces into 2D models and optimize their shape for efficient seaming and adjustment.

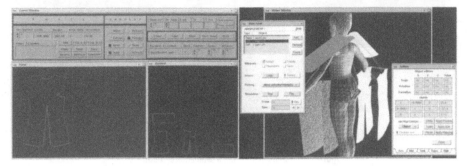

Figure 12.2 Building garment patterns with seams, and their placement around a virtual body.

12.3 Garment Assembly and Simulation

At the heart of any computer simulation tool is the calculation of adequate shapes and animations using programmed algorithms, which should be produced with minimal control from the designer.

12.3.1 Mechanical Simulation

Cloth animation techniques have evolved closely with the available computational power and graphical possibilities. The first models, pioneered by [5], were geometrical, and thus aimed to reproduce the expected shape of the cloth in some particular situations. Real mechanical simulation then appeared with [6], and computed cloth deformation only by numerically simulating the mechanical behavior of elastic surfaces. Since then, many techniques have been investigated, with various compromises between accuracy, simulation speed and versatility.

12.3.1.1 Mechanical Simulation Techniques

The cloth behavior is described by a set of laws relating how the material is deformed when it is subjected to given constraints. The main behavior parameters are extracted from experimental characterization [7–9]. Various mechanical models can then be defined, with various complexities and degrees of approximation. No analytical solutions exist in the usual cases, and a numerical integration process is required to compute the animation and rest position using discretization in space and time.

Among available schemes, the model can be described using continuous expressions of energy derivatives based on the surface geometry. These continuous models are then discretized for minimization or integration over time. Such models were described for example in [10] for modeling the elastic behavior of cloth and in [11] and [1] using Lagrange equations.

A more accurate approach would consider computing energies using elementary deformations of discrete elements, and minimizing the global system using continuity between the elements as constraints. These finite-element techniques are very efficient for computing well-defined mechanical systems accurately, but their computation requirements are still very high, and they do not seem to be adequate to support dynamic constraints such as complex collision effects. Most of their applications to cloth simulation [12–14] restrict the problem to the elastic simulation of simple fabric geometries with well-established constraints and without the complex evolving collisions to which real garments are subjected.

Conversely, the simplest mechanical models consider a discretization of the cloth material itself as point masses which are linked to each other by interactions that reproduce the mechanical behavior of the fabric. Numerical integration then computes the motion of these particles. Implementations of various complexities can be performed, the simplest being the "spring–mass" system, in which point masses are linked to their neighbors by linear springs. Spring–mass models have been implemented in several cloth simulation systems, such as in [15] (small-scale simulation of the fabric threads) and [16–18] (efficient integration techniques).

12.3.1.2 A Simple and Efficient Elastic Model

Finding the best compromise between accuracy and simulation efficiency is a key issue in mechanical simulation. These parameters must be considered not only for the mechanical model, but also for the geometrical description (mesh refinement) and issues related to collision reaction and friction accuracy. Hence it is useless to consider a very accurate description of the elastic behavior when the mesh is too coarse to describe elementary wrinkle patterns and relate geometrical contacts accurately for friction computation. As normal applications restrict a simulated garment to only a few thousand mesh triangles, simple models implemented as particle systems often offer the best compromise. Ref. [19] presents a very efficient model which is an improvement of the simple spring–mass model to deal with its most important accuracy shortcomings. Deformation and wrinkling realism of rough mesh surfaces can then be improved by geometrical techniques, such as presented in [20].

12.3.1.3 Numerical Integration

Particle system models usually translate into huge ordinary differential equation systems describing the particle motions, which have to be integrated efficiently. While the Euler method used by early systems is usually inefficient, higher order Runge–Kutta methods, as used in [17] and [19], give good results. Such explicit integration steps are very simple to compute, but these schemes may exhibit instabilities because of the numerical stiffness of particle systems, which increases with the discretization and material rigidity. An accurate adaptive time step control scheme is thus required. Implicit integration methods, such as presented in [18], which are not subject to instability, may also be considered, but they require much more complicated and expensive computations for each step. The adequate method depends on the simulation context, and on whether it is accuracy or stability considerations that limit the allowable time step.

12.3.2 Collision Detection and Response

An accurate mechanical model is essential. However, the cloth shape is mainly determined by the body which wears it. It is essential to find geometrically which object parts are interacting (detection), and then to produce accurately the corresponding reaction on the cloth motion (response).

The main issue is to master the complexity of the problem due to discretization. The cloth surface, as well as the body surface, is represented by polygonal meshes that can have several thousand polygons each. Testing each pair of polygons for potential collisions is an unrealistic task. Many optimized algorithms have been developed for that purpose, either based on space subdivision or hierarchization (voxelization, octree), object hierarchization (bounding-box hierarchies), spatial projection and ordering.

12.3.2.1 Curvature-based Hierarchical Collision Detection

In the case of cloth simulation, bounding-box hierarchies are adequate algorithms for collision detection, since the topology of the animated meshes mostly remains constant and therefore a constant precomputed hierarchy can be used. However, designing a very general cloth simulation framework requires the detection of self-collisions in the cloth surface, which may bend, wrinkle and crumple in very complex patterns. This kind of detection is, however, very inefficient, as all the adjacent elements of the mesh are seen as "colliding" by the detection algorithm. Ref. [21] details an adapted version of a hierarchical algorithm which deals with this issue. It is based on the consideration that self-collisions only occur within surfaces that are bent enough to produce a "loop". Hence self-collisions should only be detected within surface regions that are curved enough to exhibit them (Fig. 12.3).

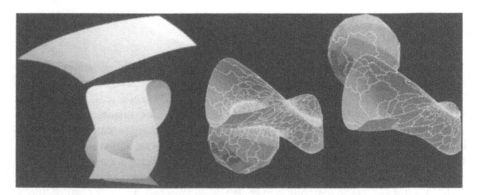

Figure 12.3 Curvature-based self-collision detection, implemented in a hierarchical algorithm.

In addition to bounding boxes, curvature information has been added in the elements of the hierarchy for performing this test. Furthermore, the algorithm takes advantage of element adjacencies by replacing the bounding-box test by a curvature test in that case. The implementation of this scheme has provided a very efficient framework where collision detection is not the bottleneck for simulation performance anymore, and where self-collision detection has only a very minor performance impact.

12.3.2.2 Constraint-Based Collision Response

As soon as the distance separating two objects is small enough to consider that they are interacting, a "feedback" should be performed on their behavior. Collision response aims to reproduce this interaction in an accurate way, primarily to avoid unrealistic interpenetration of the objects, and secondly to simulate realistic bouncing and friction effects.

Traditional collision response techniques use potential repulsion fields to model the reaction forces, which are intense and highly discontinuous. Though being a "physical" response easily integrated into the mechanical model, this solution is impractical because of the high nonlinear penalty forces, which are hard to simulate numerically and which cannot render precisely the discontinuous reaction of a solid contact.

In an approach introduced in [16], collisions were handled as geometrical constraints, using kinematical correction on the constrained elements; positions and speeds were corrected according to the mechanical conservation laws to fit the constraints precisely. This approach allows us to skip the potential walls used to enforce the constraints. More recently, [17] used a similar method to handle friction effects. This approach has been extended in [19] by a more general framework, performing corrections not only on positions, but also on speeds and mostly on accelerations. In this new scheme, the corrections only damp the kinematical difference between the colliding elements according to momentum conservation laws, ensuring reduction of the mechanical energy and stability. Such an approach, which does not rely heavily on position correction, can be integrated into the mechanical model in a better way, and ensures good response stability. Furthermore, active constraints can be included in this general scheme, such as seaming "elastics" modeled as additional acceleration contributions.

While this scheme, which allows numerous collisions to be handled without any significant impact on the performance of mechanical simulation itself, has shown itself to be quite robust, it may fail to give an appropriate response in some very particular situations of interacting collisions. Instead of complicating the geometrical computations to solve these marginal cases, a collision orientation correction scheme has been implemented [16], which reorients collisions which do not match the orientations of the majority of neighboring collisions within a contact region. Such an algorithm efficiently recovers initially inconsistent geometrical collision configurations, and contributes to the robustness of the global system for handling very general simulation contexts (Fig. 12.4).

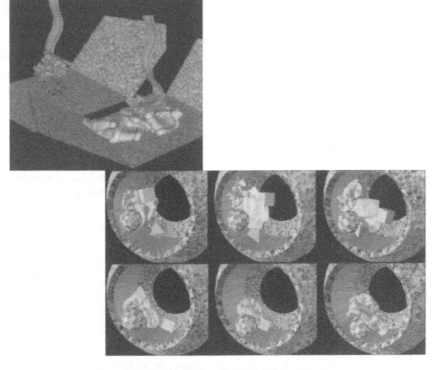

Figure 12.4 Complex Collisions: The Falling Ribbon and the Dryer

12.3.3 Smoothing and Wrinkling

In the eternal quest for computation speed, the most efficient technique is to use as rough a mesh as possible to simulate our cloth objects. Not only do rough meshes imply less data to compute, but they also allow higher simulation time steps, thanks to better numerical stability. However, when using a standard flat triangle mesh representation the deformation possibilities are reduced by the maximum curvature allowed by the discretization, which cannot of course be smaller than the size of an element.

In cloth simulation, realism results mainly from the appearance of wrinkling and buckling on the surface. Obtaining these essential features in a fast simulation system can be done through techniques that render them as sub-element details on rough meshes. This is obtained by combining smoothing algorithms to fast wrinkling algorithms that modulate pre-defined wrinkle patterns according to the surface geometrical deformation.

12.3.3.1 Smoothing Rough Meshes

Ref. [22] details an efficient algorithm for smoothing rough meshes with interpolation surfaces defined by the mesh vertices and orthogonal to normals defined on

Figure 12.5 The interpolation patch, a tetrahedron rounded to a sphere, and smoothing a rough horse.

each vertex (Fig. 12.5). The main idea is to build the smooth surface out of these normals from any arbitrary point of a triangle using a very simple geometric construction.

From any polygon point **P** represented by its barycentric coordinates, the algorithm first computes the corresponding Phong normal **N** using interpolation of the vertex normals **Ni**, and then builds for each polygon vertex **Pi** an associated vertex **Qi** by constructing a circular arc passing through **Pi** orthogonally to **Ni** and crossing orthogonally the line defined by **P** and **N**. Along that line, all the vertex contributions **Qi** are then blended into a single point **Q** using a normalized quadratic function defined on the barycentric coordinates. The interpolation surface described by **Q** is smooth and passes through each vertex **Pi** orthogonally to the normals **Ni**.

Unlike the requirements of most techniques in the literature, this technique avoids complex preprocessing such as setting up local coordinates, computing curve parameters, or any constraining recursive subdivision scheme to reach the given location. Any polygon point defined by barycentric coordinates can be constructed "on the fly" when it is needed, without any preprocessing or storage. This scheme therefore allows dynamic subdivision algorithms to be easily implemented to smooth polygonal meshes adaptively.

12.3.3.2 Geometric Surface Wrinkles

Given a mesh deformation, generally expressed as the length variation of the mesh edges from a given initial length, an algorithm extensively described in [20] computes surface wrinkling using a quick and easy geometrical algorithm.

Most wrinkles appear in a fixed place. For instance, garment wrinkles usually fall into similar patterns at those places where the fabric is deformed. For a computer graphics designer, it is convenient to define these wrinkles by drawing them in the same way as textures are usually drawn, rather than relying on modeling and a mechanical simulation to be accurate enough to render small wrinkles in the expected location. The proposed algorithm modulates the wrinkle amplitude according to local surface deformation to produce realistic animations (Fig. 12.6).

Wrinkles are designed as a texture heightfield, usually stored as a texture bitmap. The wrinkling amplitude is then obtained dynamically by comparing the current length of the mesh edges with their native length which defines the "rest" state of

Figure 12.6 Geometrical wrinkles reacting dynamically to surface geometric compression.

Figure 12.7 Dynamic wrinkles: initial surface mesh, wrinkle pattern, wrinkled cloth surface, animation.

the surface. A smooth law is used to turn this length difference into wrinkle amplitude. This law relates approximately the buckling necessary to preserve surface metric length along a given direction during compression. It is parameterized by constants which relate the wrinkle's local reactivity to the deformation along the edge's orientation, which are precomputed from the initial wrinkle pattern. The local wrinkle amplitudes are then averaged on each mesh vertex and smoothly interpolated over the mesh polygons using a normalized quadratic function. In order to relate the wrinkle shape evolution depending on various deformation configurations, several wrinkle patterns can be defined and dynamically blended on the same surface.

Displaying the wrinkles can be performed in several ways depending on the available rendering frameworks. The simplest way is to use the texture definition as bump mapping modulated by the dynamically computed amplitude. Displacement mappings can also render deep deformations accurately. Wrinkles can also be rendered as perturbations of a dynamically refined mesh using the interpolation algorithm detailed above. Combining this geometrical wrinkle scheme with the interpolation scheme described above allows very realistic wrinkled cloth animations to be produced using fast and simple simulation models based on rough geometries (Fig. 12.7).

12.3.4 Integration in a Garment Simulation System

Only an efficient combination of the presented technologies within a suitable user interface can enable a designer to produce attractive and realistic garment models. Ref. [3] describes a 3D interface for garment creation and simulation on virtual

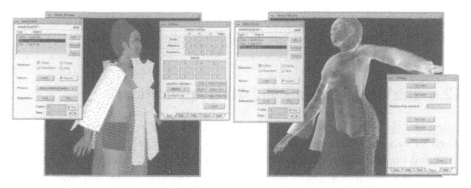

Figure 12.8 Building garments using mechanical simulation and seaming.

characters, using the technologies described in [21] (collision detection), [19] (efficient simulation) and [20] (geometrical wrinkles).

The 3D interface is basically an animation management tool allowing interactive object manipulation and mechanical simulation. 2D garment patterns are imported and placed around a 3D virtual body in a suitable initial position. Then a simplified mechanical simulation pulls the pattern seam borders together and the garment is merged to its initial position on the body (Fig. 12.8).

Finally, the body can be animated and the garments move along with it (Fig. 12.9). At any time, user interaction is possible in order to alter the motion, or to perform 3D editing on the cloth using interactive cutting and seaming.

Full creativity is available as none of the algorithms are bound to any particular context. Hence garments are not bound to remain simulated on bodies and may fly, fall and crumple with the contact of any object. Interactive editing furthermore

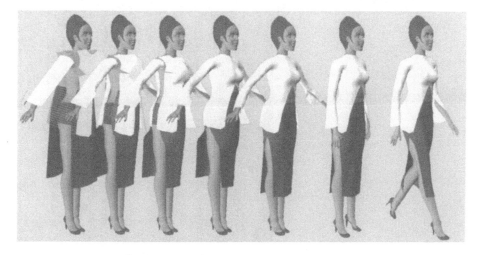

Figure 12.9 Animating garments on an animated virtual body.

expands the possibilities, and VR-specific tools are available, such as stereographic display or motion trackers, for controlling object displacements.

12.4 The Virtual Catwalk and Other Applications

Using the system presented, a fashion show exhibiting several garment models worn by various top models has been created virtually (Fig. 12.10). Some of the garments presented are tight garments, such as skirts or trousers, whereas another creation is a wedding dress with a large train. A complex decor and high-quality rendering were used.

The versatility of the model is exhibited here. Hence the system can successfully simulate skirts and trousers steadily maintained on the body using friction only, as well as realistic wrinkles appearing as the wedding dress train glides over the floor.

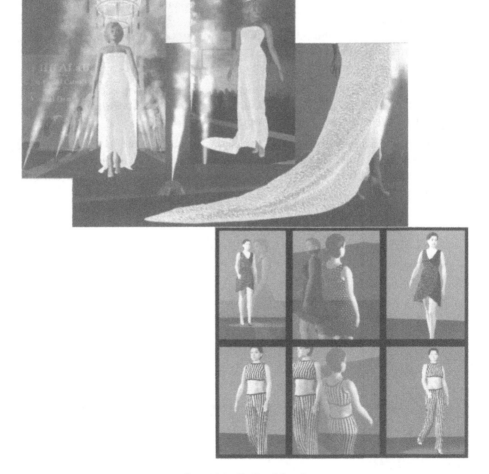

Figure 12.10 The Virtual Catwalk.

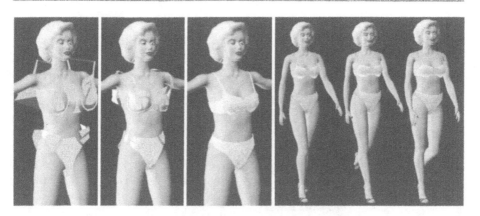

Figure 12.11 Building and simulating underwear.

The same mechanical model was used for all the simulations, demonstrating the versatility for reproducing cloth in various contexts.

While computer graphic realizations are still the main use of the system, many computer-aided design applications are also available. For instance, the framework has been used in underwear design and testing (Fig. 12.11). Complex models are designed using the system and then simulated on the body.

In this application, the underwear patterns are designed from a model description and then turned into a very refined surface mesh for mechanical simulation. During the fitting, the color gradient along the mesh edge shows the repartition of the deformations on the fabric, which helps to visualize whether the cloth is fitted or not, and therefore gives hints to improve the design (Fig. 12.12). By reducing the friction, the garment can quickly reach its most relaxed position on the body, while turning on the friction again maintains it realistically as the body is moving (Fig. 12.11).

In order to demonstrate the capacity of the system to produce virtual garment models related to reality, a fashion show mixing virtual models with their real counterparts has been produced.

This virtual show is presented in parallel with a "real" fashion show. It alternates fully rendered sequences of walking virtual models with simpler sections during which the real models exhibit the actual garments (Figs. 12.13 and 12.14).

This sequence has definitely demonstrated the usability of the software for producing long and complex scenes using many different models (Fig. 12.15).

12.5 Perspectives

These results are only a small preview of the future potentialities of a complete simulation system that combines industry-standard design tools with powerful mechanical computation and virtual reality techniques for rendering garment models on realistic animated virtual characters. Future developments are going on

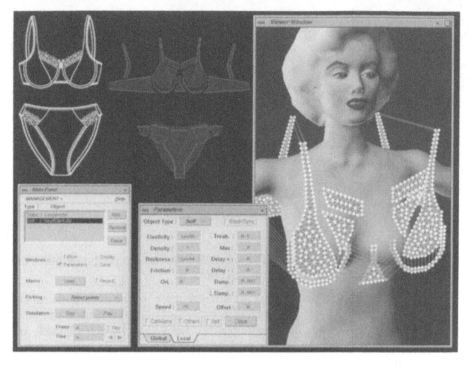

Figure 12.12 Underwear design.

Figure 12.13 Fashion design models and their virtual counterparts.

to bring fashion creation and visualization to the desk of the fashion designer as well as to materialize the dream garments of anyone.

Acknowledgements

We are grateful to the Swiss Fonds National pour la Recherche Scientifique for funding the projects related to this work, as well as to Marlène Poizat for her design skills, and to all the people who contributed to this work with technical help and suggestions, as well as illustration design and text reviewing.

Figure 12.14 More virtual fashion models.

Figure 12.15 Fashion show.

References

[1] M. Carignan, Y. Yang, N. Magnenat-Thalmann, and D. Thalmann, Dressing animated synthetic actors with complex deformable clothes, *Computer Graphics (SIGGRAPH'92 Proceedings)*, 26(2), 99–104, Addison-Wesley, 1992.

[2] H.M. Werner, N. Magnenat-Thalmann, and D. Thalmann, User interface for fashion design, *Graphics, Design and Visualization (ICCG'93 Proceedings)*, pp. 165–172, 1993.

[3] P. Volino, N. Magnenat Thalmann, S. Jianhua, and D. Thalmann, The evolution of a 3D system for simulating deformable clothes on virtual actors, *IEEE Computer Graphics and Applications*, September 1996, pp. 42–50.

[4] B.K. Hinds, J. McCartney, and G. Woods, Pattern developments for 3D surfaces, *Computer-Aided Design*, 23(8), 583–592, 1991.

[5] J. Weil, The synthesis of cloth objects, *Computer Graphics (SIGGRAPH'86 Proceedings)*, 24, 243–252, Addison-Wesley, 1986.

[6] D. Terzopoulos, J.C. Platt, and H. Barr, Elastically deformable models, *Computer Graphics (SIGGRAPH'97 Proceedings)*, 21, 205–214, Addison-Wesley, 1987.

[7] W.E. Morton and J.W.S. Hearle, *Physical Properties of Textile Fibers*, The Textile Institute/ Butterworths, Manchester and London, 1962.

[8] S. Kawabata, *The Standardization and Analysis of Hand Evaluation*, Hand Eval. and Stand. Committee of the Textile Machinery Society of Japan, Osaka, 1975.

[9] W.J. Shanahan, D.W. Lloyd, and J.W.S. Hearle, Characterizing the elastic behavior of the textile fabrics in complex deformation, *Textile Research Journal*, 48, 495–505, 1978.

[10] D. Terzopoulos, and K. Fleischer, Deformable Models, *The Visual Computer*, 4(6), 306–331, Springer-Verlag, 1988.

[11] Y. Yang, and N.Magnenat-Thalmann, Techniques for cloth animation, *New Trends in Animation and Visualization*, pp. 243–256, John Wiley & Sons Ltd, 1991.

[12] J.R. Collier, B.J. Collier, G. O'Toole, and S.M. Sargand, Drape prediction by means of finite-element analysis, *Journal of the Textile Institute*, 82(1), 96–107, 1991.

[13] T.J. Kang, and W.R. Yu, Drape simulation of woven fabric using the finite-element method, *Journal of the Textile Institute*, 86(4), 635–648, 1995.

[14] J.W. Eischen, S. Deng, and T.G. Clapp, Finite-element modeling and control of flexible fabric parts, *Computer Graphics in Textiles and Apparel (IEEE Computer Graphics and Applications)*, pp. 71–80, 1996.

[15] D.E. Breen, D.H. House, and M.J. Wozny, Predicting the drape of woven cloth using interacting particles, *Computer Graphics (SIGGRAPH'94 Proceedings)*, pp. 365–372, Addison-Wesley, 1994.

[16] P. Volino, M. Courchesne, and N. Magnenat-Thalmann, Versatile and efficient techniques for simulating cloth and other deformable objects, *Computer Graphics (SIGGRAPH'95 Proceedings)*, pp. 137–144, Addison-Wesley, 1995.

[17] B. Eberhardt, A. Weber, and W. Strasser, A fast, flexible, particle-system model for cloth draping, *Computer Graphics in Textiles and Apparel (IEEE Computer Graphics and Applications)*, 52–59, 1996.

[18] D. Baraff and A. Witkin, Large steps in cloth simulation, *Computer Graphics (SIGGRAPH'98 Proceedings)*, 32, 106–117, Addison-Wesley, 1998.

[19] P. Volino and N. Magnenat-Thalmann, Developing simulation techniques for an interactive clothing system, *Virtual Systems and Multimedia (VSMM'97 Proceedings)*, Geneva, Switzerland, pp. 109–118, 1997.

[20] P. Volino and N. Magnenat-Thalmann, Fast geometrical wrinkles on animated surfaces, *WSCG Proceedings 1999*, Plzen, Czech Republic, 1999.

[21] P. Volino and N. Magnenat-Thalmann, Efficient self-collision detection on smoothly discretised surface animation using geometrical shape regularity, *Computer Graphics Forum (Eurographics'94 Proceedings)*, 13(3), 155–166, Blackwell Publishers, 1994.

[22] P. Volino and N. Magnenat-Thalmann, The SPHERIGON: a simple polygon patch for smoothing quickly your polygonal meshes, *Computer Animation '98 Proceedings*, 1998.

13
Artificial Garments for Synthetic Humans in Global Retailing

G.K. Stylios and T.R. Wan

Abstract

This chapter puts forward the concept of global retailing or remote shopping, and describes and discusses new interdisciplinary technologies which have been developed and integrated in the fashion, textiles and apparel industries. The concept of global retailing will enable customers to see themselves performing "Virtual Wearer Trials" of garments and manufacturing companies to trade without having to sell to retailing shops. The contribution of a physically based drape cloth model with collision detection able to animate garments on fully skinned virtual humans is discussed. The model is based on cloth mechanics so that it can produce realistic animations of any draped cloth. The mechanical properties as well as the performance and sewing optimization predictions are generated in an online information service system called Cybertex. Personal data details such as shape and body measurement can be measured by the use of body scanners or simulated using geometry. Consequently, three systems are integrated together: cloth simulation, human body measurement and reconstruction, and a network of technical and trade data. The three systems are connected via an interactive visualization network.

13.1 Introduction

In the Research Centre of Excellence COMIT, at the University of Bradford, and under the generic name of Intelligent Textile and Garment Manufacture, we have been carrying out important research projects for industry. These projects deal with understanding important interactions between materials, machines and humans in order to provide the next generation of textile and fashion technologies. These new technologies advocate the much-needed own technology concept, which in itself is innovative and can stretch the imagination of managers and technicians to produce innovative applications and products in their own sector.

Textile materials are not like steel, plastic or concrete. They are very diverse, highly deformable, not uniform, nonlinear and visco-elastic, and are to some extend time dependent. Therefore a solution for one material is not necessarily the same one for another material, and hence generic approaches to future development must be specialized and interdisciplinary. Textile and fashion products have a short market life and their demand is dependent upon fashion styles, prices etc.; consequently flexibility and quick response in design and production are paramount.

This chapter highlights the integration of three important project research areas attempting to introduce new ways of designing, selling and producing garments; hence the title of "Global Retailing", which is an area of enormous interest because it challenges the conventional way of buying, selling, producing and distributing clothes. The three areas are: the simulation and animation of garments and humans, which is dealt with in our Artificial Clothes for Synthetic Humans project; the online exchange of technical and trade data which is dealt with in our Cybertex project; and the online synthetic human modelling system covered by our Synthetic Reality project. These technologies are available at our Research Centre of Excellence COMIT; the Centre for Objective Measurement and Innovation Technologies which today has 350 member companies who are users of advanced technologies. High street names such as Austin Reed, Aquascutum, and Laura Ashley are some of the member companies using COMIT as a resource centre.

13.2 The Concept of Global Retailing

The new philosophy of the 21st century for society will be based upon the concept of "living without frontiers" [1], with companies able to "compete globally". Research and development can now provide the required techno-infrastructure for the "global retailer" which will force restructuring of the industry and provide new possibilities in consumer buying methods and new opportunities in the supply chain.

Corporate strategists are already urging companies to develop electronic retailing or "buying by wire", and there are large companies which have committed themselves to this. Let us consider a scenario of providing techno-intelligence for buying a garment. The time has come when, in the comfort of our homes, we can decide to buy our clothing. The flowchart in Fig. 13.1 highlights the online link between the so-called global retailer, our home and the textile industry. It is possible that we could have the despatch of a tailored garment within two days. The reality is that even a garment virtual wearer trial may not be far away. Our work in 3D modelling and visualization at the fabric/garment/human interface has produced a fully skinned synthetic human model based on real body shape data, dressed with a garment which has been simulated and animated for a Virtual Wearer Trial.

The simulation of the garment is based on a physical model which uses real fabric mechanical properties in modelling the drape behaviour of the fabric. Collision detection algorithms enable the garment to be animated on a geometric model of a fully skinned synthetic human, which is in turn animated by modelling skeleton locomotion [2].

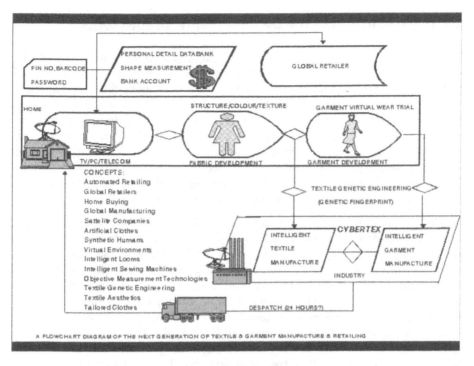

Figure 13.1 Global retailing.

This concept is therefore based on three systems which are integrated with each other: the real shape/body characteristics; the modelling, animation and visualization of the draped garment on the synthetically real human; and the online electronic communication network of exchange of textile technical and trade data for products and processes, as shown in Fig. 13.2.

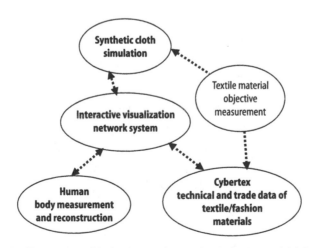

Figure 13.2 The interaction of the three systems that contribute to the concept of global retailing.

13.3 Introduction to the Dynamic Fabric Drape Model

Fabric materials are assumed to be continuum shell structures. It is realized that they display macrostructural properties [3] and therefore behave quite differently from other industrial materials, for instance steel and rubber. Successful application of finite element/finite difference methods has only been seen thus far in the engineering of materials other than textiles. Great efforts using different approaches to modelling cloth have been made [2, 4–7]. However, the interest in these efforts is more in the visual appearance rather than simulating the actual cloth behaviour in accordance with its engineering principles. More compromises have therefore had to be introduced, and modelling real fabric behaviour in terms of engineering principles remains a very difficult area of research.

In order to model fabric behaviour more accurately, our previous drape model [2] has been expanded into a new model, which uses the concept of finite elements. For the configuration of very thin shell materials like fabrics, we assume that there is a neutral surface between the top and bottom surfaces of the shell. The configuration of an element is shown in Fig. 13.3. Stresses in such a neutral surface can be of the membrane type but cannot be bending stresses. Although the response of the shell to loading usually involves a combination of bending and membrane actions, because these deformations are very small it is possible that they can be treated independently. In our case, although the corresponding deformations of fabric can be very large, they can still be treated separately. The reasons for the treatment above are mainly due to the following facts: a great difference exists between the high stiffness of the membrane strains and the bending strains, and fabric materials can always recover their original flat shape and dimensions after being deformed. The fabric deformation behaviour can therefore be regarded as a case of a developable surface [8], in which the restriction to use small deflection theory can be relaxed. The resulting differential equations are therefore simplified and the numerical difficulties due to ill-formed coupled equations are avoided.

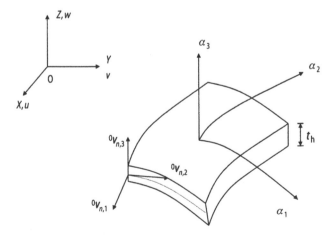

Figure 13.3 The configuration of a fabric element.

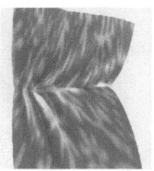

Figure 13.4 An example of fabric deformation during a sewing simulation.

Consequently, in this approach the strain components are first evaluated, corresponding to the coordinate axes aligned with the mid-surface of the shell element and establishing a strain–displacement matrix for these local strain components. Then the stiffness matrix of the element is obtained by numerical integration. The details of this approach will be reported elsewhere. The corresponding transformation between the local system and the global system can also be established, and the governing differential equations of fabrics can then be derived from the distribution of the system energies over all fabric elements of the material. The final global drape equations can be written as a general form:

$$\tilde{M}\ddot{a} + \tilde{C}\dot{a} + \tilde{K}a = F$$

where $\tilde{M}$, $\tilde{C}$ and $\tilde{K}$ are the mass matrix, damping matrix and stiffness matrix respectively. $\tilde{F}$ is the distributed external force vector applied to each node. Since a large number of nodes are used for the geometrical configuration of the loop structure, it is convenient to express the equations or matrices in an implicit form rather than in an explicit one. Since each node has been coded with node coordinates, a computer program can be used to arrange the elements of the matrices in the equations above. The solution of these equations can be found numerically [9].

It should be mentioned that in the above formulation only two basic shell assumptions are applied. The lines originally normal to the shell mid-surface remain straight and the transverse normal stresses remain zero, which is equivalent to using a general nonlinear shell theory [10].

Figure 13.4 shows an example of a complex fabric deformation during a sewing simulation, Fig. 13.5 shows an example of fabric drape over a table, and Fig. 13.6 shows an example of garment simulation. Figure 13.7 shows a sequence of a virtual wearer trial, where an effective collision detection algorithm has been used [11].

13.4 Human Body Measurement and Reconstruction

To assess a garment in a virtual environment, a synthetic human model must be present. People would also like to see themselves performing virtual wearer trials of

Figure 13.5 An example of fabric drape over a table.

Figure 13.6 An Example of garment simulation with collision detection.

Figure 13.7 Sequence of a virtual wearer trial.

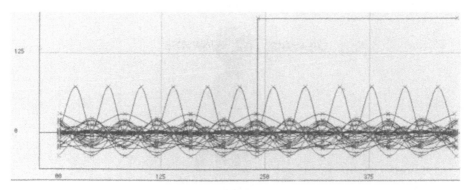

Figure 13.8 An example set of motion curves.

garments they would like to wear, as in the conventional buying of clothes. The objectives of the human body measurement and reconstruction are to provide the opportunity to users and customers to perform virtual wearer trials. To that effect their body shape must be reconstructed, and hence we have a hybrid approach of our so-called synthetically real humans concept.

In order to develop a generic geometrical human model, a skeleton model was first developed, which can be regarded as a special linkage system, like an industrial robot or a mechanical manipulator. The skeleton movement is calculated using the joint angles and its reference points. The interest in developing such a model is to focus on fabric dynamic behaviour efficiently, where a relatively simple animation model may be adequate. Then a complex synthetic human model was developed which is able to complete a number of basic body movements, like walking, running or cat-walking by a woman or a man. Figure 13.8 shows an example of motion curves, which control the skeleton joints over given time steps. These motion curves are generated in a local coordinate system relative to the position and orientation of the joints in a hierarchical structure.

In order to produce a realistic representation of individual persons, a measurement technique which can determine the human body precisely is essential. Currently there are two different approaches and two kinds of systems are being developed at COMIT. The first system uses a laser-guided camera 3D scan system, which can provide precise measurements of body data. The second system uses image recognition techniques, which provide all the 3D features and shape curves of the individual body shape plus a set of different views of the face image.

The next task is the body reconstruction in our Synthetically Real Human project. Our approach is based on a generic geometrical model of a human, the shape and size of which can be controlled or generated parametrically: either a man or a woman whose body size and shape can be synthetically changed online by providing their real size measurements as users of the system. The face characteristics can also be reconstructed online by using a camera. The latter is ongoing research which was initiated a few years ago. Figure 13.9 shows a skinned synthetic human woman on an animated skeleton.

It should be mentioned here that another task of modelling the dynamic behaviour of fabrics in garments is concerned with the interactions between the fabric and the

Figure 13.9 A skinned synthetic human woman on an animated skeleton.

synthetic human body. We therefore developed a precise technique that is able to detect collisions efficiently and reliably [9]. The collision detection algorithm presented is based on a hierarchical fabric database. In principle, we define the vertices of a garment surface according to a hierarchical structure. The collision process will start in the highest level nodes. If a distance threshold is reached, which indicates potential collisions could occur in lower level nodes, the system will search further. The same principle will be applied to each level except the base level. If the threshold is not reached, the system will skip the search to lower node levels.

13.5 Online Electronic Communication Network on Textile Technical and Trade Data – Cybertex Network

Cybertex is based on commercial data for the specification and prediction of materials such as yarns, fabrics, finishes and garments [12]. To that effect a number of measurement systems, prediction and interpretation procedures, and an industrial implementation have been established at COMIT in Bradford. Industrial companies are interacting with this facility via the Cybertex system for fast access to measurement, interpretation and prediction data for newly developed yarns, fabrics, and garments with diverse properties and performance characteristics, and for trade data.

This system is based on modelling the interaction of fabric with the machinery during processing and/or with the seam quality of the joined garment. Prediction is made of the difficulty during production and/or the maximum quality that can be achieved during sewing without problems associated with unbalanced seams, uneven seams, deformed seams, damaged stitches etc. This system can also provide advice on the amount that the property magnitudes need to be altered in order to correct the processability of the fabric, usually through finishing or re-finishing treatments, establishing the concept of engineering or re-engineering fabrics. Consequently now and in the future, whether in yarn spinning, fabric making, fabric finishing, or clothing, the key issue is to be able to use and interpret data objectively so that companies can communicate technically with their suppliers and optimize their production process using just-in-time methods. Companies connected to Cybertex are able to exchange data and specifications of products for effective customer/supplier interaction.

Each company can access optimum production requirements by accessing a given product database, unique to each company, which has visual as well as online interpreted results and report generation for easy implementation at the shop floor. Historical data can be used by each company in a number of intelligent ways, whether in routine quality assurance, product development or production optimization. Figure 13.10 shows some output examples from the Cybertex network.

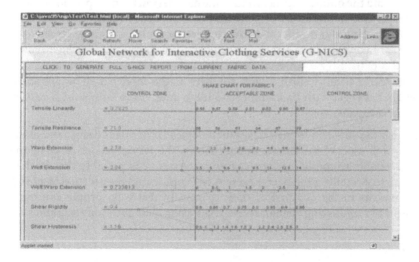

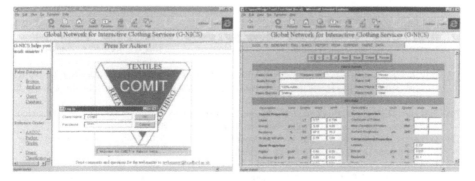

Figure 13.10 Example output from the Cybertex network.

Once we have selected or produced the right yarn and fabric for the particular tailored garment, which is simulated using our virtual wearer trial concept, the specifications of the fabric are provided in the form of a bar code which accompanies the cut fabric pieces to the sewing room of the nearest company to the home of the customer. Intelligent sewing machines can now stitch the fabric into the desired garment design with the optimum sewing machine conditions, ensuring the best achievable quality just in time. Online optimization of industrial sewing machines has already been achieved in our Intelligent Sewing Machine project [13] by a fuzzy–neural model connecting machine, material, and human. The tailor-made garment can then be dispatched to the customer in 24–48 hours.

13.6 Conclusion

This chapter has reported on the concept of global retailing and has demonstrated how three independently researched areas have been integrated for its realization: the 3D modelling of fabric, the measurement of body data for the reconstruction of humans, and the online technical and trade data network which provides real material properties. It should be emphasized that our cloth model is based on engineering principles and aims to simulate real textile behaviour of fabric/garment materials. Likewise, in the reconstruction of the body we have highlighted the possibility of using one's own measurement data as the input to the system so that a virtual wearer trial of clothes with the user as the model may be possible. The Cybertex network, with its commercial trade data, links homes with textile and garment companies.

Our aim is to provide new generic methodologies for garment design and manufacture as well as entertainment. Consequently, the fabric model in development should be able to model various textile materials. It is possible that in the near future virtual retailing will become a reality. People could see a virtual fashion show of themselves in the comfort of their lounge. In this way, people can purchase garments by conducting virtual wearer trials using their own body size and shape.

References

[1] G. Stylios, Living without frontiers: the global retailer, *International Journal of Clothing Science and Technology*, 7(4), 5–8, 1995.
[2] G. Stylios, T.R. Wan, and N. J. Powell, Modelling the dynamic drape of garments on synthetic humans in a virtual fashion show, *International Journal of Clothing Science and Technology*, 8(3), 95–112, 1996.
[3] D.W. Lloyd, The analysis of complex fabric deformation, in *Mechanics of Flexible Fibre Assemblies* (ed. J.W.S. Hearle, J.J. Thwaites, and J. Amirbayat). NATO Advanced Study Institute Series E: Applied Science No. 38, Sijthoff and Noordhoff, 1988, pp. 311–342.
[4] R. Boulic, N.M. Thalmann, and D. Thalmann, A global human walking model with real-time kinematic personification, *The Visual Computer*, 6(6), 344–358, 1990.
[5] D.E. Breen, D.H. House, and M.J. Wozny, A particle-based model for simulating the draping behaviours of woven cloth, *Textile Research Journal*, November, 663–685, 1994.
[6] P. Volino, M. Courchesne, and N.M. Thalmann, Versatile and Efficient techniques for simulating cloth and other deformable objects, *Computer Graphics Proceedings*, Annual Conference Series, 1995, pp. 137–144.

[7] B. Eberhardt, A. Weber, and W. Strasser, A fast, flexible, particle-system model for cloth draping, *Computer Graphics in Textile and Apparel, IEEE Computer Graphics and Applications*, 52–59, 1996.
[8] A.C. Ugural, *Stress in Plates and Shells*, McGraw-Hill, New York, 1981.
[9] O.C. Zienkiewicz and R.L. Taylor, *The Finite Element Method*, Vol. 2. McGraw-Hill, New York, 1991.
[10] Klaus-Jurgen Bathe, *Finite Element Procedures*, Prentice Hall, Englewood Cliffs, NJ, 1996.
[11] G. Stylios and T.R. Wan, A new collision detection algorithm for garment animation, *International Journal of Clothing Science and Technology*, 10(1), 38, 1998.
[12] G. Stylios and J.O. Sotomi, The Cybertex network, *Proceedings of World Textile Conference*, Thessaloniki, Greece. The Textile Institute, 1997.
[13] G. Stylios and O.J. Sotomi, A neuro-fuzzy control system for intelligent sewing machines, *Intelligent Systems Engineering*, IEE Publication, No. 395, pp. 241–246, 1994.

14

CATS: A Multimedia Tool for Scenographic Simulation in Theatre and TV

F. Martínez, M. Bermell, O. Belmonte, J. Sevilla, C. Romero and R. Rodríguez

Abstract

The pre-production phase of a theatre play or a TV program is a time-consuming task. The number of professionals involved in the design of the scenography and choreography of a play implies collaborative work. The work of each technician is essentially handcraft due to the lack of computer tools that offer integrated multimedia capabilities sufficient for presenting the scenographic and choreographic elements involved in a play.

In this chapter we describe a multimedia tool, CATS, for the design and presentation of a virtual *mise en scène* of a play or a TV show. We will focus the discussion on the real-time graphics module. This tool is the result of an Esprit project and its design and implementation has involved technicians in several European universities as well as people from theatre and TV.

The result is a tool to be used as a medium for discussing ideas among different artist and professionals (directors, actors, lighting technicians, choreographers, musicians etc.) and getting an accurate vision of the whole play or TV production in the pre-production phase. In addition, it can also be used as a virtual simulation for presentation purposes.

Our tool has been developed to run on low-cost platforms (PCs) using Microsoft Windows NT™.

The main challenge of CATS has been the combination of different time-consuming processes in a low-cost platform. As a result, our module is able to produce a 10–15 Hz frame rate of a medium-complex 3D lighted scene (5000 polygons) of sufficient quality inside a multimedia environment (with 2D actors moving in the 3D scene with dialogue and sound effects).

14.1 Introduction

The first step in the process of producing a play or a TV program is the pre-production phase. In this stage, the general ideas about the play or TV production are defined and discussed to reach the definitive project. Although it is neither the most expensive nor labour-intensive task, it is one of the riskiest phases in the whole project's evolution. Basically, in this step the director exchanges ideas with a group of professionals in different fields (lighting, sound, decorators, actors etc.) to study the feasibility of the different aspects of the project. As a result of this stage, the director has different material to present to the producer. Based on this material the producer studies the possibility of producing the performance.

The way in which this phase develops, as well as the final result presented to the producer, depends on each director. The use of models for discussing the scenes and presenting them is extensive, although some directors prefer to script the different scenes with the aid of drawings.

The use of computers in the pre-production stage has been limited to word processors or 3D photorealistic renderings of static scenes. In recent years, tools for composing multimedia presentations have appeared in the market (Director, HyperCard), but they are not oriented to 3D graphics, although new plug-ins for Director have 3D capabilities. The major drawback to these tools are the implicit programming languages they provide to exploit all the capabilities of the tool (in the case of Director, the language is Lingo), which are inadequate for non-programming users.

New tools and technologies have been tested in the pre-production phase of a play, mainly in the field of collaborative work and teleconferencing; a good example is the Gertrude Stein Repertory Theatre of New York [1], which use network-based applications to exchange information between the director, actors, technicians, and other professionals in different locations around the world.

In other stages of production, the use of computers is more extended (see, for example, references to specific Macintosh applications in [2]). Lighting technicians use computers to define and manage light sources. Architects use CAD tools to design the stage. In TV the use of computers is more extensive, especially in the creation of special visual effects via image processing or 3D rendering and animation in the post–production phase.

There have also been attempts to using the new Virtual Reality technologies in theatre performances, such as the "The Adding Machine" performance at Kansas University [3]. Other researchers have studied interactions between real and synthetic actors or have focused on the creation of highly interactive computer narrative spaces [4].

In this chapter, we present work performed within the European Esprit project CATS (Computer Aided Theatrical Score). The aim of CATS was to develop a computer multimedia tool for creating a virtual performance of a play or TV programme running on a personal computer under a commercial operating system. Virtual performance means a visualization of every act of the play or part of the TV program in real time, that is, interactively. The design carried out with the aid of CATS include stage design, lighting design, sound effects, actors' dialogue, actors' movements and synchronization of all the events in a time line. This tool should be useful for sharing ideas and discussing solutions among the different professionals involved in the pre-production of a performance (lighting technicians, sound technicians, director, actors, guionists etc.), as well as being able to build a virtual prototype of the future performance for presentation purposes.

14.2 User Requirements

For this work, a technical team was assembled, consisting of a group of theatre directors, lighting technicians and TV producers, which we will refer to as the "users". These professionals are people with over ten years' experience in their respective fields with an active role in the present day. The requirements of the tool were the following:

- The tool must be easy to use for non-computer-familiar users
- The cost of creating a virtual performance should be small compared with the effort employed today in the pre-production phase.
- The tool should be a real-time application.
- The tool should run on a low-cost platform such as the PC.
- Although the graphic module does not use photorealistic rendering techniques, the virtual performance must offer sufficient aesthetic quality to *suggest* aesthetical results such as lighting effects, sound effects or actors' movements.

The novelty of CATS consists in the challenge of designing and integrating the different modules to get a real-time multimedia tool running on a PC and the absence of this kind of computer tool in the field of theatre and TV scenography.

The rest of the chapter is devoted to the description of the real-time graphics module, ending with a brief view of the whole CATS tool.

14.3 General System Architecture

The architecture of CATS (Fig. 14.1) takes advantage of the facilities provided by rge Windows NT™ Operating System and OLE™ technology. These provide the underlying framework that makes possible communication between the different modules of the tool. There are five modules in CATS:

- A real-time graphics module in charge of the management and visualization of the 3D information, lighting and cameras.
- A sound and synthetic voice module in charge of creating and managing the voices of the actors as well as the special sound effects.
- A real-time synthetic actors module. This creates and manages articulated sketched actors based on assigning pre-defined movements to each actor, obtaining more complex movements by adding simple movements.
- A synchronization module, which controls the time and the state of each module in the time line.
- A core module, which controls the relationship between modules and maintains the coherence of the database.

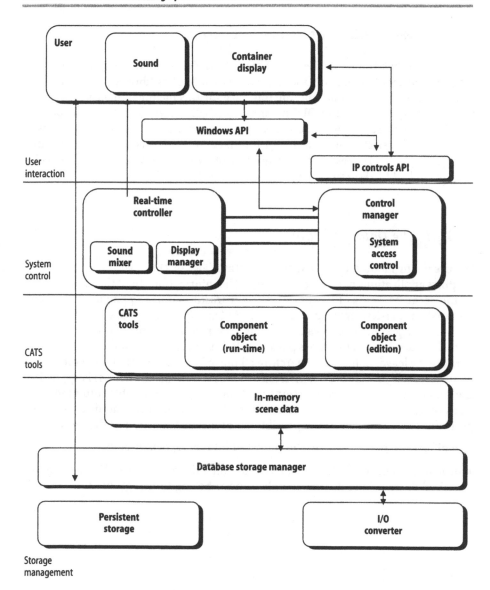

Figure 14.1 CATS architecture (© CATS Consortium 1998).

A Graphical User Interface (GUI) offers a simple interface to the user to activate the functionality offered by each module.

Each module is a component object (more concretely, an OLE document) that uses the servers included in the document (normally dynamic link libraries (.dll files)) in which the functionality of the module is implemented. Each module can offer several interfaces to the user independent of the GUI when the interface is very specific to the module (e.g. the texture tab for adding textures to 3D objects).

14.3.1 Real–Time Graphics Module Architecture

Our module has three well-separated parts: the data structure, which contains information about the active 3D scene, a set of dynamic link libraries containing the functionality of the module, and the interface for specific functionality. The third part is mainly comprised of OLE documents (OCX controls) that offer a specific interface when a service is requested (e.g. if the user chooses the option to apply a texture to the selected 3D objects, an interface for pre-visualizing and selecting textures appears). The rest is actually the core of the module. More about OLE technology applied to 3D graphics can be found in [5].

14.3.1.1 The Data Structure

We use in our module a classical data structure (Fig. 14.2) for real-time computer-graphics applications named Scene Graph. The information about the 3D structure of the scene as well as its properties (rigid trasformations applied, texture and material properties, lighting etc.) are stored in different classes of nodes that constitute a graph. Its equivalent tree is traversed each time the tool needs to refresh the scene (about 15 times per second). The nodes that contain the geometric data are the leaves of the tree. Therefore all the information contained in the nodes of higher levels (mainly rigid transformations or level of detail choices) is applied to the geometry. The user's interactions with the scene are translated into modifications of parameters inside concrete nodes of the graph. These modifications are performed each frame, making possible the real-time behaviour of the module.

The different types of node can be classified into three main groups:

• *Structural nodes*: these are in charge of building the node tree and managing the method of traversing it. Three kinds of node belong to this group: the "group"

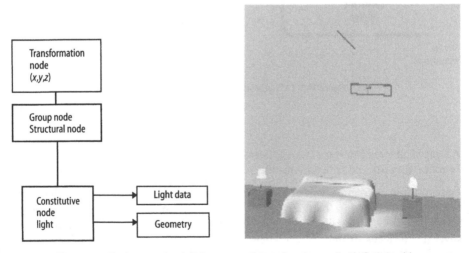

Figure 14.2 The data structure of a light source and image of a spot source (inside the rectangle).

node (which groups a bound of nodes), and the "switch" and"level of detail" nodes, which both manage the way in which the tree is traversed. This means that these nodes select the active leaves of the tree and, therefore, the 3D objects that have to be drawn each frame.

- *Constitutive nodes*: these contain the visual information of the scene. They are of three types: Geometric nodes, which store the geometrical information, lights nodes, which include data about light definition, and camera nodes, which contain the parameters of a camera.

- *Transformation nodes*: these are the nodes that apply affine transformations to the constitutive nodes, translations, rotations and scaling factors. They are named "Dcs".

All the objects in the graphics module have the same structure and are handled in the same way. More information about this subject can be found in [6].

14.3.1.2 The Functionalities

The different functionalities operate over the information stored in the Scene Graph of the active scene. The functionalities are essentially a set of methods of a class (using the concept of a class in C++) used by instances of objects of this class or using heritance. The definition of classes and their methods form several dynamic link libraries (dll) offered as a service to the component object.

Each class is referred to a different type of node of the Scene Graph and contains the methods that use the information stored in the correspondent kind of node. The "View" class is a special class derived from the common "Document" class that contains the method "DrawScene". This method traverses the Scene Graph applying the different drawing instructions. The drawing instructions are implemented with the basic drawing instructions included in the OpenGL™ library that are sent to the specific hardware of the graphic board or to the CPU as default. The "View" class is activated by external events generated by the user (such as scaling the view window or clicking with the mouse inside it) and processed by the operating system, and actually constitutes a drawing loop. The refresh rate of the scene varies depending on the complexity of the view and its value falls within a range of 5 to 25 frames per second running on a Pentium™ PC with an AGP data bus (a typical configuration at present).

14.3.2 Functional Model of CATS

There are two different modes of working with CATS: the editing mode and the simulation mode. The editing mode corresponds to the authoring part of the work. The user designs the scene and the scenography, adding lights and cameras as well as the actors' movements and dialogue. In this mode, the graphics module offers interaction with CATS via a mouse. The mouse is used to sketch the plane of a stage, and to select, move, rotate and scale 3D objects, as well as to open context menus and dialogs to give properties to 3D objects, lights and cameras. The intensive use of the mouse is the penalty for the easy-to-use requirement. The tool sacrifices accuracy to obtain the final result quickly, adhering to the philosophy that what the user is creating is not an accurate scenography or CAD model but a sketch of an idea for discussing with or presenting to other people.

In the simulation mode, the synchronization module which controls CATS is used. Following the time line, this module triggers the behaviours (actors' movements, dialogue and sound, mainly) that the user designed in editing mode. The simulation mode does not create an animation. It does not need a pre-calculation process (one of the requirement is real-time work), so the user can stop the simulation, make changes in the behaviour of any dynamic object and then come back immediately to simulation mode to see the changes carried out. For the same reason, if there is no camera planning in the designed scene, the user can navigate through the scene (that is, to see the scene from different points of view) in simulation time using the mouse.

Both the editing and simulation modes are semantically well separated by the trigger agent. In editing mode it is *the user* who activates the different functionalities of the graphic module with the mouse or the keyboard. In simulation mode is *the time* that the agent uses, reading the time line of the synchronization module, to trigger the different functionalities of the tool.

14.4 User Functionality Inside the Real-Time Graphics Module

In this section we will explain the main user functionality provided by the real-time graphics module. We will follow the same logical steps that a user would do to design a scene from scratch.

14.4.1 Stage Design

CATS is oriented towards plays or TV studio productions, although outdoor scenes can be imported from modelling tools such as Alias™. In a first approach, our module provided the user with a limited database of models representing the most common stages or environments. However, this is a very limited solution; it is likely that the models in the database will not fit the needs of a concrete performance. CATS provides a Stage Designer Tool based on a sheet of paper metaphor. This metaphor has already been exploited for designing graphical interfaces based on windows and widgets (in the style of Motif) using paper-like sketches on computers [7]. In our tool, the user designs the shape of the stage, creating a 2D design with top and front views, giving it an adequate size by using figures. Once the 2D design is finished, CATS automatically converts the 2D design to a 3D model. The 2D sketch has the role of a interface between the idea of the stage and the 3D model obtained as result, with the advantage that the system keeps the 2D sketch in a file, giving the user the opportunity to modify the idea and obtain another new 3D model based on the updated sketch. This gives our tool great flexibility and supports a design based on incremental improvements of the original idea. Other interface tools for sketching ideas in 3D worlds have been designed using other approaches [8]; one remarkable example is [9], which constitutes a direct interface between the user and 3D worlds. Our interface has two main advantages for users: it supports the possibility of modification, since the 2D sketch is stored in a file, and it is very natural for users coming from art and design, because of the extensive use of planes in these areas.

The stage design begins in the scaled black window of the tool, designing the shape of the stage's floor with the mouse (Fig. 14.3). We have chosen the mouse to approximate classical paper and pen sketching. The user approximates the desired shape by clicking and dragging the mouse to defining segments.

Once the floor is defined, the user can place two kinds of element: panels and platforms. The panel is an abstraction of a wall, and hence is any element that is placed on the floor and grows upwards normal to the floor. The platform, in contrast, can be placed on the floor, suspended in the air or attached to a panel, and represents a surface parallel to the floor but with a defined height. Both panels and platforms can be given holes to simulate windows, arches and so on (Fig. 14.4). Panels and platforms are presented in 2D as irregular quadrilaterals and are converted into irregular prisms.

The user can place these elements using the mouse and can change their colours too. An auxiliary 3D view (Fig. 14.5) is displayed when requested to show the 3D aspect of the design; thus the user has an accurate idea of the final result at any step of the design phase.

Lastly, the final 2D sketch is save into a file and CATS converts it to a 3D scene (Fig. 14.6). All the 2D elements are divided into triangles or meshes adequate for real-

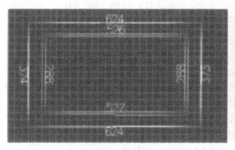

Figure 14.3 2D Design of a stage, top view.

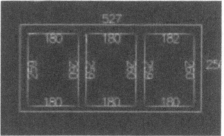

Figure 14.4 Designing the holes in a wall, front view.

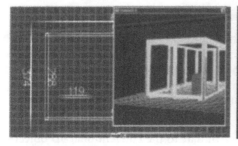

Figure 14.5 Checking the 3D aspect of the sketch.

Figure 14.6 The 3D result.

time graphics. Then, the program calculates the texture coordinates for all the geometric elements.

There are two sides to this tool. On one hand, with the Stage Designer we provide a fast and easy tool to design the basic appearance of the required stage. On the other hand, we lose in realism. The result is a simple stage that constitutes a reference (an idea) of the real stage or space where the action takes place.

The different professionals that tested the tool found it surprisingly versatile and powerful for expressing simple ideas about space, although limited in its possibilities, mainly in panels.

14.4.2 Set Design

3D objects are selected from the CATS object database and placed in the 3D stage by dragging them with the mouse. The interaction with the objects database is very easy for non-expert computer users. The user can browse in the database with a 3D visualizer that draws the selected object rotating in a small 3D window. The database is consistent concerning the model's style, and classifies the 3D models by subject. Each model has two or three levels of detail (LOD) and its complexity does not reach the normal limits for real-time rendering (< 1000 polygons); exceptions are some models of pre-defined stages.

The objects are made of nodes as described in Section 14.3.1.1. Actually, they are a higher level of abstraction. An object can be seen as a tree constituted by a group node as the root node, two DCS nodes that apply the geometric transformations to the object from its centre of gravity or from an arbitrary axis, and other nodes, ending with the leaves constituted by geometric nodes (see Fig. 14.2).

Once the user has inserted an object in the scene, he or she can translate, rotate and scale it using the left mouse button and the keyboard in a 'click and drag' fashion. So the placement and the final spatial orientation of an object are defined visually, accomplishing the easy-to-use requirement. If more accuracy is needed, the user can input the spatial coordinates of the object using the position tab of the object's dialog window. In addition to the spatial properties of the 3D object, there are a material palette and texture bitmaps that can be defined using different context dialogs activated when the user clicks the right mouse button.

14.4.3 Lighting Design

The lighting model provided by the OpenGL library consists of an Ambient–Diffuse–Specular illumination model combined with Gouraud shading. The major drawback of this model is the absence of shadows. In contrast, the lighting effects on the 3D surfaces are quite good, and this was evaluated as good enough for CATS purposes by the team of users. Also, it is an adequate model for real-time graphics.

The data structure of a light source is very similar to the conventional 3D object structure. The difference consists in the leave node, which is a light node instead of a geometric node. Associated with this data tree there is also another tree which contains the 3D representation of a lamp in the case of a finite light source.

The user handles the finite light sources like 3D objects, applying translations, rotations and scaling transformations. In addition, the user sets the light properties using a context menu. The properties include the type of source, the RGB values for Ambient–Diffuse–Specular illumination mode, and the lighting cone cut-off angle.

We have determined that the addition of a new finite light source decreases performance by around 6% (Section 14.5.1 considers this subject further). For this reason, if the scenography requires a large number of lights, the user should work by thinking about "light volumes" instead of placing the actual number of required finite light sources.

14.4.4 Camera Placement

The camera is actually a metaphor for setting the point of view of the scene. Similar to the finite light source representation, the camera concept has a geometric structure. In addition to the 3D shape, the camera's position and orientation fix the scene's point of view as in a real camera. The camera supports the same affine transformations as the 3D objects (translations etc.) and is handled using the mouse's left button. The user can see the scene through the camera as a cameraman and can adjust the field of view and move the camera in the three basic degrees of freedom "camera pan", "camera tilt" and "camera roll". The camera makes it possible to choose the best places for the real cameras in a TV studio production and facilitates the camera planning of a scene by placing several cameras and activating one or another from the synchronization module.

14.4.5 Moving Point of View

The navigation system is designed to move through the scene in both editing and simulation time. There are two basic movements with this system: Trackball Mode and Fly Mode.

The trackball mode uses the paradigm of the sphere. The user moves through the scene as though he or she is on the surface of a sphere, or as if manipulating a sphere which rotates the scene. A 3D sphere appears in the CATS user interface, which can be rotated by using the mouse. The scene's point of view changes interactively with the rotation of the sphere. In addition, the trackball provides zoom-in, zoom-out and pan modes.

The fly mode is managed with the mouse pointer. Speed can be altered by clicking the left and right mouse buttons to move the point of view forward and backward. The change of view is very useful in editing mode for checking the adequate setting of 3D objects or drawing the path of an actor's displacement. For less skilful users the GUI provides buttons for the standard positions: top, side left, side right, front and back.

14.5 Graphics Module Performance and Strategies for Resource Management

14.5.1 About Performance

The performance of the whole tool in terms of efficiency should be considered separately for the two states of work described in Section 14.2.3. In editing time, we can assume that only the module in which the user is working remains active. The system's demands on the core module during the user's operations are not frequent and should not be considered as a constant load for the system. The same assumption can be made for the GUI module. Assuming this rough approach we can consider the load imposed by the graphics module when the user is editing the scenography to be the total load. In our module we can identify two parameters directly related to the performance of the graphics module: the scene's geometrical complexity (in terms of number of polygons) and the number and type of light sources in the scene. Different types of light source have different costs of efficiency. Infinite sources are drastically less hard to compute than finite sources due to the penalty of calculating the relative position of the object with respect to the source for the second type. Given a concrete type of source, the cost grows with the number of polygon vertices and with the number of light sources.

With regard to the number of polygon vertices in the scene, we can divide the lighting model analysis into two steps. In the lighting phase the illumination model needs to compute about 12 multiplications and 5 additions per vertex. In the rasterization phase the Gouraud shading requires linear interpolation of the vertex's RGB values across each polygon [10].

Adding a new light penalizes the operations in the lighting phase described above (two sources implies making the calculations twice plus three further additions for RGB values), but it does not affect the computations of the rasterization phase. It is easy to do a test with the same geometry varying the number of lights; see Fig. 14.7).

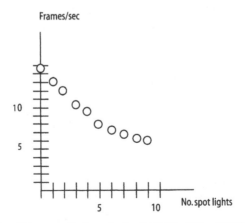

Figure 14.7 Effect of number of light sources. Hardware: Pentium II, 233 MHz; AGP bus; 128 Mbyte RAM; ATI graphics accelerator with 4 Mbyte RAM; 600 × 400 pixels viewport.

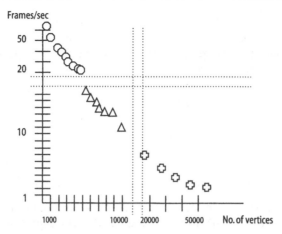

Figure 14.8 Effect of polygonal complexity. Hardware as in Fig. 14.7.

Regarding the influence of the scene's geometry on performance, it is more difficult to make estimates since the number of polygon vertices is a parameter that is involved in all the processes of a standard graphics pipeline (real or simulated). In Fig. 14.8 we show the result of increasing polygonal complexity in the graphics module.

In simulation time, the Real Time Controller (part of the core module) after looking up the table of future events and the system clock, sends messages to the different modules to produce a new step in the simulation (Fig/ 14.9). The sound/speech module presents little competition for resources (at least when using pre-recorded sound files) because the audio data is processed in the audio card, which has direct access to memory. The problem arises in the graphics and the actors modules. In addition to the ordinary computational load, there is a latency time for synchronization because the rendering is common for the two modules, since they draw in the same viewport. The Display Manager is in charge of minimizing the latency time by planning the future request of each module in the next frame.

In simulation time, the user places the point of view at a suitable position and pushes the "play" button to see the simulation. In these conditions, the Display

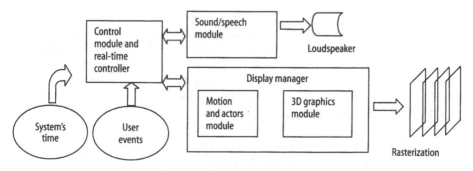

Figure 14.9 Data flow in simulation time.

Manager minimizes the latency time because there is no competition from the redrawing request. The frame rate in this situation also depends on the number of actors. In general for medium complexity scenarios (<10 000 polygons) and few actors (<10) the frame rate range is about 8 to 12 frames per second

14.5.2 Strategies for Managing Resources

The modular architecture of CATS does not imply that the modules behave independently of the rest of the system. The policy of each module must include the use of different strategies for saving and freeing resources when requested to do so by the control module. The graphics module uses different strategies to save resources.

- Use of levels of detail in the scene. Depending on the distance from the point of view to the object, the LOD nodes choose an adequate representation of the 3D object according to its geometrical complexity.
- Automatic degradation of the image. The degradation of the image is activated only in extreme cases in which the demand for resources by other modules must be met by restricting the resources available to the graphics module. The goal is to decrease the level of reality while observing the real-time constraint. The first action is to eliminate textures from the scene. The second level is to substitute Gouraud shading by flat shading. The visual impact when using these trivial techniques is high, and replacing them by other better techniques is a field for future work.

14.6 Description of the Overall CATS Tool

CATS is a multimedia system that provides the author with tools for designing scenery, actors' movements, sound and dialogue and then constructing a narrative. The authoring metaphor is a time-hierarchy style which combines the time line specification of events and the organization of the play by hierarchical composition in terms of acts, scenes and shots. In a play or a TV script the behaviour of all elements is planned from the beginning; therefore in simulation time the action goes sequentially from the beginning to the end, not allowing the possibility of choice. In this sense, CATS has a traditional approach as a multimedia system, not needing more complex approaches, such as in [11], which combine time line models with state machines to provide "some mechanism for deciding which course the narrative takes dependent of the current state of the world model".

The final result produced by CATS is a virtual performance in which actors speak and move inside a 3D environment. Many parameters in the performance can be adjusted (i.e. the tone – pitch – of the actor's voice, the colour of the lights or the duration of an actor's movement). We present now a brief description of the other modules:

14.6.1 Synthetic Actors Module

This module provides the user with synthetic human-like characters. The appearance of the actors is as line sketch based on about 30 joints (Fig. 14.10). Other, more complex, shapes are being studied, but the real-time constraint and the sharing of

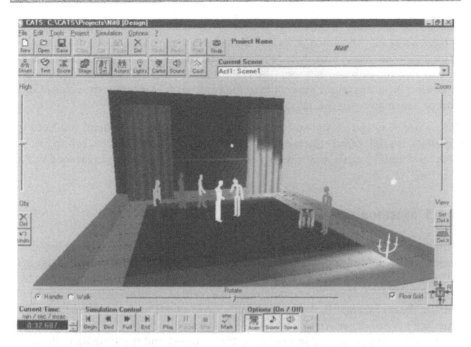

Figure 14.10 A frame of a scene in CATS during simulation. The white points are light sources.

resources with the rest of the modules makes it difficult to use more complex but more realistic shapes, such as 3D shapes with collision detection and free-form deformation.

Once the user has inserted an actor (character) into the scene, he or she has to define the actor's movements. For this purpose, the user has available a library of pre-defined basic movements, such as walk, sit down, stand up, run and bow. If the selected movement implies a displacement the user can define a path to be followed by the actor in its movement by clicking with the mouse on the stage. To build an actor's behaviour during a scene, the user must assign to the actor different move-ments from the library at different times using the time line of the synchronization module. The result is satisfactory for the main goal, which is to sketch the move-ment of an actor in the scene, but it is not realistic, specially at the boundaries of two consecutive movements (i.e. walking followed by sitting down). If the required movement is not in the database, the user has a small friendly key-frame-based editor for building his or her own movements.

The user can insert several actors in a scene and define the properties of each actor using a context menu with different tabs for directly assigning shape, voice and movement. This interface is natural for the user.

14.6.2 Sound Tool

The sound tool has two basic elements: the synthetic voice generator and the recorded sound player. The synthetic voice generator is in charge of making the dialogue of the actors in the scene. The text of the dialogue can be entered by hand or from a text file. The voice generator distinguishes the dialogue of each character by using special marks introduced in the text. The dialogue is assigned at the proper time to an actor with another tool (the synchronization tool). In the synthetic voice generator, the user assigns properties to the voice, such as whether the voice is for a man or a woman, with special tones for particular moments.

The recorded sound player executes sound files at a precise moment. It is used to introduce special sound effects in the performance. It plays standard sound files in "wav" or "midi" format and it is triggered when the "start" event is reached in the time line.

14.6.3 Synchronization Tool

With this tool (Fig. 14.11), the user synchronizes the different events along the time. The time is presented to the user as a time line. For each actor and sound (that is not dialogue) there is a time line. The user marks on the time line the main events of the performance, represented as rectangles whose vertical sides mark the start and end times of the event, and can then visually adjust two events to synchronize them. The time line metaphor was used early in the S-Dynamics system [12] (referred to in [10]) and it is implemented in many key-frame-based and multimedia tools, such as Life Forms™ or Macromedia Director™.

In addition to the direct manipulation of the synchronization tool, the GUI provides a recorder-key–based interface in which the user can "play", "pause" or go forwards or backwards along the time line. This action is automatically recognized and the scene is updated to the configuration of the current time.

14.7 Conclusions and Future Work

At present, the consortium has a first version of the tool with not all the functionality of all the modules implemented. This version runs on conventional PCs with Windows NT and has validated the architecture of CATS. Three acts of William Shakespeare's *Twelfth Night* have been implemented on this version of CATS.

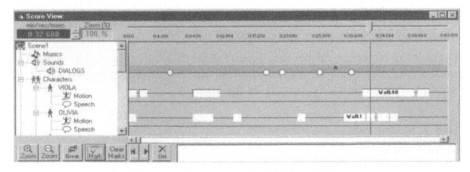

Figure 14.11 The synchronization tool with the time line.

The use of CATS as a discussion and presentation tool is also adequate for educational purposes in theatre and drama schools. Directorial students can design the ideas on a low-cost platform, a PC, using plentiful and cheap databases of sounds and 3D objects or by making the material by themselves.

Future work will be focused on the completion of the functionality of CATS. Other areas of future work are to give the 3D objects dynamic behaviour using parametric representations of motion (P-curves), to include new actor shapes, to improve the policy of the 3D module for saving resources, and to find new strategies to diminish the latency time.

Other subjects remain in technical discussion, such as the inclusion of an automatic script/play organizer that will generate the main framework of the CATS simulation from the raw text, the use of the text for quoting sound modifications (pitch) directly, and studying the possibility of implementing functionality for giving information about wardrobe and casting.

Acknowledgments

We are grateful to Salvador Bayarri, Marcos Fernandez, Inmaculada Coma and Miguel Lozano for the initial data structure of the graphics module, the run-time module, the file format definition and saving functionality, and the tool for importing Alias files, respectively.

This project has been partially funded by the EC inside the Esprit program.

References

[1] Information available via http://www.gertstein.org/.
[2] Payne, D.R. *Computer Scenographics*. Southern Illinois University Press, 1994.
[3] Unruh, D. Virtual reality in theatre: new questions about time and space. *Theatre Design & Technology*, Winter 1996, pp. 44–47.
[4] Bates, J. *The Nature of Characters in Interactive Worlds and the Oz Project*. Tech. Report School of Computer Science, Carnegie Mellon University, Pittsburgh, 1992.
[5] Hall, R. and Forsyth, D. *Interactive 3D Graphics in Windows*. Springer-Verlag, 1995.
[6] Rolf, J. and Helman, J. *Iris Performer: A high Performance multiprocessing toolkit for Real-Time 3D Graphics*. SIGGRAPH'96 Course Notes #33, New Orleans, Lousiana, 4–9 August 1996.
[7] Landay, J.A. and Myers, B.A. *Interactive Sketching for Early Stages of User Interface Design*. Proceedings of CHI'95, May 1995, pp. 29–37.
[8] Deering, M.F. The HoloSketch. VR sketching system. *Communications of the ACM*. 39(5), 54–61, 1996.
[9] Zeleznik, R., Herndon, K. and Hughes, J. SKETCH: an interface for sketching 3D scenes. *Proceedings of SIGGRAPH'96*, 4–9 August 1996, pp. 163–169.
[10] Foley, J.D., van Dam, A., Feiner, S. and Hughes, J. *Computer Graphics. Principles and Practice*, 2nd edn, pp. 868–871. Addison-Wesley, 1991.
[11] Preston, M. and Hewitt, T. Integrating computer animation and multimedia. *Proceedings of Eurographics'96*, Poitiers, France, 26–30 August 1996.
[12] Symbolics Inc. *S-Dynamics*. Symbolics, Inc. Cambridge, MA, 1985.

About the Authors

Francisco A. Martínez studied physics at the Universitat de València, specializing in electronics and computer science, ending in 1992. He began his research in telematics applied to road traffic and joined the ARTEC group (a research group specializing in real-time computer graphics) in 1995. He is now assistant professor (lecturer) in the Computer Science Department of the Universitat de València. His research areas include real-time graphics applications.

Manuel Bermell studied physics at the Universitat de València, specializing in electronics and computer science. He has worked in industry in the field of telematics applied to road transport. In 1990 he moved to the Computer Science Department of the University of Valencia. He has specialized in Windows technology applied to real-time systems. He now works in the simulation industry.

Oscar Belmonte studied physics at the Universitat de València, specializing in electronics and computer science and fundamental physics. He began his research in the ARTEC group in 1994. He has participated in projects with the local ceramic tile industry, developing tools for creating virtual and realistic environments in real time for displaying tiles. He is now assistant professor (lecturer) in the Computer Science Department of Universitat Jaume I in Castellón de la Plana, Spain.

Javier Sevilla took his degree in computer science at the Universitat Politècnica de Valencia. He joined ARTEC in 1996, collaborating on some European projects related to 3D Real-Time Graphics. He has also done research in civil simulation projects, such as a helicopter simulator. His research interest areas are 3D real-time graphics, specially 3D terrain generation.

Rafael Rodríguez took his degree in telecommunication engineering in the Universitat Politècnica de València. He belongs to the ARTEC research team. He has been researching and developing the fields of civil simulation, 3D-interfacing, synthetic actors and real-time computer graphics. His current research interests are synthetic actors for real-time graphics.

Cristina Romero took her degree in fine arts at the Universitat Politècnica de València. She collaborated in a computer animation titled "BOB" shown at the "Cinema Jove de Valencia" exhibition. She is part of the ARTEC group working on advanced real-time modelling and texturing techniques for applications with large databases. Her research interests are computer animation and modelling techniques.

15

Interpretation and Performance Assessment of Actors' Representations in Virtual Rehearsals

I.J. Palmer, W. Tang and M. Cavazza

Abstract

Virtual environments for rehearsal are useful because of their potential for distributed working and repeatability. During a rehearsal, actors' avatars must represent the actions and intentions defined by both the script and the director. In live rehearsals, assessment by the director of the actors' performance is by observation alone. However, in a virtual rehearsal environment it is possible to provide assistance in the appraisal process by analysing the avatars' motion during the rehearsal because of the digital encoding. The system described here begins with observations of events that occur at the animation engine level and progressively abstracts and refines these observations to provide a high-level behaviour and performance assessment for the director to analyse in terms of high-level "artistic" concepts. This then allows the directions to be issued that will enhance the performance in the next rehearsal.

15.1 Introduction

The application of AI techniques to dynamic environments has a long history, both in analyzing data gathered from 'real' environments and more recently from virtual environments (Badler, 1975; Nagel, 1988; Herzog, 1995). In this chapter, we describe ongoing work on a system for abstracting global goal-oriented dynamic relations between avatars. The interpretation is based on a three-layer model, the layers providing a mechanism for analyzing the time-varying scene description and the avatars' trajectories. This can then be interpreted in terms of application concepts. Multi-layered interpretation models have been proposed by the AI community, such as that used to interpret image sequences as verbal descriptions

(Herzog, 1995). We introduce quantitative analysis that takes place on the results of the third layer to measure relative performance during rehearsals.

15.2 Description of the System

The RAIVE (REALISM Artificial Intelligence Virtual Environment) system consists of a number of components. Firstly, we will consider the conceptual model of the system. Within this, the levels in the interpretation model are defined as follows:

1. Low-level event recording. This is based on changes in the state of avatars, such as changes in velocity or avatars coming into contact with objects or other avatars.
2. Medium-level processing. This takes the low-level events and examines them for patterns that might match a particular kind of simple behaviour. An example is low-level path planning, e.g. a series of changes in direction may match an obstacle avoidance trajectory.
3. High-level processing. This allows simple reasoning about the "intentions" of avatars within the given environment and the strength of these intentions, e.g. avoidance of another avatar may be quantified to be a strong aversion by maintaining a "large" separation between the avatars.

Each layer of interpretation is based on the results of the layer below (Cavazza and Palmer, 1998). From the first level, a time-ordered list of events is made available to the second level and events are taken from the head of the list, i.e. they are processed in the order that they occur. This allows simple pre- and post-condition testing that can be further refined by examining the time stamps of the events. The behaviours that are generated by the second layer are stored for querying by the third layer in a random-access storage scheme, sorted by the name of the avatar to which they apply. They maintain the time-stamp information, this being stored as start and end times for the behaviour (either of which may be left blank to signify an unknown start time or an unfinished behaviour).

15.2.1 The Graphics Event Layer

The basic level 1 information is generated as part of the graphics system's functionality as time-stamped information traces. These represent the history of changes to the graphics database. The level or granularity of event logging is user-defined for each avatar. For example, we may decide to log all velocity changes for an avatar, resulting in a sequence of time-stamped events that represent a trace of its velocity during the rehearsal, whereas we may only log collision events for a second avatar. An example of the data stored is given in Fig. 15.1.

Each event generated is added to the end of a queue of events awaiting analysis. This allows us to decouple the event processing from the graphics engine to ensure real-time graphics performance. There is a single queue for all events in the system independent of which avatar(s) they refer to. Besides velocity changes and collisions, other examples of low-level events are proximity and objects entering or

Event type: motion Time: 25 Object: Fred Position: (10,-3,50) Previous velocity: (0,0,0) New velocity: (0,0,-10)	Event type: Collision Time: 56 Object: Fred Object collided with: Bob

Figure 15.1 Examples of the event data.

leaving the scene. These are the finest grain elements on which the analysis is based. In themselves they form a description of occurrences in the system in its most primitive sense. They allow replay of sequences of actions performed by the avatars in the scene, but provide no information beyond this.

15.2.2 The Low-Level Behaviour Recognition Layer

The next level of interpretation attempts to match these low-level traces to simple behaviours. There is a set of behaviour descriptions against which traces are compared. Examples of these intermediate descriptions include "avoid", "approach", "follow" and "move-along," each of which corresponds to a different trace of events. For example, a specific set of changes in velocity in conjunction with a certain object configuration may result in an obstacle avoidance behaviour being recognised. The behaviour descriptions model a particular trace of events as a Finite State Transition Network (FSTN), against which sequences from the event queue are compared. A sequence of events may match more than one behaviour or may provide an incomplete match, so to finally decide upon a low-level behaviour it is often necessary to query the system for further information. To return to the "avoidance" example, if a sequence of velocity changes matches an "avoidance" motion, we still require that an object existed in the original path of the avatar to fully match the behaviour. This may involve querying the system to locate such an obstacle, or we may be able to infer this from the proximity of the avatar to an obstacle during the avoidance motion. Besides this avoidance motion, specific actions that are of interest during rehearsals are avatars entering a scene, moving in particular ways (e.g. moving along a wall or towards or away from objects/avatars), coming into contact with objects/avatars, and so on. These represent elements of a rehearsal that are significant factors in measuring how effective the rehearsal actually is. Figure 15.2 shows a sequence of images captured from an avatar's motion and Figure 15.3 shows an example of the state of the system during a motion interpretation. The event trace shows several changes in direction, and these are compared with transitions between states in the 'Avoidance motion FSTN'. In this case a match at this level has been found.

15.2.3 The High-Level Behaviour Interpretation Layer

The final level of interpretation builds upon the low-level behaviours to produce a model of the avatar's performance. As in the previous layer, the system takes multiple instances of the lower layer's output to try to determine a higher-level

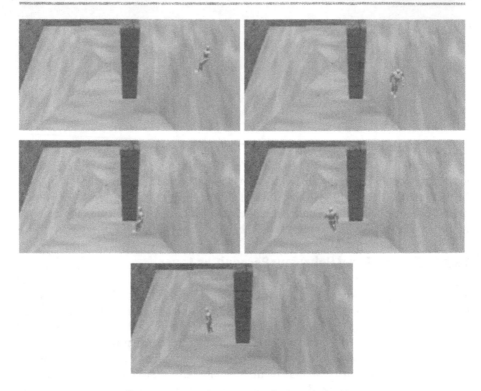

Figure 15.2 Images showing an example of an avatar's motion.

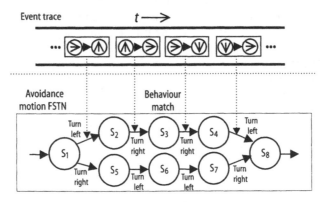

Figure 15.3 Example of detecting avoidance behaviour.

behaviour. Continuing our avoidance example, the low-level behaviour may indeed implement a higher-level "dislike" behaviour. Typically, if two actors are to exhibit a dislike for each other they will maintain a certain separation and try to avoid meetings. An avatar that exhibits the low-level avoidance of another avatar consistently, together with attempts to maximize the distance between the avatars, will be seen as exhibiting a "dislike" of the second avatar. In a rehearsal, avatars will be operating to a known script. The script would call for actors to exhibit a "dislike" of each other, so in this case the "dislike" does not need to be identified by the system. Rather, the strength of dislike and its proper realization in the course of a performance should be rated from an analysis of the motion of the avatars.

The relationship between these layers is shown in Fig. 15.4. The system tries to determine simple cause–effect relationships between sets of known occurrences on each level. The system architecture is shown in Fig. 15.5. The graphics engine is based on that of REALISM (Palmer and Grimsdale, 1994), which supports a graphics database and a set of behaviours that can be applied to objects and avatars. It has interactive and non-interactive modes of operation, supporting scripting for objects through both a custom scripting language and a C++ API. The system is extended in RAIVE to incorporate an event monitoring system that is user configurable as discussed earlier. The three layers of the interpretation scheme exist outside the graphics system and are able to read events from the event queue and query the graphics system directly.

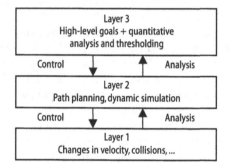

Figure 15.4 Layers of interpretation.

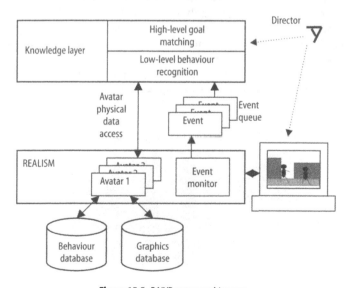

Figure 15.5 RAIVE system architecture.

15.3 Analysing Performance

In this application, the high-level goals of the avatars involved are known in advance, i.e. there is a script that is shared by all the participants. In the first instance all that is required is that this script is verified by the system, i.e. all avatars are correctly following their part of the script. This requires thresholding of the low-level behaviours that may constitute a high-level behaviour, e.g. maintaining a certain minimum distance from another avatar, having a certain relative velocity and implementing an avoidance trajectory within a certain time of nearing another avatar (see Fig. 15.6). The threshold levels form a profile for the particular behaviour, and comparing the avatar's behaviour against these profiles may yield multiple matches.

We need to measure how well a behaviour matches these profiles to provide us with a closest match. At this stage the match is based on heuristics and not on classification techniques (e.g. fuzzy logic or Bayesian networks). When we find a match, the primary behaviour should be that called for by the script. However, even if the behaviour of avatars in the system matches the script, their performance is subject to variation and this variation will be reflected quantitatively in the lower-levels. As has been discussed, the events generated at the graphics level are used to determine the low-level behaviour of avatar. The information stored with each event generated by the graphics level can be used to describe the low-level behaviour in a numerical way. This is achieved by accessing movement parameters, such as speed and direction of the movement and distance between the avatars. Instead of merely having a threshold that either accepts or rejects a particular behaviour, these values can be used to determine the strength of a behaviour. The higher-level behaviour abstractions can be drawn from the combinations of quantitative measurements and the spatial scene description at the time using a rule-based scheme.

This model can therefore serve as a basis for comparing the actions with a previous or ideal performance in terms of highly specific concepts. If one avatar is avoiding some other avatar, then from the speed of movement, separation maintained and time taken to initiate an avoidance motion we can assess how strongly the performance conveys that feeling. To achieve this we can apply weights to each of the characteristics that make up the particular behaviour that we are considering. From a director's standpoint, such a system is useful to:

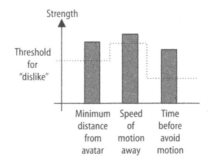

Figure 15.6 Simple thresholding of low-level behaviours.

- provide accurate measures of performance that allow ranking and comparison
- identify and quantify specific actions that account for the quality of performance

This provides the director with a quantitative measure that can be used in conjunction with the qualitative aesthetic aspects of the rehearsal.

15.4 Using Synthetic Vision

To usefully analyse the behaviour of an avatar, it is also necessary to determine what the actor can see from the avatar's position, as the relative positions, attitudes and eye contact are important elements that are not always apparent from a given 3D graphics view. These are useful because the director needs to determine that the correct actions are being taken at any time in reference to the script, and he cannot effectively view the scene from each actor's viewpoint simultaneously. While he will in general be able to view the overall orientation of the avatars, it is impossible to check the precise avatar positional relationships without repeating the rehearsal multiple times and examining the scene from different viewpoints. The need to determine that another avatar lies in the field of view of an avatar for correct identification of the "avoidance" motion has already been discussed, but this requires specific querying of the graphics database at the time when the avoidance motion was initiated. To improve upon this, a *synthetic vision* system can be used. Synthetic vision has been described for the purpose of digital actors' navigation based on the digital imaging segmentation techniques; the vision is the channel of information between the actor and its environment (Renault *et al.*, 1991; Noser and Thalmann, 1995).

We introduce an active vision concept for temporal scene description that allows the system to calculate each avatar's field of the view. This works by creating a pyramid of vision for each avatar and then clipping the object database against this volume in the same way as that used in projection viewing. An avatar's list of visible objects is generated incrementally with its movement and changes in the graphics database. The list of "visible" objects is available to the interpretation system, but it is also possible to configure the system to generate events when objects come into view (the event data is shown in Fig. 15.7). This is particularly useful for tracking the visibility of other avatars and hence analysing interpersonal attitudes that are essential to a performance. This information is added to that available at level 1 and can be used by the higher levels to assist in behaviour matching. For example, Fig. 15.8 shows an avatar "seeing" a second avatar. If the behaviour of the first avatar then matches that of avoidance and this was initiated when the second avatar

Event type: Sees	Event type: EyeContact
Time: 45	Time: 59
Object: Fred	Object: Fred
Object seen: Bob	Object seen: Bob

Figure 15.7 Examples of data for avatar "seeing" events.

Figure 15.8 General view showing view pyramids of avatars (left) and view 'seen' by avatar 1 (right).

entered the first's field of view, this will imply that the sight of the second avatar triggered this behaviour. We also define "eye contact" as occurring when two avatars' lines of sight are coincident (example event data is shown in Fig. 15.7). This is useful for reinforcing or rejecting the recognition of certain behaviours, for example prolonged eye contact would be considered as inconsistent with a 'dislike' of another avatar.

15.5 Use in the Rehearsal Environment

For use as a virtual rehearsal application we can use these quantitative behavioural descriptions as a measure of an actor's performance. Consider again a script that dictates that two characters are to dislike each other. This may be exhibited in non-verbal ways, such as moving further apart, giving a goal-directed motion that can be exhibited in several different ways dependent on the spatial scene description at the time. The quality assessment and the expense of the movement can be drawn by using a set of functions, such as length of "eye contact", average attracting speed over the defined time interval, and cost function value for the motion. The value of the cost function is the measurement of the time taken from the start position to the goal position. For example, consider the following script extract:

> Fred enters the room and sees Bob. Bob greets Fred and extends his arm to shake hands. Fred hesitates, then moves to the other side of the room and sits down, avoiding Bob's outstretched arm.

This will require that Fred exhibits a dislike of Bob, which should manifest itself in his hesitancy and the route taken by Fred. We can then use these factors to provide a measure of the effectiveness of Fred in showing his dislike of Bob. We can crudely quantify how the "dislike" is realized by measuring length of eye contact and relative motion. This will allow the director to decide if the avatars are performing well enough according to his criteria. Hence by examining information about the avatars' low-level behaviour it is possible not only to determine the behaviour of

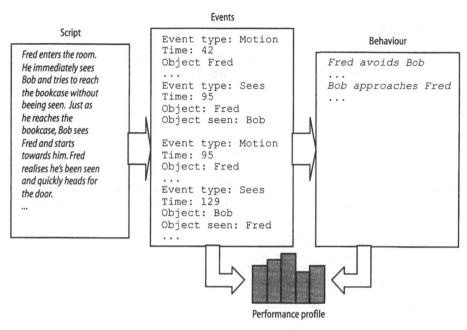

Figure 15.9 Example of the script–event–behaviour relationship

the object but also the strength of this behaviour. The system can therefore be used as a diagnostic tool for directors of virtual rehearsals. A simple example of the relationship between a script, the system events, behaviour and performance profile is shown in Fig. 15.9.

15.6 Conclusions and Further Work

The RAIVE system described here implements a three-layer system for interpreting the behaviour of avatars in a virtual rehearsal environment. As information is passed up through the layers, progressive refinement of the behaviour recognized occurs until a simple measure of the performance of the avatar is obtained against predefined criteria. This provides a director not only with a method of verifying that the script is being accurately followed, but also with quantitative data to assess the performance of the actors in the rehearsal. The performance profiles combine elements of the avatar's motion and inter-avatar relationships, and these can be directly related to aspects of the script. This can be used in combination with other non-quantitative factors (such as aesthetic ones) to make decisions about the relative qualities of different rehearsal performances.

The next step in this work is to extend and refine the set of events and behaviours that the system supports. This will allow more detailed information to be provided to the director to further inform his or her decisions. The nature of these improvements will be decided upon after use of the system in a number of test environments and productions.

Acknowledgements

Part of this work is funded by the Digital VCE under Theme 4: Image and Video Creation and Manipulation for Artificial Environments.

References

Badler, N.I. (1975) *Temporal Scene Analysis: Conceptual Description of Object Movements*, Technical report 80, Computer Science Department, University of Toronto.

Cavazza, M. and Palmer, I.J. (1998) Higher-level interpretation in virtual environments, submitted to *Applied Artificial Intelligence* (in press).

Herzog, G. (1995) From visual input to verbal output in the visual translator. *Proceedings of the AAAI Fall Symposium on Computational Models for Integrating Language and Vision*, Cambridge, MA.

Nagel, H.-H. (1988) From image sequences towards conceptual descriptions, *Image and Vision Computing* 6, 59–74.

Noser, H. and Thalmann, D. (1995) Synthetic vision and audition for digital actors, *Proceedings of Eurographics '95*, University Press, pp. 325–336.

Palmer, I.J. and Grimsdale, R.L. (1994) REALISM: reusable elements for animation using local integrated simulation models, *Computer Animation '94*, IEEE Comp. Soc. Press, pp. 132–140.

Renault, O., Thalmann, D. and Magnenat-Thalman, N. (1991) A Visual-based approach to behavioural animation, *The Journal of Visualization and Computer Animation*, 1(1), 18–21.

16
Real-Time Virtual Humans

Norman I. Badler, Rama Bindiganavale, Juliet Bourne, Jan Allbeck,
Jianping Shi and Martha Palmer

Abstract

The last few years have seen great maturation in the computation speed and control methods needed to portray 3D virtual humans suitable for real interactive applications. Various dimensions of real-time virtual humans are considered, such as appearance and movement, autonomous action, and skills such as gesture, attention, and locomotion. A virtual human architecture includes low-level motor skills, mid-level PaT-Net parallel finite state machine controller, and a high-level conceptual action representation that can be used to drive virtual humans through complex tasks. This structure offers a deep connection between natural language instructions and animation control.

16.1 Virtual Humans

Only fifty years ago, computers were barely able to compute useful mathematical functions. Twenty-five years ago, enthusiastic computer researchers were predicting that all sorts of human tasks from game-playing to automatic robots that travel and communicate with us would be in our future. Today's truth lies somewhere in-between. We have balanced our expectations of complete machine autonomy with a more rational view that machines should assist people to accomplish meaningful, difficult, and often enormously complex tasks. When those tasks involve human interaction with the physical world, computational representations of the human body can be used to escape the constraints of presence, safety, and even physicality.

Virtual humans are computer models of people that can be used

- as substitutes for "the real thing" in *ergonomic* evaluations of computer-based designs for vehicles, work areas, machine tools, assembly lines, etc. *prior to the actual construction of those spaces*
- for *embedding real-time representations of ourselves or other live participants* into virtual environments

Recent improvements in computation speed and control methods have allowed the portrayal of 3D humans suitable for interactive and real-time applications. These include:

- *Engineering*: analysis and simulation for virtual prototyping and simulation-based design.
- *Virtual conferencing*: efficient teleconferencing using virtual representations of participants to reduce transmission bandwidth requirements.
- *Interaction*: real-time graphical bodies inhabiting virtual worlds.
- *Monitoring*: acquiring, interpreting, and understanding shape and motion data on human movement, performance, activities, or intent.
- *Virtual environments*: living and working in a virtual place for visualization, analysis, training, or just the experience.
- *Games*: real-time characters with actions and personality for fun and profit.
- *Training*: skill development, team coordination, and decision making.
- *Education*: distance mentoring, interactive assistance, and personalized instruction.
- *Military*: battlefield simulation with individual participants, team training, and peace-keeping operations.
- *Design/maintenance*: design for access, ease of repair, safety, tool clearance, visibility, and hazard avoidance.

Besides general industry-driven improvements in the underlying computer and graphical display technologies, virtual humans will enable quantum leaps in applications requiring personal and live participation.

In building models of virtual humans, there are varying notions of *virtual fidelity*. Understandably, these are application dependent. For example, fidelity to human size, capabilities, and joint and strength limits are essential to some applications such as design evaluation, whereas in games, training, and military simulations, temporal fidelity (real-time behavior) is essential. Understanding that different applications require different sorts of virtual fidelity leads to the question of *what makes a virtual human right*?

- What do you want to do with it?
- What do you want it to look like?
- What characteristics are important to the success of the application?

There are gradations of fidelity in the models: some models are very advanced in a narrow area but lack other desirable features.

In a very general way, we can characterize the state of virtual human modeling along at least five dimensions, each with a wide range of realizations. Some significant datapoints along each one are listed below:

1. Appearance: 2D drawings → 3D wireframe → 3D polyhedra → curved surfaces → freeform deformations → accurate surfaces → muscles, fat → biomechanics → clothing, equipment → physiological effects (perspiration, irritation, injury)

2. Function: cartoon → jointed skeleton → joint limits → strength limits → fatigue → hazards → injury → skills → effects of loads and stressors → psychological models → cognitive models → roles → teaming

3. Time: offline animation → interactive manipulation → real-time motion playback → parameterized motion synthesis → multiple agents → crowds → coordinated teams

4. Autonomy: drawing → scripting → interacting → reacting → making decisions → communicating → intending → taking initiative → leading

5. Individuality: generic character → hand-crafted character → cultural distinctions → personality → psychological-physiological profiles → gender and age → specific individual

Different applications require specialized human models that individually optimize character, performance, intelligence, and so on. Many research and development efforts concentrate on pushing the envelope of one or more dimensions toward the right.

If the need demands it, the *appearance* of increasingly accurate physiologically and biomechanically grounded human models may be obtained. We can create virtual humans with *functional* limitations that go beyond cartoons into instantiations of known human factors data. Animated virtual humans can be created in human *time* scales through motion capture or computer synthesis. Virtual humans are also beginning to exhibit *autonomy* and intelligence as they react and make decisions in novel, changing environments rather than being forced into fixed movements. Finally, several efforts are under way to create characters with *individuality* and *personality* who react to and interact with other real or virtual people [1–6].

Across various applications, different capabilities are required as shown in Table 16.1. A model that is tuned for one application may not be adequate for another. An interesting challenge is build virtual human models with enough parameters to provide effective support across several application areas.

We have been very actively engaged in research and development of virtual human figures for over 25 years [7]. Our interest in human simulation is not unique, and others have well-established efforts that complement our own, for example [8–12], The framework for our research is a system called *Jack®*.[1] Our philosophy has led to a particular realization of a virtual human model that pushes the above five dimensions toward the more complex features. In particular, here we will look at various aspects of each of the dimensions above, primarily working toward enhanced function and autonomy.

Why are real-time virtual humans difficult to construct? After all, anyone who goes to the movies can see marvelous synthetic characters, but they have been created typically for one scene or one movie and are not meant to be reused (except possibly by the animator – and certainly not by the viewer). The difference lies in the *interactivity* and *autonomy* of virtual humans. What makes a virtual human *human* is not just a well-executed exterior design, but movements, reactions, and

---

1 Jack® is now the basis of a commercial software product distributed by Engineering Animation, Inc.

Table 16.1 Comparing applications for virtual humans.

Application	Appearance	Function	Time	Autonomy	Individuality
Cartoons	high	low	high	low	high
Games	high	low	low	medium	medium
Special effects	high	low	high	low	medium
Medical	high	high	medium	medium	medium
Ergonomics	medium	high	medium	medium	low
Education	medium	low	low	medium	medium
Tutoring	medium	low	medium	high	low
Military	medium	medium	low	medium	low

decision making which appear natural, appropriate, and context-sensitive. Communication by and with virtual humans gives them a uniquely human capability: they can let us know their intentions, goals, and feelings, thus building a bridge of empathy and understanding. Ultimately we should be able to communicate with virtual humans through all our natural human modalities just as if they, too, were real.

16.2 Levels of Control

Animating virtual humans may be accomplished through a variety of means. To build a model that admits control from other than direct animator manipulations, however, requires an architecture to support higher-level expressions of movement. While layered architectures for autonomous beings are not new [13], we have found that a particular set [14] of levels seems to provide an efficient localization of control sympathetic to both graphics and language requirements. We examine this multi-level architecture, starting with a brief description of typical graphics models and articulation structure. We then examine various motor skills that empower virtual humans with useful capabilities. We organize these skills with parallel automata at the next level. The highest level uses a conceptual representation to describe actions and allows linkage between natural languages and action animation.

16.2.1 Graphical Models

A typical virtual human model consists of a geometric skin and an articulated skeleton. Usually modeled with polygons to optimize graphical display speed, a human body may be manually crafted or more automatically shaped from body segments digitized by laser scanners. The surface may be rigid or, more realistically, deformable during movement. The latter accrues additional modeling and computational loads. Animated clothes are a desirable addition, but presently must be done offline [15, 16].

The skeletal structure is usually a hierarchy of joint rotation transformations. The body is moved by changing the joint angles and the global position and location of

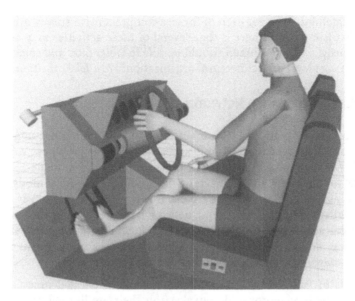

Figure 16.1 Smooth body (by Bond-Jay Ting).

the body. In sophisticated models (Fig. 16.1), joint angle changes induce geometric modifications that keep joint surfaces smooth and mimic human musculature within the body segment [17, 18]

Animated virtual humans may be controlled by real people, in which case they are called *avatars*. The joint angles and other location parameters are sensed by magnetic, optical, or video methods, and converted to rotations for the virtual body. For a purely synthetic figure, computer programs must generate the right sequences and combinations of parameters to create the desired movements. Procedures to change joint angles and body position are called *motion generators* or *motor skills*.

16.2.2 Motor Skills

Typical virtual human motor skills include:

- Playing a stored motion sequence; this may have been synthesized by a procedure, captured from a live person, or manually scripted.
- Posture changes and balance adjustments.
- Reaching (and other arm gestures).
- Grasping (and other hand gestures).
- Locomoting (stepping, walking, running, climbing).
- Looking (and other head gestures).
- Facial expressions.
- Physical force- or torque-induced movements (jumping, falling, swinging).
- Blending (coarticulating) one movement into the next one.

Numerous methods exist for each of these; a comprehensive survey is beyond our scope. What is important here is that several of these activities may be executed simultaneously: a virtual human should be able to *walk, talk, and chew gum*. This leads to the next level of architectural organization: *Parallel Transition Networks*.

16.2.3 Parallel Transition Networks

Two decades ago we realized that human animation would require some model of parallel movement execution. About a decade ago [19] graphical workstations became fast enough to support feasible implementations of simulated parallelism. Our model for a parallel virtual machine that animates graphical models is called Parallel Transition Networks, or PaT-Nets. Other human animation systems have adopted similar paradigms. In general, network nodes represent processes and arcs contain predicates, conditions, rules, or other functions that cause transitions to other process nodes. Synchronization across processes or networks is effected through message-passing or global variable blackboards.

The benefits of PaT-Nets accrue not only from their parallel organization and execution of low-level motor skills, but also from their conditional structure. Traditional animation tools use linear time-lines on which actions are placed and ordered. A PaT-Net provides a *nonlinear* animation model, since movements can be triggered, modified, or stopped by transition to other nodes. This is the first crucial step toward autonomous behavior, since conditional execution enables reactivity and decision-making capabilities.

Providing a virtual human with human-like reactions and decision making is more complicated than just controlling its joint motions from captured or synthesized data. Here is where we need to convince the viewer of the character's skill and intelligence in negotiating its environment, interacting with its spatial situation, and engaging other agents. This level of performance requires significant investment in nonlinear action models. Through numerous experimental systems we have shown how the PaT-Net architecture can be applied: games such as *Hide and Seek* [20], two-person animated *conversation* (*Gesture Jack*) [3], simulated emergency medical care (*MediSim*) [21], a real-time animated *Jack Presenter* [22, 23], and multi-user *JackMOO* [24] virtual worlds.

PaT-Nets are effective but must be hand-coded in Lisp or C++. No matter what artificial language we invent to describe human actions, it is not likely to be just the way people conceptualize the situation[2]. We therefore need a higher level, conceptual representation to capture additional information, parameters, and aspects of human action. We do this by drawing on natural language semantic concepts.

16.2.4 Conceptual Action Representation

Even with a powerful set of motion generators and PaT-Nets to invoke them, a challenge remains to provide effective and easily learned user interfaces to control, manipulate and animate virtual humans. Interactive point and click systems (such

---

2   Discussions with Bonnie Webber led to this observation.

as *Jack* and numerous other animation production toolsets) work now, but with a cost in user learning and menu traversal. Such interfaces decouple the human participant's instructions and actions from the avatar through a narrow and *ad hoc* communication channel of hand motions. A direct programming interface, while powerful, is still an offline method that moreover requires specialized computer programming understanding and expertise. The option that remains is a natural language-based interface.

Perhaps not surprisingly, instructions for people are given in natural language augmented with graphical diagrams and, occasionally, animations. Recipes, instruction manuals, and interpersonal conversations use language as the medium for conveying process and action [7, 25, 26]. The key to linking language and animation lies in constructing *Smart Avatars* that *understand what we tell them to do*. This requires a conceptual representation of actions, objects, and agents which is simultaneously suitable for execution (simulation) as well as natural language expression. We call this architectural level the *Parameterized Action Representation*, or PAR. It must drive a simulation (in a context of a given set of objects and agents), and yet support the enormous range of expression, nuance, and manner offered by language [27]. The PAR gives a high-level description of an action that is also directly linked to PaT-Nets which execute movements. A PAR is *parameterized* because an action depends on its participants (agents, objects, and other attributes) for the details of how it is accomplished. A PAR includes *applicability* and *preparatory* conditions that have to be satisfied before the action is actually executed. The action is finished when the *terminating* conditions are satisfied. Some of the PAR slots are described below:

- *Physical objects*: the list of objects referred to within the PAR. Each physical object has a graphical model and other properties.
- *Agent*: the agent who will be executing the action. Here, the user's *avatar* is the implied agent. An agent is a special type of object and has additional capabilities such as a set of actions it knows how to execute.
- *Start*: the time or state in which the action begins.
- *Result*: the time or state after the action is performed.
- *Applicability conditions*: a boolean expression of conditions (conditions conjoined with logical **and**s and **or**s) which must hold (be true) in order for the action to be appropriate to perform. These conditions generally have to do with certain properties of the objects, the abilities of the agent, and other unchangeable or uncontrollable aspects of the environment. Unlike the preconditions (see below), it would be impossible or impractical to try to satisfy the applicability conditions as sub-goals before performing the action. For *walk* one of the applicability conditions may be: *Can the agent walk?* If not, conditions are not satisfied and the action is aborted. Going across the street requires that the agent be mobile and self-propelled in some fashion. Applicability conditions may also replace an action with a more specific one: opening the door might be specialized to a sliding action if that is what this particular door calls for.
- *Sub-actions*: the breakdown of the action into partially ordered or parallel substeps. It is a collection of actions connected in a graph structure which indicates the temporal relationships (if any) between the actions (e.g. whether two actions

are to be done sequentially, in parallel, etc.). Actions ground out as PaT-Nets. Thus a PAR can describe either a complex action or a primitive action. A complex action can list a number of sub-actions that may need to be executed in sequence, parallel, or a combination of both. A primitive action is a PaT-Net. Parameters pass from PAR to PaT-Net to motion process.

In general, preparatory actions or applicability conditions may involve the full power of motion planning. The commands, after all, are essentially goal requests [28] and the smart avatar must then figure out how (if at all) it can achieve them. Presently we use PaT-Nets with hand-coded conditionals to test for likely (but generalized) situations and execute appropriate intermediate actions. Adding more general actions planners is possible since the PAR represents goal states and supports a full graphical model of the current world state [20].

- *Core semantics*: the primary components of meaning of the action, including Preconditions, Postconditions, Motion, Force, Path, Purpose, Terminating Conditions, Duration, and Agent Manner.

A PAR appears in two different forms:

- *UPAR (Uninstantiated PAR)*: we store all instances of the uninitialized PAR in a database (called the *Actionary*) in a hierarchical tree. A UPAR contains default applicability conditions, preconditions, and execution steps. This is the heart of the Actionary. Multiple entries are allowed: just as verbs have multiple contextual meanings. *Go to bed* means much more than *go to the door* because it entails preparatory (and possibly) optional actions such as *undressing* and *lying down when at the bed*.

- *IPAR (Instantiated PAR)*: an IPAR is a UPAR instantiated with specific information on agent, physical object(s), manner, terminating conditions, etc. Any new information in an IPAR overrides the corresponding UPAR default. An IPAR can be created by the parser (one IPAR for each new instruction) or can be created dynamically during execution.

16.2.5 Architecture

Figure 16.2 shows the architecture of the PAR system.

- *NL2PAR*: this module consists of two parts: parser and translator. The parser takes a natural language instruction and outputs a tree structure. For each new instruction, the translator uses the tree and Actionary database to first determine the correct instances of the physical object and agent in the environment. It then generates the instruction as an IPAR.

- *Database*: all instances of physical objects, UPARs, and agents are stored in a persistent database contained in the Actionary. The physical objects and UPARs are stored in hierarchies within their respective databases.

- *Execution engine*: the execution engine is the main controller for the agent actions. It accepts a PAR from the NL2PAR module, passes it on to the correct agent process, evaluates conditions, expands PARs if necessary, and ultimately sends agent movement update commands to the visualizer.

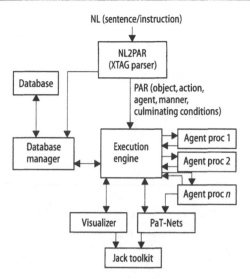

Figure 16.2 PAR Architecture.

- *Agent process*: each agent is controlled by a separate process, which maintains a queue of all IPARs it is to execute. Individual action capabilities and planning abilities may vary across agents.
- *Output graphics and human models*: we use the EAI/Transom Jack toolkit and OpenGL to maintain and control the actual geometry, scene graphs, and human behaviors and constraints. This component may be easily changed to control other articulated body models.

A language interpreter promotes a *language-centered* view of action execution, but augmented and elaborated by parameters modifying lower-level motion synthesis. Although textual instructions can describe and trigger actions, details need not be explicitly communicated. The smart avatar PAR architecture interprets the semantics of instructions for both motion generality and environmental context-sensitivity. In a prototype implementation of this architecture, called Jack's MOOse Lodge [24], four smart avatars are controlled by simple imperative instructions (Fig. 16.3). One agent, the waiter, is completely autonomous and serves drinks to seated avatars when their glasses need filling.

16.3 Discussion

This exposition has described virtual human modeling and control, with an emphasis on real-time motion and language-based interfaces. In particular, we discussed such issues as appearance and motion, autonomous action, and motor skills. A PaT-Net parallel finite state machine controller can be used to drive virtual humans through complex tasks.

We next described a first version of a Parameterized Action Representation. The PAR is meant to be the intermediate structure between natural language

Figure 16.3 Jack's MOOse Lodge.

instructions with complex semantics and task execution by a virtual human agent. An algorithm for interpreting PARs within an object-oriented system has been implemented.

We have established a role for language in action modeling. Linguistic classifications have helped us by identifying typical properties and modifiers of animate agents, such as the dimensions along which agent behavior can vary. In addition, linguistic analysis can help identify typical actions of animate agents and typical modifiers for their actions. Basing an agent and action ontology on linguistic evidence and movement models ensures extensibility. However, the development of the virtual human model from the bottom up ensures that a rich set of necessary capabilities are present.

Given this architecture, do we see the emergence of realistic human-like movements, actions, and decisions? Yes and no. On the positive side, we see complex activities and interactions. On the negative side, we're not fooling anyone into thinking that the virtual humans are real. While some of this has to do with graphical appearance, synthetic movements are still easy to pick out. Motion captured from live performances is much more natural, but harder to alter and parameterize for reuse in other contexts.

One approach to natural movement that offers some promise is to look deeper into physiological and cognitive models of behavior. For example, we have built an attention system for the virtual human that uses known perceptual and cognitive parameters to drive the movement of the eyes. Attention is based on a queue of tasks and exogenous events that may impinge arbitrarily. Since attention is a resource, as the environment becomes cluttered, task performance naturally degrades [29]. Attention can also predict the reappearance of temporarily occluded objects.

Another approach is to observe human movement and understand the parameters that shape performance. In the real world this is a physical process; in our simulated world it may be modeled kinematically if we choose the right controls. We have implemented [30] an interpretation of Laban's Effort notation to have a parameterization of agent manner. The Effort elements are Weight, Space, Time, and Flow; they may be combined and phrased to effect the performance of a given set of key poses for a character's arms, hands, and body.

Soon virtual humans will have individual personalities, emotional states, and live conversations [31]. They will have roles, gender, culture, and situation awareness [32]. They will have reactive, proactive, and decision-making behaviors for action execution [33]. They will need to have individualized perceptions of context. They must understand language so that we may communicate with them as if they were real.

The future holds great promise for the virtual humans who will populate our virtual worlds. They will provide economic benefits by helping designers early in the product design phases to produce more human-centered vehicles, equipment, assembly lines, manufacturing plants, and interactive systems. Virtual humans will enhance the presentation of information through training aids, virtual experiences, teaching, and mentoring. And Virtual humans will help save lives by providing surrogates for medical training, surgical planning, and remote telemedicine. They will be our avatars on the Internet and will portray ourselves to others, perhaps as we are or perhaps as we wish to be. They may help turn cyberspace into a real, or rather virtual, community.

Acknowledgments

Many students, staff, and colleagues in the Center for Human Modeling and Simulation have made this effort possible. Additional information and contributors may be found through http://hms.upenn.edu/.

This research is partially supported by the US Air Force through Delivery Orders #8 and #17 on F41624-97-D-5002; the Office of Naval Research (through the University of Houston) K-5-55043/3916-1552793, DURIP N0001497-1-0396, and AASERTs N00014-97-1-0603 and N0014-97-1-0605; the Army Research Lab HRED DAAL01-97-M-0198; DARPA SB-MDA-97-2951001; NSF IRI95-04372; NASA NRA NAG 5-3990; the National Institute of Standards and Technology 60 NANB6D0149 and 60 NANB7D0058; SERI Korea; and JustSystem Japan.

References

[1] J. Bates. The role of emotion in believable agents. *Comm. of the ACM*, 37(7), 122–125, 1994.
[2] J. Bates, A. Loyall, and W. Reilly. Integrating reactivity, goals, and emotion in a broad agent. In *Proc. of the 14th Annual Conf. of the Cognitive Science Society*, pp. 696–701, Hillsdale, NJ, 1992. Lawrence Erlbaum.
[3] J. Cassell, C. Pelachaud, N. Badler, M. Steedman, B. Achorn, W. Becket, B. Douville, S. Prevost, and M. Stone. Animated conversation: rule-based generation of facial expression, gesture and spoken

intonation for multiple conversational agents. In *Computer Graphics*, Annual Conf. Series, pp. 413–420. ACM, 1994.

[4] P. Maes, T. Darrell, B. Blumberg, and A. Pentland. The ALIVE system: full-body interaction with autonomous agents. In *Computer Animation* (eds. N. Magnenat-Thalmann and D. Thalmann), pp. 11–18. IEEE Computer Society Press, Los Alamitos, CA, 1995.

[5] K. Perlin and A. Goldberg. Improv: a system for scripting interactive actors in virtual worlds. In *ACM Computer Graphics*, Annual Conf. Series, pp. 205–216, 1996.

[6] D. Rousseau and B. Hayes-Roth. *Personality in Synthetic Agents*. Technical Report KSL-96-21, Stanford Knowledge Systems Laboratory, 1996.

[7] N. Badler, C. Phillips, and B. Webber. *Simulating Humans: Computer Graphics Animation and Control*. Oxford University Press, New York, NY, 1993.

[8] R. Earnshaw, N. Magnenat-Thalmann, D. Terzopoulos, and D. Thalmann. Computer animation for virtual humans. *IEEE Computer Graphics and Applications*, 18(5), 20–23, 1998.

[9] S.K. Wilcox. *Web Developer's Guide to 3D Avatars*. Wiley, New York, 1998.

[10] J. Hodgins, W. Wooten, D. Brogan, and J. O'Brien. Animating human athletics. In *ACM Computer Graphics*, Annual Conf. Series, pp. 71–78, 1995.

[11] M. Cavazza, R. Earnshaw, N. Magnenat-Thalmann, and D. Thalmann. Motion control of virtual humans. *IEEE Computer Graphics and Applications*, 18(5), 24–31, 1998.

[12] K. Perlin. Real time responsive animation with personality. *IEEE Trans. on Visualization and Computer Graphics*, 1(1), 5–15, 1995.

[13] R. Brooks. A robot that walks: emergent behaviors from a carefully evolved network. *Neural Computation*, 1(2), 1989.

[14] D. Zeltzer. Task-level graphical simulation: abstraction, representation, and control. In *Making Them Move: Mechanics, Control, and Animation of Articulated Figures* (eds. N. Badler, B. Barsky, and D. Zeltzer), pp. 3–33, Morgan-Kaufmann, San Francisco, 1990.

[15] M. Carignan, Y. Yang, N. Magnenat-Thalmann, and D. Thalmann. Dressing animated synthetic actors with complex deformable clothes. *ACM Computer Graphics, Proc. SIGGRAPH '92*, pp. 99–104, July 1992.

[16] D. Baraff and A. Witkin. Large steps in cloth simulation. *ACM Computer Graphics, Proc. SIGGRAPH '98*, pp. 43–54, July 1998.

[17] J. Wilhelms and A. van Gelder. Anatomically-based modeling. *ACM Computer Graphics, Proc. SIGGRAPH '97*, pp. 173–180, July 1997.

[18] B.-J. Ting. Real time human model design. PhD thesis, CIS, University of Pennsylvania, 1998.

[19] N. Badler and S. Smoliar. Digital representations of human movement. *ACM Computing Surveys*, 11(1), 19–38, 1979.

[20] T. Trias, S. Chopra, B. Reich, M. Moore, N. Badler, B. Webber, and C. Geib. Decision networks for integrating the behaviors of virtual agents and avatars. In *Proceedings of Virtual Reality International Symposium*, 1996.

[21] D. Chi, B. Webber, J. Clarke, and N. Badler. Casualty modeling for real-time medical training. *Presence*, 5(4), 359–366, 1995.

[22] T. Noma and N. Badler. A virtual human presenter. In *IJCAI '97 Workshop on Animated Interface Agents*, Nagoya, Japan, 1997.

[23] L. Zhao and N. Badler. Gesticulation behaviors for virtual humans. *Proc. Pacific Graphics*, pp. 161–168, 1998.

[24] J. Shi, T. J. Smith, J. Granieri, and N. Badler. Smart avatars in JackMOO. In *IEEE Virtual Reality Conf.*, 1999.

[25] N. Badler, B. Webber, J. Kalita, and J. Esakov. Animation from instructions. In *Making Them Move: Mechanics, Control, and Animation of Articulated Figures* (eds. N. Badler, B. Barsky, and D. Zeltzer), pp. 51–93. Morgan-Kaufmann, San Francisco, 1990.

[26] B. Webber, N. Badler, B. Di Eugenio, C. Geib, L. Levison, and M. Moore. Instructions, intentions and expectations. *Artificial Intelligence J.*, 73, pp. 253–269, 1995.

[27] N. Badler, B. Webber, M. Palmer, T. Noma, M. Stone, J. Rosenzweig, S. Chopra, K. Stanley, J. Bourne, and B. Di Eugenio. Final report to Air Force HRGA regarding feasibility of natural language text generation from task networks for use in automatic generation of Technical Orders from DEPTH simulations. Technical report, CIS, University of Pennsylvania, 1997.

[28] N. Badler, B. Webber, W. Becket, C. Geib, M. Moore, C. Pelachaud, B. Reich, and M. Stone. Planning for animation. In *Computer Animation* (eds. N. Magnenat-Thalmann and D. Thalmann). Prentice Hall, 1996.

[29] S. Chopra. Where to look? Automating some visual attending behaviors of virtual human characters. *PhD Dissertation*, CIS, University of Pennsylvania, 1999.

[30] D. Chi. Animating expressivity through Effort elements. *PhD Dissertation*, CIS, University of Pennsylvania, 1999.

[31] K. Thorisson. Real-time decision making in multimodal face-to-face communication. *Proc. Second Annual Conf. on Autonomous Agents*, ACM, 1998.

[32] J. Allbeck and N. Badler. Avatars á la snow crash. In *Proc. Computer Animation*. IEEE Press, 1998.

[33] W.L. Johnson and J. Rickel. Steve: an animated pedagogical agent for procedural training in virtual environments. *SIGART Bulletin*, 8(1–4), 16–21, 1997.

17
Dialogue Design for a "Virtual Interactive Presenter"

Marc Cavazza

Abstract

With the advent of 500-channel digital TV, there is a need for sophisticated user interfaces that would enable the user to take full advantage of programme diversity. This paper describes the design of a conversational interface to an Electronic Programme Guide (EPG.) After reviewing dialogue modelling issues, we introduce our approach, based on a specialization of speech acts theory. On the basis of linguistic data, we suggest that besides specialized speech acts, it is necessary to consider an interpretative approach to speech act recognition.

17.1 Introduction and Objectives

With the advent of 500-channel digital TV, the selection of programmes will become an increasingly difficult, if not impossible, task. Since TV guides themselves will come under electronic formats (as Electronic Programme Guides, EPG), selection of TV programmes will largely become a user interface issue. It is thus necessary to develop new interfaces to the EPG that enable the users to take full advantage of the diversity of channels offered. However, even in the perspective of digital TV, traditional computer interfaces are not suited to the majority of consumers and may not achieve effectiveness for the particular task of programme selection. Human–computer dialogue, in particular agent-based dialogue, in which the user interacts with a friendly character through speech recognition, would represent the ideal user interface and is deemed to increase user acceptance of human–computer dialogue. The VIP (Virtual Interactive Presenter) project[1] aims

---

1 Partners of the VIP (LINK Broadcast Technology) project include the University of Bradford, Cambridge University, the BBC, Sony DNSE and Advance Communications plc.

at developing such an intelligent interface based on a conversational character communicating with the user through speech recognition and speech synthesis.

In this chapter, we discuss the dialogue techniques for the implementation of a conversational interface to an EPG. While speech recognition and parsing analyse user input to produce instructions to the system, dialogue techniques formalize the conversational exchanges between the user and the system, hence supporting the process of programme selection. Dialogue techniques are a subset of Natural Language Processing (NLP) techniques, and as such they rely on linguistic descriptions of dialogues, knowledge representation and control strategies. After a discussion of the specific nature of information access in an EPG in terms of conversational interfaces, we will review the principles behind state-of-the-art dialogue systems. We will then introduce our own approach based on specialized speech acts to be used for the refinement of user requests. Finally, on the basis of available linguistic data, we will discuss the important problem of speech act recognition.

17.2 Information Access in an EPG

In this section, we discuss some knowledge representation problems associated with an EPG. An EPG is a structure containing schedule data, organized around a description of categories and genres that should be meaningful to both the content provider and the user. In the remainder of this chapter, we should use the term *category* to refer to programme categories such as "movies", "entertainment", "sports", "news" etc., while specific programmes will be referred to as *instances* of a given category. We should also use the term *subcategory* for any category subordinated to the main categories (e.g. movie genres are subcategories of "movies"), regardless of the number of levels in the category hierarchy.

An EPG can be naturally represented through a hierarchical structure such as a tree because of the way categories, subcategories and instances are described. However, hierarchical structures are also known to be faced with many limitations when it comes to represent contextual differences (Cavazza, 1998a), and EPGs are no exception to this difficult problem. As hierarchical structures their natural mode of consultation is that of *browsing*. Browsing essentially assumes two basic conditions. Firstly, there should be a meaningful entry point into the classification. This is usually the case through high-level categories or genres such as films, documentaries or sports. Secondly, it should be possible to follow the taxonomic links to navigate from one category down to the final programme instances. Browsing as a model for information retrieval however suffers from a certain number of limitations. In this context, agent-based dialogue should essentially be considered an alternative to browsing. A conversational approach can provide guidance during the selection process, making it both natural and efficient. Also, the conversational agent can apply dynamic filters that go beyond the explicit hierarchical organization of the EPG, hence implementing mechanisms that are closer to the actual user's selection process.

In the selection of a programme, we can consider that user preferences are best described through *feature structures*. Features are distinctive properties of programme contents. They can correspond to generic information, such as programme genre and categories, forming part of the EPG hierarchical description. However, non-taxonomic information, such as starting time, parental rating, pricing information, or cast, also constitutes important description features. We should refer to the latter as *specific* features that can distinguish a given programme from related programmes within the same category. Finally, there is a need to accommodate idiosyncratic attributes, such as "entertaining", "boring", "funny", etc. Though there is some common ground knowledge about these features (political debates would rarely appear as entertaining), their detailed interpretation depends on specific user preferences. As these are not part of the EPG description, they have to be computed dynamically through the use of inference rules and/or some elementary form of user model. A related problem is the use of categories that do not appear as such in the set of editorial categories supporting the EPG, one example being "soap". The extension of such categories can also be computed through inference rules mapping these categories to the best matching editorial categories. Figure 17.1 represents a sample description for an instantiated feature structure corresponding to a user selection. The *connotation* field represents the user personal categorization of the programme (here, "entertaining"). These have to be computed dynamically depending on common sense knowledge that can, however, be superseded by user-specific information. The main category *movies* is further refined into the movie genre *western* and the subcategory *classic* that distinguishes more recent westerns from those of the 1950s–60s. Hence the *classic* feature only stands as *classic as a western*. The specific features include pay-per-view information, parental guidance and cast. These are important features in the interactive selection of a programme that may be the subject of specific requests such as "I want something my kids can see" or "I want a western with John Wayne". Finally, the *instance* field contains the set of programmes that match a particular description.

The whole dialogue process will be centred on the construction and refinement of such feature structures, through the interpretation of user replies in terms of filters to be applied to the EPG contents. Having adopted a feature-based representation for the user selection, there is a natural relation between the semantics of user replies and the features used in programme selection. Namely, if the semantic lexicon for the system is based on semantic features, these can be aggregated to constitute the informational content of user requests (Cavazza, 1998b).

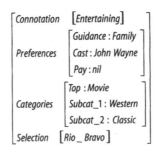

Figure 17.1 A feature structure.

17.3 Dialogue Modelling in Information Access Applications

Several levels of formalization are usually described in Human–Computer Dialogue systems. These are generally referred to as the *dialogue model*, the *task model* and the *user model*, though these may overlap in practical implementations. We should briefly introduce some of the main approaches, essentially from the perspective of information access dialogues.

- The *dialogue model* represents the structure of exchanges between the user and the system. It is usually based on a linguistic theory such as speech acts (Searle, 1959; Austin, 1962), or structural dialogue theories (Roulet, 1985; Pernel, 1994). An important trend in recent years has been the development of plan-based models that identify utterances to communicative actions (Cohen and Perrault, 1979). Speech acts theory provides a classification of dialogue utterances in terms of their communicative effects, including those related to "non-literal" interpretation. As the communicative actions essentially transform the beliefs of the speakers, their effects have often been formalized through belief logics (Sadek, 1996; Cohen and Levesque, 1990). Another aspect of dialogue modelling is the formalization of dialogue control functions (Bunt, 1989, 1994) such as greetings, acknowledgements, repair and request for repair that establish and maintain contact between the speaker and the hearer. Even though these are established in the framework of inter-human conversational dialogue, a subset might be required for the implementation of a natural human–computer conversational dialogue.

- The *task model* is a specification of the operations to be carried by the system in response to the various user requests. As far as formalisms are concerned, it can follow traditional methods for task modelling in human–computer interaction, but more often uses plan-based representations. These representations can provide a unifying framework between linguistic phenomena, planning data and user models through the notion of *intentions*. However, this notion proves difficult to handle in practical implementations. In the specific case of information access dialogue, the task model can also be related to the organization of data in the database. For instance, the AGS dialogue system for telephone-based access to weather information (Sadek, 1996) relies on a semantic network that structures information according to semantic proximity.

- The *user model* is not part of every dialogue system. It is fully justified whenever user preferences might impact on the course of dialogue and there is a direct benefit in tracking and recording them. Simple implementations of user models can however prove useful in priming the dialogue and recording preferences that span across an entire dialogue session.

In the field of human–computer interaction, many projects have addressed conversational assistants (Kurlander and Ling, 1995; Nagao and Takeuchi, 1994; Perlin and Goldberg, 1995). These are generally animated characters with which the user interacts through spoken dialogue. The adoption of an agent-led dialogue can influence the nature of exchanges between the system and the user. One of the major advantages of dialogue systems over simple speech-based interfaces is that user utterances are potentially shorter, consisting mainly of replies to system prompts. This simplifies both speech recognition and parsing. This point is evidenced in the sample dialogues in MGuide (1998), Bunt (1994), Busemann *et al.* (1997) and (Sadek, 1996), where the average length of users' replies tend to be 5–7 words. This appears to be related to the fact that the user only issues brief replies to system prompts. Yankelovich *et al.* (1995) also recognize the impact of directive prompts over more open conversational dialogue in terms of user replies. In some cases (see e.g. Sadek (1996)), it should be noted that the user's opening requests tend to be significantly longer than the remainder of the dialogue, which is essentially led by the system.

As a first step towards the specification of user–computer dialogue, we have collected linguistic data on possible user replies, forming a preliminary corpus. This corpus is based on user interviews and the design of tentative dialogues by several developers, also referring to dialogues described in the literature about comparable applications (Sadek, 1996; Busemann *et al.*, 1997). It is meant to constitute a starting point for the investigation of linguistic surface form, as well as the description of application-specific speech acts. This simulated corpus mainly includes user replies at various stages of dialogue. Several formulations of some replies have been provided in application of the habitability principle (Ogden and Bernick, 1995).

This constitutes a different approach than the traditional "Wizard of Oz" (WOz) experiments. There were several reasons why we did not conduct a WOz experiments at an early stage, among which the fact that the kind of suggestions spontaneously produced by a human "wizard" might be quite different from those automatically generated by the system. This leaves open the possibility of setting up a WOz experiment at a later stage, after a partial implementation of the dialogue module.

The vocabulary size for this initial corpus is approximately 400 words, with a small proportion of proper names. Implemented dialogue systems have been described with vocabularies as small as 40 words (Nagao and Takeuchi, 1994). This is also because complex dialogue situations can be generated dynamically from a small set of speech acts and a limited vocabulary. Obviously, systems with larger vocabularies will have the potential of interpreting a larger number of requests and are required to operate on EPG categories and contents. The average length of user replies in the corpus is six words. From this, we can estimate that the system prototype should be able to handle vocabularies of 500 to 1000 words, proper names accounting for approximately 20% of the total vocabulary. This corpus has been used as a starting point for the description of application-specific speech acts. Figure 17.2 represents a sample potential dialogue between the system and the user, the details of which will be discussed in Section 17.4.

17.4 From Speech Acts to "Search Acts"

Many recent approaches to human–computer dialogue have been inspired by speech acts theory (Searle, 1959; Austin, 1962). Speech acts characterize dialogue utterances beyond their literal meaning in terms of the intended actions that they

System: What would you like to see? [greetings]
User: Something entertaining [provides a selection feature]
System: What about a movie? [computes a compatible entry point in the EPG] (1)
User: Yes, a comedy please [accepts category and selects sub-category] (2)
System: There are two comedies tonight: "Sleepless in Seattle" and "Kindergarten Cop"
[proposes two programme instances from the selection] (3)
User: I don't like Schwarzenegger [rejects the *cast* feature] (4)
System: What about "Sleepless in Seattle" [updates selection by filtering on rejected feature]
User: Anything else? [ambiguous rejection]
System: Still a comedy? [updates selection + enquires about category]
User: No

Figure 17.2 A sample dialogue and its interpretation (see also Fig. 17.4).

are supposed to trigger on the hearer's side (Cohen and Perrault, 1979). In the case of information access dialogues, this amounts to classifying utterances into categories such as *Inform, Request, Reject* (Traum and Hinkelmann, 1992) that map to elementary actions in the information access task. The practical implementation of speech acts theory has often been more difficult than initially envisioned, because of the difficulties of properly identifying speech acts from the user's utterances (Sadek, 1996; Traum and Hinkelmann, 1992). More fundamental criticism has challenged the validity of speech acts theory (Bourdieu, 1982; Ghiglione and Trognon, 1993), but we should not review it here.

We will not refer to speech acts theory as our ultimate theoretical background. Rather, we will adapt some recent proposals in dialogue research inspired by speech acts to the specific needs of our application. In doing so, we shall try to be consistent with the approaches we refer to. However, the fact that some important problems, like speech act identification (Traum and Hinkelmann, 1992), are still to find appropriate solutions will sometimes lead us to *ad hoc* solutions.

Within the field of human–computer dialogue, Bunt (1979) has established a list of 24 elementary speech acts, and this has been simplified by Lee and Wilks (1996), who use a subset of 20, in four categories. The design of more specific speech acts is an interesting trend in dialogue research. Busemann *et al.* (1997) have described specialized speech acts such as proposing, accepting, rejecting, cancelling or fixing a meeting. The Discourse Resource Initiative (Allen and Core, 1997) has established a preliminary list of specialized speech acts, including specific categories that would influence the addressee's future actions, such as *Action-directive* or *Info-request*.

Our central hypothesis is that the forms of query refinement can be described through a well-identified set of speech acts. This is what we should call search acts, a specialization of speech acts previously described such as *Inform* or *Request*, tuned to the specific requirements of our application. We should consider that both the user and the system generate speech acts. The system generates prompts, which tend to present possible choices from which the user will select a programme. The user, in turn, accepts or rejects suggestions and refines the current description. The process of agent-led dialogue is equivalent to the definition of a specialized set of speech acts that are constrained by the nature of operations that differentiate between programmes. As we shall see, it is possible to further refine this model to take advantage of both the conversational approach and the feature-based description for programme contents. We will rely on the basic assumption that the agent and the user speech acts are *asymmetrical*. The agent mainly drives the user into providing information for the selection of programmes. The user enquires about the availability of programmes, replies to selections and issues direct commands to the system. This asymmetry also relieves us from dealing with theories of cooperation or belief ascription (Lee and Wilks, 1996). Instead of updating each other's beliefs, as in classical speech act theory, the user and the system operate on a common feature-based description that serves as a filter to access information in the EPG. The latter points may depart significantly from mainstream speech act theory.

At this stage, we will consider the following list of speech acts for the user, not considering those dealing with dialogue control:

- *Refine* (Subcat | Feature). This speech act refines the current selection by specifying an additional subcategory or feature. For instance, in reply to the suggestion "Would you like a movie?" whenever the user replies "Yes (acceptance of category), a thriller please (specifying a subcategory)" or "Do you have any with Sean Connery?" (acceptance of the category, specifying the *cast* feature). Whenever the user asks for a specific instance, this is identified as a specific selection (see the *Select* speech act).

- *Forbid* (Cat | Subcat | Feature | Instance). The *Forbid* speech act expresses dislike for a specific category, feature or instance, which should be recorded by the system for the whole duration of the dialogue (e.g. "I don't like sitcoms").

- *Reject* (Latest | Instance | Cat | Subcat). This speech act corresponds to the explicit and non-ambiguous rejection of the current suggestion and/or selection proposed by the system. Because some properties are not open to negotiation, rejection of a feature should be interpreted as rejection of the current selection as a whole (e.g. "I'm not paying for that"). The alteration to the current selection, and hence future suggestions from the system depends on the *Reject* parameter. A non-motivated rejection (e.g. negative reply) is considered as rejecting the *latest* suggestion.

- *Select* (Cat | Subcat | Feature | Instance). Through the *Select* speech act, the user can specifically ask for a given category or feature. If the user selects a subcategory as an entry point, the current description should by default add categories of which the subcategory is a subclass. An example is "Do you have any adventure movies?", which should add the *movie* category to the description filter.

- *Enquire* (Feature). The *Enquire* speech act accesses the value of a given feature for the current selection. It does not alter the selection itself. Examples of enquiries include *cast*, *starting_time* or pricing information in the case of pay-per-view movies.

- *Request* (Filter). Through this speech act, the user can explicitly ask for a complex selection (e.g. "I'd like an action movie that my kids can watch, too"). This is often used for opening dialogue, especially when the user gets acquainted with the system. The filter parameter represents the conjunction of features requested by the user.

- *Backtrack-New-Request* (Filter). This speech act is similar to *Request*, but is used in the course of the dialogue and brings a complete shift in focus (e.g. "I'd rather watch the cricket match" when replying to a movie selection). It is hence different from both Partial-Accept and Partial-Reject speech acts below. The surface form as well as the context can play a role in its proper recognition.
- *Partial-Accept* (Filter). In the case of partial acceptance, the system should compute what should be left aside and what should be kept from the current selection. For instance, consider the dialogue of Fig. 17.3. The initial filter (F1) brings the system to propose a selection (S1). The user, by acknowledging only part of the selection, induces in turn the new filter (F2).

User: What movie do you suggest then?
System: What about "Against all odds" on channel 55
User: Can I have another movie with James Woods?

$Movies(x) \wedge Subcat\_1(x) \wedge Subcat\_2(x)$	(F1)
$F_1, F_2, ..., F_n \wedge Cast(x, James\_Woods) \wedge Channel\_55(x)$	(S1)
$Movies(x) \wedge Cast(x, James\_Woods)$	(F2)

Figure 17.3 A *Partial-Accept* speech act.

- *Partial-Reject* (Filter). The latter speech act we propose is characterized as accepting the main category but rejecting the subcategory and/or providing an additional criterion. The dialogue of Fig. 17.2 can be interpreted as a *Partial-Reject* (Fig. 17.4). It is also required to properly handle the difference between *Partial-Accept* and *Partial-Reject* speech acts. Some surface linguistic forms, like the occurrence of explicit markers for negation or preference, can provide useful cues.

$Entertaining(x) \supset Movie(x)$	(I1)
$Movie(x) \wedge Comedy(x)$	(F2)
$Movie(x) \wedge Comedy(x) \wedge Cast(x, Schwarzenegger) \wedge S'$	(S3)
$Movie(x) \wedge \neg Cast(x, Schwarzenegger)$	(F4)

Figure 17.4 A *Partial-Reject* speech act.

- *Direct-Command* (Command). This speech act is dedicated to interface control (e.g. "can I see the trailer?").
- *Choose-from-Selection* (Selection). This speech act can be applied only in response to the system proposing to choose between different categories or instances. It is used to select an item within the proposed list.

The agent's role can be specified through a set of speech acts which will in turn suggest categories, subcategories, and instances or will enquire about specific criteria generating such selections (the latter if the current dialogue status does not permit it to make such a suggestion directly). The generation of speech acts by the system follows a simple goal: to reach a point where a small number of instances can be presented to the user. This goal can be pursued on the basis of local operators only, constantly refining the feature description.

The system can in turn make use of the following specific speech acts (again not considering dialogue control acts):

- *Suggest* (Category | Subcategory | Instance). The system suggests a possible refinement to the current selection, which should induce the equivalent of a *Refine* speech act.
- *Suggest-Selection* (Instances). A list of possible instance programmes.
- *Select-Between* (Categories | Subcategories). The system proposes alternative categories or alternative subcategories.
- *Request-Refine* (Subcategory). The system asks for a refinement to the current selection, without explicit suggestions.
- *Request-Confirm* (Category | Subcategory). In ambiguous cases, the system asks for a confirmation that a given category is still valid (e.g. "Still a comedy?").
- *Propose-Action* (Action). Used by the system to propose the display of trailers etc. for the selection.
- *Inform* (Feature). The system in reply to a user enquiry, outputs the value of a given feature for the current instance selection or another named instance.

17.5 The Interpretation of User Replies

The interpretation of user replies should provide three different kinds of information:

- the identification of the speech act itself
- the set of content features conveyed by the sentence, assembled following syntactic links when appropriate
- the generation or updating of a filter that represents a query to the database

The first step of interpretation is obviously the linguistic processing of the user reply. Traditional parsing techniques can assemble semantic structures, which contribute both to the recognition of speech acts and semantic features to be incorporated as parameters for the EPG search. We have prototyped this approach with a TFG (Tree-Furcating Grammar) parser (Cavazza, 1998b) which is a fully implemented parser that integrates syntax and semantics. However, the final parser for the system might make use of dependency-based parsers still based on some form of lexicalized trees. Figure 17.5 represents the parsing of a user reply, "Is there a movie with James Woods?". Elementary trees associated with each word are combined using two operations (Substitution and Furcation), Semantic features attached to these words are assembled synchronously to these operations. The overall process of interpretation is represented in Fig. 17.6.

Identification of speech acts from user replies varies in difficulty. *Acceptance* is often just a matter of surface variation. *Rejection* can be slightly more complex, as

User: When's the next news bulletin?
System: Would you like to see the news bulletin on channel 55?
User: I only watch the BBC news.

$$News(x) \wedge Channel\_55(x) \qquad (F1)$$
$$News(x) \wedge BBC(x) \qquad (F2)$$
$$Channel\_55(x) \supset \neg BBC(x) \qquad (I3)$$
$$News(x) \wedge BBC(x) \wedge \neg BBC(x) \supset \bot \qquad (F4)$$

Figure 17.5 Parsing with a TFG prototype (see text).

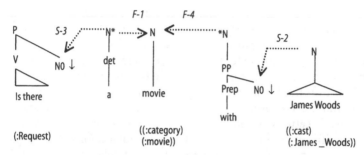

Figure 17.6 Overall interpretation of user replies.

there is a need to properly distinguish related speech acts, such as *Forbid* ("I don't like sitcoms") or *Partial-Reject*.

One classical example of the interpretation of the illocutionary nature of a speech act is that of interpreting enquiries such as "Is there any kind of X?". When issued in a neutral context such as the opening of a dialogue, that statement behaves as *Request*. However, when used as a reply to a current selection in the course of the dialogue, it should be interpreted as either a *Refinement* or even depending on the context, a *Backtrack-New-Request* speech act. This means that speech act recognition also relies on context. In some cases, speech act recognition cannot be directly inferred from syntactic markers or semantic features. Let us consider the dialogue of Fig. 17.7.

The reply needs to be interpreted in a context where the system is suggesting a news programme on a channel that is not the BBC (F1). Thus if we interpret it in terms of addition to the current filter, we end up with a logical contradiction (F4). The problem here stands in the fact that the speech act cannot be easily be inferred from

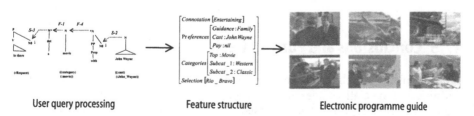

User query processing   Feature structure   Electronic programme guide

Figure 17.7 A contradictory interpretation.

the surface structure and developing the sentence into its corresponding logical form can provide a solution.

Speech act recognition once again appears to be a complex process that can make use of surface syntactic markers, lexical semantics, dialogue context and even logical interpretation. Further, it might be the case that the correct identification of a speech act is more a circular interpretative process. In such a process, both user input and the current context would play a role. While this would be quite complex to implement as a single mechanism, it should be kept in mind for the actual design if the identification procedures.

We have used a logical formulation, mainly for descriptive purposes. In using a logical formulation, it is not the truth value of the formula that matters, but its role as a filter, or its extension. However, the fact that formulas can result in logical contradictions can be used as a tool for interpretation as well. We should not equate this formula with the meaning of the sentence but rather its interpretation in the context of an information access dialogue. We still consider that a more appropriate definition for the meaning of the sentence stands in its linguistic content in terms of lexical features. These still appear in the formula, as predicate labels. Further, a significant difference exists between the logical formula acting as a filter, and the conjunction of features describing a particular programme fitting the description. However, part of this description can be actively reincorporated into the filter through a user reply. That kind of reply acts as a kind of *grounding* process (Traum and Allen, 1992), incorporating a feature from the current selection into an explicit element of the search filter. It is all the more important that such features could be relevant to the user while the system might not have an appropriate relevance model. In other words, while the model cannot use the full description of an instance as the basis for the next filter, the user has the power to do so through specific speech acts, such as *Partial-Accept* or *Partial-Reject*, that ground specific instance features into the search filter. Another problem related to the use of logical formulas is to determine what should be rejected when the user rejects the current suggestion. It is clear for instance that the rejection of a category should lead to the rejection, unless explicitly specified, of any of its subcategories, though there is no such explicit mention in the formula itself. On the other hand, rejection of the current selection could result in the withdrawal of the most specific predicate, so that default backtracking would take place at the immediate superclass. However, simple logical formulas, such as those previously introduced, do not capture the taxonomic relations between predicates, and this calls for further investigation either at the formalism level or at the inference procedure level.

17.6 Conclusions and Further Work

We have proposed a dialogue model for information access dialogues, based on the definition of specialized speech acts that can account for the cooperative refinement of feature structures. The proposed set of speech acts is consistent with recent trends in dialogue research and preliminary linguistic data collected. The asymmetrical nature of speech acts between the user and the system is a natural consequence of adopting user-led dialogue.

The problem of speech act recognition from user utterance does not admit a simple solution in the general case. Most proposed methods rely heavily on surface linguistic forms (Traum and Hinkelmann, 1992), including specific markers for e.g. negation or rejection. We have evidenced some cases in which the proper identification of a speech act had to be deferred until the user reply was interpreted in terms of a logical filter. The relations between semantic interpretation and speech act recognition thus demand further investigation.

At this stage, we have not addressed dialogue control and dialogue repair, which would require more experimental data in the form of full dialogue transcripts. We rely on the fact that specialized speech acts can accommodate some phenomena related to dialogue repair, such as shift in focus. Finally, the dialogue model also needs to be extended to take into account dynamic assessment of dialogue progress. This is required for the inclusion of visual feedback, which in the case of conversational characters can be implemented through elementary facial expressions, and provides an additional channel for user feedback without overloading the dialogue process itself.

Acknowledgements

The images in Fig 17.6 were provided by the BBC, courtesy of Adam Hume. Although the final version of the VIP prototype will use the BBC's system of programme classification, the categories presented here are illustrative only and as such do not reflect the current or future status of the BBC's system for programme classification. David Kirby and Adam Hume are thanked for their assistance with editorial categories. Steve Parnell is thanked for his assistance during early stages of the project.

References

Allen, J. and Core, M. (1997). DAMSL: Dialogue act markup in several layers. *Draft contribution for the Discourse Resource Initiative.*

Austin, J. (1962). *How to Do Things with Words.* Oxford University Press, Oxford.

Bourdieu, P. (1982). *Ce que parler veut dire.* Fayard, Paris.

Bunt, H.C. (1989). Information dialogues as communicative action in relation to information processing and partner modelling. In *The Structure of Multimodal Dialogue* (eds. Taylor, M.M., Néel, F. and Bouwhuis, D.G.), North-Holland, Amsterdam.

Bunt H.C. (1994). Context and dialogue control. *THINK Quarterly* 3(1), 19–31.

Busemann, S. Declerck, T., Diagne, A., Dini, L., Klein, J. and Schmeier, S. (1997). Natural language dialogue service for appointment scheduling agents. In *Proceedings of ANLP'97*, Washington DC.

Cavazza, M. (1998a). Textual semantics and corpus-specific lexicons. In *LREC'98 Workshop on Adapting Lexical and Corpus resources to Sublanguages and Applications*, Granada, Spain.

Cavazza, M. (1998b). An integrated TFG parser with explicit tree typing. In *Proceedings of the Fourth TAG+ workshop*, IRCS, University of Pennsylvania.

Cohen, P.R. and Levesque, H.J. (1990). Persistence, intention and commitment. In *Intentions in Communication* (eds. P. Cohen, J. Morgan and M. Pollack). Morgan-Kaufmann, San Francisco.

Cohen, P.R. and Levesque, H.J. (1995). Communicative actions for artificial agents. In *Proceedings of the First International Conference on Multi-agent Systems* (ICMAS'95), San Francisco.

Cohen, P.R. and Perrault, C.R.. (1979). Elements of a plan-based theory of speech acts. *Cognitive Science*, 3(3), 177–212.

Ghiglione, R. and Trognon, A. (1993). *Ou va la pragmatique?* Presses Universitaires de Grenoble.

Kurlander, D. and Ling, D.T. (1995) Planning-based control of interface animation. *Proceedings of CHI'95 Conference*, ACM Press, New York, pp. 472–479.

Lee, M. and Wilks, Y. (1996). An ascription-based approach to speech acts. In *Proceedings of the 16th International Conference on Computational Linguistics (COLING'96)*, Copenhagen.

MGuide (1998). *Guidelines for Designing Character Interaction*. Microsoft Corporation. Available online at http://www.microsoft.com./workshop/imedia/agent/guidelines.asp.

Nagao, K. and Takeuchi, A. (1994). Speech dialogue with facial displays: multimodal human–computer conversation. In: *Proceedings of the 32nd Annual Meeting of the Association for Computational Linguistics* (ACL'94), pp. 102–109.

Ogden, W.C. and Bernick, P. (1996). Using natural language interfaces. In *Handbook of Human–Computer Interaction* (ed. M. Helander), Elsevier Science Publishers.

Perlin, K. and Goldberg, A. (1995). Improv: a system for scripting interactive actors in virtual worlds. In *Proceedings of SIGGRAPH'95*, New Orleans.

Pernel, D. (1994). Gestion des buts multiples de l'utilisateur dans un dialogue homme–machine de recherche d'informations. *PhD Thesis*, University of Paris XI.

Poesio, M. and Traum, D. (1997). Representing conversation acts in a unified semantic/pragmatic framework. In *Proceedings of the AAAI Fall Symposium on Communicative Actions in Humans and Machine*, Cambridge, MA.

Sadek, D. (1996). Le dialogue homme–machine: de l'ergonomie des interfaces à l'agent dialoguant intelligent. In *Nouvelles Interfaces Homme–Machine* (ed. J. Caelen). OFTA, Paris: Tec & Doc (in French).

Searle, J. (1959). *Speech Acts*. Cambridge University Press, Cambridge.

Traum, D. and Hinkelmann, E.A. (1992). Conversation acts in task-oriented spoken dialogue. *Computational Intelligence*, 8(3).

Traum, D.R. and Allen, J.F. (1992). A "Speech Acts" Approach to Grounding in Conversation. *Proceedings of the International Conference on Spoken Language Processing* (ICSLP'92), pp 137–140.

Yankelovich, N., Levow, G.-A. and Marx, M. (1995). Designing speech acts: issues in speech user interfaces. *Procedings of CHI'95*, Denver.

18

Virtual Humans' Behaviour: Individuals, Groups, and Crowds

Daniel Thalmann, Soraia Raupp Musse and Marcelo Kallmann

Abstract

In this chapter, we first try to identify which mechanisms should be simulated in order to implement truly virtual humans or actors. We start from a structure linking perception, emotion, behavior, and action. Then we emphasize the central concept of autonomy and introduce the concept of Levels of Autonomy. Finally, we propose a new abstraction for specification of behaviours in complex virtual environment simulations involving human agents, groups of agents, and interactive objects endowed with different levels of autonomy.

18.1 Introduction

Virtual human agents (hereafter referred to simply as virtual humans, agents, or virtual actors) are humanoids whose behaviours are inspired by those of humans [1]. They can be equipped with sensors, memory, perception, and behavioural motives that allow them to act or react to events. They can also be much simpler, such as being guided by users in real time or interpreting predefined commands. The term *group* will be used to refer to a group of agents, and the term *object* for an interactive object of the environment. Agents, groups, and objects constitute the entities of the simulation.

A virtual actor inhabits a world which is dynamic and unpredictable. To be autonomous, it must be able to perceive its environment and decide what to do to reach the goal defined by its behavior. The relevant actions must then be transformed into motor control actions. Therefore the design of a behavioral animation system raises questions about creating autonomous actors, endowing them with perception, selecting their actions, their motor control and making their behavior believable. They should appear spontaneous and unpredictable. They should give an illusion of life, making the audience believe that an actor is really alive and has its own will. As stated by Bates [2], the believability of an actor is made possible by the emergence of emotions clearly expressed at the right moment. The apparent emotions of an actor and the way it reacts are what give it the appearance of a living being with needs and desires. Without it, an actor would just look like an automaton. Moreover, the use of emotions makes actors placed in the same context react differently. By defining different emergence conditions on different actors for their emotions, the generated emotions are guaranteed to be different, and consequently the derived behaviors are different.

High-level behavioral autonomy concerns the ability to simulate complex behaviours. The most common method for simulation of simple acts of cognition is to use a rule-based system [3]. In this chapter we consider that the ability to simulate decision processes, memory, learning activities and the performing of specialized actions can be included in the agents (agents-based applications), groups (groups-based applications) or in the objects (objects-based applications).

Different parameters of agent simulation can be defined in order to achieve the desired compromise between different requirements. Among others, interactivity, complex behaviours, intelligent abilities and frame rate of execution are directly related to the level of autonomy (LOA) that each entity of the simulation might have. Based on LOAs, we may then introduce three kinds of behavioural autonomy: guided, programmed and autonomous. Here, guided behaviour represents the lower level of autonomy where the behaviours have to be informed by an external process (user, other system, etc.). Programmed control implies the use of a notation (language) to define possible behaviours, which the entity is able to translate into internal behaviours. Autonomous behaviour concerns the capability of acting independently exhibiting control over their internal state [4].

18.2 Background Work

The use of behavioral animation in generating computer animation is a well-explored domain. Reynolds [5] described the first use of a behavioral model to produce flocking behavior. Badler *et al.* [6] created a task planner and a biomechanical model for virtual humans illustrated with by soldiers. Tu and Terzopoulos [7] created autonomous fishes living in a physically modeled virtual marine world. Hodgins *et al.* [8] described dynamic athletic behaviors. Unuma *et al.* [9] modeled human figure locomotion with emotions.

Other papers have presented behavioral architectures. Brooks [10, 11] developed a subsumption architecture built in layers of behaviors. Maes [12] presented an action selection model where action selection is an emergent property of activation/inhibition dynamics among actions. Beer *et al.* [13] developed neural networks for insects. Ahmad *et al.* [14] described hierarchical concurrent state machines for behavior modeling and scenario control. Blumberg [15, 16] described an action selection model and created autonomous creatures.

Some papers have presented interactive systems involving virtual creatures. Maes *et al.* [17, 18] designed a full-body interaction system with a virtual dog. Perlin [19] described seemingly emotionally responsive virtual actors using random noise functions.

Research in autonomy has also focused on social behaviors. Mataric [20] extended Brooks's work to create complex group behavior produced from simple local interactions. Bécheiraz *et al.* [21] presented a model of nonverbal communication and interpersonal relationships between virtual actors. The Oz project [2, 22–24] focused on the creation of believable autonomous agents that exhibit rich personalities in interactive dramas.

Several works have discussed the various ways of simulating and interacting with virtual agents. Zeltzer [25] presents a classification of levels of interaction and abstraction required in different applications. More recently, Thalmann *et al.* [26, 27] proposed a new classification of synthetic actors according to the method of controlling motion, interaction and control of face and body. Noser and Thalmann [28] have described an L-system animation to model autonomous agents able to learn using synthetic vision and perception issues. Brogan *et al.* [29] and Bouvier [30] have also presented groups and crowd simulations using particle systems and significant dynamics. In recent work, a crowd model has been introduced using different abstractions of behaviors, such as the term *guided crowd* [31].

Kallmann *et al.* [32] introduced the concept of smart-objects to specify entities containing interaction information of various kinds: intrinsic object properties, information on how to interact with it, object functionality, and also the expected agent behaviors. Applications based on agent–object interactions allow human factors engineers to test and analyse designed environments [33]. An example of such an application is presented by Johnson *et al.* [34], whose purpose is to train equipment usage in a virtual environment.

18.3 Modeling the Properties of Virtual Humans

18.3.1 Introduction

For the modeling of actor behaviors, the ultimate objective is to build intelligent autonomous virtual humans with adaptation, perception and memory. These virtual humans should be able to act freely and emotionally. They should be conscious and unpredictable. But can we expect in the near future to represent in the computer the concepts of behavior, intelligence, autonomy, adaptation, perception, memory, freedom, emotion, consciousness, and unpredictability? First, we will try to define these terms. More details may be found in [35].

- *Behavior* for virtual humans may be defined as the manner of conducting themselves. It is also the response of an individual, group, or species to its environment.
- *Intelligence* may be defined as the ability to learn or understand, or to deal with new or trying situations.
- *Autonomy* is generally defined as the quality or state of being self-governing.

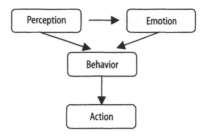

Figure 18.1 Structure of the behavioral model

- *Adaptation*: an artificial organism is adaptive as long as it may "survive" in more or less unpredictable and dangerous environments.
- *Perception* is defined as the awareness of the elements of environment through physical sensation.
- *Memory* is generally defined as the power or process of reproducing or recalling what has been learned and retained, especially through associative mechanisms.
- *Emotion* may be defined as the affective aspect of consciousness; this is a state of feeling, a psychic and physical reaction subjectively experienced as strong feelings and physiologically involving changes that prepare the body for immediate vigorous action.
- *Consciousness* may be defined as the quality or state of being aware, especially of something within oneself, or the state of being characterized by sensation, emotion, volition, and thought.
- *Freedom* for a virtual actor may be defined as the extent to which its future behaviour is unpredictable to somebody.

In the following sections we will try first to identify which mechanisms should be simulated in order to implement truly virtual humans or actors. We can start from the structure proposed by Becheiraz and Thalmann [36] and shown in Figure 18.1. It links perception, emotion, behavior, and finally action. Then we will discuss the important concepts of memory. Autonomy is a central characteristic that will be discussed in more detail in Section 18.4, where *Levels of Autonomy* will be introduced. Unfortunately, other properties, like freedom and consciousness, or even intelligence, are still extremely hard to model. We will concentrate our efforts on behavior, autonomy, perception, memory, emotion, and action.

18.3.2 Perception

Perception is defined as the awareness of the elements of the environment through physical sensation. In order to implement perception, virtual humans should be equipped with visual, tactile and auditory sensors. These sensors should be used as a basis for implementing everyday human behaviour, such as visually directed locomotion, handling objects, and responding to sounds and utterances. A simulation of the touching system should consist in detecting contacts between the virtual human and the environment. The most important perceptual subsystem is the vision system. A vision-based approach for virtual humans is a very important perceptual subsystem and is, for example, essential for navigation in virtual worlds. It is an ideal approach for modeling a behavioral animation and offers a universal approach to pass the necessary information from the environment to the virtual human in the problems of path searching, obstacle avoidance, and internal knowledge representation with learning and forgetting characteristics. Vision-based behavioral models have already been described by Renault *et al.* [37] and Reynolds [38]. In [37], each pixel of the vision input has the semantic information giving the object projected on this pixel, and numerical information giving the distance to this object. So it is easy to know, for example, that there is a table just in front, 3 meters away. With this information, we can directly deal with the problematic question: "What do I do with such information in a navigation system?".

At a higher level, we may decompose perception as suggested by Becheiraz and Thalmann [36]. An actor's perception may include only the objects and the other actors in its neighborhood. But in this case, it limits the possible behaviors because only the presence and the characteristics of an object or an actor are used to select a behavior. The actions of the actors and their consequences are not taken into account. The perception module should then produce three types of perception. The first type is the perception of the presence of objects and actors. This is called *perception of objects*. The second type is the perception of actions of actors. This perception is called *perception of actions*. The last type is the perception of actors performing actions on objects. This is called *perception of events*. The result of a perception is composed of three lists of objects, actions and events. Perception of events is slightly more complex because events themselves are decomposed into three classes: desirable events, events happening to another actor, and potential events which may or may not occur. When the perception of an actor, one of its actions and the object involved together match the definition of a desirable event, it is perceived. The perception of an event happening to another actor is similar to that of desirable events, except that the actor is always different from the one perceiving the event. The perception of potential events is made in two steps. A potential event may actually occur after a certain time, or it may never happen. So at first a potential event is perceived, and later it is either confirmed or unconfirmed. The perception of the nature and the characteristics of an object, an actor or an action is not easily done from their 3D representation. Recognizing an action through motion is difficult as well. The solution adopted is to categorize every object, actor and action based on its nature and characteristics.

18.3.3 Emotion

Emotion may be defined as the affective aspect of consciousness; this is a state of feeling, a psychic and physical reaction (as anger or fear) subjectively experienced as strong feelings and physiologically involving changes that prepare the body for immediate vigorous action. Virtual humans should be capable of responding emotionally to their situation as well as acting physically within it. Apart from making the virtual humans more realistic, visible emotions on the part of the virtual humans could provide designers with a direct way of affecting the user's own emotional state. Virtual humans will therefore be equipped with a simple computational model of emotional behaviour, to which emotionally related behaviour such as facial expressions and posture can be coupled, and which can be used to influence their actions.

An emotion is an emotive reaction of a person to a perception. This reaction induces him or her to assume a body response, a facial expression, or a gesture, or select a specific behavior. An emotion takes place between a perception and a subsequent reaction. Two different persons can thus have different reactions to the same perception, according to the way they are affected by this perception.

Ortony *et al.* [39] describe an emotional model. The generated emotions belong to three classes which are the same as the perception classes. The emotions are generated in reaction to objects, actions of agents and events. The class of emotions caused by events is partitioned into three groups of emotion types. The first group concerns the emotions caused by potential events. The second group concerns events affecting the fortune of others and the last one concerns events affecting the well-being of the actor. Each class is characterized by emergence conditions for each of its emotions and variables affecting its intensity. The emotions felt by an actor are caused by its perception. Although some perceived objects, actors or actions are necessary for the emergence of an emotion, they may not possess some required qualities with sufficient intensity to produce an emotion effectively felt by the actor.

18.3.4 Behavior

Behavior is often defined as the way in which animals and humans act, and is usually described in natural language terms which have social, psychological or physiological significance, but which are not necessarily easily reducible to the movement of one or two muscles, joints or end effectors. Behavior is also the response of an individual, group, or species to its environment. Based on this definition, Reynolds [5] introduced the term and the concept of *behavioral animation* in order to describe the automating of such higher level animation. Behavior is not only reacting to the environment, but should also include the flow of information by which the environment acts on the living creature as well as the way the creature codes and uses this information.

Behavior may be described in a hierarchical way. The behavioral model decomposes a behavior into simpler behaviors which may themselves be decomposed into other behaviors. Each level of this hierarchical decomposition contains one or more behaviors which are performed either sequentially, or concurrently. A level of the hierarchy containing several behaviors to be performed sequentially is called a behavior. Each behavior of a behavior sequence is called a behavioral cell. A behavioral cell contains behaviors which are performed either concurrently or exclusively when inhibition rules are specified. The behaviors contained in a behavioral cell are either behaviors or elementary behaviors. A behavior allows recursive decomposition in the hierarchy of a behavior. An elementary behavior is situated at the bottom of the hierarchical decomposition and encapsulates a specialized behavior which directly controls one or more actions. A behavior is executed by recursively performing each of the behavior, behavioral cell and elementary behavior entities at each level of the hierarchical structure of the behavior. At the top is a behavior entity with a finite state automata composed of at least one behavioral cell. The active behavioral cell is then performed. The state of each of its behaviors or elementary behaviors is evaluated. Then, for each active behavior or elementary behavior, the inhibition links, if any, are applied. Only active and non-inhibited behaviors or elementary behaviors are performed. This process is applied recursively down to the bottom of the behavior hierarchy, terminating with the elementary behaviors. The actions encapsulated by their specialized behaviors are then performed.

A high-level behavior uses in general sensorial input and special knowledge. A way of modeling behaviors is to use an automata approach. Each actor has an internal state which can change each time step according to the currently active automata and its sensorial input. In the following we use behavior and automata as synonyms. To control the global behavior of an actor we use a stack of automata. At the beginning of the animation the user provides a sequence of behaviors (the script) and pushes them on the actor's stack. When the current behavior ends the animation system pops the next behavior from the stack and executes it. This process is repeated until the actor's behavior stack is empty. Some of the behaviors use this stack too, in order to reach subgoals by pushing themselves with the current state on the stack and switching to the new behavior, allowing them to reach the subgoal. When this new behavior has finished the automaton pops the old interrupted behavior and continues. This behavior control using a stack facilitates to an actor to become more autonomous and to create its own subgoals while executing the original script.

18.3.5 Action

Based on perceptual information, the actor's behavioral mechanism will determine the actions it will perform. Actions may be of several degrees of complexity. An actor may simply evolve in its environment, it may interact with this environment or it may even communicate with other actors. We will emphasize three types of action: navigation and locomotion, grasping, and ball games.

Actions are performed using a common architecture for motion [40]. The motion control part includes five generators (keyframing, inverse kinematics, dynamics, walking and grasping) and high-level tools to combine and blend them. The action module [41] manages the execution of the different actions used by a behavior by animating a generic human model based on a node hierarchy [40]. It allows the concurrent or sequential execution of actions by managing smooth transitions between terminating and initiating actions.

The animation is driven by a behavioral loop. The role of the behavioral loop is to update the state of the virtual world corresponding to the new time. At each new iteration, the new time is incremented by a discrete time step. To update the state of the virtual world, the loop must update the state of each object and actor. In the case of an actor, the perception is done first; then its emotions are generated before its behavior and its actions are performed:

    repeat
        for each object and actor

```
            perception
    for each actor
            emotions generation
    for each object and actor
            behavior execution
    for each object and actor
            actions execution
```

18.3.6 Memory

Memory is generally defined as the power or process of reproducing or recalling what has been learned and retained, especially through associative mechanisms. This is also the store of things learned and retained from an organism's activity or experience as evidenced by modification of structure or behavior or by recall and recognition.

To implement a concept of memory into a virtual human is not very complex, as memory is already a key concept in computer science. For example, Noser and Thalmann [42] propose a dynamic occupancy octree grid to serve as a global 3D visual memory and to allow an actor to memorize the environment that it sees and to adapt it to a changing and dynamic environment. The actor's reasoning process allows it to find 3D paths based on its visual memory by avoiding impasses and circuits. The global behavior of the actor is based on a navigation automaton representing the automaton of an actor which has to go from its current position to different places, memorized in a list of destinations. It can displace itself in known or unknown environments.

18.4 Autonomy and Levels of Autonomy

18.4.1 Autonomy

Autonomy is generally defined as the quality or state of being self-controlled. Bourgine [43] defines an autonomous system as a system which has the abductive capacity to guess viable actions. As stated by Courant *et al.* [44], in cybernetics as well as in cognitive psychology autonomy has always been strongly connected with self-organization. Hence computer scientists sometimes prefer to take the following definition of autonomy "the capacity of a system to maintain its viability in various and changing environments".

The need to have autonomous behaviour for virtual humans arises in several situations:

- in virtual environments where users can have aid from virtual humans for learning, equipment training etc.
- in computer-generated films, the more autonomous behaviour that is built into the virtual humans, the less extra work there is to be done by the designer to create complete scenarios
- in simulation of real-life events, such as building evacuation in the event of fire

Table 18.1 Comparison between different LOAs.

	Guided	Programmed	Autonomous
Memory	Generally not provided	Generally not provided	Connected with others parameters internally to agents
Learning	Not provided	Not provided	Can be present
Autonomy	Low	Medium	High
Self-control	Not provided	Not provided	Result of a behavioural complex process using other internal parameters
Perception	Generally not provided	Should be provided	Can be vision, structure-oriented and connected to other parameters, e.g. action
Behaviour	Driven-oriented	Program-oriented	Agent-oriented. Result of behavioural process using other parameters, e.g. perception
Action	Driven-oriented	Program-oriented	Agent-oriented decision
Motion	Driven-oriented	Program-oriented	Motion planning based

- in interactive games, autonomous human-like behaviour is necessary in order to maintain the illusion in the user that the virtual humans are real ones

Different parameters of agents' simulation can be defined in order to achieve the desired compromise between different requirements. Among others, interactivity, complex behaviours, intelligent abilities and frame rate of execution are directly related to the level of autonomy (LOA) that each entity of the simulation might have. Based on the Level of Autonomy (LOA), we may then introduce three kinds of behavioural autonomy: guided, programmed and autonomous. Guided autonomy represents the lower level of autonomy, where the behaviours must be informed by an external process (user, other system etc.). Programmed control implies the use of a notation (language) to define possible behaviours, which the entity is then able to translate into internal behaviours. Guided or programmed agents can be useful depending on the application. When less compromise with complex behaviours is necessary in the simulation, agents that are "less autonomous" can represent the best performance in terms of execution frame rate and interactivity. Table 18.1 presents some comparison data between these three kinds of LOA.

The classification presented in Table 18.1 shows the main differences between the three kinds of agent control. In any case, some systems can be developed by mixing the type of control in the same simulation. For instance, an agent could have a programmed or guided motion, but also memory with learning processes in order to achieve new behaviors, which might have greater priority than the programmed or guided behaviors.

Table 18.2 exemplifies the three kinds of agent autonomy using two different agent tasks: (1) agent goes to a specific location; (2) agent applies specific action.

18.4.2 LOA Related to Groups of Agents

In the case of crowd simulation, we usually intend to have lots of virtual human agents, but avoid dealing with individual behaviours. In contrast to the last section, our goal here is to describe methods to provide intelligence focused in a common group entity that controls its individuals. Figure 18.2 shows the correlation between these two parameters.

Table 18.2 LOA present in different agent-oriented tasks.

Agent LOA	Agent goes to a specific location	Agent applies a specific action
Guided	Agent needs to receive during the simulation a list of collision-free positions	Agent needs to receive information about the action to be applied
Programmed	Agent is programmed to manage the information of a path to follow while avoiding collision with other agents and programmed obstacles	Agent is programmed to manage where and how the action can occur
Autonomous	Agent is able to perceive information in the environment and decide a path to follow to reach the goal, using the environment perception or the memory (past experiences)	Agent can decide about an action to be applied. This action can be programmed, imitated or existent in the memory (past experiences)

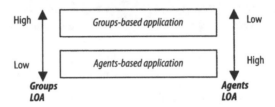

Figure 18.2 Correlation between groups and agents LOA.

We have called the crowd and group applications groups-based applications, where individual complexity is less required. In this case, the intelligence abstraction can be included in the groups, providing more autonomy to the groups instead of the individuals. On the other hand, agents-based applications concern more complex individuals, as shown in the last section. Some different classes of techniques have been discussed in the literature depending on the number of elements being controlled and the sophistication of the control strategy [3]: particle [45], flocking [5] and hybrid systems, mixing particle, flocking and reactive behaviours [31].

The methods presented in Table 18.3 are characterized by emergent behaviours: a global effect generated by local rules [3]. Although some crowd simulations seem to be formed by autonomous agents, this is not completely true. In fact, normally this concerns simple individuals controlled by complex groups' behaviours. However, some rule-based behavioural animation can be used in simulations formed by small groups, as characterized in Table 18.4 [3].

Considering levels of autonomy (LOA), we have classified the crowd behaviours into three groups:

1. Guided crowds, whose behaviours are defined explicitly by the users
2. Programmed crowds, whose behaviours are programmed in a script language
3. Autonomous crowds, whose behaviours are specified using rules or other complex methods

Table 18.5 exemplifies this classification of crowd autonomy using two different crowd tasks: "group goes to a specific location", and "group reacts to matched event".

Table 18.3 Table modified from the original [3] in order to include hybrid systems [31].

Method	Particle systems	Flocking systems	Hybrid systems
Structure	Non-hierarchical	Levels: flock, agents	Levels: crowd, groups, agents
Participants	Many	Some	Many
Intelligence	None	Some	Some
Physics-based	Yes	Some	Can be
Collision	Detect and respond	Avoidance	Avoidance
Control	Force fields	Local tendency in the flock structure	Pre-defined, rules and guided

Table 18.4 Behavioural method to simulate complex behaviours.

Method	Behavioral systems
Structure	Can present hierarchy
Participants	Few
Intelligence	High
Physics-based	No
Collision	Avoidance
Control	Rules

Table 18.5 LOAs present in different group-oriented tasks.

Crowd LOA	Group goes to a specific location	Group reacts to matched event
Guided	Group needs to receive during the simulation a list of positions "in-between" in order to reach the goal	Group needs to receive an information about the matched event and the reaction to be applied
Programmed	Group is programmed to manage the information of a path to follow avoiding collision with other agents and programmed obstacles	Group can manage events and reactions, which are programmed
Autonomous	Group is able to perceive information in the environment and decide a path to follow to reach the goal, using the environment perception or the memory (past experiences)	Group can perceive a matched event and decide about the reaction to be applied. This reaction can be also programmed or existent in the group memory (past experiences)

By considering the hierarchy existent normally in crowd systems (crowds, groups and agents), complex structures such as memory and decision making can be defined at the group level, in this case optimizing the fact that the agents do not need to have this information.

18.4.3 LOA Related to Objects

Whenever the simulation needs to handle complex agent–object interactions, many difficult issues arise. Such difficulties are related to the fact that each object has its own movements, functionality and purposes.

There is a range of growing complexity for possible agent–object interactions in a virtual environment. Examples are actions like grasping a fruit or automatic doors that open when agents are nearby, and also complex actions like entering a lift.

One can consider that agents' perceptions can solve all the necessary reasoning and planning processes to achieve some simple tasks, such as a single hand's automatic grasping of small objects [46]. But this is not possible for interactions with objects that have an intricate proper functionality, as in the lift example (Fig. 18.4). Moreover, even for simpler interactions, such as our grasping example, we did not consider semantic aspects, e.g. recognizing through sensors whether or not a given fruit can be eaten.

A first approach to overcome these difficulties is to maintain a table with some semantic and grasping information for all graspable objects [47]. Another approach models all possible object interaction features, such as its functionality and semantic information, containing also a complete description of all the possible interactions it can offer to the agent [32].

In fact, each time more information related to the object is given, its level of autonomy (LOA) is increased. In the scope of simulations in virtual environments, increasing the LOA of an object will make it move from a guided state through a programmed state until it achieves a completely autonomous state. In the lowest LOA, the object knows only the possible movements to be applied to its parts. In the highest LOA, the object has all the interaction information necessary, in the form of pre-defined plans, to take control over the agent to make it perform the interaction. In the mid-term, the programmed object controls its moveable parts based on the agent decisions taken during the interaction.

Table 18.6 illustrates how an agent must proceed according to the different LOAs for three different interactive objects of the environment: a door that opens with a simple lateral translation movement, a direction sign, and a two-stage lift.

Depending on the LOA of each object, different sensors (see Table 18.1) are required to exist in the agent in order to perform an interaction. Such sensors can

Table 18.6 LOA present in different object-oriented tasks.

Object LOA	Door	Sign	Lift
Guided	The agent has to move its arm to an attainable and meaningful location on the door, and control its movement until the door opens	The agent recognizes that the sign has an arrow and recognizes the direction shown	The agent recognizes where the call button is, how and when the door opens, how and where to enter inside the lift, when and how to go out, etc.
Programmed	The agent has to move its arm to the right place, but the door opens by itself	The agent recognizes the sign, but the direction is given with no recognition	The agent accesses the current lift state and decides only its moves accordingly
Autonomous	The door takes control of the agent, telling it exactly the place to put its hand and how to complete the movement of the door	The sign gives a new direction to go for each agent that passes nearby	The lift takes control of the movements of the agent and gives it a complete plan, based on primitive actions, to perform the interaction

be difficult to control and are expensive in terms of both computer memory and computer processing time. To minimize such side effects, and depending on the application, it can be interesting to use highly autonomous interactive objects. This means adopt the strategy of leaving inside each interactive object a list of available pre-defined plans that are automatically updated depending on objects' internal states.

18.4.4 A New Abstraction for Specification of Behaviours

As presented in the preceding sections, our new paradigm for defining the LOA of virtual human agents considers that the "intelligence" is not only included in the virtual human agents, but can also be included in groups and objects. In this section, we describe this new paradigm, mentioning examples of different simulations where the autonomy abstraction is variable for the entities of the simulation. Considering the abstraction levels (guided, programmed and autonomous behavior), we present a schema that includes the entities group and object, as showed in Fig. 18.3.

We can thus classify a simulation in terms of the autonomy distribution among its entities, i.e. a simulation (S_i), can be translated as a function of three components (agents, groups and objects), as follows:

$S_i = f(\text{LOA(Agents)}, \text{LOA(Groups)}, \text{LOA(Objects)})$

In this way, depending on the application, one can choose the best distribution of autonomy to adopt. In general, if the simulation wants to focus on the behaviour of a given entity, this entity might have a maximum LOA.

Interesting cases may arise when we choose to have different LOAs among individuals of the same entity type. For example, consider the case of a simulation of autonomous agents, with a limited set of sensors, interacting with objects. The objects of the environment which are simple enough to be guided by such agents can be initialized as guided, while other more complex objects can be initialized with more autonomy. A consistent strategy of priorities and negotiation must be adopted in simulations where two entities with high LOA need to achieve a common task. One example is when an autonomous agent receives from an

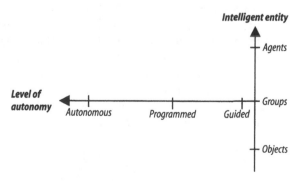

Figure 18.3 Level of autonomy vs. intelligent entity.

Figure 18.4 Agents interacting with a lift. Image generated using a lift programmed as a smart object [32].

autonomous object a complete plan to achieve some interaction task. In this case, the agent will use its sensors to validate, or even ameliorate, the given plan. For this to happen, both entities must be capable of negotiating, having a common notion of priorities. A similar negotiation is needed when an autonomous agent is required to follow a behavior that comes from its current autonomous group control.

These simulations are exemplified by the following description of three simulations:

1. Simulation of autonomous agents in a train station, which involves interaction with several objects: chairs, counters and a lift. Most of them are guided objects, while the lift, which has a complex functionality, is autonomous. Thus we consider that the overall object autonomy is medium (programmed). The agent can perceive and interact with the different kinds of objects, sit down on the chair, buy a ticket at a counter and take the lift. However, due to the limited set of agent perceptions no negotiation is done between the agent and the lift; the agent just accepts the autonomous behaviour of the lift (Fig. 18.4).

2. Simulation of groups of agents involved in a political demonstration. The groups have their motion programmed but are autonomous concerning their perception of other agents and their ability to react to the proximity of others (Fig. 18.5). As in example 1, we have chosen to represent this mixed control as medium LOA. The agents are just programmed according to the groups' behaviours.

3. Simulation of a party populated by autonomous groups. The groups have two possible emotional statuses: SOCIAL (representing groups that prefer to walk and meet others instead of eating) or HUNGRY (the opposite idea). Through the

Figure 18.5 Political demonstration where autonomous and programmed groups are able to interact with others and react as a function of it. Image generated using a crowd simulation framework [48].

Figure 18.6 Autonomous groups interacting with autonomous objects. Image generated by mixing a smart object control [32] inside the crowd simulation framework [31].

meeting of groups, the emotional status can be dynamically changed as a function of sociological rules [48]. If a group decides to eat something, the autonomous object table [49] controls the interaction with the table of food (Fig. 18.6).

18.5 Conclusions

We have proposed in this chapter a new abstraction to be considered in order to distribute autonomy among the entities of a simulation. The idea we have dealt with here concerns the possibility of improve the frame rate of execution as well as optimizing the complexity required by distributing some knowledge and autonomy to other entities in the simulation: groups and objects. This paradigm has been tested in the context of a Virtual City project [50] because we have to simulate several virtual human agents that can act in different ways and apply different actions.

Acknowledgements

The research was sponsored by the Swiss National Research Foundation, the Federal Office for Education and Science (in the framework of the European Projects COVEN and eRENA), FUNDEPE, CAPES and CNPq (Brazilian offices of Education and Science).

References

[1]   Meyer, J.A. and Guillot, A. From SAB90 to SAB94: four years of animat research. In *Proceedings of Third International Conference on Simulation of Adaptive Behavior*, Brighton, UK, 1994.

[2]   Bates, J. The role of emotion in believable agents. *Communications of the ACM*, 37(7), 122–125, 1994.

[3]   Parent, R. *Computer Animation: Algorithms and Techniques*, http://www.cis.ohiostate.edu/~parent/OxfordPress.html.

[4]   Wooldridge, M. and Jennings, N. Intelligent agents: theory and practice. *Knowledge Engineering Review*, 10(2), 1995.

[5]   Reynolds, C. (1987) Flocks, herds, and schools: a distributed behavioral model, *Proc. SIGGRAPH '87, Computer Graphics*, 21(4), 25–34, 1987.

[6]   Badler, N.I., Phillips, C., and Webber, B.L. *Simulating Humans: Computer Graphics, Animation, and Control*. Oxford University Press, New York, 1993.

[7]   Tu, X. and Terzopoulos D. Artificial fishes: physics, locomotion, perception, behavior, *Proc. SIGGRAPH '94, Computer Graphics*, pp. 42–48, 1994.

[8]   Hodgins, J.K., Wooten, W.L., Brogan D.C., and O'Brien, J.F. Animating human athletics. *Proceedings of SIGGRAPH '95*, pp. 71–78, Los Angeles, CA, 6–11 August 1995.

[9]   Unuma, M., Anjyo, K., and Takeuchi, R. Fourier principles for emotion-based human figure animation. *Proceedings of SIGGRAPH '95*, pp. 91–96, Los Angeles, CA, 6–11 August 1995.

[10] Brooks, R.A. A robust layered control system for a mobile robot. *IEEE Journal of Robotics and Automation*, RA-2(1), 1986.

[11] Brooks, R.A. A robot that walks; emergent behaviors from a carefully evolved network. *MIT AI Lab Memo 1091*, February 1989.

[12] Maes, P. "How to do the right thing, *Connection Science*, 1(3), 1989.

[13] Beer, R.D., Ritzmann, R.E. and McKenna, T. (eds.) *Biological Neural Networks in Invertebrate Neuroethology and Robotics*. Academic Press, 1993.

[14] Ahmad, O., Cremer, J., Hansen, S., Kearny, J., and Willemsen, P. Hierarchical, concurrent state machines for behavior modeling and scenario control. In *Conference on AI, Planning, and Simulation in High Autonomy Systems*, Gainesville, Florida, 1994.

[15] Blumberg, B.M. Action-selection in hamsterdam: lessons from ethology. In *Third International Conference on the Simulation of Adaptive Behavior*, pp. 108–117, Brighton, UK, 1994.

[16] Blumberg, B.M. and Galyean, T.A. Multi-level direction of autonomous creatures for real-time virtual environment. In *Proceedings of SIGGGRAPH '95*, pp. 47–54, August 1995.

[17] Maes, P. Artifical life meets entertainment: lifelike autonomous agents. In *Communications of the ACM*, 38(11), 108–114, 1995.

[18] Maes, P., Darell, T., Blumberg, B., and Pentland, A. The ALIVE system: full-body interaction with autonomous agents. *Proceedings of Computer Animation '95*, pp. 11–18, Geneva, Switzerland, 19–21 April 1995.

[19] Perlin, K. Interacting with virtual actors. *Visual Proceedings of SIGGRAPH '95*, pp. 92–93, Los Angeles, CA, 6–11 August 1995.

[20] Mataric, M.J. From local interactions to collective intelligence. In *The biology and Technology of Intelligent Autonomous Agents* (ed. Luc Steels). NATO ASI Series F, Vol. 144, pp. 275–295, 1995.

[21] Bécheiraz, P. and Thalmann, D. A model of nonverbal communication and interpersonal relationship between virtual actors. In *Proceedings of Computer Animation '96*, Geneva, 1996

[22] Reilly, W.S.N. Believable social and emotional agents. *Technical Report CMU-CS-96-138*, School of Computer Science, Carnegie Mellon University, December 1996.

[23] Loyall, A.B. and Bates, J. Personality-rich believable agents that use language. *Proceedings of the First International Conference on Autonomous Agents*, Marina del Rey, California, February 1997.

[24] Mateas, M. An Oz-centric review of interactive drama and believable agents. *Technical Report CMU-CS-97-156*, School of Computer Science, Carnegie Mellon University, Pittsburgh, PA, June 1997.

[25] Zeltzer, D. Task-level graphical simulation: abstraction, representation and control. In *Making them Move: Mechanics, Control and Animation of Articulated Figures* (ed. N. Badler, B. Barsky, and D. Zeltzer), pp. 3–33, 1991.

[26] Thalmann, D. A New generation of synthetic actors: the interactive perceptive actors. *Proc. Pacific Graphics '96*, National Chiao Tung University Press, Hsinchu, Taiwan, pp. 200–219, 1996.

[27] Cavazza, M., Earnshaw, R., Magnenat-Thalmann, N. and Thalmann, D. Motion control of virtual humans. *IEEE Computer Graphics and Applications*, 18(5), 24–31, 1998.

[28] Noser, H. and Thalmann, D. (1996) The animation of autonomous actors based on production rules, *Proceedings Computer Animation '96*, 3–4 June 1996, Geneva, Switzerland. IEEE Computer Society Press, Los Alamitos, California, pp. 47–57, 1996.

[29] Brogan, D.C., Metoyer, R.A., and Hodgins, J.K. Dynamically simulated characters in virtual environments. *IEEE Computer Graphics and Applications*. 18(5), 58–69, 1998.

[30] Bouvier, E., Cohen, E., and Najman, L. From crowd simulation to airbag deployment: particle systems, a new paradigm of simulation. *Journal of Electronic Imaging*, 6(1), 94–107, 1997.

[31] Musse, S.R., Babski, C., Capin, T., and Thalmann, D. Crowd modelling in collaborative virtual environments. *ACM VRST '98*, Taiwan

[32] Kallmann, M. and Thalmann, D. Modeling objects for interaction tasks, *Proc. Eurographics Workshop on Animation and Simulation*, 1998.

[33] Badler, N. Virtual humans for animation, ergonomics, and simulation. *IEEE Workshop on Non-Rigid and Articulated Motion*, Puerto Rico, June 1997.

[34] Johnson, W.L. and Rickel, J. Steve: an animated pedagogical agent for procedural training in virtual environments, *Sigart Bulletin*, 8(1–4), 16–21, 1997.

[35] Magnenat Thalmann N., Thalmann D. Creating artificial life in virtual reality. In *Artificial Life and Virtual Reality* (eds. Magnenat Thalmann, N. and Thalmann, D.). John Wiley, Chichester, 1994, pp. 1–10.

[36] Becheiraz, P. and Thalmann, D. A behavioral animation system for autonomous actors personified by emotions, *Proc. First Workshop on Embodied Conversational Characters (WECC 98)*, Lake Tahoe, USA.

[37] Renault, O., Magnenat-Thalmann, N., and Thalmann, D. A vision-based approach to behavioral animation, *The Journal of Visualization and Computer Animation*, 1(1), 18–21.

[38] Reynolds, C.W. An evolved, vision-based behavioral model of coordinated group motion. In *From Animals to Animats* (eds. Meyer, J.A., Roitblat, H.L., and Wilson, S.W.), Proc. 2nd International Conf. on Simulation of Adaptive Behavior, MIT Press, 1993.

[39] Ortony, A., Clore, G.L., and Collins, A. *The Cognitive Structure of Emotions*. Cambridge University Press, 1990.

[40] Boulic, R., Capin, T., Kalra, P., Lintermann, B., Moccozet, L., Molet, T., Huang, Z., Magnenat-Thalmann, N., Saar, K., Schmitt, A., Shen, J., and Thalmann, D. The HUMANOID environment for interactive animation of multiple deformable human characters. *Proceedings of EUROGRAPHICS '95*, pp. 337–348, Maastricht, The Netherlands, 28 August–1 September 1995.

[41] Boulic, R., Bécheiraz, P., Emering, L., and Thalmann, D. Integration of motion control techniques for virtual human and avatar real-time animation. *Proc. VRST '97*, ACM Press, pp. 111–118, September 1997.

[42] Noser, H., Renault, O., Thalmann, D., and Magnenat Thalmann, N. Navigation for digital actors based on synthetic vision, memory and learning, *Computers and Graphics*, 19(1), 7–19, 1995.

[43] Bourgine, P. *Autonomy, abduction, adaptation*, in *Proc. Computer Animation '94* (eds. Magnenat Thalmann, N. and Thalmann, D.). IEEE Computer Society Press, 1994.

[44] Courant, M., Beat Hirsbrunner, B., and Stoffel, B. Managing entities for an autonomous behaviour, in *Artificial Life in Virtual Reality* (eds. Magnenat Thalmann, N. and Thalmann, D.). John Wiley & Sons, 1994.

[45] Reeves, W. Particle systems – a technique for modeling a class of fuzzy objects, *ACM Transactions on Graphics*, 2(2), April 1993.

[46] Huang, Z. *et al.* A multi-sensor approach for grasping and 3D interaction, *Proc. Computer Graphics International '95*, Leeds, Academic Press, pp. 235–254.

[47] Levison, L. Connecting planning and acting via object-specific reasoning, *PhD thesis*, Dept. of Computer & Information Science, University of Pennsylvania, 1996.

[48] Musse, S.R. and Thalmann, D. A model of human crowd behavior: group inter-relationship and collision detection analysis. *Proc. Workshop of Computer Animation and Simulation of Eurographics '97*, September 1997. Budapest, Hungary.

[49] Kallmann, M. and Thalmann, D. A behavioral interface to simulate agent–object interactions in real time. *Proc. Computer Animation '99*, IEEE Computer Society Press, 1999.

[50] Farenc, N. *et al.* A paradigm for controlling virtual humans in urban environment simulation. *Applied Artificial Intelligence Journal*, Special Issue on Artificial Intelligence (in press).

19

An Inhabited 3D Oil Platform for Immersive CSCW

Roland Mark Banks

Abstract

This chapter describes the implementation of an application jointly developed by BT Laboratories and Telenor Research to explore the possibilities for group-to-group collaboration within spatially immersive display environments such as the VisionDome™ and RealityCentre™, using a distributed software platform. The application investigated the issues surrounding the networking of our respective systems and the potential benefits to the oil and petrochemical industries in using telepresence as a means of collaboration.

We consider the usability of the system, and the network and hardware issues encountered during the trial and its technical implementation, as well as a more general discussion of the merits and implications for the oil and telecommunications industries.

19.1 Introduction

Early in 1998 a small team within BT formed a collaboration with the Applied Media Technology (AMT) research group within Telenor, Norway's leading telecommunications operator, to conduct a unique experiment. Our aim was to network our respective immersive virtual reality systems to provide an inhabited teleconferencing space – integrating video with the sharing of information between remote participants, within a computer-generated environment.

Two main issues arose from this experiment: (1) how does a co-located group interact and control a shared data set and (2) how is this experience extended to a second group located over 800 miles away?

The visual display systems used in the experiment are commonly referred to as RealityCentres[1]. RealityCentres [1, 2] provide a workable virtual reality experience

---

1   RealityCentre is a trademark of Silicon Graphics, Inc.

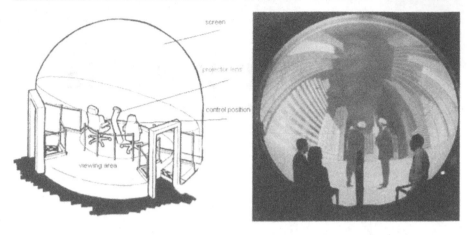

Figure 19.1 The VisionDome at BT Labs and interior view showing pre-recorded material.

for a small group of people to interact without the need for a headset. Increasingly, RealityCentres are used in AEC, engineering and petrochemical applications. The application used to illustrate this immersive collaborative environment is based on a petrochemical scenario.

This chapter provides an overview of (1) RealityCentres, (2) the research aims of the experiment, (3) the technical implementation of the experimental system and (4) conclusions which are leading to further research in this area.

19.2 Background

In May 1998 the Visualization Summit [3] took place in Oslo, Norway – aimed primarily at delegates from the oil, gas and AEC sectors highlighting the benefits of immersive computer-supported collaborative working (CSCW).

The VisionDome [4] (Fig. 19.1) at BT Laboratories provided the setting for one half of the link-up between BT in the UK and the Summit in Oslo. Manufactured by Alternative Realities Corporation[2] (ARC), the VisionDome is a hemispherical display system with a 180° field of view provided by a special projector lens. Fifteen people can be accommodated within a five-metre diameter, eliminating the need for restrictive head-mounted displays, while promoting group interaction. A high degree of visual realism is attained as a combined result of the optics, display properties and computing power.

BT has been using the VisionDome as a research platform for a number of years to investigate various aspects of advanced teleconferencing environments – application design, sense of presence, spatial audio systems [5] – and to conduct human factors evaluation.

---

2   VisionDome is a trademark of Alternative Realities Corporation (http://
www.virtual-reality.com/)

The remote half of the demonstration involved the Visionarium in Oslo – a semi-immersive RealityCentre comprising a large horizontally curved screen with a 150° horizontal by 40° vertical field of view, powered by a Silicon Graphics supercomputer. It enables a relatively large group of people to visualize complex information such as seismic and geological data, and review computer-aided design/manufacture (CAD/CAM) databases. Accommodating up to 35 people, there are facilities for fairly large groups to meet and interactively edit large databases or conduct a fly-through of a new building design. Since the first RealityCentre was opened by Silicon Graphics in 1994 at Theale, near Reading, UK, the concept has caught on – there are now around forty[3], and as many as five are opened each month.

19.3 Why an Oil Platform?

An ever-increasing number of RealityCentre users include large multinational oil companies, who wish to explore the possibilities of collaborative working for data visualization, design review and architectural walk-through. With the advent of powerful new computing architectures, object-oriented VR toolkits and application programming interfaces (APIs) the creation of distributed virtual environments is now a much quicker and simpler process; however, the networked group-to-group interaction aspects have largely been neglected.

Virtual reality techniques have been applied to many industrial applications, including CAD/CAM, virtual manufacturing, product development and rapid prototyping. The oil industry is one such beneficiary of these new technologies, highlighted by the notable success of the Conoco Caister Murdoch (CMS2) visualization, designed with CADCentre[4] software and implemented in the MAVERICK system [6]. The typical cost savings of such a project emphasize the effectiveness of modern visualization tools. A RealityCentre or VisionDome installation brings further benefits by enabling a large group to work together in ways not possible with desktop systems.

The design, construction, and maintenance of oil platforms is a hugely complex task, involving a great number of engineers, managers, designers, accountants and others. In bringing together the various members of a project team for a design review session or to assess construction details, a greater appreciation of the development cycle is conveyed to every member of the team, bringing tangible benefits to the entire process. Feasibility studies can be backed up with a broad range of supporting data, and costly engineering mistakes can be avoided much earlier by recognizing potential problem areas and design conflicts.

Immersive CSCW has been greatly enhanced by technological advances during the last few years – higher resolution projectors, edge-blending technology and vastly more powerful computers. Life-size three-dimensional imagery can enhance selected applications, particularly large-scale visualizations where the sense of

---

3   Source: Silicon Graphics customer magazine *Know*, issue 1
4   http://www.cadcentre.co.uk/

"being there" is important. In designing applications, the challenge is to seamlessly integrate audio, video and computer-generated components and provide a natural interface so that users can obtain information quickly and unambiguously.

By understanding the issues involved the telecommunications industry is better placed to support the network and service requirements of such systems, the characteristics of the applications and the needs of the users themselves from both technological and human factors standpoints.

19.4 The Scenario

The demonstration took place in May 1998 over two days during the Visualization Summit, and simulated a minor emergency onboard an oil platform – two critical sections of the pipework had collided during drilling, causing a leakage in the drill string and a subsequent explosion. Telenor played the role of the multinational oil company, and BT acted the part of the experts onboard the oil rig. Both groups had to follow the procedure that would occur in a real-life situation and try to prevent further catastrophe. The task was to control the leakage and prevent the pipes from colliding further, before deciding what course of action to take.

Several different scenario ideas were initially explored. Figure 19.2 shows an example of one of the earlier designs, showing the possible sequence of events during the demo.

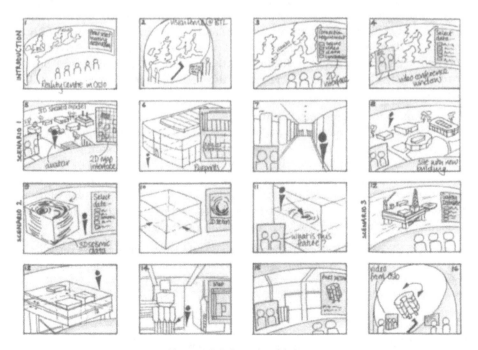

Figure 19.2 Early storyboard designs.

Figure 19.3 Screenshots from the introductory animation sequence.

Preceding the main demonstration was an introductory animation sequence (Fig. 19.3) illustrating the scenario to the audience, in which a remotely operated vehicle (ROV) inspected parts of the lower structure of the platform. The users were presented with a three-dimensional view of a fictitious oil platform in the North Sea, with information of relevance to the task displayed at specific points above and below the oil platform and at the point of collision. A panel of buttons is located in 3D space to the right of the main model, which can be used to rotate the image and select real-time pressure readings, weather charts and other data. The more familiar videoconferencing elements of live video and audio were an integral part of the environment: a video stream of the remote group was overlaid onto the model and digital MPEG movie files were displayed as texture-mapped polygons.

The physical appearance of the environment was modelled with industry-standard tools such as 3D Studio MAX, which was also used for early visualization and concept designs. The oilrig was based upon real 3D data from StatOil[5], who also provided some real-time movie footage for the textures. Geometry was subsequently converted to Virtual Reality Markup Language (VRML) format and imported into the demo.

19.5 Navigation and Interaction

The issues surrounding the interaction between participants within the environment are an important consideration when designing such an application. Navigation should be as intuitive as possible in a virtual environment, impacting upon the users' perceptions of the quality of interaction and their sense of presence of the overall experience. While these subjective measures are difficult to quantify, it

---

5 http://www.statoil.com/

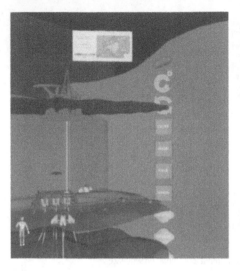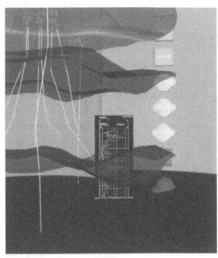

Figure 19.4 Images from the application showing oil platform, avatar and information panels.

seems obvious that natural, unhindered navigation acts as an aid to overall communication. If users have to struggle with the interface, this will affect their ability to use the tools in their fullest capacity.

User interface and design considerations played a major role in the application development, with the distinction between an inhabited space and traditional CAD/design review systems highlighted by the inclusion of lifelike texture-mapped avatars representing the users (Fig. 19.4). The nature of the VisionDome dictates that special considerations must be made when designing application software due to the larger field of view, increased peripheral space and the impact of greater information density upon spatial awareness.

The software was developed as a prototype demonstration, and therefore we were limited to the mouse as an input device, both for navigation and interaction. Movement was made by a combination of dragging the mouse and pressing the alternate mouse buttons (using a Silicon Graphics three-button mouse); however, moving around the environment was not as easy as we had expected. It was often difficult to determine the precise location of other people within the world because the disparity between the field of view in the VisionDome and Visionarium (particularly in the vertical axis) meant that we were not always aware of each other. As such we relied partially on audio cues to judge their position – a degree of verbal coaxing was necessary to direct them to the point of interest.

As a result of the trial, suggested improvements for navigation and the user interface include:

• The use of force feedback, haptic interfaces and speech recognition technology to enhance the experience.
• The inclusion of more effective control mechanisms such as 6 degrees of freedom input devices, and an effective mapping between the control method and movement within the environment.

- Realistic physical constraints where appropriate. The simulation of gravity and accurate collision detection may be more applicable to certain kinds of software, for example manufacturing and training simulations, than to many virtual environments. Some VEs allow the user to follow the terrain or a convenient ground plane, of importance especially in building interiors where walking through objects could result in the user becoming disorientated. Steed [7] considers techniques for efficient collision detection and navigation.

- Context-sensitive navigation techniques. A selection of methods might be available, of which the most appropriate can be chosen according to the task, such as flying through space or the ability to teleport to a specific point. Large virtual environments where there is greater chance of becoming lost may benefit from waypoints, trails, virtual cairns [8] or point of interest (POI) navigation methods, as described by Mackinlay et al. [9].

- Intelligent agents to suggest and provide a range of supporting information, to search relevant databases, locate team members and organize meetings.

- More appropriate placement of multimedia elements. Users found difficulty obtaining the optimum viewing position for content within the world and selecting icons proved especially frustrating. The ability to align orientation to an object would be a convenient feature.

19.6 Discussion

Communication is perhaps the most important aspect of a collaborative virtual environment. Speech is the most widely used, although text chat, whiteboards and file transfer tools are popular additions to many VR systems.

We found that facial expression and gestures were limited when communicating with the other group. Natural eye contact was hindered due to the positioning of cameras and the low light levels required in both environments. Lighting difficulties are now partially alleviated with the arrival of newer VisionDome technology, and much brighter projectors with improved image clarity and colour definition enable relatively normal lighting conditions to be tolerated while still producing bright images onscreen.

In terms of user representation, avatars helped to convey some of the missing gestural cues and establish the users as inhabitants in the environment. The appearance of the avatars is completely customizable – clothes, hairstyle and general appearance.

Key aspects of communication we need to consider further are

- How communication is initiated, who has control of the interaction, and how different interaction techniques impact upon task performance. A similar technique to desktop conferencing software could be implemented where the chairperson relinquishes control of the floor to one of the participants, or a system that allows only the person holding a designated token to speak.

- The visual and audio feedback presented to the user. How does the use of gestures, eye contact (which was limited in our trial) and social protocols relate to the effectiveness of interaction?

- How group dynamics affect communication within immersive environments. Twenty or thirty people may be co-present; they probably cannot all interact in the same manner at once.
- Bandwidth requirements and network usage. Further trials would enable us to have a better understanding of the demands placed upon the underlying network and characterize the application more fully in terms of usability and performance.
- Whether we can we link up other systems at the same time, and how many simultaneous groups constitute an effective working team.

19.7 Conclusions

The BT/Telenor collaboration provided a unique opportunity to investigate a networked CSCW tool that could be used by the oil industry. Although purely a prototype demonstration system, the application gave us an insight into many of the technical and usability challenges associated with implementing a group-working environment, and furthered our understanding of the wider issues of telepresence in an immersive context. Further trials could enable a more comprehensive analysis and collation of user feedback, as well as a study of the effectiveness of immersive, semi-immersive and desktop environments when networked together. Each places unique constraints upon an application in terms of user interface, design, and interaction style.

The future will see many more applications of this type, particularly in RealityCentre installations, which are becoming increasingly commonplace, giving opportunities for the telecommunications industry to capitalize on the desire for high-end networked CSCW tools.

Appendix I

Implementation

The Visionarium uses a three-projector display system, whereas the VisionDome has a single curved hemispherical display, so the demo was tailored to meet the needs of both environments. There was extra display space in the former for additional data either side of the main demo window (Fig. 19.5), with the world occupying the centre region. The VisionDome poses some problems in this respect by nature of its curved display surface. ARC, however, has a unique solution, which is to replace the OpenGL system libraries with customized versions, resulting in the correctly distorted spherical shape.

The acoustic properties of domes pose certain challenges too. It is well accepted that spherical display surfaces are inherently problematic, and the VisionDome is no exception. On this occasion we opted not to use a spatial audio system, instead routing the audio feed from Oslo through a mixing desk, giving a limited amount of control.

Figure 19.5 View in Visionarium showing videoconferencing windows and 3D model.

Distributed Object-Oriented Virtual Reality Environment (DOVRE)

The application uses version 0.5 of Telenor's DOVRE [10] application programming interface (API): a C++ object-oriented framework for the development of distributed multi-user VR systems. DOVRE has been used by Telenor in a wide range of applications, and as a platform to conduct trials investigating collaborative learning in virtual environments [11].

It has a number of key features including

- Highly scalable architecture. Our trial consisted of two groups, although it can support hundreds of simultaneous inhabitants.
- Supports common file formats including DXF and VRML.
- Support for various interaction devices – mouse, joystick, Polhemus tracker. The actual hardware implementation is hidden from the programmer, who can easily create new interaction classes.
- Class and node representation. A hierarchical system of scene-graph nodes represents properties of the scene including geometry, lighting, billboards, audio and transformations.
- Operates across a heterogeneous computing platform. Currently DOVRE exists for the Silicon Graphics IRIX 6.x operating system, Linux and Windows for the Intel platform. OpenGL is typically used for rendering.
- Client–server architecture using TCP/IP. Telenor is also investigating other protocols and network technologies where appropriate, including ATM and multicast. It is also following the development of the MPEG-4 standard.
- Message system for inter-object communication. Objects can have their own behaviour and state, acting autonomously upon events they receive.
- Object-oriented programming (OOP) paradigm, allowing extensibility, flexibility and data encapsulation.

As noted by Bian *et al.* [12], object-oriented programming techniques and message-driven event models greatly simplify the task of creating a virtual environment. In DOVRE the low-level graphics and rendering operations are taken care of by the VR rendering engine, and network commands can be handled transparently. The VR programmer is left to concentrate mainly on describing the events and actions that each object must handle, and the organization and behaviour of the scene.

Appendix II

Networking the environments

To achieve relatively good video quality and application performance our network configuration (Fig. 19.6) consisted of an ISDN 6 (384 kbps) connection to handle audio and video traffic between BT Labs and the Visionarium. An additional ISDN 2 (128 kbps) channel was dedicated solely to application data (such as user location and events) over TCP/IP. This was anticipated as a typical configuration for an application of this type; however, a higher bandwidth connection such as ISDN 30 might be desired in situations where video and audio quality take precedence.

A dual-processor Silicon Graphics Onyx2 Infinite Reality computer (single graphics pipe) resided at BT Labs running the software as client, with a similar three-pipe machine acting as server at the Visionarium. The distinction between client and server operation in DOVRE is purely the fact that clients can connect to a server – a client can run in an unconnected state.

An Ascend MAX 1600 router (Fig. 19.7) provided a total of eight ISDN channels, and a VC2300 video codec handled video and audio encoding/decoding at BT. The Visionarium was set up in a similar configuration, although an Ascend Pipeline 50 was used for TCP/IP access using two ISDN channels plus a Tandberg ISDN 6 videoconferencing system. The local network at BT was isolated from the main BT intranet for security reasons.

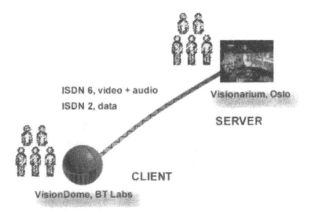

ISDN 6, video + audio
ISDN 2, data

Visionarium, Oslo

SERVER

CLIENT

VisionDome, BT Labs

Figure 19.6 Basic network configuration between BT Labs and Visionarium.

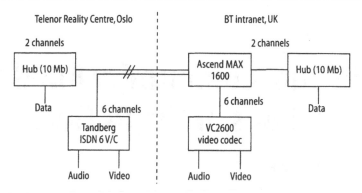

Figure 19.7 Simplified network topology between BT Labs and Visionarium.

Acknowledgements

Thanks to my project colleagues at BT: Andy Auchterlonie, Luke Harmer, Peter Lawrence, Peter Platt, Doug Traill, Mark Wilkinson, and Alison Willard.

I would also like to thank our partners in the collaboration from Telenor: Lars Nilsson, Ola Øldegård, Espen Ottar, Asbjørn Ousland, Karl Anders Øygard, Bjørnar Nørstebø, and Heidi Rognskog

StatOil kindly provided data and models.

References

[1] Isdale, J. Spatially immersive display systems, *VR News*, 7(4), 23–26, 1998.
[2] Silicon Graphics Reality Centre Web site. http://www.sgi.com/realitycenter/over-view.html.
[3] Visualization Summit, Oslo, Norway. 6 May 1998. http://www.sgi.com/newsroom/press_releases/1998/may/vrsummit.html.
[4] Walker, G., Traill, D., Hinds, M., Coe, A., and Polaine, M. VisionDome: a collaborative Virtual environment, *British Telecommunications Engineering Journal*, 16, October 1996.
[5] Rimell, A. and Hollier, M. Design and implementation of 3-dimensional spatial audio for immersive environments, *Proceedings of the Institute of Acoustics*, 19(6), 87–94, 1997.
[6] Cook, J., Hubbold, R., and Keates, M. Virtual reality for large-scale industrial applications, *Future Generation Computer Systems* 14, 157–166, 1998.
[7] Steed, A. Efficient navigation around complex virtual environments, *Proceedings of Virtual Reality Software and Technology*, 15–17 September 1997, ACM VRST'97, pp. 173–180.
[8] Willard, A. and Platt, P. The ramblers guide to virtual environments, Presented at the IEE colloquium *The 3D Interface for the Information Worker*, 19 May 1998.
[9] Mackinlay, J.D., Card, S.K., and Robertson, G.G. Rapid controlled movement through a virtual 3D workspace, *Computer Graphics*, 24(4), 171–176, 1990.
[10] Distributed Object-oriented Virtual Reality Environment (DOVRE). http://televr.fou.telenor.no/html/dovre.html.
[11] Ødegård, O. and Øygard, K.A. Learning in collaborative virtual environments – impressions from a trial using the Dovre framework, *Telektronikk*, 92(3–4), 51–58, 1996.
[12] Bian, T., Rongming, Z., Qiantu, W., and Guanzhong, D. Message-driven object-oriented programming: a promising solution to virtual reality construction, *IEEE International Conference on Intelligent Processing Systems*, 28–31 October 1997, IEEE, Vol. 2, pp. 1742–1746.

20

3D Virtual Community Building Applications in the PANIVE Architecture

Chris Flerackers, Nic Chilton, Rae Earnshaw, Wim Lamotte and Frank Van Reeth

Abstract

PANIVE (PC-based Architecture Networked Interactive Virtual Environments) is an extensible architecture in which various networked virtual environment applications can be realized. This chapter describes our efforts in realizing applications in the area of "3D virtual community building", in which people can virtually meet each other, speak to each other, interact with each other, etc. in a virtual equivalent of conventional social communities.

The overall architecture will be discussed briefly. Some attention will be given to the realization of the audio component in the system (speech input and 3D sound output) that supports intuitive interaction among the participants in a shared virtual environment.

The main part of the chapter discusses and illustrates some demonstrative example applications that highlight the potential for realizing 3D networked virtual communities in the architecture.

20.1 Introduction

A virtual community can be seen as an infrastructure that will allow many users to participate in a shared interactive 3D environment. The community would need to be able to support a large number of users over a range of communication networks. The elements required for such a system model were described in Virtual Society (Honda *et al.*, 1995), and have been implemented in systems that have been developed by adapting the capabilities of existing technology. Dias *et al.* (1997) discuss the issues of scalability of large-scale Networked Virtual Environments. Capin *et al.* (1997) discuss the representation of (and interaction with) virtual humans in this kind of environments.

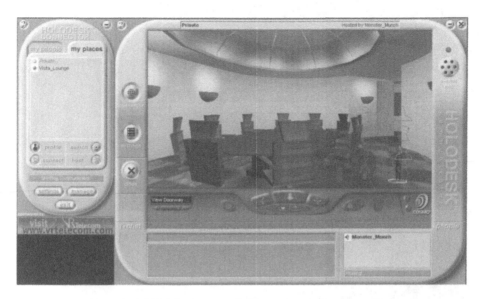

Figure 20.1 The Holodesk™ connector and communicator inside a private office.

These systems are based around a virtual reality display device that should be able to maintain the model database of the multi-user virtual environment in real time. Additional to this is a toolkit that would allow the user to interact naturally. This would include the ability to allow communication, whether verbally or textually, as a minimum, but ideally also support elements of computer-supported cooperative work (CSCW), such as the ability to share and view multimedia files. Seligmann and Edmark (1997) discuss the automatic generation of 3D virtual environments to support multimedia communication between people in a CSCW context.

Many of the available systems are based around Web browsers with VRML 2.0 plug-ins, but this in itself can prove troublesome (Broll, 1997), as the scripting side of VRML2.0, to provide the network communications and interactivity, is completely browser dependent. We briefly highlight three systems in the Web browser category.

20.1.1 The Holodesk[1]

The Holodesk™ system (Fig. 20.1) is a multi-user VRML97 world that utilizes the Cosmo Player 2.1 to view shared worlds. The system is based on hybrid architecture. The user's system consists of a "connector" that connects to the server and allows searches of users and worlds and maintains an address book for the user, and a "communicator" that uses Internet Explorer with the Cosmo Player plug-in to interact in worlds and text and audio chat.

---

1 http://www.holodesk.com/

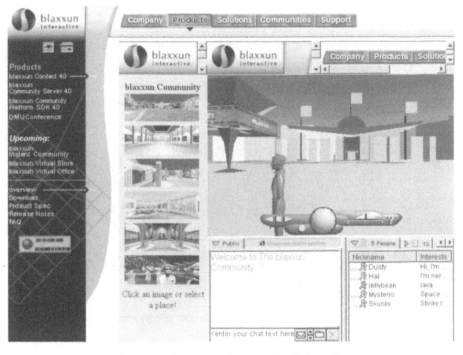

Figure 20.2 Blaxxun Contact browser inside a 3D-chat world.

The system comes with a predefined set of avatars and template worlds. However, rather than general worlds for anyone to enter, a user creates a world based on one of the templates and invites other users in. The main server contains information on users and worlds; however, it is not the server for worlds, as when a user "hosts" an environment the world database is placed on the user's machine and served to other the invited users. The avatars provided have a predefined set of key-frame actions that are easily accessible in the user interface.

As well as the real-time communication options of audio and text-chat, the system supports collaborative working by allowing the importing and sharing of files as well as viewing them, within the environment of slideshow presentations. The performance speed of the system is mainly good, as connections are made with the host of a world rather than centrally, although this is dependent on the host's network connection.

20.1.2 Blaxxun Contact[2]

The Contact system (Fig. 20.2) comprises a VRML plug-in to view worlds, and utilizes a Web browser for access and functionality, such as online chat. The system is based on a client–server hierarchy and is initially set up to connect to a server that

---

2 http://www.blaxxun.com/

Figure 20.3 Sony Community Place browser connecting to a multi-user world.

provides a variety of public worlds, although the client-side browser allows connection to any Blaxxun server. The basic system is mainly a 3D chat environment. The avatars have in-built key-frames that are triggered by keywords in the text typed in the chat window. In addition to the Contact browser, server software is available to allow the hosting of your own worlds. The system has been designed to be extensible and the availability of an SDK allows the development of new systems. The system supports 3D worlds in VRML and Superscape's Viscape, and offers HTTP and MIME support for development of a tailored system.

20.1.3 Community Place Browser[3]

The Community Place browser (Fig. 20.3) is a VRML 2.0 browser that supports Java-enhanced worlds. The browser interface has toolbars for navigation as well as the use of click-and-drag navigation with the mouse. The system is based on a client–server hierarchy with the database model being installed on the client system rather than downloaded from the server. The main use of the browser is for connecting to Community Place multi-user worlds. Depending on the level of features built into a world, a user may have a selection of avatars and gestures to choose from. The browser also works in combination with Web browsers to allow worlds to have features requiring HTTP and MIME support.

In additional to the browser the Community Place system has CP Bureau, server software to host multi-user VRML worlds, and CP Conductor, which allows VRML worlds to be constructed.

---

3   http://vs.sony.co.jp/ and http://www.community-place.com/

Table 20.1 Summary of the functionality of the systems.

	Holodesk	Blaxxun Contact	Sony Community Place
Real-time Communications	Audio and online text chat	Online text chat (and text-to-speech facility)	Text chat in multi-user state
Multimedia support (e.g. video, audio)	Audio chat	Support for video and audio files	Only via a Web browser
CSCW	Importing/sharing of documents and slide-shows with VR representations	Limited trading of objects supported.	Limited
Performance speed	Very good, as the server of the world is the owner's machine	Reasonable, though can be slow with many users	Good for standard VRML
Performance dependability	Performance dependent on speed of connection of host user of world	Number of users on main server	Number of users in a world (though dependence reduced by use of local scripting)
Natural interaction	Avatar gestures provided as key-frames plus audio chat	Gestures provided only as triggers to	Gesture behaviours
Interface usability	Uses Cosmo player plus key-frames. Very easy to use. Can navigate and communicate simulta-neously: "Walk'n'Talk"	Navigation via a panel in the browser. Communica-tion via text chat prevents "Walk'n'Talk"	Click-and-drag navigation, easy to use buttons
Navigation	Cosmo Player's click-and-drag and "dashboard" tools	A dashboard that has a directional dial	Click-and-drag plus toolbar of directional arrows
Main function	Meetings for small numbers of (invited) participants	General public space for "3D chat"	VRML browsing/multi-user virtual community (via CP bureau)

20.1.4 Comparison

The functions available in the three systems can be compared as in Table 20.1.

Section 20.2 provides a brief general overview of the PANIVE architecture. Some illustrative applications realized in PANIVE are described in Section 20.3. Conclusions and directions for future work are given in Section 20.4.

20.2 Architectural Overview of PANIVE

20.2.1 General Overview

20.2.1.1 Client–server

PANIVE is implemented as a client–server architecture (Fig. 20.4) using the DirectX set of libraries: DirectDraw for supporting 2D drawing and video

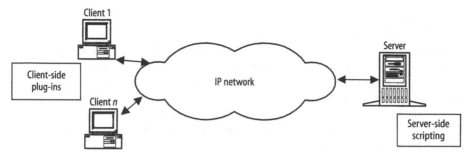

Figure 20.4 General overview of the PANIVE architecture

functionality, Direct3D for realizing the 3D drawing functionality, DirectPlay for organizing the networking components and the clustering of clients into groups and sessions, and DirectSound for delivering the audio functionality. For a more detailed outline of the implementation of PANIVE, the interested reader is referred to Coninx *et al.* (1999).

20.2.1.2 Extensibility

The PANIVE environment is extensible on two levels: (1) at the server-side by means of server-side scripting and (2) at the client-side by means of client-side plug-ins.

Server-side scripting allows new behaviour in a 3D virtual environment to be defined by means of script development in VBScript and/or JScript. Events generated by a user client (e.g. clicking with the mouse, entering a new world, colliding with a certain object) are sent to the server, upon which corresponding script commands are executed and transmitted to the clients. The server is utilized to synchronize the event/commands and to make sure that the appropriate commands are sent to the proper clients.

Working through a client side plug-in (implemented in C++) delivers similar functionality, but has the additional advantages of real-time interaction (i.e. no delay has to be taken into account between generation of an event and the invocation of a corresponding command) and high execution speed (compiled vs. scripted). A disadvantage of the client-side plug-in infrastructure compared with server-side scripting is the higher level of difficulty involved in the programming (C++ as compared to scripting) and the potentially more complicated synchronization of the event/commands (which now partly needs to be done at the client-side).

20.2.1.3 Avatar M

The motion of avatars in PANIVE is implemented by means of the client-side plug-in infrastructure, and as such it is extensible. Currently, a combined physically based motion/vertex interpolation scheme is provided. In the physically based motion implementation, each avatar is given a point mass on which the influence of various forces is taken into account. The source of the applied forces is either generated interactively (e.g. by pulling the mouse) or through the environment itself (e.g. through gravitational and/or frictional force). The model exploits various mutually interacting parameters to perform the basic physically based calculations, such as avatar position/velocity/acceleration, avatar orientation, avatar mass, external friction/gravitation, normal of (as well as distance to) the surface underneath the avatar, etc. For each frame, the model generates a transformation matrix for the local coordinate axis of the avatar.

Superimposed on the physically based motion is a vertex interpolation scheme in which key positions of the geometry of the avatar are used to generate free-form deformations (Coquillard and Jancene, 1991) in the avatar motion.

The avatar view presented to the person controlling the avatar at issue can be (1) a first person view, (2) a third person view, or (3) a freely determined view having no relation to the position of the avatar.

20.2.2 Audio in PANIVE

The audio support in PANIVE is two-fold: firstly, it is used to position the content of pre-defined audio files (typically .wav files) into a 3D environment. This position can be either static or dependent upon the (possibly moving) position of any 3D object or character within a PANIVE 3D environment. The sounds at issue can be playing continuously, or can be dependent upon event-triggers. Secondly, audio can be captured from a speaking person and be transmitted across the network to each person that is located close enough (in the 3D environment) to the speaker. This latter type of sound is located at the position of the avatar representing the speaker; it replaces traditional textual chatting interaction (based upon typing) with verbal interaction.

The experiments are done with a sound system for the PC clients in the network which is based on the DirectX Foundation platform. The DirectPlay part of the DirectX functionality realizes the network management and makes it possible to communicate transparently over different protocols. DirectPlay also contains the functionality to divide different people into different groups. Each person and each group gets its own unique ID.

The DirectSound3D part of the DirectX Foundation platform allows us to play sound in a 3D (virtual) environment. The functionality of this part is so extensive that it can even simulate the Doppler effect when the sound has a speed and direction. One can also adjust the cone and direction of the sound. Even the fall-off of the sound can be adjusted. Exploiting the sound functionality further enhances the experience of being present in the simulated 3D environment.

The key problems when transmitting sound over a network are the available bandwidth and the delay originating from the use of the network. Audio compression is used to reduce the volume of data that is gathered when capturing a sound. Using the Audio Compression Manager (ACM) of the Windows platform makes the realized sound system independent of the compression format at issue. The ACM provides functions to select one of the installed formats and then just compresses all the data delivered by the application. The integration of the ACM makes our sound system very expandable in the use of compression formats because new compression formats installed on the system are accessible via the ACM.

The network delay is kept to a minimum by using the DirectSound3D functionality. DirectSound3D makes use of sound buffers. These are buffers which contain the sound data to be played. The sound buffers are just flat sequential amounts of memory that are viewed as cyclic buffers. DirectSound supports sending notifications to the application when the buffer is played up to a specific position. The application can then react on these notifications by replacing the processed sound data by new data received from the network. The application will, however, never write the data from the network immediately to the sound buffers of DirectSound but it will first buffer the received data in a larger buffer that takes care of the fluctuations in network traffic. This is a simple but effective solution to delay equalization, in order to ensure smooth playback of time-dependent sound information.

20.3 Some Virtual Community Building Applications

20.3.1 Virtual Playgrounds

A first set of applications that PANIVE can host involves environments in which children can play networked virtual alternatives of real games; in fact, this kind of application fired the initial trigger for developing PANIVE. We enlist here a few demonstrative games that are implemented:

- "Four on a row", "Checkers": 3D models (and accompanying scripts) of these traditional board games are put into a PANIVE environment. Two people play the games by interacting with the 3D model. Multiple people can enter the playground and view what is happening in the game. Figure 20.5 shows a screenshot of the prototype "Four on a row" setting.

- "Find the treasure": in this application, children are confronted with a task to find a certain object (or set of objects in random order, or a set of numbered objects in a particular order) within a 3D environment. The PANIVE feature that allows travel between several "worlds" is exploited in this kind of application. Visual cues ("3D geometrical pointers") as well as audible cues (a weakly humming 3D sound positioned near the object(s) to be found) can be used to support the search process.

- "Hide and seek": as a variant on the above theme, children have to find each other (i.e. each other's avatar representation) in a certain 3D environment. Figure 20.6 shows a snapshot of a floating island scene which is used in this context.

- "Remote control of a virtual object": in this kind of virtual playground application, children can use virtual control devices to control virtual objects in a virtual setting: e.g. a virtual toy boat on a virtual pool or a virtual toy car on a playing ground.

Figure 20.5 Snapshot of a game setting in PANIVE.

Figure 20.6 Snapshot depicting part of a "hide and seek" 3D environment.

On average, the scripting part of this kind of gaming applications takes a few (1–3) days of programming by a specialist. The 3D modelling part depends upon the complexity one has to bring into the scene at issue, and can vary from a few hours to several weeks, or even months for a complex "multi-world" environment.

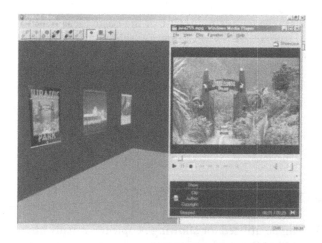

Figure 20.7 Screenshots of environments for launching PC applications from within PANIVE: **a** playing music and **b** playing video sequences.

20.3.2 Personalized 3D Interface

As the PANIVE client is implemented under the MS Windows platform, it is possible to develop scripts and 3D environments as a personalized 3D interface to launch multimedia PC applications. Simple scripts can be developed to launch from within a 3D environment (e.g. by clicking on certain objects and hence launching the appropriate commands) programs to play video or music on your PC client, or Web browsers to contact WWW sites etc. Figures 20.7(a) and (b) show some snapshots for launching audio- and video-playing applications.

20.3.3 Virtual Interactive Studios

VISTA – Virtual Interactive Studios for TV-Applications – is a European Esprit HPCN research project in which the PANIVE architecture will be used to support remote interaction with a virtual television studio. One of the basic ideas behind VISTA involves the creation of interactive TV programmes that are situated in a virtual setting. PANIVE is used in this context for various levels of functionality: (1) the client–server architecture gives the basic means to interconnect various people interacting with each other and the virtual scenery; (2) the client allows the participating people to have their own view on the virtual scenery; (3) a "specialized" client is utilized to generate a signal to be broadcast; (4) yet another client is provided for the director of the programme to select/control the virtual camera that is used to generate the view which is to be broadcast.

20.3.4 Virtual 3D Meeting Place

In a general context, PANIVE can be utilized for allowing people to virtually meet and interact with each other within a 3D virtual environment. The 3D setting can be an artificially generated environment or can be modelled after an existing context. Figure 20.8 shows a screenshot in which a part of a 3D model of an existing town market-place is depicted. Readers interested in related work dealing with automatically generating multimedia communication environments are referred to Seligmann and Edmark (1997).

The basic means of mutual interaction between people in such environments is that of natural speech. The audio functionality described in Section 20.2.2 is heavily exploited in this context.

Figure 20.8 Screenshot of a virtual meeting place environment, modeled from an existing market-place.

20.4 Conclusions and Directions of Future Work

The main objective of our work around PANIVE is to create an infrastructure in which various applications in the area of networked virtual environments can be realized. This chapter gives an overview of the PANIVE architecture and describes some illustrative applications in it in the area of 3D virtual community building.

Future work will manifest itself on three levels:

- System level: a main effort we foresee on this level involves the distributing of the server architecture over multiple physical servers, which will allow us to involve more simultaneous users to be participating in one or more 3D environments and which also will allow us to cover a larger geographical spread.

- New application domains: we plan to implement 3D environments and accompanying scripts and plug-ins that will allow us to develop intrinsic connections between the real world and a 3D virtual environments; interactions in the real world action will induce reactions in the real world (e.g. switching on a physical light by switching on a virtual representation of the light switch, control in general of apparatus through a virtual interface, ...) and actions in the real world will induce reactions in the 3D virtual environment (e.g. depiction of the content of a Web-cam into a virtual screen, monitoring in 3D environments the status of physically measured meters and valves, ...).

- New applications within a certain domain; e.g. we plan the development of new virtual playground games for children.

Acknowledgements

Part of this work is funded by the European Esprit research project VISTA. We would like to thank all the people at ANDROME who contributed in one way or another to the realization of the environments realized in PANIVE; especially the creative help of Paul Akkermans, Liesbeth Beckers, Geertrui "Mokke" Beullens and Bart "Pokke" Van Bael is greatly appreciated.

References

Broll, W. (1997) Distributed virtual reality for everyone – a framework for networked VR on the Internet, *Proceedings of IEEE Virtual Reality Annual International Symposium 1997 (VRAIS '97)*, pp. 121–128.

Capin, T.K., Pandzic, I.S., Noser, H., Magnenat-Thalmann, N. and Thalmann, D. (1997) Virtual human representation and communication in VLNET, *IEEE Computer Graphics and Applications*, 17(2), 42–53.

Coninx, K., Van Reeth, F., Flerackers, M. and Flerackers, E. (1999) The implementation of PANIVE: a PC-based architecture for networked interactive virtual environments, in *Digital Convergence: The Information Revolution* (eds. J. Vince and R. Earnshaw), pp. 327–340, Springer-Verlag, London.

Coquillard, S. and Jancene, P. (1991) Animated free-form deformation: an interactive animation technique, *Proc. SIGGRAPH '91*, 25(4), 23–26.

Dias, T.K., Singh, G., Mitchell, A., Kumar, P.S. and McGee, K. (1997) NetEffect: a network architecture for large-scale multi-user virtual worlds, *Proc. ACM VRST97*, pp. 157–163.

Flerackers, C., Alsema, F. and Van Reeth, F. (1999) TypoToons: An interactive TV-application through a networked virtual environment, *ISAS'99 Conference*, Orlando, July 1999.

Honda, Y. *et al.* (1995) Virtual society: extending the WWW to support a multi-user interactive shared 3D environment. *Proceedings of VRML'95*, ACM Press, pp. 87–94.

Lea, R. *et al.* (1997) Community Place: architecture and performance. *Proceedings of VRML '97 Symposium*, ACM, pp. 41–49.

Seligmann, D.D. and Edmark, J.T. (1997) Automatically generated 3D virtual environments for multimedia communication, *Proc. WSCG97*, pp. 494–503. Also available at `http://www.multimedia.bell-labs.com/projects/archways/publications/WSCG97/`.

21

Telepresence – the Future of Telephony

Graham Walker

Abstract

BT is a leading international supplier of telepresence in the form of telephony. Telepresence enables "people as content", and there are rapidly developing and wide-ranging opportunities for broadband, mobile, multimedia telepresence services. In marked contrast with the relatively ubiquitous and consistent telephone, our vision for future telepresence services encompasses a wide variety of "terminals", ranging in physical scale from personal wearable devices through more conventional desktop or living room hardware to immersive room-based systems. This chapter focuses on our desktop work, outlining our vision for both business and residential services, and reporting early results from user experiments.

21.1 Introduction

Telephony is a basic form of telepresence – enabling human interaction at a distance, creating a sense of being present at a remote location. As the UK's leading supplier of telephony for over a century, BT has a built a deep and wide-ranging understanding of the technical, user and social aspects of a service which we take for granted as part of everyday life.

Looking to the future, BT Labs has an extensive research programme on diverse forms of multimedia telepresence [1]. As a service provider, we continue to take an integrated multidisciplinary perspective, with contributions ranging from network protocols, APIs and coding algorithms, through service management and distributed system optimization, to user interface design, ethnography and the study of business trends.

In marked contrast with the relatively ubiquitous and consistent telephone, our vision for future telepresence services encompasses a wide variety of "terminals", ranging in physical scale from personal wearable devices through more conventional desktop or living room hardware to immersive room-based systems. This chapter focuses on our desktop work, outlining our vision for both business and residential services, and reporting early results from user experiments. Complementary papers complete the picture, covering projects on wearable telepresence and larger-scale collaborative environments [2, 3].

In Section 21.2 we clarify our wide-ranging definition of telepresence, positioning it as the future of telephony. In the following section we describe projects on Desktop Telepresence, addressing both business and residential applications. We outline current technical implementations and early user feedback, and discuss plans for future work. The threads are drawn together in the Discussion and Conclusions, which highlight the wealth of opportunity for innovative services and stress the importance of multidisciplinary collaboration in bringing them successfully to market.

21.2 Background

Before discussing current research activities, it is appropriate to clarify our definition of "telepresence" and to confirm its importance in future communications services. Telepresence, or human presence at a distance, covers a range of remote interaction and collaboration applications. The inclusion of both spatial and temporal distance is important, since we see a continuum from real-time communications such as a phone call or video-conference through to services such as email and asynchronous groupware. Another key aspect is that the content, such as text and audio chat, images and documents, is largely produced by the users of the service. This important consideration is often overlooked in the early development of content-hungry online information services, but is stressed by Dertouzous [4]:

> ...a major misconception: the world's preoccupation with content instead of work. In today's industrial world economy, activities involving traditional content such as newspapers, books, magazines, radio and TV programs, and Web pages account for about 5% of the economy... activities involving information work account for 50 percent. Both information content and information work will flow over the Information Marketplace

This wide-ranging definition of telepresence has been recognized by leading commentators as the "killer application" for the Internet [5]. It emphasizes the role of the user as consumer *and* producer of "content", both in business and leisure-driven services, and informs a programme of research which seeks to understand "people as content".

In addressing telepresence as the future of telephony, we can identify a number of key dimensions in which future services will extend the existing user experience. Figure 21.1 highlights three "axes" along which telephony will develop, confirming the multidimensional stretch of the imagination that is needed when addressing the potential of telepresence:

• *Information integration*: telephony is predominantly an empty audio channel, the same empty audio channel day-in, day-out, where the users make all of the content and interest in real-time. In future services, there will be opportunities to

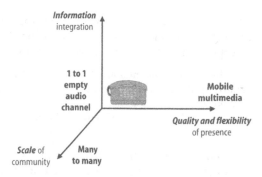

Figure 21.1 Telepresence – new dimensions in telephony.

have some form of persistent context, a backdrop of shared information or applications such as a spreadsheet or perhaps a 3D engineering model.

- *Quality and flexibility of presence*: video telephony remains a relatively small market, and mobility is largely restricted to voice and low-bandwidth data, but future telepresence services will embrace a wide diversity of mobile, multimedia environments. Terminal equipment will range in scale from room-based spatially immersive audio-visual displays to personal wearable devices, with an increasingly important role for a diversity of contextually-aware devices.

- *Scale of community*: conferencing applications notwithstanding, most telephony remains a 1:1 interaction. In the future we will see a growth in community services which support many-to-many telepresence.

All these axes raise substantial research challenges, and in the following section we will outline specific areas of project work which are addressing both technical and user assessment issues for "desktop telepresence".

21.3 Desktop Telepresence

Current telepresence services are predominantly delivered to the telephone and desktop computer for business applications, while the telephone also dominates the residential market. This chapter considers the future of both the office desktop and also the domestic living room, where some form of PC/TV/telephone hybrid will increasingly supplement conventional telephony. We outline our vision, describe initial application demonstrations, and report early results from user experiments.

21.3.1 Business

In a business setting, the commercial drivers for telepresence include increased flexible and remote working, greater use of geographically distributed teams, the rise of organizational models such as the extended enterprise or virtual business, growth in global collaborations and round-the-clock working. One vision for telepresence is of a persistent, shared online space, which reflects and augments the communications channels available in the real world. Desktop telepresence in this context means integrating communications services and social presence into the data-dominated landscape of the Internet and corporate intranets:

> We keep hearing about the Net and the millions of new people using it every day, so why don't I ever run into any of them there? Current visions of the 'National Information Infrastructure' make it sound like a big, vacant reference library. Instead, it should be more like a town, with many people interacting with each other as they go about their activities. (*Pavel Curtis*)

For example, a large screen hanging on the wall of a homeworker might provide a window onto a virtual world providing contact with remote colleagues and their activities analogous to the peripheral awareness of a communal physical office space.

21.3.1.1 Conference Call Presence

An initial step towards this vision is Conference Call Presence, an early commercial development from our research. CC Presence is an audiographic conferencing service, combining a regular multi-party PSTN audio conference with a T120 data conference [6]. A control window provides a static view of a virtual meeting space, linking the audio and data conferences (Fig. 21.2). The visual representation of the conference participants offers significant advantages over standard audio conferencing, with facilities for turn-taking and chairman control, a link to personal contact details, and private chat capability.

Key application features include:

• Window on the conference – an intuitive graphic meeting room-based user interface.

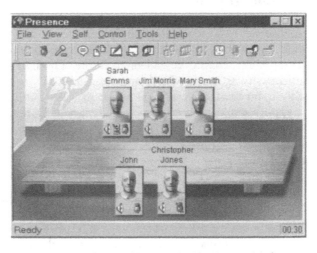

Figure 21.2 Conference Call Presence, virtual meeting room interface.

- Chair control – for large or formal conferences a chairperson can be appointed with executive powers.
- Invitation of additional participants – useful if you have forgotten to invite someone or need to quickly bring an expert into a meeting.
- File transfer – the electronic equivalent of passing documents across the meeting room table.
- Whiteboarding – works like an overhead transparency projector (OHP) to allow users to make remote presentations visible to all participants. Useful also for brainstorming and capturing issues.
- Application sharing – a word processor, spreadsheet or other application on the PC of any participant can be shared and everyone else can take it in turns to contribute to the document or manipulate the figures.
- Chat – a text tool useful for passing notes publicly or privately to other participants without interrupting the flow of the meeting.

However, it is important to note that the "application" is only part of the picture, in that conferencing and telepresence generally are ultimately a "service", which must consider aspects such as setup, directories, and billing.

Key service features for CC Presence include:

- No need for specialist equipment – requires only a PC with an Internet connection and an ordinary telephone.
- Software distributed free – making it cost-effective to roll out within teams and organizations.
- Conferences easily arranged – either over the telephone or from a Web site at any time 24 hours a day.
- No notice required – conferences can start immediately.
- Conferences are easy to join – simply click on an email attachment. No lengthy dialogues with operators or numbers to remember.
- The service can be used away from base – with a mobile phone and a laptop PC equipped with a modem.
- You can take part with only a phone – but of course you will not benefit from the visual element.

For our research vision, CC Presence is important in that it introduces a virtual meeting space as the conference interface, albeit a fixed viewpoint with simple, static avatars. It promotes a sense of copresence in a shared space, in contrast with the conventional "through the window" paradigm for videoconferencing services.

21.3.1.2 The Forum

In business applications we cannot rely on the "Gee this is fun!" factor of some virtual world applications. One of the biggest difficulties with such worlds is navigation. If we are to create effective business meetings online we should employ simple navigation while retaining the strengths of the spatial metaphor. To address

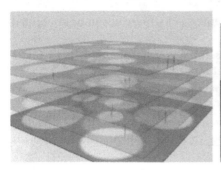

Figure 21.3 Forum Contact Space and Meeting Space interfaces.

this issue we have developed a concept called *symbolic acting*, which is used in The Forum, a research project building on the virtual meeting space offered by CC Presence. The Forum is divided into two parts: the Contact Space and the Meeting Space.

The Forum Contact Space is addressing problems and paradoxes discovered as part of the analysis of flexible workers in BT's remote working trials. The Contact Space is not an application in which you do your work, it is a space for "hanging out" in, a place to manageably meet your colleagues or people you "ought" to interact with if only you worked in the same office or building. For example, when you are writing a document on, say, JavaScript, the Contact Space Agent puts your avatar in the "JavaScript" interest area in the visualization on your desktop [7]. This will put you in "visual proximity" with other people in your Contact Space system working in a similar area without you having to navigate you avatar. Put simply, you let the system do the walking.

In the illustration of the Contact Space (Fig. 21.3), the ground plane shows circles representing all the Interest Groups belonging to the working group as gathered by the Contact Space Agent. You can see avatars located in the space, positioned by the system depending on their desktop activity and subject matter. The transparent layers represent the "action" layers where specific user-defined activities are treated as special cases to position people on these planes when conducting these activities. This opens up the users to "meeting" others doing similar activities but with differing subjects. As the system moves the avatars around it orientates the viewpoint or direction of view of the avatar towards other people in the space who have similar long-term interests.

The Forum Meeting Space is similar in approach to the Contact Space but is focused more on synchronous meetings and is based round audio conferencing in a more direct extension of CC Presence. Symbolic acting again means that while you do your normal activity on the desktop machine, the avatar representing you acts out the symbolic meaning of your activity. For instance, if you have a window obscuring the visualization of the Space your avatar is seen to be looking at a document. In this way everyone knows who is looking at the reviewing document without the user having to control both your desktop and their avatar in the Space. It is like having your own method actor!

In the illustration of the Forum Meeting Space (Fig. 21.3) we see three avatars representing people present in an audio conference. Navigation is turned off in this application. Documents can be dragged from the computer desktop and placed on the desk visible between the avatars. To share a document the person drags the icon onto the centre of the table. Others at the meeting will see your avatar slide the document onto the table.

The Forum Meeting Space and Contact Space are integrated into a consistent client–server architecture. Each client represents a user, and uses VRML sent from the server to display the space and the avatars of other users in that space. The server keeps track of the position and state of the users within the spaces and ensures that all the clients are updated with this information as users move and interact with the world. The server also communicates with an agent server, which suggests moves around the world dependent on the users' desktop activity. At the client, other components can be used to provide extra functionality to the spaces, such as voice over IP and data conferencing.

21.3.2 Residential

There are also opportunities for telepresence in a residential setting. As more homes come "online", residential telepresence is already moving beyond the telephone, with services such as networked PC gaming and chat spaces. Personal email, a basic form of telepresence frequently referred to as the "killer application of the Internet", has been a leading driver in the growth of residential Internet penetration.

Looking to the future, services such as online shopping and interactive TV, although initially dominated by *1:many* broadcast content with a limited back channel, will also evolve to support *many:many* telepresence. The human contact of real-world shopping can be as important as the final transaction, and both student–tutor and student–student interaction are an essential element of conventional learning. These social aspects will need to be reflected in online inhabited implementations. Our residential telepresence vision would also extend to "attending" a live football match from an armchair in your living room, while experiencing a sense of co-presence with fellow supporters comparable with watching the game on a large-screen TV in a bar or pub.

21.3.2.1 Inhabited TV

Our work on residential shared spaces has focused in particular on the concept of Inhabited TV: the combination of collaborative virtual environments and broadcast TV to create a new entertainment and communications medium [8]. The defining feature of this medium is that an online audience can socially participate in a show that is staged within a shared virtual world. The producer defines a framework, but it is the audience interaction and participation which brings it to life. A broadcast stream may then be mixed from the action within the virtual world and transmitted to a conventional viewing audience, either as a live event or sometime later as edited highlights.

Inhabited TV extends traditional broadcast TV and more recent interactive TV by enabling social interaction among participants and by offering them new forms of control over narrative structure (e.g. navigation within a virtual world) and greater interaction with content (e.g. direct manipulation of props and sets). It seeks to harness the creativity of the audience by offering them an opportunity for "fifteen Megabytes of fame". Such telepresence services raise research challenges in technical implementation, content, interface and service management.

In addressing these issues we have pursued a programme of experiments in inhabited TV, working in collaborations with Sony, the BBC, Channel 4, Illuminations and Nottingham University [9]:

- *NOWninety6* [10], a virtual poetry performance, occurring simultaneously in a physical theatre and in a virtual world. This was staged as part of a Nottingham arts festival in autumn 1996.
- *The Mirror* [8], six public online virtual worlds, run alongside the UK BBC television series *The Net* in spring 1997. The broadcast in this case was based on edited, recorded footage. Figure 21.4 shows an interactive game from "Play" world in The Mirror.
- *Heaven & Hell – live*, a live one-hour television broadcast in autumn 1997 on the UK's Channel 4 from inside a public virtual world.

In each event there were four types of participants (or "levels of participation"), illustrated in Fig. 21.5:

- passive *viewers*, either watching broadcast television or watching a single projected view in a theatre (in the case of *NOWninety6*)
- online *inhabitants*, embodied within the virtual worlds and able to interact and take part

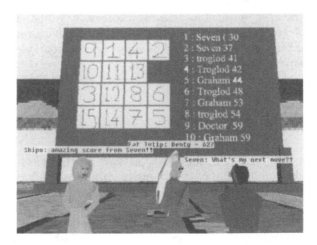

Figure 21.4 Inhabited TV – avatars competing in The Mirror [8].

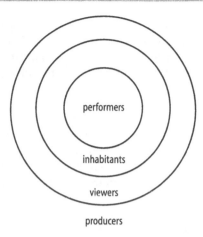

performers

inhabitants

viewers

producers

Figure 21.5 Layered participation in Inhabited TV.

- professional *performers* or correspondents, also embodied in the virtual worlds, providing content and coordination
- the *production* team, including camera operators, director and technical support, who worked behind the scenes to make each event happen

The three experiments are summarized in Table 21.1, using the layered participation framework. They raised a number of significant issues with the creation of Inhabited TV. In particular, a mismatch in expectations between virtual world "inhabitants" and TV "viewers" was identified as a major obstacle to the success of

Table 21.1 Layered participation in experimental Inhabited TV events.

	NOWninety6	The Mirror	Heaven & Hell – live
Performers	Six poets performing sequentially over a two-hour show Audio and body tracking	Celebrity "super avatars" introduced for a small number of special events – debates and a game show Text chat and interaction capabilities similar to the inhabitants	Celebrity host and two game-show contestants Audio for the TV broadcast, and assistants to provide text, navigation and interaction in the online world Also three reporters with TV broadcast audio in addition to online interactivity
Inhabitants	Sixty, participating in groups of ten "angels" from locally situated silicon graphics workstations Audio chat capability	Over two thousand registered "citizens", recording 4500 online hours over a seven-week period from their home PCs Text chat, shared behaviours and collaborative tasks	135 "lost souls", participating in the one-hour live broadcast from their home PCs Text chat and collaborative tasks Also 800 users of the associated Web site chat and newsgroup during the broadcast
Viewers	Two hundred at a live performance, with the virtual world simultaneously projected into the cinema	Half a million viewers of the BBC2 series *The Net* saw edited highlights and reporting on the worlds	An estimated 200 000 viewers of the Channel 4 TV broadcast

this new medium. For example, a viewer demands a fast-paced and largely undemanding experience, while an inhabitant expects something much more leisurely and personally involving. The details of these lessons are discussed elsewhere [11], and the next section will focus on a fourth more recent experiment – *Out of this World* (OOTW) – that sought to address these issues by staging a fast-paced Inhabited TV show. Whereas previous experiments had delivered the virtual worlds over the public Internet and broadcast the result on national television, OOTW used a high-speed LAN for the participants, with the output projected for the viewers in an adjoining theatre. This simulated the infrastructure that could be available as digital TV evolves, and allowed us to experiment with more sophisticated forms of control and interaction in the virtual worlds.

21.3.2.2 Out of this World

OOTW was a public experiment with Inhabited TV that was staged in front of a live theatre audience. The event was staged as part of *ISEA: Revolution,* a programme of exhibitions and cultural events that ran alongside the *9th International Symposium on Electronic Art* (ISEA'98) that was held in Manchester in the UK in September 1998. There were four public performances of OOTW in the Green Room theatre over the weekend of 5–6 September. These were preceded by two days of construction, testing and rehearsal. OOTW was implemented in the MASSIVE-2 system [10].

Like *Heaven and Hell – Live,* OOTW was a game-show. This choice allowed a direct comparison to be made between the two experiments. Given the issues referred to above, the design of OOTW was motivated by two key questions:

• Could we involve members of the public in a fast-moving TV show within a collaborative virtual environment? In particular, could we clearly engage the inhabitants with the performers and with one another, could they keep up with the action, what would they contribute, and would they enjoy the experience?

• Could we produce a coherent broadcast from the action within the CVE? In particular, would the broadcast output be recognizable as a form of TV and would it be entertaining to watch?

The remainder of this section provides an overview of OOTW, including the participation model, content, and a critical reflection on its success.

OOTW Implementation The show featured a competition between two teams (the "aliens" and the "robots"), to escape a doomed space station. Each team was led by a paid performer who was wearing an immersive VR headset and was tracked (both head and hands) using electromagnetic trackers. Teams comprised four members of the public (drawn from those entering the theatre) seated at networked PCs in the production area (in "real" Inhabited TV, these people would be at home). These inhabitants could navigate using a standard PC joystick, and took part in four collaborative games. The show was fronted by a virtual host who appeared in the world as a live video texture on a large virtual screen. The inhabitants and performers all wore microphone-headsets and were able to talk to one another

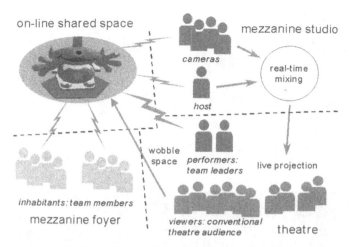

Figure 21.6 *Out of this World* participant structure.

using packetized network audio. The host also has a microphone, and audio spot effects were triggered automatically at various points in the games. The participant structure for OOTW is outlined in Fig. 21.6.

To create the live audio/video feed into the theatre we made use of standard outside broadcast methods. There were four virtual cameras, each with its own operator. These fed into an outside broadcast mixing desk (with input, preview and transmission monitors), together with a direct view of the host and a video tape (VT) player for additional, pre-recorded, linking footage. An experienced television director was responsible for directing and video mixing. An additional technician operated the VT, and audio was mixed separately by an audio engineer through the house PA. All of these people were on a talk-back circuit to allow them to coordinate their actions. Figure 21.7 illustrates some of the participants and elements of the "broadcast" output.

There were a total of four rehearsals and four performances over a period of three days.

OOTW Assessment We now present an initial assessment of the extent to which the two goals described above (involving the public in a fast-moving enjoyable show in which they were engaged with the performers; and producing a coherent and entertaining broadcast output) were met by OOTW. This assessment is based on post-event discussions with the viewing audiences, feedback from the performers, inhabitants and production team and opinions from press reviews. Notes were taken during the audience discussions and these were supplemented with various personal reflections via email immediately after the event and at post-event meetings.

- *Did we produce coherent, face-pace interaction within a CVE?*
  Our overall sense is that we succeeded in staging a game-show in a CVE where members of the public interacted with actors around a loosely structured script. The inhabitants were clearly central components of the show. The pace of the action was rapid, at least in terms of our previous experience of CVEs. The games were mostly playable and generally recognizable in form.

Figure 21.7 Scenes from *Out of this World*: the director and her assistant; an inhabitant; introducing the Alien team; the end of the show; inside the spaceship; immersed performer next to the screen in the theatre.

- *Did we produce a coherent and entertaining broadcast output?*

We believe that the broadcast was coherent and recognizable as TV, again to a level that we hadn't achieved with previous experiments. Indeed, as we shall see below, viewers' reactions to the piece mostly focused on the content of the show and seemed to take it as read that this was a form of television – the technology was mostly transparent.

In contrast, the content of OOTW attracted considerable criticism, as the following paragraphs now describe.

- *Lack of empathy with the show and its characters*
  Several viewers commented that they did not warm to the show or feel empathy with its characters. Major contributing factors to this may have been the lack of expressive capability of the avatars and the low quality of the audio. With the exception of adding some gestural capability to the team leaders through the use of immersive interfaces, neither of these issues was directly addressed by OOTW. Furthermore, applying our game design principles may have resulted in a more sparse, albeit coherent, landscape that contributed to the feeling of emptiness.

- *Lack of legend and the importance of community*
  A further subtle factor in this lack of empathy may have been a lack of legend. Our actress commented that her character lacked a sense of history. There was no established background to the show – why were the participants on this space station? How long had they been there? What had happened previously? This lack of a shared history made it difficult to establish an interesting dialogue between the performers and inhabitants or to improvise interesting content around the framework of the show. Our impression is that a common reaction among participants was to resort to stereotypes to fill this void, in this case based on the gender division between the teams – a major concern with the show from some viewers. Thus, although OOTW did succeed in establishing engagement between the performers and inhabitants through the collaborative nature of its games, the resulting relationship wasn't especially interesting.

Future Inhabited TV should invest greater effort into developing interesting characters and narratives. This might be achieved though the more central involvement of authors, scriptwriters and producers early on in the development process. However, it might also emerge naturally from long-term online communities – a strength of CVE technology. In many ways, the latter approach was successfully demonstrated in The Mirror, where a sense of community was established over six Inhabited TV shows.

We therefore argue that OOTW partially addressed the issues of coherence and pace raised by earlier experiments. In particular, our production software allowed us to script and direct a framework within which the public and our actors could engage one another. However, the content of OOTW was more problematic and content should be a major focus of future work. We can summarize with the following quote from *The Times* [12]:

> At this stage Inhabited Television is merely an interesting diversion hinting at greater things. One suspects it will be some time, and several more surreal previews, before the system can generate material strong enough for television.

21.4 Discussion

In progressing both the Forum and our work on Inhabited TV, we can identify many specific areas that afford seemingly endless scope for further work. For example, more realistic avatars, fluent multi-modal interaction or novel approaches to navigation could all improved the telepresence experience, and are

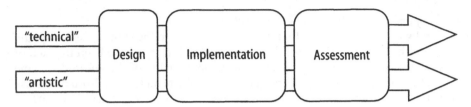

Figure 21.8 Complementary disciplines in a simple three-stage project model.

indeed components of our research programme. However, in this brief discussion we chose to highlight our general approach of multidisciplinary working as being key to future progress.

Figure 21.8 is a simplistic representation of what is in reality an imprecise and often unstructured "process". Dertouzos uses the terms "techie" and "humie" as a loose distinction between technologists with an IT or physical science background, and humanists or those with a grounding in art, design or the social sciences [4]. Such terminology can overemphasize a divide in skills and outlook which we are seeking to bridge, but it remains largely appropriate while we retain an emphasis on narrow specialisms in most higher and further education courses. Within our projects at BT Labs, we have on occasion used the anglicized "java-bods" and "arty-bods"!

Figure 21.8 shows a progression through three stages: design, implementation and assessment. This naïve linear sequence in practice involves complex feedback inter-stage loops, and ultimately becomes a cycle provided that there is continued discovery and learning. At each stage, the interaction between disciplines is essential to innovation and understanding:

- *Design* requires a mix of user-driven "pull" informed by social and market studies with "push" from innovative concepts, tempered by a sound awareness of current technical possibilities and probable future developments. Paper-based storyboards can be particularly valuable at this stage, although tools are increasingly available which facilitate "draft" computer-based models and animations, which can be evolved into the next stage.

- *Implementation* demands close teamworking between content and interface designers and developers with more traditional programming skills. Again, tools and development environments are increasingly helping to blur the handover between disciplines.

- *Assessment* again requires close interaction between the disciplines in designing experiments which yield complimentary "techie" and "humie" data. For example, typical goals might be to understand the links between technical performance and user acceptability, or to build a user interaction profile that can be used to predict network traffic or optimize resource allocation.

Both the Forum and the Inhabited TV work are loosely structured around this process. Key contributions in implementing a tangible application demonstrator to unify the potentially disparate interests include:

- longitudinal studies in the office and home to inform our understanding of user needs, and of the societal impact of new technologies

- quality and creativity in interface design, linked to formal assessment of the user interaction
- technical innovation and quantitative performance measurement down to a detailed network level

21.5 Conclusions

Telepresence is the future of telephony: in a diversity of multimedia applications, delivered to a range of physical terminals. We have described leading-edge application experiments in "desktop telepresence" for both business and residential services. The Forum is addressing the workplace needs of a distributed team, and work on Inhabited TV is exploring a vision which integrates greatly increased viewer interaction and participation into traditionally passive broadcasting.

The experiments are conceived to address the breadth research challenges which we face in delivering commercially successful services. It is our experience that whilst technologists, social scientists and designers continue to make discipline-specific advances in these integrated projects, the most important advances and insights are typically the result of multidisciplinary interactions.

Acknowledgements

The author would like to thank his colleagues at BT Labs for helping to initiate and creatively progress the projects referred to in this chapter. Many of the projects also involve commercial and academic partners, and their contribution both to the work and the related concepts is gratefully acknowledged.

References

[1]   Sheppard, P.J. and Walker, G.R. (eds.) *Telepresence*, Kluwer Academic Publishers, 1999.
[2]   Dyer, N. and Bowskill, J. Ubiquitous communications and media: steps toward a wearable learning tool, *BCS Conference on Digital Media Futures*, Bradford, April 1999; this volume, Chapter 5.
[3]   Banks, R. An inhabited 3D oil platform for immersive CSCW, *BCS Conference on Digital Media Futures*, Bradford, April 1999; this volume, Chapter 19.
[4]   Dertouzos M. *What Will Be: How the New World of Information Will Change Our Lives*, HarperCollins, 1997.
[5]   Bell, G. and Gray, J.N. The revolution yet to happen, in *Beyond Calculation: the Next Fifty Years of Computing* (eds. Denning, P.J. and Metcalfe, R.M.), Springer-Verlag, 1997.
[6]   Conference Call Presence. `http://www.conferencing.bt.com/assets/p&s/presence.htm`.
[7]   Davies J. and Revett M., Networked information management, *BT Technology Journal*, 15(2), 1997.
[8]   Walker, G.R. The Mirror – reflections on Inhabited TV, *Br. Telecommun. Eng.* 16(1), 29–38, 1997.
[9]   Benford, S., Greenhalgh, C., Brown, C., Walker, G.R., Regan, T., Rea, P., Morphett, J. and Wyver, J. Experiences with Inhabited Television, *Proc. CHI'98*, ACM Press, Los Angeles, May 1998.
[10] Benford, S.D., Greenhalgh, C.M., Snowdon, D.N. and Bullock, A.N. Staging a poetry performance in a collaborative virtual environment, *Proc. ECSCW'97*, Lancaster, Kluwer Academic Press, 1997.
[11] Benford, S., Greenhalgh, C., Craven, M., Walker, G.R., Regan, T., Morphett, J. and Wyver, J. Inhabited Television: broadcasting interaction from within collaborative virtual environments (in preparation).

[12] *The Times*. TV from another planet: something virtually different. Interface section, 7 October 1998, London.

22

A Journey to the Hemispheric User Interface – Creative and Technical Achievements

Janice Webster

Abstract

The search is still on for a physical place that will allow one person or a group of people the chance to be totally immersed and engaged with a real-time computer-generated experience. The Hemispherium™ is a new stepping stone on this journey. It has been described as the next "step-change" in group immersive VR [1]. The development of the design will be described in this chapter and compared with the now established Reality Centre experience.

This chapter also includes a technical overview and illustrates the creative achievements with reference to VR in museums and heritage sites, the built environment, and for education and entertainment. It highlights the technical challenges, the importance of teamwork and a shared vision to develop a new virtual reality experience.

In presenting this "Journey to the Hemispheric User Interface" the author draws on her experience of working with Trimension and Silicon Graphics as Industrial Partners and with the Technical Director and Technical Manager in the Virtual RealityCentre, University of Teesside.

22.1 Introduction

In 1997 the Virtual Reality Centre, University of Teesside, opened a group immersive Virtual Reality Auditorium (cinema) to seat up to 20 persons. The design is based on the Silicon Graphics RealityCentre, version 1, which was opened in the SG Headquarters in Theale, June 1995.

Thus the journey to the Hemispheric User Interface started: a journey to develop a more immersive VR experience for a single user and also for group working (Figs. 22.1 and 22.2). The Hemispherium™ was officially opened in December 1998. The

Figure 22.1 Hartlepool Headland User Meeting.

Figure 22.2 Developers discussing proposed Town Centre development, Middlesbrough.

screen is 180° by 180°, with seven projectors to fill the screen with high-resolution images (Fig. 22.3).

This chapter describes the design process and references user experiences in the VR auditorium and the Hemispherium™. It describes the technical design decisions and illustrates the uses.

22.2 Virtual Reality Auditorium

The Auditorium is a black soundproofed room, 8 m × 18 m. It was conceived as an interim solution before the building for the Hemispherium™ existed. It was built in order to gain experience of creating virtual environment models, learn how to technically manage and maintain such a facility, and most importantly engage with the public and private sector sponsors, clients and developers during 1997/98.

Figure 22.3 Bird's-eye view from the flight chair in the Hemispherium™.

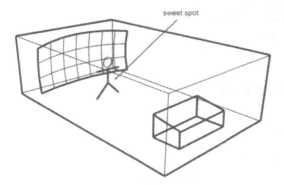

Figure 22.4 VR Auditorium sketch.

The display screen is 7 m × 2.5 m, with a 140° field of view horizontally and 40° vertically (Fig. 22.4). Three projectors (Fig. 22.5) are synchronized to produce the edge-blended seamless image, which is generated by an Infinite Reality computer. Controls to interact with the virtual environment models are located at a control desk to the rear of the auditorium. Joystick control can be positioned closer to the screen, normally at the "sweet spot".

The three projectors are ceiling mounted and positioned to give a clear line over the heads of seated users.

22.3 User Expectations of the Experience

There is a sense of mystery, expectation and anticipation about entering the Auditorium for the first time. User surveys indicate that it:

• should be a very interactive experience

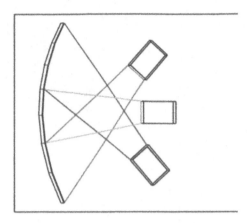

Figure 22.5 Plan views of projectors and screen.

- might be like an arcade game
- should be visually realistic, even filmic
- may cause sickness

22.4 User Responses

22.4.1 General

One VR Centre objective is to provide VR awareness training. This covers the many aspects of VR, from low-cost solutions using VRML to Quicktime VR plus periph-eral devices, VR environment modelling software and hardware, and group immersive VR, such as the VR Auditorium. The "trainees" are almost too varied to describe. They include children, students, parents, teachers, community council-lors and managers from the public and private sector. This paper is not about a research survey into their responses; however. such a varied audience influenced the VR Centre Team during 1997/1998. This is reflected in the eventual design for the Hemispherium™. In summary it was noted that:

- the quality of the image was poorer than expected
- the feeling of immersion was only good at the sweet spot
- there was an engagement with the virtual environments
- it is a somewhat passive experience
- it is much better than headset VR
- better audio clues are required

22.4.2 Case Studies

The responses from clients were different, more positive. In fact, it has become difficult to manage the increase in demand from community groups, local

Figure 22.6 Angel of the North.

authority leaders, heritage groups and decision-makers from the built environment sector. The VR Auditorium for such clients is turned into a:

• decision-making room
• promotional space
• marketing tool
• concept design development tool
• sculptors "extra brain cells" (Fig. 22.6)

The functionality of the VR Auditorium was increased during 1997 so that multimedia presentations could also be made before, during or after the VR "show". This was not envisaged at the outset but has turned out to be an essential element of the room. In comparison the new Hemispherium™ is, as yet, only configured to display VR models.

22.4.3 Specific Case Study

The VR Centre can be set up as a training simulator. This specific case study was carried out on behalf of the Civil Aviation Authority and used software from ETC. The training in question was designed for Fire Commanders to allow them to "virtually" take command of disasters at airports. The study confirmed that the experience was "very real". For such training it was reported that:

• it is essential to have audio synchronized with the visual clues.
• the humans in the scene were unrealistic.
• the realism of the virtual environment models of the airport, fire engines etc. was good enough. In comparison, when shown to museum curators the models were regarded as poor.
• the sense of immersion and engagement was average to good.
• the brightness and clarity of the image were satisfactory.

22.5 VR Auditorium – Summary

The VR Auditorium continues to provide an essential learning facility. For the demonstrator or presenter it is a space where the audience can be intimately involved with the screen image – even walk up to it and explain what is happening in a very intuitive way. In 1998 there was still the vision to build a better experience. Additional funding was secured and the decision made to retain the interim VR Auditorium and build a second immersive VR experience based on a 180° by 180° dome screen. The Hemispherium™ is the result.

22.6 Birth of the Hemispherium™

Our human field of view is about 200° horizontal and 130° vertical. Several years ago Barbour [2] and Kalawsky [3] reported how the larger field of view images in domes increase the subjective feelings of naturalness, expansiveness, depth and "reality".

At the start of the project the industrial Partner, SEOS, recommended a 6 m dome to be mounted vertically with three high-resolution projectors to fill the central field of view and a fish-eye lens projector to "soft-fill" the floor and sky. They had just completed a dome simulator for a military client. In this design the cockpit is located just behind the "sweet spot" and is the interface. This was a possible solution.

At the outset the design team had few criteria, and certainly not the name. The first sketch (Fig. 22.7) was the largest clue.

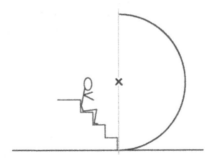

Figure 22.7 Concept sketch.

22.6.1 Technical Challenges

The technical summary of the VR Auditorium highlighted the need to pay particular attention to:

• viewing angles
• quieter air conditioning

- more sensitive controls on the flight chair
- more space at the control desk, for up to four people, not two
- better visual immersion
- safeguard against power cuts

And especially

- projector reliability
- better edge blending of the images
- sustainable colour balance
- double the refresh rate
- brighter image, better contrast

The latter five points were regarded as critical to sustaining and maintaining interest in this new design. At this stage detailed costs were not the key issue.

22.6.2 Design Criteria Based on Experience

The design team also identified the need to have:

- multi-participant control
- ambionic surround sound
- a flight chair at the "sweet spot" with a range of controls
- high-resolution images over all of the screen, since many of the Centre's existing models include buildings, roads, parks and rivers
- the Centre globally networked

22.6.3 Projector Configuration

By early summer 1998 the VR technical team proposed that it would be cost-effective to consider using six projectors to produce high resolution images over the whole of the screen (Fig. 22.8).

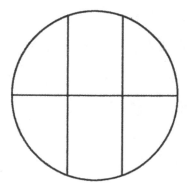

Figure 22.8 Six projector configuration showing central horizon-line seam.

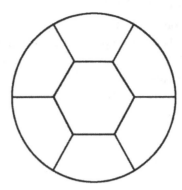

Figure 22.9 Seven-projector configuration with hexagonal central image and six equal sectors.

The major disadvantage envisaged was the central blend. After many lengthy discussions with the technical partners at Trimension Systems Limited, sister Company to SEOS, a seven-projector solution was chosen (Fig. 22.9). This eliminates the central horizon line blend, in retrospect a good design decision.

22.6.4 Design of the Stage-Set

There was also the challenge of how to create a stage for the people – in fact, how to design the stage-set to keep that sense of mystery, excitement and participation and how to ensure that a person could be located in the flight chair at the "sweet spot" with no barriers in the way. At last, there was a role for an interior designer!

The design was labelled "fasten your seat belts" by the Publicity Officer of the University. A phrase that turned out to be true (Fig. 22.10).

The final platform design is toughened glass so that there is the opportunity to view beneath the chair (Fig. 22.11). There are safety rails for the four other chairs on the front row.

Figure 22.10 Fastening the seat-belt in the flight chair.

Figure 22.11 View of flight chair on glass plate.

22.6.5 Hemispheric User Interface

The word *hemispheric* conjures up the concept of floating, levitating and perhaps zero gravity. The user interface is either adored or hated – it makes some people frightened and others exhilarated. One fact emerges – this interface is unique.

Imagine being fastened into a modified racing car seat that is fixed to a glass floor. Once the seat-belt is secure the flight chair is propelled by a hydraulic ram out into "space" towards the screen until the eyes are in line with the edge of the 6 m screen. The flight chair controls allow positioning anywhere in the virtual environment. Peripheral vision is filled by high-resolution images; in fact, the surface is covered by over 9 million pixels. Audio signals are designed to enhance the experience.

The name Hemispherium™ was invented and trade-marked.

22.7 Technical Summary

The Hemispherium™ uses a fully immersive PRODAS dome display, with seven channels of high-resolution PRODAS projection onto a 6 m hemispherical dome screen that is mounted vertically. The dome is manufactured of lightweight GRP material and finished with a matt white optical coating. The PRODAS projectors are geometrically corrected and seamlessly edge blended using a seven-channel DigiBlend edge blending and colour correction system. The dome surface is covered with over 9 million pixels. This single rich image portrays levels of computer-generated realism that allow design decision-making of anything, ranging from an entire galaxy to a detailed view, at a very enlarged scale, of a Roman artefact; from a new road layout to a reconstruction of a 13th century Priory (Fig. 22.12).

The main computer is a Silicon Graphics Onyx 2 with 10 processors and three graphics pipelines. It has 40 Gbyte of disk space, 2048 Mbyte of main memory and

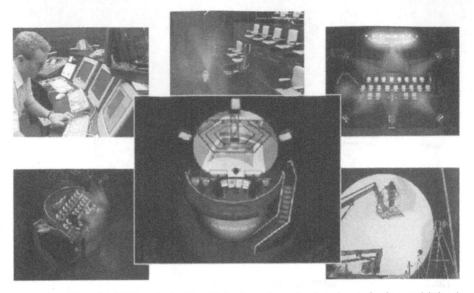

Figure 22.12 Views of the VR Hemispherium™ model, showing seating and projector layout, plus the control desk and "final coat of paint".

64 Mbyte of texture memory. 3D surround sound is produced by 12 speakers, driven by a LAKE sound card.

The flight chair is a modified racing seat. The controls and additional fixing and safety belts were designed by the VR Centre Technical Director and Design Workshop Manager at the University of Teesside. One disadvantage is that there are no constraints for the feet, and swinging legs can cause interference between the projectors and the screen. The final location is adjustable for different age ranges (Fig. 22.13).

Figure 22.13 User participation – fastened in, but not projected fully out to the "sweet spot".

Figure 22.14 At the controls in the "sweet spot" position.

22.8 Does the Technology Work?

Most of the technical challenges have been addressed. The edge blending is rated as excellent by the professional team and users. The colour balance and brightness are average. Projector reliability is still a concern, but is being addressed by the suppliers. Access to the projectors necessitates closure of the facility for two days. General maintenance is scheduled between client sessions.

The general seating arrangements for 20 people are tight in the space available; however, group dynamics are still good. The flight chair (Fig. 22.14) is excellent.

Technical expertise with sound systems within the VR Centre team was minimal at the outset. Knowledge is growing, but there is much more work to be done in linking the audio to the graphics models.

22.9 Design and User Summary

It is too soon to predict the importance of this design. The Design Team for the new Planetarium at the American Museum of Natural History realized that they had the opportunity to "ride through the galaxy", rather than "gaze up at the stars". The Eurofighter simulation group realized that they could "look up or down" and still have the same level of realism.

This is another stimulating experience for learning and fun (Fig. 22.15). It is as possible to fly back in time into a Saxon village in AD 600 as it is to drive over a new bridge for the Millennium. The challenge is still how to arrange to have more than one flight chair. Multi-participant control is a challenge to the VR community in general, as is a full 360° screen.

Figure 22.15 Engaged with the project.

22.10 Conclusions

The ability of synthetic worlds to stimulate our senses by wholly computer-generated environments is now an accepted experience.

The public at large tends to think that the computer-generated special effects in film are virtual reality. The word *virtual* is used and misused in many contexts.

The journey to the Hemispheric User Interface set out with a mission to break through one important aspect for group immersive VR experience and single task-oriented training: to create high-resolution images to fill the human peripheral vision using real-time computer generated environments.

Version One is an overwhelmingly successful project in this respect. Time will tell as to whether this 180° × 180° system will find the same niche in the market-place as the less-immersive Reality Centre design.

References

Hughes, D. (1998) *Launch of the Hemispherium™*, Innovation and Virtual RealityCentre, University of Teesside, UK, 11 December.
Barber, C.G., Meyer, G.W. (1991) Visual cues and pictorial limitations in photorealistic images, *SIGGRAPH91, Course Notes*, C9, IV-1–IV-36.
Kalawsky, R.S. (1993) *The Science of Virtual Reality and Virtual Environments.* Addison-Wesley, Reading.
Parkin, B. (1998) Making virtual domes a reality, *7th TILE98 Conference Proceedings*, pp. 66–67.

About the Author

Janice Webster has a first degree in Interior Design. She has been using computer-aided visualization systems since the mid 1980s. In 1988 she established the MSc Computer Graphics Applications course (CAGTA). In 1994 she was appointed Director of the Institute of Design at the University of Teesside with a mission to develop computer-related design tools for designers. During this time she introduced VR and rapid prototyping technologies and became involved in establishing a Virtual RealityCentre.

Since 1997 she has established the VR Centre as a Centre of Excellence. As Executive Manager her key responsibilities are innovative and imaginative project initiation plus marketing and promotion of the Centre across Industry, Commerce and Education. The VR Centre Team has developed from six people in February 1997 to 30.The Centre is still growing. The latest development has been the design and construction of a unique immersive VR experience called the Hemispherium™. She is a founder member of the Reality Centre Special Interest Group (RCSIG – 1997) and was Chair in 1998, and is also a member of the Networking Centres of Excellence Management Group in the Northern Region and the Sophia Antipolis/North-East technology initiative (SANE).

Author Index